About Island Press

Island Press is the only nonprofit organization in the United States whose principal purpose is the publication of books on environmental issues and natural resource management. We provide solutions-oriented information to professionals, public officials, business and community leaders, and concerned citizens who are shaping responses to environmental problems.

In 2003, Island Press celebrates its nineteenth anniversary as the leading provider of timely and practical books that take a multidisciplinary approach to critical environmental concerns. Our growing list of titles reflects our commitment to bringing the best of an expanding body of literature to the environmental community throughout North America and the world.

Support for Island Press is provided by The Nathan Cummings Foundation, Geraldine R. Dodge Foundation, Doris Duke Charitable Foundation, Educational Foundation of America, The Charles Engelhard Foundation, The Ford Foundation, The George Gund Foundation, The Vira I. Heinz Endowment, The William and Flora Hewlett Foundation, Henry Luce Foundation, The John D. and Catherine T. MacArthur Foundation, The Andrew W. Mellon Foundation, The Moriah Fund, The Curtis and Edith Munson Foundation, National Fish and Wildlife Foundation, The New-Land Foundation, Oak Foundation, The Overbrook Foundation, The David and Lucile Packard Foundation, The Pew Charitable Trusts, The Rockefeller Foundation, The Winslow Foundation, and other generous donors.

The opinions expressed in this book are those of the author(s) and do not necessarily reflect the views of these foundations.

Reconstructing Conservation

Finding Common Ground

Edited by

BEN A. MINTEER

and

ROBERT E. MANNING

ISLAND PRESS

Washington • Covelo • London

Copyright © 2003 Island Press

All rights reserved under International and Pan-American Copyright Conventions. No part of this book may be reproduced in any form or by any means without permission in writing from the publisher: Island Press, 1718 Connecticut Avenue, N.W., Suite 300, Washington, DC 20009.

ISLAND PRESS is a trademark of The Center for Resource Economics.

No copyright claim is made in the work of David N. Bengston, Rolf Diamant, David C. Iverson, Nora Mitchell, employees of the federal government.

Library of Congress Cataloging-in-Publication Data

Reconstructing conservation : finding common ground / edited by
Ben A. Minteer and Robert E. Manning.
    p. cm.
Includes bibliographical references and index.
  ISBN 1-55963-350-6 (hard cover : alk. paper) — ISBN 1-55963-355-7
(pbk. : alk. paper)
  1. Nature conservation—United States—History. 2. Nature
conservation—United States—Philosophy. 3. Nature conservation—United
States—Social aspects. I. Minteer, Ben A., 1969– II. Manning, Robert E., 1946–
  QH76.R43 2003
  333.7′2′0973—dc21

                      2003009198

British Cataloguing-in-Publication Data available

Cover artwork taken from "Billings Farm and Museum from Mt. Peg" by Vermont artist, Sabra Field. This print was commissioned by the Woodstock Foundation, and is symbolic of the long-term stewardship of the lands in and around Woodstock, Vermont, including the Billings Farm & Museum and the Marsh-Billings-Rockefeller National Historical Park, as well as the conceptual and practical reconciliation of nature and culture outlined in this book.

Printed on recycled, acid-free paper ✹
Manufactured in the United States of America
09 08 07 06 05 04 03   10 9 8 7 6 5 4 3 2 1

This book is dedicated to Laurance S. Rockefeller in appreciation for his interest in and support for this project, and in respect for his lifelong and productive engagement in conservation thought and practice.

The Woodstock Foundation was very pleased to join with our colleagues and friends at the University of Vermont, the National Park Service, and The Trust for Public Land in sponsorship of a seminar on the history, values, and practice of conservation.

In their task of "reconstructing conservation" for the new century, the participating scholars addressed a wide range of questions of ethics and practice and found common ground in the essential humanity of conservation. Conservation, both as an idea and a practice, must be concerned with the total relationship between humans, culture, and the natural environment. It has roots in theory, science, ethics, aesthetics, and in the real places where people live and work, whether urban, suburban, rural, or wild. The time is upon us and the opportunity is great—not just for conservation of the land but also for renewal of the human spirit.

This fundamental connection between land and the human spirit was essential to the philosophies of George Perkins Marsh and Aldo Leopold, and it is basic to my own conservation philosophy. It was especially fitting that part of the seminar took place in Woodstock, Vermont, where my wife Mary and I focused much of our conservation interest for many years. There, working in partnership, the Woodstock Foundation's Billings Farm & Museum and the Marsh-Billings-Rockefeller National Historical Park preserve and interpret a cradle of American conservation—the boyhood home of Marsh and a place that has known the hand of thoughtful stewardship over two centuries.

From the conserved farm and forest of Woodstock, from the verdant rural countryside of Vermont, and from the probing ideas of the scholars whose work is represented here, we take renewed hope, rooted in our legacy of conservationism and poised to address the challenges before us. As it did in the time of Marsh, once again the message and vision of conservation will go forth across the nation from the hills of Vermont.

—LAURANCE S. ROCKEFELLER, Chairman Emeritus,
The Woodstock Foundation, Inc.
May 1, 2003

CONTENTS

Foreword   xi

Part I. Introduction   1

  1. Conservation: From Deconstruction to Reconstruction   3
      Ben A. Minteer and Robert E. Manning

Part II. Nature and Culture Reconsidered   17

  2. Writing Environmental History from East to West   19
      Richard W. Judd

  3. The Nature of History Preserved; or, The Trouble with
     Green Bridges   33
      Robert McCullough

  4. Going Native: Second Thoughts on Restoration   43
      Jan E. Dizard

  5. Conservation and Culture, Genuine and Spurious   57
      Luis A. Vivanco

Part III. Reweaving the Tradition   75

  6. Expanding the Conservation Tradition: The Agrarian Vision   77
      Paul B. Thompson

  7. Regional Planning as Pragmatic Conservationism   93
      Ben A. Minteer

  8. Building Conservation on the Land: Aldo Leopold and
     the Tensions of Professionalism and Citizenship   115
      Susan Flader

  9. Scott Nearing and the American Conservation Tradition   133
      Bob Pepperman Taylor

10. Conservation and the Four Faces of Resistance   145
       Eric T. Freyfogle

11. Conservation and the Progressive Movement:
       Growing from the Radical Center   165
       Curt Meine

Part IV. New Methods and Models   185

12. Conservation: Moral Crusade or Environmental
       Public Policy?   187
       Bryan Norton

13. Social Climate Change: A Sociology of Environmental
       Philosophy   207
       Robert E. Manning

14. Reconstructing Conservation in an Age of Limits:
       An Ecological Economics Perspective   223
       David N. Bengston and David C. Iverson

15. The Implication of the "Shifting Paradigm" in Ecology for
       Paradigm Shifts in the Philosophy of Conservation   239
       J. Baird Callicott

16. An Integrative Model for Landscape-Scale Conservation
       in the Twenty-First Century   263
       Stephen C. Trombulak

**Part V. Reconstructing Conservation Practice:
Community and the Future of Conservation
Stewardship**   277

17. Community Values in Conservation   279
       Patricia A. Stokowski

18. Stewardship and Protected Areas in a Global Context:
       Coping with Change and Fostering Civil Society   297
       Brent Mitchell and Jessica Brown

19. Reinventing Conservation: A Practitioner's View   313
       Rolf Diamant, J. Glenn Eugster, and Nora J. Mitchell

20. Conservation Stewardship: Legacies from Vermont's Marsh   327
       David Lowenthal

Part VI. Conclusion   333

21. Finding Common Ground: Emerging Principles for
       a Reconstructed Conservation   335
       Ben A. Minteer and Robert E. Manning

Notes   351
About the Contributors   401
Index   405

FOREWORD

The ideas and fundamental principles underlying *Reconstructing Conservation* resonate with each of us and the missions of our institutions. Indeed, many of the concepts and principles that emerged from the original seminar in Vermont (which are now part of this book) reflect the evolving ways we are developing and conducting our respective programs of conservation education, scholarship, and practice. The Woodstock Foundation, for example, operates its Billings Farm & Museum in programmatic partnership with Marsh-Billings-Rockefeller National Historical Park. Working side-by-side, these two institutions carry on the conservation efforts of multiple generations of careful stewards on lands in and around George Perkins Marsh's boyhood home in Woodstock, Vermont, celebrating and interpreting the principles of conservation stewardship for thousands of visitors every year. The National Park Service's Conservation Study Institute has recently been created to study and extend new models of conservation based on collaborative approaches to blending nature and culture in more harmonious and mutually reinforcing ways. The School of Natural Resources at The University of Vermont is fully engaged in an interdisciplinary program of education and research designed to transcend the traditional natural resources and environmental fields of study. And, the Trust for Public Land is part of a network of state, regional, and national conservation groups, public agencies, private corporations, and three local towns, all working to protect the land, water, wildlife, and economy of the headwaters of the Connecticut River. We credit Ben Minteer and Bob Manning, organizers of the original seminar and co-editors of this book, for the genesis of these thoughtful, progressive, and optimistic ideas, and applaud the many contributors for their eloquent delivery of insightful papers.

The seminar held in the fall of 2001 was a provocative and engaging series of sessions, alternating between scholarly presentations and challenging discussions of their practical implications. But these sessions were limited to those of us privileged to participate. As sponsors, we resolved to make this work more widely accessible, and we are delighted that this book has now come to fruition. A groundbreaking convergence of scholarly reflection and professional insight, *Reconstructing Conservation: Finding Common Ground* is an illuminating, critical, yet ultimately hopeful, assessment of the rapidly changing worlds of conservation thought and practice. The editors have assembled a prominent, multidisciplinary group of scholars and professionals, all of whom are either known for their work in shaping our scholarly understanding of conservation, or for advancing strategies by which conservation is carried out by citizens and professionals on the ground. As a consequence, we believe *Reconstructing Conservation* will be viewed as a landmark contribution to the history and philosophy of conservation and the practice of conservation stewardship in our communities and on the landscape.

The authors' main charge in the book, to rethink and revitalize our conservation bequest for a new generation of scholars, professionals, and citizens, has perhaps never been more urgent. Nor, in some ways, has it been more challenging. As the editors observe in their introduction, the intellectual and practical challenges confronting those working to sustain a commitment to conservation during this period of great conceptual and political tumult in environmental thought and policy should not be underestimated. In responding to many of these challenges in the pages that follow, the contributors to *Reconstructing Conservation* have engaged in a rich and multilayered conversation—one that is interdisciplinary, probing, and prospective. Their collective work and vision is a fine example of what is possible when forward-thinking academics and practitioners make common cause on a subject of great mutual significance and public concern.

From our perspective, one of the main strengths of *Reconstructing Conservation* is this very fluid integration of scholarly inquiries into the depths of conservation thought and practitioner insights into the real work of conservation stewardship. By bringing theory and practice together, this approach also uncovers many of the shifts underway within the academic and professional conservation communities. Among the more important and promising of these changes is the expanded public and civic nature of conservation, and the establishment of meaningful conservation partnerships across traditional organizational and institutional boundaries. These emerging developments clearly represent a change in the way conservation is conceived, and valued, and carried out as a collective enterprise.

Conservation was once practiced in back rooms from seemingly distant places. People from the eastern United States wanted to protect the west. People of the Western Hemisphere wanted to save the forests and rain forests of far off continents. The work was important and good, and was crafted in response to the challenges of the time, yet from our perspective today, some fundamental ingredients were absent. *Reconstructing Conservation* shows us that a new type of conservation is emerging. Work once done primarily in boardrooms is now being conducted in town halls and school gymnasiums and involves many stakeholders. Organizations, communities, and government agencies work in partnership toward common goals that balance the interests of ecology, recreation, economy, and local traditions.

This type of collaboration within the wider conservation community is happening across the spectrum. African nations are now working across borders with local people to create trans-nation peace parks that are good for both wildlife and people. New land trusts proliferate, working from the grassroots to protect local and regional resources. Right here in Vermont, our recognition and celebration of the interconnections between ecology, economy, and community spirit have led to creative government, organization, and community partnerships designed to sustain the vitality of the northern forest. The concepts and principles of *Reconstructing Conservation*, then, are much more than good scholarly thinking; they reflect the way conservation is done on the ground, an acre at a time, in partnership, embodying the core democratic principals of participation and self-determination.

As co-sponsors of the seminar at which the early versions of these essays were first presented, we are especially delighted to see the publication of *Reconstructing Conservation* by Island Press. This book itself serves as a fine example of the great potential of creative conservation partnerships. It represents the shared conviction of our organizations that the convening of leading scholars and practitioners to deliberate over the meaning and work of conservation is essential to charting an intelligent and productive course for the further development of conservation thought and practice. Indeed, the thoughtful dialogue initiated at the seminar has coalesced into a "common ground" embodied in our collective conservation inheritance and a forward-reaching set of unifying principles for the future. We hope the essays in *Reconstructing Conservation* will continue to spark dialogue and debate that will help unveil new cooperative strategies and solutions to our enduring conservation challenge.

Donald D. DeHayes, Dean, School of Natural Resources, University of Vermont

David A. Donath, President, The Woodstock Foundation, Inc.

David Houghton, Director, Northern New England Field Office, The Trust for Public Land

Nora J. Mitchell, Director, Conservation Study Institute of the National Park Service

Part I

Introduction

Chapter 1

Conservation: From Deconstruction to Reconstruction

BEN A. MINTEER AND ROBERT E. MANNING

The idea for the present volume was born in discussions with our colleagues about the changes rippling through the academic environmental community at that time, the mid- and late 1990s. Of these, perhaps the most significant was the appearance of a set of high-profile critiques questioning the very foundations of environmental thought and practice from the vantage point of the end of the twentieth century. Led by William Cronon and his now well-known debunking of the American wilderness idea, these arguments had generated more than a few sparks across a wide range of scholarly and professional fields.[1] Indeed, Cronon's and others' work seemed to issue an indirect yet provocative challenge to scholars and practitioners engaged in the study and management of human–environment relationships. As academics with an interest in the integrity and contemporary vitality of the American conservation tradition, we can say that these deconstructive arguments certainly got our attention.

Although the revisionist papers appearing in Cronon's oft-cited collection, *Uncommon Ground,* were focused more on coming to terms with the consequences of the cultural mediation of our knowledge of nature and models of ecological change in postwar environmentalism, Cronon's own dismantling of the meanings and images associated with the American wilderness idea suggested that the earlier conservation movement was also implicated in the broader critique. In particular, Cronon singled out the nature romanticism of Henry David Thoreau and John Muir and the primitivism of Frederick Jackson Turner as examples of how American thinking about wilderness had been saddled with utopian myths that represented a flight from lived human history and an escape from the hard problems presented by modern urban and industrial life.[2] If Cronon was right, it meant that our thinking about wilderness had been at best intellectually lazy in its acquiescence to these wrongheaded ideas about our place in the world. At worst, it had been morally irresponsible, especially in its neglect of urban and rural conditions and the men and women who toiled in the fields and in the factories, away from an idyllic and imaginary "pristine" nature.

Cronon's criticism of the wilderness concept and, more generally, the deconstructivist assessment of the commitments and strategies of late-twentieth-century environmentalism are now part of the environmental studies canon. They have been joined by a growing and broadly sympathetic literature, including further interdisciplinary critiques of the wilderness idea,[3] attempts to demystify significant contemporary conservation concepts such as that of biodiversity,[4] and projects exploring the historically neglected dimensions of class, culture, and authority in the management of parks and wildlife.[5] For the most part, we believe this critical turn has provided a useful service. It has, for example, exposed the previously unreflective presuppositions of contemporary environmentalism, holding traditional and widely accepted interpretations of concepts such as wilderness and biodiversity to the fire of critical scrutiny. Even though the academic and popular environmental community's response to Cronon and his followers has been at times overly defensive and less constructive than we might have liked, these critiques have nonetheless stimulated an important and potentially transformative debate about the conceptual foundations of environmentalism as we move into the first decades of the twenty-first century.

Yet, as we said before, it is also true that these penetrating criticisms of modern American environmentalism have issued an undeniable challenge to those who would defend the "classical" conservation tradition—the period running roughly from George Perkins Marsh to Aldo Leopold (and perhaps to the publication of Rachel Carson's *Silent Spring*)—as practically viable and intellectually relevant in the new "deconstructivist era." After all, the mostly unquestioned realism about nature during this time and the nascent "modernist" ecological understandings of the era's principal thinkers would seem to make the tradition a prime candidate for systematic debunking and demythologizing. Nevertheless, we believed that there was still much of value in the tradition, even if we also conceded its very real philosophical and scientific limitations as a template to guide current and future thought and practice. How, we wondered, should we go about reading the conservation tradition in this new, highly charged, and seriously self-conscious academic environment?

To answer this question, we decided to do what most academics do when faced with an intellectual crisis of epic proportions: we held a seminar. In this we were also following the model established by Cronon and his colleagues, given that the papers appearing in his *Uncommon Ground* began their lives in a seminar held at the University of California, Irvine, in the early 1990s. For our project, we wanted to create an appropriate forum in which both the scholarly and practitioner communities could come together and attempt to fill the deconstructionist void. We believed it was important to bring these two groups into an open dialogue with each other, and we hoped that the opportunity for increased traffic between the theory and practice of conservation would help achieve a balance of "intelligent practice" and "practical intelligence" at the seminar.

Our primary task was an ambitious one: to assess the meaning and relevance of our conservation inheritance in the twenty-first century and to chart a course for revising the conventional narratives and accounts of the tradition so that a "usable past" might be uncovered that could inform present and future conservation efforts. In the fall of 2001, then, we organized and held an invited, interdisciplinary seminar in Vermont focused on the challenges of "reconstructing" conservation thought and practice in the wake of the earlier deconstructive efforts. The seminar participants were a select group of leading academics and professionals nationally and internationally known for their work in conservation scholarship or the practice of conservation in local communities and on the landscape. They approached our project's goals with great intellectual seriousness and creativity, and their energy held steady over the nearly five full days of plenaries, panels, and roundtable discussions. This enthusiastic response suggested to us that we had managed to start a conversation not only compelling in its conceptual scope and orientation but also timely in its asking of hard questions of the conservation tradition regarding its role as a guide for a new age's relationship with its environment.

In hindsight, we think the physical settings of the talks had more than a little to do with what we (naturally) think of as the success of the seminar. The symbolism of our chosen locations for the events in Vermont was hard for the participants to ignore. The first half of the seminar took place in the majestic John Dewey Lounge in the University of Vermont's historic Old Mill building, underneath a portrait of the great American philosopher (and the university's most famous graduate). Dewey's influential 1920 book *Reconstruction in Philosophy* not only inspired the title of the present volume; it also served as a model for our desired mix of judicious criticism of the conservation tradition with the development of a positive, forward-looking vision for conservation thought and practice in the twenty-first century.

The second half of the seminar was held in the small historic village of Woodstock, Vermont. Woodstock was the home of George Perkins Marsh, whose 1864 book *Man and Nature* was, as Lewis Mumford memorably put it, "the fountainhead of the conservation movement."[6] It was here, in the hills and valleys of Vermont, that Marsh made his initial observations of human effects on the environment and began formulating his original ideas about the proper course of the human–nature relationship. Woodstock is also the site of Marsh-Billings-Rockefeller National Historical Park, the first unit of the National Park System devoted to studying and interpreting conservation for the public. The park houses the National Park Service's Conservation Study Institute, which conducts a program of research, education, and practice on conservation as applied to national parks, public lands, and beyond.

In the drive south from Burlington to Woodstock, then, our seminar participants were, in a very real sense, bringing their meditations on the American conservation tradition back to the birthplace of the national conservation impulse. Laurance S. Rockefeller, who with his wife, Mary French Rockefeller, gifted the lands constituting the park in Woodstock to the nation, had passionately stated his hope at the park's dedication that the park and its affiliated programs would carry on the tradition of sending "the message and vision of conservation across the nation from the hills of Vermont." In our view, there was no better place to discuss the prospects of reconstructing conservation than at the University of Vermont and in Woodstock.

Given the unusually high caliber of the participants, it should not have been surprising that the presentations and discussions at the seminar surpassed our expectations. Moreover, the conversations took on a compelling life of their own over the course of the agenda in Burlington and Woodstock. Although the deconstructivist critique had catalyzed our decision to bring the project participants together in Vermont, the panel presentations and ensuing discussions went much further than these initial beginnings. It was obvious to us, in fact, that in many cases our contributors had already moved beyond the confines of this tendentious debate about the cultural foundations of environmentalism set down in the mid- and late 1990s. We believed this was a healthy development. While remaining sensitive to the changed atmosphere of conservation in light of these critical projects, the seminar participants were clearly less interested in providing partisan defenses of the deconstructive enterprise or knee-jerk rejoinders to it than they were in looking forward, probing the structure and substance of a reconstructed and revised conservationism for the future.

By taking part in this project, the seminar participants were not only stepping into the breach with regard to the tensions that have marked the deconstructivist debate over wilderness and environmentalism; they were also entering a larger and, we think, ultimately more important discussion about the proper course of future conservation scholarship and action. This larger discussion, however, has also been marked by considerable academic and professional debate and divisiveness in recent years. Any careful survey of the scholarly and popular literature in conservation, for example, will reveal a host of conceptual and methodological polarizations that have worked to divide individuals and "camps" within the diverse fields of conservation thought and practice. A representative list of these oppositional elements might include the following:

- Conservation versus preservation
- Conservationism versus environmentalism
- Anthropocentrism versus biocentrism/ecocentrism
- Instrumental value versus intrinsic value
- Utility versus aesthetics
- Efficiency versus equity
- Nature as construct versus nature as essence
- Moral pluralism versus moral monism
- Urban/rural environmentalism versus wilderness environmentalism
- Eastern (U.S.) versus western (U.S.) perspectives
- Regional focus versus national focus
- Working/cultural landscapes versus pristine nature
- Stewardship versus hands-off management policies
- Grassroots action versus centralized approaches
- Citizen environmentalism versus expert/bureaucratic environmentalism
- Models of ecological disturbance versus models of ecological order
- Conservation theory versus conservation practice

Some of these tensions are captured in the aforementioned deconstructivist critique, though many speak to additional commitments and goals that are debated in academic and professional conservation circles. Of course, this list is by no means exhaustive. We also do not wish to suggest that a subscription to one or more of the commitments on the left or the right entails an endorsement of all the claims and tenets on that side of the aisle. But we do believe this list captures some of the major philosophical and strategic disagreements within conservationism, both past and present. And though some of these divisions seem to be slowly disappearing, or at least moving toward some degree of conceptual compatibility (e.g., the debate over equilibrium-based and disturbance-based ecological models), others remain firmly in place and even appear to have deepened in recent years (e.g., anthropocentrism versus biocentrism/ecocentrism, the constructivist–essentialist debate).

We know that many of our participants probably believed they had a stake in one or more of these debates at the seminar, yet we were struck by the degree to which they attempted to move beyond these imposed categories and their entailments. Even when it was apparent that some of the presenters were interested in working along one side of an argument, for example, they sought to develop complementary rather than adversarial projects, or they worked to shore up weaknesses and fill conceptual holes in the conservationist literature. This is not to say that the divisions represented in the foregoing list were somehow magically erased in Vermont, nor to suggest that many of these opposing ideas do not provide a useful way of thinking about some of the real tensions in our understanding of conservation thought and practice. We only point out here that our participants were not beholden to "either-or" logic in the framing of their discussions and proposals for reconstruction. This independence was probably best demonstrated by the numerous pleas for philosophical compatibility and tactical cooperation at the seminar and by the participants' awareness of the need to move beyond rigid ideology and the constraints of historically entrenched positions and arguments in their respective fields.

The specific questions that emerged through the individual presentations and discussions at the seminar formed a crosscutting pattern of historical reflections, philosophical investigations, social scientific studies, and practical considerations of the past, present, and future of conservation initiatives on the landscape. Among the questions raised by these lines of inquiry were the following:

- Why and how have the intellectual and social histories of conservationism ignored certain subjects and movements, and how might these accounts be revised to accurately reflect the peoples, places, and ideas left out of these histories?
- What is the role of human agency in natural and cultural landscapes, and how do we come to terms with the demands and responsibilities of conservation stewardship?
- What are the limitations and lessons of early-twentieth-century Progressive conservationism for conservation in the first part of the twenty-first century?
- How should we understand the philosophical and value bases of conservation in light of new histories, new methodologies, and new analytic models in the natural and social sciences?
- What, if any, should be the overarching goals of conservation in a contemporary environment characterized by social, ethical, and methodological pluralism?
- How do questions of class, identity, and community shape the material prospects of conservation on the ground?
- What are the descriptive and normative features of community-based conservationism, and how do these approaches promise to engage citizens more effectively in conservation practices?

These questions and others like them filled our five days in Vermont that fall. And they would continue to engage the participants as they returned to their own places to reflect and write about them for this book.

This Book

The book you hold in your hands brings together the mature versions of the ideas and arguments first advanced at our seminar. The chapters reflect not only the authors' original statements about the prospects of reconstructing conservation but also their subsequent thinking on these issues in light of their dialogues with other seminar participants over the course of the Vermont meetings. The contributors represent an impressive range of scholarly fields and professional disciplines. On the academic side, they offer perspectives informed by history, philosophy, political theory, sociology, economics, anthropology, historic preservation, legal studies, and conservation biology. Our professional/practitioner contributors bring considerable experience and leadership in the stewardship of protected areas and cultural landscapes, both domestic and international. Together, they provide the volume with an unusually broad yet conceptually integrated vision for rethinking past and present conservation thought and practice to meet the needs and circumstances of a new, post-deconstructivist era.

Although each contributor brings his or her own unique perspective, interests, and experience to the discussion in the ensuing chapters, we believe the chapters are linked by several broad and intersecting lines of argument that advance the larger project of reconstructing conservation. We will revisit these threads in more detail—in a set of emerging principles for reconstructing conservation—in our conclusion to this volume. A brief outline of larger concepts here, however, offers a useful thematic orientation to the chapters that follow.

Revising and Expanding the Conservation Tradition

The recent publication of new and impressive biographies of key conservation thinkers such as George Perkins Marsh, John Wesley Powell, and Gifford Pinchot serves to remind us of the enduring significance of the conservation tradition.[7] Yet these treatments appear at a time in which a number of new, alternative histories have greatly extended our view of the populist and social dimensions of the American conservation impulse.[8] Both historical approaches—taking fresh stock of the pillars of the tradition, and expanding the conservation story to include people and places traditionally left out of the canon—are represented in the present volume. In several of the chapters that follow you will find new, critical perspectives on many of the towering figures of conservation, including those thinkers we might consider the historical "bookends" of the movement: George Perkins Marsh, who is discussed in the chapter by David Lowenthal, and Aldo Leopold, who figures prominently in the chapters by Susan Flader, Curt Meine, Eric T. Freyfogle, and J. Baird Callicott. But you will also come across a number of forgotten or underrepresented voices and movements in the tradition that hold the potential to deepen and enrich the conservation story. In the chapter by Bob Pepperman Taylor, for example, you will read about the "oppositional" form of conservationism developed by Scott Nearing. Likewise, Ben A. Minteer's chapter introduces the "pragmatic conservationism" of Lewis Mumford into the intellectual history of conservation philosophy. In his chapter, Robert McCullough acquaints us with the shared "humanism" of conservationist/planner Benton MacKaye and architect Clarence Stein. Richard W. Judd's chapter uncovers the historic "eastern" model of conservation practiced by rural New Englanders on their farms and in their forests. And Paul B. Thompson's chapter resurrects the earlier agrarian thinkers and their ideas about the relationship between subsistence, moral character, and political economy. Together, these authors' reconsiderations of the conservation tradition and their attempts to expand its historiographic and philosophical borders provide some of the pieces of a new, rewoven conservation history.

Reconciling Nature and Culture

Not surprisingly, many of the chapters in this book engage, directly and indirectly, the deconstructivist critique of the idea that we can achieve an unmediated understanding of nature independent of the interpretive frameworks of culture. From Jan E. Dizard's discussion of the (often ignored) intertwining social and ecological dimensions of new efforts in ecological restoration to McCullough's plea for establishing common ground between historic preservation and traditional nature conservation, many of the contributions provide fascinating glimpses of how a reconstructed conservation might come to terms with its interwoven natural and cultural dimensions. Other chapters in this vein offer a revised conservation agenda that includes the built and cultivated environments as well as the natural (e.g., the chapters by McCullough, Judd, Thompson, Minteer, and Freyfogle), suggesting that a geographic rapprochement of nature and culture, in addition to the conceptual, is in order. As Luis A. Vivanco reminds us in his chapter, however, there are considerable perils associated with adopting an essentialist understanding of culture in any such reconciliation, a move that can expose troubling issues of power and justice in conservationist discourse and practice.

Reviving Progressive Conservation

It is difficult to think about the "professional" conservation movement of the first decades of the twentieth century apart from the moral language and institutions of American Progressivism: the "gospel of efficiency" in natural resource management, the rise of scientific expertise in public administration, and a democratic suspicion of corporate capitalism. Several chapters in this book mark a return to such Progressivist themes, offering critical assessments of their liabilities but also recognizing their potential to inform a retooled conservationism in the twenty-first century. Flader's discussion of Aldo Leopold's evolving views on the importance of conservation citizenship and Taylor's chapter on Scott Nearing's "Progressive homesteading" reveal the positive and destructive features, respectively, of the earlier Progressive impulse. Meine's call for a return to the "radical center," however, holds out the hope that in this new era, conservationism can retrieve its Progressive roots in the search for common cause across party, class, and ideological lines.

Revising Conservation Inquiry

Several of the chapters in this volume argue for changes within the academic disciplines that investigate the conservation tradition. Judd, for example, presents a brief for an "eastern" approach to the study of environmental history as a counterpoint to the dominant "western" model in the field. Minteer suggests that environmental philosophers need to develop more sophisticated intellectual histories by revisiting the ideas and intellectual influences of environmental thinkers, such as Mumford and the regional planners, whose works are underrepresented in the field's narratives. In his chapter, Meine argues for a more nuanced conservation history, one that recognizes the dynamic and diverse foundations of the movement and its rich interweaving of science, philosophy, policy, and social practices. Robert E. Manning, in his chapter, makes a case for more sociological analyses of conservation philosophy and presents the results of some empirical studies of environmental values and ethics to support a methodologically pragmatic approach to studying environmental commitments. In a similar manner, Bryan Norton advances a new analytic model for environmental ethics, one that is more problem oriented and is couched in a larger "multi-criteria" adaptive management framework. And David N. Bengston and David C. Iverson call for economists to incorporate a more serious regard for ecological limits and to recognize social values beyond utility maximization in the quest for ecological sustainability.

Linking Conservation Theory and Practice

A key and recurring theme of our project is the need to connect the *theory* about conservation with grounded discussions of the *activity* of conservation on the landscape. The chapters by Lowenthal, McCullough, Flader, and Patricia A. Stokowski demonstrate how the insights of conservation history and social thought can inform more intelligent practice, from improved stewardship and community conservation efforts to new and fruitful alliances between the professions that study and inform conservation actions. The chapter by Rolf Diamant, J. Glenn Eugster, and Nora J. Mitchell and the chapter by Brent Mitchell and Jessica Brown both illustrate how thoughtful practitioners can help conservation theorists to understand the strategic and political constraints facing conservation activities, as well as to recognize opportunities for reconstructing conservation on the ground. Similarly, Stephen C. Trombulak's chapter provides a conservation biologist's view of the importance of securing biological and ecological processes through a "dominant use" system of land designation, an approach he suggests will protect biodiversity values alongside human economic development. By linking theory and practice in this manner, we hope the present volume not only helps keep theorists grounded in their work but also sets the stage for bringing the reconstruction discussion down from the tower of the academy and into communities and institutions, where it may be engaged by citizens and environmental professionals who are building conservation on the landscape.

Coping with Change through Adaptation

Many of the chapters in this volume address the challenges presented by manifestations of change in contemporary conservation, in both social and ecological contexts. In his chapter, Callicott explores the evolving paradigms of ecological thought in the scientific community and discusses the implications of the emerging "flux-of-nature" model for contemporary philosophies of conservation. A similar discussion may be found in Dizard's chapter, which emphasizes the need for responsible environmental management in light of nature's perpetual motion. In their chapter, Bengston and Iverson illustrate how new ecological knowledge and changing social values have challenged the assumptions of traditional economic thinking about the environment and how an adaptive ecological economics offers an appropriate model for valuing a plurality of ecological goods and systems in a new era of conservation. And the chapters by Diamant, Eugster, and Mitchell and by Mitchell and Brown provide helpful discussions of some developing trends in conservation practice, many of which attempt to cope with the numerous social and ecological changes that characterize the contemporary scene.

Defending Pluralism, Embracing Community

One general conclusion that seems to draw nearly unanimous consent among our authors is that a reconstructed conservation in the twenty-first century will be a very diverse enterprise. It will be multi-foundational in its philosophical commitments (Minteer) and pluralistic in its value and ethical justifications (Manning; Bengston and Iverson). Indeed, as Norton suggests in his chapter, environmental and conservation-related problems involve choices among competing goods, which must be experimentally integrated into environmental policies, not reduced to any single value. Norton and others (e.g., Diamant, Eugster, and Mitchell; Mitchell and Brown) indicate that the specific strategies and goals of conservation, too, will be as different as the publics that propose them and the landscapes they ultimately concern. Alongside this recognition and defense of pluralism in conservation thought and practice is the embrace of community that appears in many of the chapters. In particular, several chapters advance elements of a community-based conservationism, a project that connects a concern for human social well-being with the stewardship of our built and natural surroundings (e.g., the chapters by Flader, Meine, Thompson, and Stokowski). In several cases, these pleas for community are accompanied by warnings of the dangers of moral individualism and fragmentation and the resulting loss of land health and landscape-level thinking in conservation planning and action (e.g., the chapters by Freyfogle and Trombulak).

The Responsibilities of Stewardship

Finally, many of the chapters that follow argue for the necessity of the practice of intelligent stewardship in a reconstructed conservation. In a sense, the more theoretical contributions to this volume provide much of the conceptual justification for conservation stewardship in the twenty-first century, inasmuch as they offer readings of environmental thought and action that firmly embed human values and goals in the landscape. David Lowenthal's recovery of George Perkins Marsh's ideas about the nurturing of stewardship for present and future generations and Dizard's point about the importance of responsible stewardship in the face of a constantly changing ecological order remind us of the costs of relinquishing our obligations to promote a sustainable and healthy environment through sensitive intervention in natural systems. Thompson's chapter on the agrarian conservation vision, too, suggests how the tradition's impulse to ensure that productive processes are passed down through the generations provides a normative framework for community-level stewardship. Diamant, Eugster, and Mitchell and, in their chapter, Mitchell and Brown discuss stewardship from a practitioner's perspective and illustrate its continuing practical and conceptual significance in their fields.

These are some of the more significant themes we believe flow out of the nineteen contributed chapters in this volume. There are certainly many others, and we hope that part of the value of this book is its ability to inspire further discussion of the issues and arguments advanced herein. We believe that the chapters, taken together, demonstrate that a reconstructed conservation, one that draws upon the strengths of the tradition while revising and refitting it to meet the changed circumstances and needs of the present, can move us into a more positive relationship with our intellectual bequest and our biophysical surroundings. In this, we once again draw inspiration from John Dewey, who set the standard for such a process in his aforementioned *Reconstruction in Philosophy*:

> A plea for reconstruction cannot, as far as I can see, be made without giving considerable critical attention to the background within which and in regard to which reconstruction is to take place. Far from being a sign of disesteem, this critical attention is an indispensable part of interest in the development of a philosophy that will do for our time and place what the great doctrines of the past did in and for the cultural media out of which they arose.[9]

The chapters in this book are organized in the following manner. Part II, "Nature and Culture Reconsidered," contains chapters by Judd, McCullough, Dizard, and Vivanco and explores the contested meaning of the human presence in the landscape, including the question of how we are to cope with the lack of universally clear and absolute distinctions between nature and culture in the histories and practices of conservation. Part III, "Reweaving the Tradition," brings together chapters by Thompson, Minteer, Flader, Taylor, Freyfogle, and Meine and is concerned with the historical refocusing of our conservation narratives and the assessment of their legacies for current and future inquiry and action. In part IV, "New Methods and Models," contributions by Norton, Manning, Bengston and Iverson, Callicott, and Trombulak provide fresh analytic approaches relevant to understanding the values and science of conservation, including new ways of conceptualizing conservation goals on the landscape. Part V, "Reconstructing Conservation Practice: Community and the Future of Conservation Stewardship," contains a series of chapters (by Stokowski; Mitchell and Brown; Diamant, Eugster, and Mitchell; and Lowenthal) that explore the growing dependence of conservation efforts on community action, including the leading role of stewardship ideals and behaviors in this process. In the concluding chapter, we present and discuss twelve emerging principles for a reconstructed conservation, distilled from the preceding chapters. We think these principles provide a useful summary of the book, and we hope they will stimulate further discussion and reflection on the conservation impulse in the years ahead.

We would like to acknowledge the generous support of The Woodstock Foundation, the National Park Service's Conservation Study Institute, The Trust for Public Land, and the University of Vermont's School of Natural Resources. We would also like to thank the following individuals for their suggestions and their commitment to this project over the course of its development: Don DeHayes, Rolf Diamant, David Donath, David Houghton, Nora Mitchell, Bryan Norton, and Bob Pepperman Taylor. We are grateful to our editors at Island Press, Barbara Dean, Barbara Youngblood, and Laura Carrithers, for their enthusiasm about this volume and their efforts in helping to bring it to fruition. Last, we thank Elizabeth Corley and Martha Manning for their good advice, kind patience, and unwavering support.

Part II

Nature and Culture Reconsidered

Writing Environmental History from East to West

RICHARD W. JUDD

Environmental history emerged in the United States in the early 1970s as a subset of the country's western history, having absorbed as its dominant themes the panorama of untrammeled nature and a vast public domain. Well into the 1980s, recruits came predominantly from this parent field, and environmental history continues to bear the imprint of these beginnings. Of the fifty-two articles about the United States published in the first five volumes of *Environmental History* (1996–2000), twenty focused on the West (including Alaska), thirteen on the country at large, eleven on the East, five on the Midwest, and three on the South. Just as the New England synthesis—Puritan cohesion, declension, Yankee individualism—dominates early American history, the western framework—Native harmony, frontier exploitation, conservation consciousness—provides the paradigm for environmental history.[1]

It seems fitting that the West, with its open spaces and monumental landscapes, serves as a font for environmental history. After all, Frederick Jackson Turner's commentary on the American West laid the foundations for the discipline, and the grand scale of this Turnerian landscape gives environmental history much of its epic quality. A generation of prominent western historians such as Fred A. Shannon, Walter Prescott Webb, James C. Malin, Wallace Stegner, Ray Allen Billington, and Paul W. Gates were equally influential in sensitizing environmental historians to the shaping influence of aridity, openness, and formative frontier institutions.[2] Moreover, the nation's best-known conservation achievements—the first national forests, national parks, wilderness areas, federal dams, and soil conservation efforts—were carved out of these western spaces. Even today, the public sees conservation as tantamount to saving these western natural resources and scenic wonders.

Regionalism and History

Transcending this regional bias is difficult, given the discipline's philosophical perspective and its methodological demands. The cross-disciplinary approach in environmental history research adds layers of complication to the historian's already full agenda, discouraging transregional approaches. Regionalism, moreover, is the bedrock of environmental history. Linking people to a particular natural landscape, the ultimate test of environmental history, usually requires a tight geographic focus: a story rooted in place. Yet environmental historians, like all historians, are encouraged to generalize. Compelled by the belief that a society connected to its past is better prepared to face its future, historians seek the universal in the particular— the regional, in this case. Too often, this means writing as though the western experience were the norm, against which all other environmental history should be judged. Thus, the basic questions raised in the discipline's early years have endured: how did contact with primitive open space influence American culture, and how did an aggressively capitalist society disfigure a fragile virgin land? Reassessing these questions is important because the paradigms American historians use have wider significance. As an Asian historian recently wrote, U.S. environmental history has "indelibly marked the field worldwide."[3]

Given these influences, the East hangs in the shadow of the West in this particular field. Most courses in environmental history, if Bruce Piasecki's 1984 "Sampler of Courses and Programs in Environmental History" is still representative, gravitate to western themes such as the rectilinear survey, the passing of the frontier, the public domain, reclamation, the dust bowl, national parks, and wilderness protection. Even our basic eastern texts, William Cronon's *Changes in the Land,* Carolyn Merchant's *Ecological Revolutions,* and Timothy Silver's *New Face on the Countryside,* are modeled on a basic western premise in which a pioneering encounter with raw nature impoverished a region's ecological mosaic. Moving beyond this approach not only aligns environmental history with environmental and cultural conditions in the East but also offers a foundation for reconstructing the broader fields of conservation and environmental history. Drawing on some new themes emerging in the field, I would like to imagine an environmental history written from east to west rather than west to east, with a different set of questions, concerns, and definitions. This literature reminds us that the East, like the West, reveals, in the words of Eric Purchase, the "bedrock truth about how Americans treat the land."[4]

In discussing historiographic differences as fundamental as these, it is useful to identify those cultural and natural features that define the East as distinctive from the West. The following list includes those that seem most significant to environmental analysis.[5] Subsequent discussion will elaborate.

Western Regionalism	Eastern Regionalism
Frontier landscapes	Long-settled landscapes
Mobility	Stability
Conquest and disintegration	Reciprocity and ecological reintegration
Rootlessness and "newness"	Tradition and folkways
Individualistic land use	Traditional constraints on land use
Alienated work	Teleology of work
Commons exploitation	Commons environmentalism
Federal conservation	State conservation
Economic gyration	Gradual economic ascent
Earth monuments	Pastoral landscapes
Ecological conquest	Disintegration
Cultural rootlessness	Newness
"Pristine" wilderness	"Recovering" wilderness
Aridity (slow succession)	Humidity (rapid succession)
Large-scale history ("big sky")	Small-scale history ("Thoreau's swamp")

Long-Settled Lands

Setting aside the Spanish Southwest, the greatest length, continuity, and intensity of settlement are found in the East. The frontier disappeared along the Appalachian front as early as 1810, and in many places forest clearing peaked in the 1840s, leaving only the most remote mountain regions untouched.[6] Entire industries—ice and charcoal production, tanning, shipbuilding, live-oaking—emerged and disappeared before much of the West was settled. Stone walls, cellar holes, and forgotten cemeteries, sheltered by old-growth forests, attest to the fact that what the East lacks in geographic scale it makes up for in chronology. The effacement of an integrated ecology is not *the* story in the East; rather, it is one of several scenarios that emerge out of a long history of disruption and rebirth in a settled landscape.

This long durée gives us an opportunity to step back from the initial pioneering pulse and take stock of the culture–nature interaction over the long haul. It changes our perspective in several ways. First, the oscillations of deforestation and reforestation, depletion and renewal, settlement and abandonment, and pollution and recovery suggest reciprocity rather than nature-as-victim. This long, nonlinear history casts our relation to nature as a meeting of equals. Forests now cover 90 percent of Maine, 87 percent of New Hampshire, and more than 75 percent of Vermont; nineteenth-century figures were largely the reverse. In today's Connecticut, 25 percent of the flora and 30 percent of the fish are introduced species. As David Foster notes, these changes comprise "one of the most remarkable environmental stories in U.S. history," but this is a story in which nature and culture are truly interactive: culture disrupts; nature rebounds; and culture responds. "What began as an opposition," Kent Ryden says, "has slowly evolved into a balance."[7] One era's ecological disaster becomes the next era's textured landscape.

Second, studying long-settled landscapes forces us to think about the importance of tradition and folkways, acquired over several generations of continuous habitation, in shaping the environment. The western experience was—and is—predicated on mobility, evoking images of raw culture confronting raw nature, a kind of atomistic free-for-all in which profit is the singular motive driving a rootless and traditionless people. George Perkins Marsh once described Americans as a people who rendered "all things, the works of nature or the works of man, the woodland and the meadow, the river and the highway, . . . in a condition of perpetual fluctuation and change." This addiction to change, he noted, was "unfavourable for the execution of permanent improvements," since it required "a very generous spirit in a landholder to plant a wood on a farm he expects to sell." Perceptive here as always, Marsh understood why geographic mobility and conservation do not go hand in hand. According to landscape historian John Warfield Simpson, colonial Americans had no historical links with the land, so they were unlikely to people it with the myths and spirits of their ancestors. This disconnection, the freedom from reference and context, "made it easier for them to alter the landscape with little guilt or self-restraint."[8]

Colonial Americans were indeed newcomers in a new land, but Turnerian bias—new lands, new ideas—blinds us to the place of tradition in early land use. Most environmental historians, following William Cronon, have assumed a starkly capitalist orientation in the earliest Euro-American colonies, a set of values that structured colonists' relation to nature. This assumption borrows from a larger controversy among colonial and early national historians over capitalist and precapitalist mentalité, but environmental historians enter this debate heavily influenced by the western pioneering experience, in which advanced capitalist impulses and Turnerian individualism were in full flood. In fact, colonial society was not constructed out of thin air; recent historians such as Timothy H. Breen, David Grayson Allen, David B. Hall, and Martyn J. Bowden emphasize the transfer of Old World culture and customs to this resource-rich land.[9] These transfers suggest a narrative different from the environmental declension found in western history. Brian Donahue's work on early Concord and my own on northern New England suggest a set of Old World traditions that encouraged collective management of such resources as soil, water, meadow hay, forage, timber, muck, game, fish, clams, fodder, peat, and fuelwood.[10] Early on, Americans made their pact with private property, but in a variety of interesting ways land use followed communal expectations.

The persistence of these communal traditions after the American Revolution is exemplified in a flood of petitions to New England state legislatures between 1800 and 1840 asking for local collective powers to manage resources such as fish, game, and timber. These in turn reflect a broader pattern of common rights and constraints. Mutually agreed-upon measures for hunting, fishing, logging, foraging, and grazing were among the "habits of mutuality," as southern historian Steven Hahn put it, that persisted in the early national period despite the market revolution and its ideology of open access or private enclosure. As Richard Andrews points out, "environmental policies of many kinds existed in America from the earliest period of European colonization."[11] Here again, the image of society reinventing itself on the frontier blinds us to the role of tradition in shaping American land use.

Third, studying long-settled landscapes brings into focus a kind of cultural familiarity with the land that is not as apparent in the western experience, and this, too, has implications for environmental history. As Hal

Baron noted in his history of Chelsea, Vermont, eastern farmers who resisted the nineteenth-century rural-to-urban and east-to-west migrations nurtured a strong sense of place and belonging, and here, in these multi-generational links to the land, we can observe the genesis of a meaningful cultural geography and test this powerful construct against the idea of frontier rootlessness.[12] Generations of southern mountain people, for instance, used the ridges and hollows near their homes as a sort of commons, a place to run cattle and hogs, hunt bear, fish, harvest plants and herbs, gather berries, and cut firewood; women acquired intimate knowledge of local flora essential to subsistence, craft, and commodity production. Thus, we can add to the several ways of knowing nature and place—exploratory knowledge, scientific knowledge, romanticized knowledge—a concept of folk knowledge that historians are only now coming to appreciate. Mountain people saw the forest not simply as board feet but, as historian Donald Davis asserts, also as a "living matrix of plants, animals, and shared memories." This folk knowledge in turn cultured a sense of ownership: "They regarded this country as their country, their common," Gifford Pinchot discovered during his work at Biltmore. "And it was not surprising, for they needed everything usable in it—pasture, fish, game—to supplement the very meager living they were able to scratch from the soil." Margaret Brown, who studied southern Appalachian peoples, adds that "in a way foreign to a modern reader, love for the land came from use." Familiarity and folk knowledge brought a realization, as Menominee Indian leader Verna Fowler once put it, that "you have . . . only have one home," a place where your ancestors were buried and where your "children's children . . . will have to live."[13]

Alienated Work and the Ethics of Land Use

Plumbing the rhetoric of place in long-settled lands reveals a more nuanced set of motives behind the use of nature. American historians uniformly comment on the rapaciousness of early farmers, loggers, and hunters, but we actually know little about how these participants defined their role in the continental shift from wilderness to "fruitful field," in Timothy Dwight's memorable phrase.[14] Activities such as farm clearing, logging, trapping, dam building, and fishing were utilitarian tasks, but rural producers also saw their work with nature in teleological terms, as a way of bringing order to a chaotic natural world. Work was the signature they left on the land, the mirror of their aspirations, and, like Dwight, they celebrated the agrarian scene emerging from the gloomy forest. New England agrarian literature cast nature and landscape as dynamic forms, responding to floods, fires, mountain slides, insect plagues, climate changes, and other sometimes mysterious natural forces, and readers were exhorted to mold the latent energies in their forests, swamps, soils, rivers, and climates to a greater purpose. Farming and logging had subtle moral implications. To assume a one-dimensional frontier impulse—individual profit from supposedly inexhaustible resources—obscures this teleology of work and oversimplifies the meaning behind changes in the land.[15]

Whether or not this teleology included a conservation ethic is worthy of debate. When the American pioneers "scrape[d] epidermis against bark on the primitive frontier," John Opie pointed out in his recent environmental history textbook, they saw themselves "belligerently at war with nature."[16] This terse statement summarizes our general understanding of the rural petty producer in nineteenth-century America, east or west. Donald Worster blamed the dust bowl of the 1930s on profit-maximizing Great Plains farmers who took pride in "busting" the sod and failed to accept the primacy of grass in a grasslands ecology. But this alienation from the land, Worster went on to explain, was at least in part a product of the Plains farmers' classic western orientation: they were "newcomers" on the last frontier of American agriculture and therefore lacked a sense of place. If indeed mobility explains in part their relation to the land, can we extrapolate that the East's more persistent farmers transcended this alienation?[17] Given the complex associations acquired in the process of using the land over several generations, we may ask: did those who "stayed behind," as Hal Baron put it, harbor a stronger concern for their environment? "Without romanticizing . . . a very difficult life," Margaret Brown asserts, "it is accurate to say that . . . ecological knowledge borne of use and spiritual traditions . . . encouraged them to imbue that use with meaning." According to Donald Davis, the onset of corporate logging in the southern Appalachians triggered an intuitive conservationist reaction among mountain people, not only because heavy logging contributed to flooding and soil erosion but also because it undermined local food- and folkways. "Daughters forgot which herbs their mothers hunted in the woods," Brown writes, "due, in part, to the fact that the woods weren't there any more." Environmental historian Kathryn Newfont found examples of what she calls a "commons environmentalism" as late as the 1970s campaigns to prevent clear-cutting in the southern Appalachian national forests.[18]

We need to know more about how established farmers, loggers, trappers, or rural wage earners—as opposed to pioneers—viewed the exploitation of nature. What they felt about nature was complicated, of course, by their own role in destroying it. Not only this, but they seem to have lacked the overarching vision we associate with mainstream conservation today—the sense of spiritual beauty in wilderness conditions or the abiding faith in scientific forest management. Commons environmentalism, to use Newfont's term, seems to center on specific local uses—fishing, hunting, berrying, wood gathering. New England farmers, for instance, crusaded to save their forests, because forests were useful in a variety of ways, but they were equally eager to drain every swamp in sight, because swamps were *not* useful. Grassroots conservation is as complicated as it is fascinating, and the East, with its long history of petty resource extraction, provides an excellent venue for launching an exploration of its scope and parameters.[19]

America's Earliest Conservation Efforts

The East offers other approaches to reconstructing conservation history. As the first region in the country to deplete its forests, soils, fisheries, and wildlife resources, the East pioneered many conservation measures, typically under state, rather than federal, auspices. State fish commissions, formed in New England in the 1860s, became the nation's first permanent conservation agencies. They amounted to official recognition, as legal historian Arthur McEvoy put it, "that the North American frontier was not, after all, boundless."[20] These early efforts in turn raise questions about the social origins of conservation policy—the degree to which conservation emerged out of class struggles between groups with vested interests in nature. Mill owners, farmers, and fishers advanced conservation claims in their struggle over New England rivers; game laws and forestry measures were similarly contested along class lines, generating conservation rhetoric. These early conservation battles, fought out at the state and local levels, profiled the class and cultural biases of the participants much more clearly and frankly than national debates, in which issues were more abstract and universal.[21]

The East also provides a longer perspective on the industrial revolution and its environmental consequences. Industrialism in the West was ushered in with huge capital outlays and advanced technology; the environmental changes it brought were typically sudden and unilateral. In the East, nature was, in historian Theodore Steinberg's phrase, "incorporated" into the emerging system of markets, machines, and cities in a more gradual and complex fashion. Viewing the industrialization procession from its beginnings, at the shift from domestic to market production, permits a careful assessment of this profound change in relations to nature. Recent histories of industrialization in New England by John Cumbler and Diana Muir assess this shift over the course of a century and across an entire bioregion. They show that environmental changes were part of a much broader pattern: domestic production becoming more marginal, families growing smaller, land more scarce, agriculture more scientific, legal and political thought more proactive, land use more intense, soil more compacted, streamflow more erratic, rivers more polluted—the ecology *and* the workforce more impoverished.[22]

Over the course of this eventful century, nature proved to be variously accommodating, resilient, and resistant. It surfaced in unexpected ways among the crowded tenements and factories, and because New Englanders pioneered this urban-industrial transformation, they were the first to come to grips with its unanticipated natural consequences. This expansive viewpoint shows how a broad spectrum of victims, villains, and heroes interacted with the environment—capitalists, factory workers, farmers, inventors, judges, health officers, and engineers, all of whom shaped, survived, or challenged the early industrial revolution. Collectively, their response anticipated the aggressively active state and the new notion of public good that emerged a century later in the environmental era. In this eastern urban-industrial context, nature itself was defined differently, as a heavily constrained but still intractable biota manifest in microbes and millponds and embedded in a reworked landscape of machines, cities, and regionwide flows of energy, capital, materials, and people. Here again, historical depth and continuity help portray nature as an agent, rather than a victim, of history.[23]

Preservationist Challenges, Historical Reconstructions

Our domesticated eastern nature, freighted with history and tradition and altered to almost unrecognizable dimensions, presents a unique set of contemporary preservationist challenges, and these, too, have implications for reconstructing conservation history. Samuel Hays, who surveyed the environmental movement region by region in his monumental *Beauty, Health, and Permanence: Environmental Politics in the United States, 1955–1985,* found a close connection between the strength of environmental sentiment and the presence of dramatic landscape features that served as sources of regional identity and foci for preservationist politics.[24] In the West, these iconic features tend to be culturally decontextualized earth monuments such as the Grand Canyon or Yellowstone's geysers. The markers of eastern identity are more typically pastoral, distinctive not because of their natural *or* their cultural attributes but because these two are so inextricably combined. The Adirondack forest, the Maine coast, the Chesapeake shore, or the Great Smoky Mountains, for instance, are valued not only for their natural beauty but also for their significance as iconic working landscapes. These associations expand our definition of the redemptive landscape, but they also complicate the preservationist mandate. Many of the islands off the Maine coast, for instance, were deforested by fishermen nearly four centuries ago, and continuous sheep-pasturing kept them treeless. Is this condition "natural," or should they be allowed to grow back to spruce thickets? The "balds" in Great Smoky Mountains National Park present similar management questions.[25]

Defining "natural" makes wilderness management problematic in the East as well. Here there are no "pristine" landscapes comparable to those in the West, but to the casual observer the dynamic eastern forests can *look* primeval after only a few decades of recovery. It was this relatively rapid ecological succession that inspired the Eastern Wilderness Areas Act of 1974, as a companion to the 1964 Wilderness Act, aimed at roadless federal lands in the West. But as policy analysts Lloyd Irland and Christopher Klyza suggest, eastern wilderness is enmeshed in a web of history. These well-trammeled eastern lands have complex multiple meanings, as storehouses of biodiversity; sources of jobs, taxes, and raw materials; and cultural and recreational resources. Thus, despite similarities in the two wilderness acts, the East is "developing its own approach to the wilderness question," as Irland puts it, by adapting to a situation in which the boundaries between nature and culture, trammeled and pure, are less distinct.[26]

The East's iconic cultural landscapes and its recovering wilderness remind conservation historians and policy makers that nature indeed has a history, and we cannot effectively separate the ecological and cultural components of this story. In the United States, ecologists typically study natural processes hypothetically, by excluding any consideration of human intervention, past or present. By contrast, their British counterparts act on an understanding that ecologies have been shaped by human hands over millennia, and these cultural influences have become a part of the natural process.[27] In the East, where the Euro-American landscape is centuries old, the British approach seems more relevant. Wilderness management in a forest littered with abandoned hunting blinds, skid roads, cellar holes, and rock walls must recognize that defining "natural" is not as simple as it seems. In the West, where monumental natural features command the eye and where altitude, severe climate, and competition for soil moisture slow the succession process, nature can seem timeless, absolute, and separate from history. The eastern forest, with its legacy of disturbance and its explosive ecological succession, challenges the idea that nature and culture can be viewed as separate entities. Thoreau, for example, found the Maine woods authenticating in part because it invoked the lore of logging, hunting, guiding, exploring, and timber surveying: it was a cultural, as much as a natural, place.

The Problem of Scale

Finally, the scale of the natural environment in the eastern United States changes certain management prerogatives, and this, too, has implications for reconstructing conservation history. Western wilderness areas are measured in millions of acres; those in the East, in tens of thousands. These islands of wildness are no less precious, but they present unique challenges. "Scale is an important feature of the conservation proposal," public land law expert Debra Donahue observed about western rangelands. "Successful biodiversity conservation . . . must encompass whole landscapes."[28] In the East, where nature is closer, more intimate, and more fragmented, this principle must be modified to accommodate landscapes shaped and sized in a variety of ways.

The scale of eastern conservation and environmental history also requires flexible thinking. Western writers treat history in epic slices encompassing huge watersheds, grasslands, or mountain ranges—"ocean-like landscape[s] over which powerful currents and forces flow . . . unimpeded," as landscape historian John Warfield Simpson puts it.[29] Eastern history tends to be more focused, as the New England town studies of the

1960s and 1970s suggest. In this regard, Thoreau's fixation on intimacy in nature appreciation is instructive; as ecologist Daniel Botkin points out, Thoreau rarely mentioned the vast Katahdin wilderness outside his essays in *The Maine Woods*. "In contrast, it was the biologically rich swamp, surrounding him so closely with life that distant vistas were obscured and size became irrelevant, that held the deepest meaning." Botkin concludes that we cling, mistakenly, to the assumption that "only a big wilderness can provide an experience of the wild."[30] And what about big environmental history? Is an eastern alewife stream as relevant, historically, as the Columbia River? John Hanson Mitchell's suggestive history of Scratch Flat, a small parcel of land near the Nashua River, ranges across fifteen thousand years of environmental change and continuity, offering endless possibilities for understanding the nature–human dialectic. Diana Muir begins her environmental history of New England at a small suburban pond near Boston, where eradication of the beaver in 1632 leads to a discussion of food chains, aquatic botany, moose, nesting cavities, siltation, eutrophication, peat accumulation, and the like. Kevin Dann's history of Lewis Creek, a minor flowage basin on the eastern shore of Lake Champlain, expands into a discussion of natural science, ecology, botany, folklore, and the history that makes up the watershed's sense of place.[31] As they traverse these local landscapes rich in images, stories, and natural processes, Mitchell, Muir, and Dann challenge our sense of appropriate scale in history. Gayle Brandow Samuels focuses her environmental history on individual trees, such as Connecticut's Charter Oak, but like the lone sylphium Aldo Leopold discovered in a neglected corner of a midwestern cemetery, her trees have deep roots in the history of the land, leading outward to the community, the watershed, or the bioregion.[32]

So where does this survey of eastern environmental history lead us? Nature East is altered, relative, intimate, and fragmented, built and rebuilt over time, a cultural as well as a natural process. Can this model cast a shadow as well? Perhaps not like that of the West, but if we acknowledge this different regional reality, if we search out the unique as well as the universal in each landscape history, then we can pull together the elements of a truly national environmental history. "There is no mistaking the Northeast today for a pristine landscape," Christopher Klyza tells us, but he quickly reminds us that all across the continent, just as in the East, Native Americans manipulated nature for millennia before Europeans ever saw the "forest primeval." Every wilderness, in short, is a recovering wilderness, a land with a history. Relatively natural nature is a supremely eastern idea, but it is not at all inappropriate elsewhere. The East helps us reconstruct the conservation story for a more settled continent, a modern world in which nature persists in the engineered landscape. And by defining nature in complex ways, eastern history points to a defense of the environment appropriate to our modern humanized landscapes—engineered landscapes that are, by now, far more typical of the American scene. What applies in the East, then, now applies everywhere, even in today's West. Reconstructing conservation history—from East to West—should be of interest to all historians.

Chapter 3

The Nature of History Preserved;
or, The Trouble with Green Bridges

ROBERT MCCULLOUGH

In 1995, a now familiar volume of essays titled *Uncommon Ground: Toward Reinventing Nature* examined the many ways in which our natural environments are devised by culture. Nature, according to the book's editor, William Cronon, is not nearly so natural a concept as people typically assume. More important, Cronon argues that by placing certain privileged natures apart from the broader nature in which we all participate, we succumb to an illusion that obscures our immediate surroundings. We also create natures enjoyed only by privileged segments of our society. The book seeks greater awareness of this cultural-mindedness in our environments, with the hope of building more just and sustainable relationships with the places we call home—by another name, community.[1]

One essay, that by Cronon, focuses on wilderness. Its title, "The Trouble with Wilderness; or, Getting Back to the Wrong Nature," proved prophetic in the amount of turmoil it created, and continues to create, within the environmental movement. The essay was republished in the inaugural issue of *Environmental History* in January 1996, accompanied by critiques from three conservationists, Samuel Hays, Michael Cohen, and Thomas Dunlap. Cronon then provided a rejoinder to their criticisms.[2]

Today, these articles are well-trampled ground to many, and I resurrect them with some hesitation—in fact, trepidation. Yet together they raise profound questions for my discipline, historic preservation—questions all the more significant for the absence of any intention by the authors to ask them. For example, if wilderness, that lofty pilgrimage church of environmentalism (cathedrals house too many rituals for some cultural tastes), is entirely an invention of past and present cultures, or a socially constructed abstraction, as Cronon suggests, isn't everything farther down the

mountain cultural as well? And, if cultural interpretations offer the clearest vantage points for observing these environments, shouldn't our emphasis be one of identifying and preserving cultural resources rather than
natural ones?

This begins to look like an opportunity for a strategic acquisition by historic preservation, and we might call the emerging conglomerate "Ecology
of Cultural Landscapes and Built Environments," offering at least partial
recognition to shareholders of the environmental movement. Such a
merger might also give our discipline a chance to discard the word "historic," a term that too frequently prompts division rather than unison.

Yet a serious note of warning underlies Cronon's comments, a note that
rings true for both the historic preservation and environmental movements. If we defend wilderness and wild nature (substitute cultural landscapes and the built environment) in such a way that we fail to engage
fundamental human problems (poverty, education, adequate housing, safe
and healthy working places, overpopulation, transportation), two important consequences ensue and our efforts become self-defeating. First, we
fail to generate broad-based public support for a conservation ethic. Second, we risk relinquishing that body of support to those who would discard resources for the sake of grasping short-term economic gain. Cronon
believes, and I think he is right, that we won't find solutions to human
problems through abstract ideals about nature (substitute "history"). This
type of escape simply won't do. Instead, we must find and confront a
middle ground where a broad range of human problems can be addressed
in visibly successful ways.

This quest for middle ground—by another name, community—is (or
should be) as fundamental to historic preservation as it is to natural resource conservation. Trends during the 1990s suggest that we (historic
preservationists) seem to be moving in this direction, despite the absence
of any literary forum wherein the type of acute self-criticism in which
Cronon engages can take place. For example, on May 4, 2002, Richard
Moe, president of the National Trust for Historic Preservation, addressed
the National Press Club in Washington, D.C. His speech, titled "A New
Pride in Our Past, a New Day for Our Cities," offered cautious optimism
for the nation's urban centers, today showing signs of recovery. Moreover, a
fair share of the credit, he believes, belongs to historic preservation.

Anticipating surprise at this claim from members of his audience, Moe
explained that the preservation movement is no longer the vocal band of

outsiders that people imagine it to be. This comment alone acknowledges preservation's difficulty in establishing an identity of broad appeal. Instead, Moe continued, the discipline has matured into a sophisticated national movement dedicated to the look and livability of America's communities. Here, substitution of the word "community" for "city" is no casual proxy. In response to a question from the audience at the conclusion of his remarks, Moe stressed that, today, historic preservation is all about building and preserving communities—by another name, middle ground.

At first glance, this emphasis on community seems at least worthy but not necessarily earthshaking. Yet, upon reflection, the full implications loom large. Preserving community means engaging all aspects of community structure. In turn, this means establishing alliances, or at least working relationships, with the many disciplines that contribute to community: housing, commerce, transportation, education, social services, public utilities, conservation commissions. The list is a long one, and nothing less can be expected to really solve human problems. This is precisely the point that Cronon is making. In truth, the goals are so closely parallel and the task so enormous that one wonders why cultural and natural resource protection have remained separate for so long in America. Clearly, this is at least one of the central questions for any seminar examining methods of reconstructing conservation.

This lengthy stage-setting has been necessary to frame that single issue. But if we plan to move in this direction, then a broad range of other questions must also be considered. Many of them surface in the writings of Cronon, Hays, Cohen, and Dunlap, again providing evidence of the important connections between natural and cultural resource conservation. Many of these concerns, too, are closely aligned to questions posed by the seminar that led to this book. The final tally may show more questions than answers, but many of the important ones seem to point toward that fundamental middle ground. We should lose no time in beginning our dialogue.

History as a Cultural Construct

Cronon states the paradox of wilderness preservation in this way: it is a resource untouchable by humans, but unless we humans manage it very consciously, it is unlikely to survive. The paradox of preserving historic buildings and cultural landscapes might be phrased in this manner: these are symbols to be set apart from the forces of change, but even the seemingly neutral act of interpreting them as symbolic introduces change. Or, as Michael Cohen observed, "in the broad sweep of history, all except change is illusion."3

Let's, for purposes of discussion, accept the argument that wilderness is mostly a human invention and investigate the parallels to history, which we might define as either pristine truth or the ultimate cultural construct. Cronon's trouble with wilderness is not its human lineage, and he regards the resource as no less worthy of protection for wearing the garb of culture. Rather, his concern is for policy decisions weakened by a failure to recognize the resource's true nature. Miscalculated policies, in turn, become obstacles to solving the larger human problems at stake. In other words, by blindly pursuing an unattainable perfection in a wilderness removed from any human intervention, we lose sight of more compelling human objectives.

Such positing raises a number of important considerations for historic preservation. For one thing, if wilderness, the least human (or most perfect) of the earth's resources, is a cultural phenomenon, in what ways should this shape our attitudes toward more mundane cultural resources? Cronon asks, "What is the true nature of wilderness?" Today, we might ask: "What is the true nature of history revealed in our landscapes and buildings? Have we set the past apart, giving it a symbolism that transcends its practical human value? Are these symbols appreciated, or even recognized, only by a privileged few? Do we, in the pursuit of truth, knowledge, or symbols, seek an ultimately elusive past and, in the process, misconceive its true nature or worth? More important, what are the consequences and costs of any such misconceptions in human terms?

Just as Cronon places greater emphasis on the second concern, that of costs and consequences, debate about the true nature of history may be secondary to any assessment of whether the policies that flow from our preservation ethic truly address human needs. Nevertheless, being mindful of the former is crucial because it reinforces the need to constantly connect with the latter. Moreover, reconsidering the nature of history preserved is an exercise that ultimately may benefit those engaged in natural resource conservation. Cronon believes that wilderness, as a cultural resource, deserves protection. If so, doesn't the discipline that regularly engages in dialogue about methods for preserving cultural resources have something to offer? Today, any effort to sort these complexities seems incomplete unless both of the two disciplines are present.

As Thomas Dunlap remarks, some of the connections made in other countries are absent in America. He points to Australia, where wilderness, housing for workers, and human landscapes are all part of environmental history and where labor unions have joined forces with environmentalists to protect the Great Barrier Reef. He writes: "We need a framework that will integrate city and country, factory and forest, daily life and wilderness experience."[4]

Dunlap's plea is not a new one. Benton MacKaye pursued an equally comprehensive ordering, and his writing surfaces in a great variety of contexts. A 1929 essay titled "A New England Recreation Plan," which appeared in the *Journal of Forestry,* underscores the need to combine both the primeval and the mechanistic. MacKaye wrote: "And so the forest is the root of man's society as the city is its head and flower. A civilization without its city would be a headless one; and a civilization without its forest is a rootless one. Forest and city must grow side by side in any balanced civilization." More than seventy years have elapsed, but this integration of cultural and natural resources continues to prove elusive.[5]

MacKaye, too, emphasized the importance of preserving backyard wild places, exactly the type of activity that Cronon believes is lacking today among wilderness advocates. In 1947, as president of The Wilderness Society, MacKaye issued a memorandum to all members asking them to seek out and preserve neighborhood patches of wildland. The effort was part of a nationwide campaign to build a broad base for wilderness preservation. Although MacKaye scattered his ideas far and wide, many of them never taking root, nearly all are united by a single thread—a fundamental humanism that defined both the man and his thinking throughout a long life.

That humanism, too, provided a foundation for the enduring friendship between MacKaye and architect Clarence Stein. The pair first met on July 10, 1921, at the Hudson Guild Farm near Netcong, New Jersey, where the Appalachian Trail was conceived. MacKaye's proposal for the Appalachian Trail was published in the *Journal of the American Institute of Architects* that fall, and Stein, who chaired the institute's Committee on Community Planning, provided an introduction to a reprint of the article that same year. The friendship that began that summer flourished for more than half a century, until 1975, the year both men died, MacKaye at ninety-six and Stein at ninety-three.

That two men of such vastly different backgrounds should prosper in friendship from so improbable a beginning point as the Appalachian Trail is an intriguing part of their story. Stein, urbane and worldly, was educated in New York City at the Workingman's School, established by the New York Society for Ethical Culture. He became a planner of new towns, his outlook shaped by the living conditions of the urban poor and their shabby neighborhoods. MacKaye, a forester, socialist, regional planner, and writer, rebelled against the exploitation of labor and natural resources in the name of capitalism. The friendship of Stein and MacKaye, kindred spirits in humanism, is a beacon for the protection of cultural and natural resources during the twenty-first century, a metaphor to guide alliance between the two fields. This is a friendship, too, that can shape future environmental thought, much as Thomas Cole and William Cullen Bryant, depicted in the famous Asher B. Durand painting *Kindred Spirits,* influenced twentieth-century environmentalism.[6]

Neither the balanced civilization envisioned by MacKaye and Stein nor the practical alliances at work in Australia are unprecedented. Octavia Hill, an Englishwoman who pursued social and housing reforms, was impressed with a Massachusetts organization, the Trustees of Public Reservations. That body was created in 1890 by legislative act to hold title to scenic and historic lands. Hill returned to England to help form Britain's National Trust for Places of Historic Interest or Natural Beauty in 1894. Ironically, more than fifty years later, in 1949, America's National Trust for Historic Preservation was chartered, but without direct ties to natural resources.

If we are to reconsider the nature of history as a cultural construct, Kevin Lynch's 1972 book *What Time Is This Place?* deserves another reading. Lynch focused on the connections between social and environmental change, noting that "history is time" and "the environment is the clock by which we tell time." Seeking a particular use of old and new to provide reassurance in the face of change, he argued, "A desirable image is one that celebrates and enlarges the present while making connections with past and future." Although intolerant of the inhuman qualities of urban renewal and its great psychological and social costs, Lynch questioned some of the doctrines and purposes of historic preservation. Past events, he reasoned, may give us a sense of proportion to help us bear our present difficulties, but efforts to preserve all of the past would be life-denying. Instead, he argued, guarantees of, or limits on, the rate of change might be more effective than either preservation or a policy of no regulation at all.[7]

Many in the historic preservation field did not welcome Lynch's assessment. In particular, his separation of remote history from the immediate past, one or two generations deep, seemed untenable. To Lynch, the latter possessed much greater value in helping society cope with the stresses of environmental change, and the former could be relegated to a public attic, circulated periodically. I didn't, and still don't, agree that the remote past lacks utility. Evidence of its use is all around us in my adopted state, Vermont. I didn't, and still don't, believe that Lynch adequately addressed an American ethic that often places the burden of proving that the destruction of resources isn't necessary on those who would conserve them. Instead, a presumption that resources can be preserved in the face of change, at least in some form, seems to be a much better point of beginning.

Yet today, efforts to poke holes in Lynch's arguments and to defend historic preservation seem to push us into the very same camp of wilderness advocates whom Cronon criticizes. For those who cling too closely to the past, Lynch points to the inevitability of change. For those who cling too closely to wilderness as a nature apart from humankind, Cronon points to the certainty of human influence. Perplexing as these concerns may be, one thought is strikingly clear in reconsidering Lynch's book: it is pregnant with the same quest for solutions to present human problems that Cronon seeks. Lynch's introductory words are telling: "Throughout the discussion, the reader will find a strong emphasis on the present—where we are and must live—and on the necessity and desirability of change. This will at times be disturbing."[8]

Without flinching from the staunch belief that our cultural heritage is of enormous social value, David Lowenthal also affirms the certainty of change. In his 1985 book *The Past Is a Foreign Country,* he observes that recent interest in history, propelled in part by the historic preservation movement, has revealed quite starkly how much the present actually changes the past. He and Cronon alike sound a note of warning that we risk misconceiving the past (substitute wilderness) if we think of it as a fixed truth from which no deviation should occur. And, as does Lynch, Lowenthal suggests that a fusion of past and present offers a more realistic alternative, arguing that our heritage remains alive and comprehensible only if that fusion takes place.[9]

Cultural Resource Advocacy

The task, then, becomes one of developing models for accommodating change in order to achieve a successful fusion of past and present, cultural and natural. At this point, an example may help to distill these concerns

and at the same time illustrate several points, among them (1) the suscep-
tibility of history to cultural construction (as opposed to a truth apart); (2)
the potential breadth of division between cultural and natural resource
conservation; (3) avenues of commonality despite that potential breadth;
and (4) consideration of the question of whether historians can or should
act as resource advocates, a question some may find vexing.

In Vermont, skirmishes are being fought at the sites of historic metal
truss bridges. In this state, most were built during the twentieth century,
many after the infamous 1927 flood. They represent distinctive features on
the landscape and also define spatial gateways into village centers. (It may
be just coincidence, but nearly all are painted green.) Many people regard
these bridges as neither strong enough nor wide enough to carry modern
vehicles safely. Yet communities able to look beyond a coating of rust
sometimes recognize the visual contributions these structures offer. Inevitably, a question arises: can we replace the old bridge with a new one exactly like it?

If that occurs, a very small segment of the population will understand
that we have lost a piece of history and that the new bridge is a deception
rather than a truth. Yet isn't it symbolism that transforms the bridge into
something more than just a physical object of painted steel? And isn't this
symbolism entirely a cultural construct, as susceptible to interpretation and
shifting perceptions as Cronon's wilderness? More important, as we chase
our tails trying to solve this conundrum, do we lose sight of more pressing
human problems at stake? If so, what are the true costs to our plural
environments?

At first glance, forests and green bridges may seem so far apart that the
likelihood of any broad alliance appears remote. Yet the gap is probably not
so vast after all. Not surprisingly, people often ask why rusted steel bridges
are worth preserving. One response, often successful, is that our communities and landscapes are patchworks of natural and cultural resources and
that changes to incidental parts can ultimately transform the whole. This
process occurs in small increments and is very similar to stream bank erosion, which is often readily visible to those posing the questions. Moreover,
biologists tend to prefer the preservation of existing bridges because this
avoids damage to stream banks caused by the construction of new and
larger bridges, almost always on a different alignment. If a coalition can be
forged here, why not in Benton MacKaye's backyard wild places?

The division between cultural and natural resource protection also poses irony in more subtle ways. Why, for example, does the type of critical self-scrutiny prompted by Cronon and others seem to surface more readily in the field of natural resource protection than in that of historic preservation? Part of the answer may be that the latter has something important to offer the former—an inclination to consistently reexamine canons fundamental to the discipline, together with a number of forums in which that inquiry can take place.

Historic preservation, too, may be able to offer something in return. If the battle is for fusion of past and present, as Lowenthal argues, or for middle ground, as Cronon suggests, the question then becomes the degree to which history and nature, as cultural constructs, can be altered without compromising sustainability for all human and nonhuman species. Historic preservation has struggled long and hard with part of that question and has developed very specific models, now standard, to describe the subtleties of change that take place. Many of these models assume the necessity of combining past and present, much as Lowenthal advises.

Of the participants in the seminar that preceded this book, how many paused to consider the color, texture, light, and space of their immediate environment? Its contribution to their ability to focus on important questions? The John Dewey Lounge, housed in the University of Vermont's historic Old Mill building, is a careful restoration, by definition an effort to accurately return a resource to a specific period in its history. Yet it is only one small part of a much larger rehabilitation project that begins just down the hall. In contrast to restoration, rehabilitation involves preserving an old building by adapting it to a new use. Change is not only permissible; it is often recognized as the surest means to extend a building's life. Yet change should not compromise the building's underlying historic integrity—manifest in its character-defining features. Thus, an ability to continue interpreting the building's history, mentally separating it from the changes that have taken place, is essential.

Here, more specific models, such as the secretary of the U.S. Department of the Interior's Standards for Historic Preservation Projects, become important. Initially, finding an appropriate new use is fundamental—a use that will fit into the old building without destroying its history. Beyond that, repairing historic materials, when possible, is preferable to replacing them. If deteriorated beyond repair, these materials should be replaced in kind. Essential new features, elevators, accessibility systems, lighting, or fire safety doors, for example, can be introduced in unobtrusive locations or designed to fit comfortably with older features. Nor is the restoration of a single room necessarily incompatible with rehabilitation taking place elsewhere in the structure.

Other terms, including "preservation" and "reconstruction," also have special meanings and are applied in different circumstances. We in historic preservation don't seem to battle over such questions in the same way those in natural resource conservation do. Each term means something different, yet each recognizes that certain degrees of truth in history are acceptable, in fact unavoidable. Ironically, Kevin Lynch found these distinctions perplexing. Part of the explanation may be that historic preservation has always been tethered by the practical limits of its goals. Most buildings must be justified in economic terms, and we are usually satisfied just to say that at least part of history survives. Stated more precisely, we are often content if efforts to introduce the new are approached with a sincere respect for the past.

Conclusion

One final question deserves consideration. Are those of us engaged in these battles as advocates properly able to step back and give fair thought to the public needs at stake? To the ephemeral qualities of cultural constructs? Or do we become so vested in a particular outcome—so personally committed to one cause—that we lose sight of the larger struggles occurring around us? More important, do we recognize the far-reaching consequences of our actions? Do we engage the broader public, building new green bridges of a collaborative nature and adding to our constituencies in the process, or do we ultimately extend the divide? Bringing our two bodies of thought to bear on this question will, I believe, strengthen and balance both.

Chapter 4

Going Native:
Second Thoughts on Restoration

JAN E. DIZARD

Nearly a century and a half ago, George Perkins Marsh warned of an imminent catastrophe: we (European immigrants to North America) were clearing forests, altering rivers, and introducing non-native species of plants and animals (and pathogens as well) to an extent that seemed certain to change forever—and for the worse—the nature of nature. A diplomat in Turkey and Italy, Marsh saw at firsthand the permanent damage that deforestation and overgrazing had wrought. Marsh, like his contemporaries and many who followed their lead, thought nature was like an extraordinarily complex machine. As with a machine, every part is, in principle, indispensable. When a forest is cleared, everything changes, down to the microorganisms in what was once the forest floor. When a river is dammed, the effects ripple up- and downstream. In his remarkable *Man and Nature* (1864), Marsh systematically surveyed the disturbances, depletions, and degradations that several thousands of years of human activity had produced, beginning first in the Mediterranean region and then in Europe. *Man and Nature* was, in effect, Marsh's warning to his fellow Americans: learn from these errors and do all you can to moderate appetites and improve forestry and agricultural practices.

Although he worried about what the environmental disruptions would mean for the future, Marsh was not simply a doomsayer. He held out hope that, with a fuller appreciation of the intricate workings of nature, humans could become less destructive of the natural world and learn to work with instead of against nature. The word "sustainability" had not yet been introduced into the vocabulary, but that is clearly what Marsh had in mind. He was at least guardedly optimistic about our capacity to learn from past mistakes. He was, as his biographer, David Lowenthal, aptly put it, a "prophet of conservation."[1] Things may never be what they once were, but we needn't rush headlong toward certain calamity. With care, understanding, and self-restraint, nature's bounty might continue to nourish us, literally and figuratively. Were he alive today, Marsh would no doubt marvel at the resilience of his native Vermont. Whether this resilience would have caused him to revise his assessment of the relationship between "man and nature" is a far more complicated question than I can address here. What I do want to address is where the line of analysis begun by Marsh has taken us.

Needless to say, we have seen precious little of care and self-restraint in the century and a half since Marsh published *Man and Nature*. When concern for the environment began to arouse the public in the 1970s, the Progressive Era conservation movement that Marsh helped inspire had very nearly run its course, not because its mission had been accomplished but because it had never been taken seriously. The only major exception to this generalization involves the way we have managed game fish and game animals. Hunters and fishers, albeit with foot-dragging,[2] helped promote and have strongly supported a conservation-minded game management policy, which has meant that most game species are thriving.[3] The federal agencies charged with ensuring sustainable use of public lands and those whose mission also included educating private landowners to become better stewards of their holdings were simply not equal to the pressures from the United States Congress and the White House, not to mention governors and state legislatures, each reflecting the intense lobbying of the extractive, agricultural, and recreational interests. The reawakened environmental movement had little sympathy for conservation, which seemed scarcely more than a fig leaf masking wasteful and blatantly unsustainable practices. Rejecting the language of conservation and suspicious of sustainability, contemporary environmentalists have been steadily drawn toward efforts to protect as much of the planet as possible from the bulldozer, chain saw, and plow. Since there are precious few places left that can be called, with a straight face, "pristine," it did not take long for the desire to protect the environment to metamorphose into a desire to reclaim and restore lands to at least an approximation of their presumed original condition.

The reason seems simple enough: what was here before humans began modifying the flora and fauna, and the land, air, and water on which they depend, had been tested by the force of natural selection over many thousands of years and were, thus, ideally suited to be where they were. Every step removed from the original ensemble of flora and fauna is a step toward decline and instability. Marsh captures this nicely:

Nature, left undisturbed, so fashions her territory as to give it almost unchanging permanence of form, outline, and proportion, except when shattered by geological convulsions; and in these comparatively rare cases of derangement, she sets herself at once to repair the superficial damage, and to restore, as nearly as practicable, the former aspect of her dominion.[4]

Decades before plant ecologist Frederic E. Clements and ecologist Eugene Odum introduced the concepts of succession and climax, Marsh described undisturbed nature existing in "a condition of equilibrium . . . which, without the action of man, would remain, with little fluctuation, for countless ages."[5] Thus, had the hand of man been stayed, things would have remained as nature intended. It follows that if we can remove the handprint of man, equilibrium will be our reward. Instead of a world careening toward calamity, we might achieve a world in which large swaths of land are more or less intact; and if the swaths can be made large enough, they may be a decisive counterpoise to the disturbed and degraded lands that are beyond reclaiming. Wherever possible, nature's regulation should be preferred to human manipulation.

In this spirit, a diverse group of biologists, ecologists, and environmental activists, working loosely under the umbrella of "restoration ecology," has been making a serious bid for defining what it means to be an environmentalist. In the early 1970s, an environmental management regime called "natural regulation" became policy in Yellowstone National Park. This meant, among other things, no more culling of elk as well as closure of the dumps that had long been a magnet for grizzlies and, inevitably, tourists eager to see them. It also meant that park personnel labored to create a park that closely resembles what the first white person most likely saw when he arrived on the scene.[6] In a similar vein, RESTORE: The North Woods, a New England–based organization, is gathering support for its initiative to get a very large portion of Maine's forest declared a national park, thus putting the forest safely out of the reach of loggers. Finally, a variety of projects are involved in restoring degraded habitats. These projects range in scale, some little more than demonstration projects and others quite large. Among the latter, the most notable, perhaps, is the attempt to restore millions of acres in the Great Plains states to their condition before agriculture and cattle and sheep grazing, a project known as the Buffalo Commons.

Although the latter are a heterogeneous batch of initiatives, they do have some important features in common that are worth noting before we turn our attention to two examples, the Chicago Wilderness Habitat Project and the Buffalo Commons project. Each of these otherwise diverse initiatives is defined by the goal of mitigating, insofar as possible, the effects humans have had on the targeted landscape. With things back more nearly to their original condition, we will have no need to fear for the collapse of the natural world that sustains all living things.

There are several things wrong with this way of thinking. In its most ideologically pure and extreme version, the view of nature on which these initiatives rest is suspect. "Undisturbed nature" is an oxymoron. There are, of course, all sorts of large and small perturbations that have both local and global environmental repercussions. Less dramatically, though just as relentlessly, organisms, as the distinguished evolutionary geneticist Richard Lewontin has shown,[7] are ceaselessly busy modifying their environment—to their own advantage in the short run and typically to their grief in the long run. Stability, like beauty, is in the eye of the beholder. The notion that what the area we now call Yellowstone National Park was like two hundred years ago would have remained in that condition, like some diorama, is unlikely. We know the geologic record of the area for the past two hundred years, so we can say that the topographic features have been stable. But there is no way to know what the frequency of fires might have been (or whether they were ignited by lightning or Indians) and how the proportions of species would have varied over time in response to fires, unusually heavy snowfalls, droughts, and the whole host of smaller variations and disturbances that would have constantly kept things stirred up.[8]

Put another way, to argue that the undisturbed (by humans) is to be preferred to the disturbed is to court a serious and disabling teleology. It is to argue that what was here before us was *meant* to be here. By implication, this view implicitly means that we really do not belong: we have simply imposed ourselves. Surely this is untenable. Nothing is meant to be this way or that. There are, to be sure, reasons why, at any moment in time, things are arranged in a certain way, but to attribute to such an arrangement a meaning, much less some compelling moral standing, is tantamount to reinventing the thoroughly discredited theory of "special creation." That this way of thinking is now couched in the cool, analytic language of ecology rather than in the language of theology does not make the theory any more worthy. It is curious, to say the least, that such discredited notions continue to resurface. It is alarming when scientists lend their authority to them.

Of course, preferring habitats restored to their original condition over habitats that are modified by human artifice puts those who claim to know what belongs where in a powerful position. Biologists and ecologists can claim a privileged voice in the making of environmental policy to the extent that they can tell us what nature intended this or that place to be like. There is immense value in knowing what the prairie was like before pioneering sodbusters began their labors, just as there is value in preserving and restoring unique ecological systems on a scale sufficient to capture our natural history. But it is something else again to throw the weight of science behind the desire to erase as much as possible the traces of human effects on the environment. There are good reasons to worry about the future, but these worries should not drive us toward embracing one particular slice of what was, after all, a very dynamic and fluid past, if only because there is no reason to believe that the original condition is suited to the ways in which we now live and the stresses our way of life inevitably puts on the environment. The pristine may have been what Marsh and many others claim for it (a balanced, stable, finely tuned system), though I have my doubts, but then it surely follows that our incursions and modifications make a return improbable. In the bargain, science gets politicized.

The second and related problem with this set of environmental initiatives is that it essentially sets up a tacit dichotomy between "good" and "bad" nature. This is an old problem. There have always been those who resist the temptation to valorize "rocks and ice," spectacular views from soaring mountaintops, and towering trees to the exclusion of an interest in the prosaic stuff near home. In the late nineteenth and early twentieth centuries, the dean of American natural history writers, John Burroughs, though no opponent of saving wilderness, took exception to the ways in which John Muir and others made it seem that wilderness was the only thing really worth treasuring. In our own day, nature writer John Hanson Mitchell has expressed a similar sentiment:

Wilderness and wildlife, history, life itself, for that matter, is something that takes place somewhere else, it seems. You must travel to witness it, you must get in your car in summer and go off to look at things which some "expert," such as the National Park Service, tells you is important, or beautiful, or historic. In spite of their admitted grandeur, I find such well-documented places somewhat boring. What I prefer . . . is that undiscovered country of the nearby, the secret world that lurks beyond the night windows and at the fringes of cultivated backyards.[9]

Expressing this same general point of view earned noted environmental historian William Cronon the concerted wrath of the environmental movement for his having the temerity to challenge the orthodoxy of wilderness preservation.[10] The point is not to dismiss wilderness, much less efforts to restore bruised and battered landscapes to something approaching what Aldo Leopold would call "land health," which I take to mean land capable of sustaining a robust variety of living things, including humans. Instead, Cronon argues, and I agree, the point is to put these efforts in historical and cultural perspective, lest we lose sight of the larger and pressing need to figure out ways in which we can lighten the burden we are imposing on all of nature. Without this, setting aside this or that spot will only ensure more intense pressure on the land outside the reserves. It is hard to see any net gain in this, for man or nature. I shall return to these broad matters after examining the Chicago Wilderness project and the proposal for creation of the Buffalo Commons.

The Trouble with Restoration

Historically, most restoration initiatives have been small in scale. Leopold's effort to restore a bit of precontact Wisconsin prairie on his land was typical. The Chicago Wilderness project pushes the scale well beyond Leopold's patch of restored prairie but still has to be regarded as more a demonstration project than anything else. If the goal is to recover historical ecosystem functions and reverse the trend toward radical habitat modification, very large areas will be required. This has led some proponents of restoration to propose ever more sweeping projects, among the grandest of which is the Buffalo Commons, an effort being promoted by the Great Plains Restoration Council (GPRC). The GPRC hopes to restore a million acres of prairie reaching from Mexico to Canada *as the first step* toward the goal, according to their mission statement, of allowing "all native Plains animal cultures the open space, health and ancestral freedom to prosper" (http://www.gprc.org/about). Although neither the Buffalo Commons nor the Chicago Wilderness project can be taken as paradigmatic for all restoration projects, each reveals problems that should give us pause. Certainly, there must be a place for restoration in any rethinking of conservation, but by itself, restoration is a shaky basis upon which to build a new model of conservation. Before we proceed, let me briefly describe each of these restoration projects.[11]

In the 1970s, a small group of environmentalists began small-scale restorations in patches of abandoned railroad rights-of-way and in some public forestlands in and around the Chicago metropolitan area. Over time, a broad coalition of environmental organizations, public agencies, and ad hoc citizen groups formed, and the restoration efforts grew in scale. Maps of municipal and county forests led the restorationists to look for abandoned properties, neglected and degraded watercourses, and greenbelts buffering subdivisions, shopping malls, and industrial "parks" that could provide links to these otherwise isolated public forests. The project acquired a name: Chicago Wilderness. The idea must have seemed so counterintuitive as to be compelling, if only for the irony involved in imagining wilderness in the heart of one of the country's largest cities. Large numbers of volunteers became engaged in identifying and inventorying non-native flora, and piece by piece the aliens were removed and replaced with the plants that were native. The goal was to produce a more or less connected series of landscapes that resembled the prairie and oak savanna that greeted the first European settlers to the area.

By the mid-1990s, when controversy erupted, thousands of volunteers had invested thousands of hours in the project. In the process, many had become serious, albeit amateur, botanists and all had acquired a deeper knowledge of their immediate surroundings and natural history. Controversy flared as the bits and pieces began to fit into the larger pattern. It turned out that many of those not bitten by the bug of restoration liked the trees and shrubs that lined their backyards and that shielded them from the noise and dirt of the freeways and malls. What could be more natural than trees, they wondered, and what gives restorationists the right to cut down trees and replace them with prairie grass? The objections grew more pointed when it became clear that maintaining the prairie would require not only the cutting of trees and clearing of brush but also the application of herbicides and periodic fires to keep the aliens out and maintain the natural life cycle of a prairie. Restoration efforts met with stiffening resistance, and several counties banned further restoration initiatives. As of this writing, restoration efforts have been largely put on hold, and those that proceed are circumscribed by a host of restrictions.

The enthusiasm the legions of volunteers had for the original prairie is impressive but should not blind us to the fact that, for some, enthusiasm became zealotry. Everything non-native was scorned, and those who could not or would not see the light were disparaged. What started out as a grass-roots (no pun intended), open, if not exactly democratic, initiative that managed to enlist a remarkable array of organizations and individuals became a divisive and polarizing presence precisely because the proponents of prairie restoration could not accept the fact that not only are there different ways to "love nature," there are also different natures to love. Restorationists loved the original prairie because it didn't need human manipulation—it was an instance of a climax community—but, paradoxically, maintaining the restored areas requires constant intervention to keep alien plants from reappearing. Far from returning nature to an unmanaged pristine whole, the restorers created a landscape that required quite heavy-handed management regimes, which the unconverted found unacceptable. As impressive as the outpouring of volunteers was, events revealed that the coalition assembled beneath the banner of the Chicago Wilderness project was broad but not deep, and it could deepen its roots only in terms of its own quite narrow agenda.

The Chicago experience suggests that urban areas are good for small-scale demonstration projects, much like the vegetable gardens urban residents coax into fertility where buildings have been razed and lots left vacant, but that as the scale increases, the number of people who feel put upon grows exponentially. It is one thing to have a tract that replicates, more or less, what the early settlers saw; it is another thing altogether to argue that any and all departures from that standard represent loss, degradation, and defilement. Even though, by the early 1990s, Chicago Wilderness could boast 20,000 acres of restored prairie in Chicago and the surrounding counties, this was but a tiny fraction of the total land area of the former prairie. Only at the most symbolic level could it be said to matter. Many multiples of 20,000 would be needed even to begin to provide a counterweight to the abuses heaped upon the former prairie by industry, agriculture, and urbanization. Too much symbolic freight got loaded onto the effort, and, as a result, the capacity to keep things in perspective was lost. In the end, people and prairie could no more coexist in the late twentieth century than they could in the middle of the nineteenth, though the reasons for the conflict certainly have changed over the past century and a half.

People might pose a problem for the proponents of the Buffalo

Commons, though they at least have the advantage of having many fewer people with whom to deal. The idea of a Buffalo Commons occurred to Frank and Deborah Popper, both planning professionals, while they were commuting on the New Jersey Turnpike—precisely the context in which the mind is likely to wander toward thoughts of empty spaces "where the buffalo roam." Aware of a demographic shift that was producing a steady population decline in the Great Plains, they got the idea that maybe the Plains was simply not meant to be home to more than a handful of intrepid souls. They knew that attempts to settle and make a living had been repeatedly thwarted by the elements—droughts came regularly; bitterly cold and long winters were routine; irrigation was becoming both expensive (even when subsidized) and problematic over the long run as the water table subsided—and by an equally erratic and punishing agricultural economy. The population on the Plains would swell and then slowly decline as climate and debt wore away the settlers' resolve. And then a new cycle would commence, only to repeat the dispiriting experience of the earlier wave.

By the late 1980s, when the Poppers had their epiphany, the third downward turn of this cycle was well under way. Towns were literally being shuttered up. Today, there are dozens of counties all across the Plains states where the population density is less than five people per square mile (this was the population density Frederick Jackson Turner used to define the frontier). With the population shrinking, the Poppers reasoned, why not rethink, on a grand scale, what should be done on and to the Great Plains? Research into the economic and demographic history of the Great Plains quickly confirmed their hunch: the Plains cannot sustain the sorts of agriculture that the three waves of settlers have tried to practice. There is not enough water, cattle overgraze and exhaust the range, and intensive cropping leads to soil erosion. The net result is a predictable coincidence of disasters, ecological, economic, and social. It was time, they wrote in 1987, to find a more sustainable way to use the Great Plains.

They coined the term "Buffalo Commons," at the time thinking of it as a metaphor, not a blueprint. The Poppers explained:

> We conceived the Buffalo Commons in part as a literary device, a metaphor that would resolve the narrative conflicts—past, present and most important, future—of the Plains. In land-use terms, the Buffalo Commons was an umbrella phrase for a large-scale, long-term

restoration project to counter the effects of the three [boom-and-bust] cycles. We wrote that in about a generation, after the far end of the third [current] cycle had depopulated much more of the Plains, the federal government would step in as the vacated land's owner of last resort. . . . The Buffalo Commons would not mean buffalo on every acre; but where Plains land uses were not working well either environmentally or economically, replacement land uses that treated the land more lightly would become inevitable. The federal government would oversee the replacement, and the new land uses would fall between intensive cultivation/extraction and pure wilderness. The Buffalo Commons used metaphor as a way to give form and words to the unknowable future.[12]

The Poppers' proposal echoes John Wesley Powell's recommendations for how the Plains should be settled. A little more than a century ago, Powell argued that the soils and climate on the Plains were not suitable for intensive agriculture of the sort practiced in the Midwest.[13] History clearly has absolved Powell, and the Poppers were sure that a repeat of this history would prepare the way, finally, for a new, environmentally appropriate departure. It might yet do so, but after the 2000 elections, it is hard to imagine a conservatively governed nation getting enthusiastic about the federal government acquiring huge chunks of the ten Plains states. But even if the Poppers' vision winds up being ignored by the federal government, as Powell's was earlier, the idea has excited interest and gathered support. Indeed, the idea of the Buffalo Commons has begun to be put into practice on a rather large scale, thanks to billionaire Ted Turner.

In recent years, Turner has been buying up ranches all across the Plains states, and he now stands as the nation's largest private landowner. Claiming some million acres, most of it in the Plains, he and his son have decided to restore their holdings to their original condition. Teams of botanists have been removing alien grasses and planting native grasses in their stead. Cattle are out; buffalo are in. Restoration on this scale is, to say the least, quite remarkable, whether it works on its own terms or not. Even if the restoration is only partially successful, it is likely that Turner's properties will stand in vivid contrast to the public and private lands around his ranches. Native grasses are adapted to the arid climate and will no doubt slow soil erosion, and since buffalo do indeed roam, unlike stay-at-home cattle, the grasses are much less likely to be overgrazed. Buffalo also don't do nearly the damage to riparian habitats that cattle are notorious for doing, and this means that riverbanks and stream banks will not be destroyed. In turn, this will mean better habitat for fish. Turner will no doubt be the envy of his neighbors.

On a far less grand scale, other ranchers have begun raising buffalo and restoring at least some native vegetation on their land.[14] Some Plains Indians have embraced the Buffalo Commons idea and begun to commit tribal lands to the restorationist cause. It remains to be seen, of course, whether this will end in a patchwork (with a few very large patches, to be sure) or the conversion from traditional land uses will make the patches steadily expand until they fuse into one large, more or less contiguous block of restored Great Plains. There are many hurdles to be faced. One, surely, is the hold cattle ranching has on the imagination.[15] Ranchers are not likely to replace cattle with buffalo on a large scale. There seems to be little doubt that buffalo could once again thrive on the Plains, but if the Buffalo Commons is to thrive, the buffalo will have to be a good investment. Ted Turner can afford expensive hobbies, but even he was recently obliged to take notice when the bottom dropped out of the market for buffalo meat. In a news release in early 2002, Turner announced that he was planning to open a chain of restaurants featuring buffalo in hopes of boosting the flagging market for the meat.

Another hurdle is one the restorationists in Chicago imposed upon themselves. The vision of a restored habitat becoming self-perpetuating, returned to the balance it once exhibited, is deeply misleading. Quite apart from the important question of how we ought to think about precontact habitats and whether they ever were balanced, now that the prairie and the Great Plains have been disturbed and are surrounded by non-native species of all sorts, with more sure to come, restorationists have signed on to a program that requires constant monitoring and management to keep "bad nature" from ruining "good nature." Ecologist Steve Gatewood is one of the few advocates to frankly acknowledge this. In 1998, as executive director of the Wildlands Project, an umbrella organization covering many restoration efforts, he reported on a proposal to "rewild" an area in Florida, noting that "any landscape, including wilderness, will be a managed one because humans will have to work constantly to sustain its ecological integrity."[16] This is precisely the sort of vigilance that contributed to the opposition to restoration in the Chicago area as residents began to resent the continual interventions. The one thing the Chicago Wilderness project had going for it was its volunteer base—the work of restoring was done inexpensively. But the Great Plains lacks people, so it is hard to imagine restoration of the Plains being done on the cheap.

Again, Turner can afford to hire a crew of plant and wildlife biologists, but it is hard to imagine where the money would come from for a fully realized Buffalo Commons. One need only look at the fiscal history of the National Park Service to begin to imagine the difficulty of sustaining the funding that would be required for maintenance of the Buffalo Commons once it was restored to its original condition. It is wishful thinking, to be charitable, to imagine that once restored, an area will stay that way on its own. If support falters, and it is hard to imagine that support would be unwavering over the long run, ground would quickly be lost. Of course, if the goal is worthy, then the price and the risks of even partial success might be worth it.

Is the Goal of Restoration Worthy?

The Chicago Wilderness Habitat Project risked political capital by insisting on a definition of environmentalism that asked too much for too little demonstrable good. Yes, some people are gratified to see prairie grass instead of buckthorn, but most people do not see buckthorn, much less aspen, maple, or birch, as a scourge. Some of this may be chalked up to ignorance, but more than a lack of knowledge of prairie ecology is involved here. There are a bevy of value preferences implicit in restoration, values that appeals to natural history or to the young science of ecology cannot vindicate. If the goal of environmentalists is to create as large a constituency as possible committed to environmental stewardship, the Chicago experience should be read more as a cautionary tale than as a model. The plain truth is that people resented being told that the nature they appreciated was bad and that they were ignorant and misguided. The Chicago restorationists came to sound suspiciously like evangelists who knew the one true path and who insisted that anyone rejecting that path was an enemy of the earth.

Restoration has been praised because it has engaged a lot of sincere and earnest people in taking a direct personal interest in the environment that surrounds them.[17] It can do this, but the price can be high, and the risk of alienating people who would conceivably be willing to support a more flexible and nuanced environmentalism is also high, as the Chicago experience clearly indicates. If restoration were merely a metaphor, as was the Poppers' initial conception of the Buffalo Commons, there would be little with which to quarrel. But when restoration is taken literally, the mischief begins. Dogmatism appears, lines are drawn, and, before we know it, there is only one "nature" worth valuing and taking seriously. Thus, when the Poppers' metaphor was picked up and instantiated in the Great Plains Restoration Council, the metaphoric quality of the Buffalo Commons evaporated. Just as wilderness as metaphor, in Chicago or anywhere else, is fine but becomes something else again when it is taken literally, so it is with a preference for habitats largely cleansed of human disturbance.

After the participatory dust settles, it turns out that restoration works best when it is carried out by a few hands, hired or otherwise, on privately owned lands. If The Nature Conservancy and Ted Turner want to restore native flora and fauna to their lands, they can do it, politics be damned. And if Turner's restaurants compel McDonald's restaurants to feature a buffalo burger special and thus the price of buffalo climbs, the Buffalo Commons may be more or less realized. This may be good for people and the environment, not because the Great Plains will have been restored to its original condition but because cropping buffalo will have become profitable. Absent this eventuality, the Great Plains and the Chicago Wilderness project will, for different but converging reasons, founder.

There is one final reason to regard restoration with caution. Restoration proceeds on the premise that lands reclaimed and restored should be used sparingly, if at all, by humans. This puts restorationists squarely at odds with the millions of people who use the out-of-doors recreationally, particularly those who engage in traditional activities such as fishing, hunting, and trapping. As I noted in passing earlier, sportsmen and sportswomen were among the earliest and most enthusiastic supporters of stewardship and conservation. Indeed, were it not for their efforts—and the millions of dollars they have spent on research, habitat improvement, and game management—our wildlife would be in desperate shape. Environmentalists who pursue a course that antagonizes a core base of support for conservation risk shrinking support for stewardship when they should be seeking ways of expanding it.

This is not to say that restoration has no place in a renewed conservation agenda. Restoration, in fact, has always been a part of the conservation vision. The U.S. Fish and Wildlife Service, in cooperation with private organizations, most notably Ducks Unlimited, has vigorously promoted the restoration of prairie potholes in the United States and Canada. This obviously benefits migratory waterfowl, but the benefits extend well beyond more ducks. Trout Unlimited has similarly promoted the restoration of rivers and streams. What makes these sorts of restorations distinctive is that they do not require people to keep out. On the contrary, they are designed to enhance the environment so that people can get more enjoyment and pleasure from nature.

The problem with the Chicago Wilderness and Buffalo Commons projects is as simple as it is painful: each project asks us to return to an idealized past that cannot be recaptured on a scale that meaningfully addresses our very real environmental woes. Millions of buffalo on the Great Plains and prairie grasses waving in the legendary Chicago wind won't make a nick in the environmental challenges we face. At best, they will provide playgrounds for those fortunate enough to be able to avail themselves of a walk on the prairie fragment or who can afford a week of elk and buffalo hunting or trout fishing on a Turner ranch.

If stewardship and conservation are to be revivified in the twenty-first century, we must start where we are, not where we were. This will entail several complicated concessions. First, and most important, nature is in constant flux, and our attempts to engineer it will rarely, if ever, work exactly as planned. Second, we need to accept the fact that we cannot hermetically seal ourselves off from nature. We can have wildlands, but we will have to accept their boundedness and the burden of maintaining them—no matter the scale, they will not be self-organizing, much less self-replicating. There will have to be sufficient political will generated to pay the tab for managing the land in a fashion likely to be sustainable for the long term. Finally, if we ask people to pay, it is only reasonable that they should expect some benefit in return, including the benefit of being able to enjoy the fruits of conservation.

Acknowledgments

I wish to acknowledge the constructive criticisms of an earlier draft of this paper offered by Leo Marx. In addition, David Lowenthal was extraordinarily generous with his time and gave me encouragement to proceed when I most needed it. Needless to say, I am also indebted to Ben Minteer and Robert Manning for organizing the seminar at which an early version of this paper was presented, and to the participants whose papers and comments helped me think more clearly about these matters than I otherwise might have.

Chapter 5

Conservation and Culture, Genuine and Spurious

LUIS A. VIVANCO

The idea that successful conservation depends on attention to social relations and cultural context has been gaining legitimacy beyond the narrow realms of environmental anthropology and sociology. Conservation philosophers, biologists, field practitioners, and policy makers have increasingly adopted the languages of value pluralism, multiculturalism, and cultural diversity to acknowledge the complex ways that social differentiation and cultural ideologies influence the success or failure of conservation initiatives. This is especially true among those who work where the traditionally Western discourse of nature conservation confronts indigenous peoples and ethnic minorities with very different ideas about the boundaries between themselves and their natural surroundings.[1]

The apparent embrace of "the human element" through the languages of cultural diversity and social relations deserves serious attention, although it is not a new or original set of issues among conservation theorists and practitioners.[2] Perhaps it is more interesting these days to ask why it is necessary to declare their legitimacy or necessity at all, or in a tone that implies that to do so is a surprising, counterintuitive, or even transgressive paradigm shift. Conservation is, after all, presumably about limiting and redefining people's social relationships with natural ecosystems and processes in ways that apparently protect the latter from the former. If so, anthropological perspectives can certainly offer valuable lessons to help people understand the values and beliefs that underlie the ways they relate to the natural environments in which they live. The "culture" concept is not reducible to mere differences in values, however. With its attention to holism and integration—the view that such components of a sociocultural system as worldview, economy, politics, religion, and so on, are interrelated—the culture concept has proven its relevance as a tool for understanding the complex ways people continually adapt to, use, and recreate their material environments. Viewed on their own terms, such adaptations reflect the plasticity of human activities, based as they are on very specific meanings of reality, worldviews, and forms of social organization unique to particular groups of people.[3] As an applied concept, culture has become a key element in international development schemes, based on the recognition that local technologies and social institutions are often uniquely adaptive and that programs succeed by building upon, not sweeping aside, local situations, needs, and traditions.[4]

As I will argue here, conservationists already make certain epistemological assumptions about culture and social relationships, sometimes self-consciously acknowledged, sometimes not. Conservation biologist Nick Salafsky, for example, observed that "conservation is first of all a human social issue. Conservation activities are primarily designed to modify human behaviors that affect biodiversity."[5] This view—that social relations and cultural context are relevant because they illuminate why people think and act the way they do so that conservationists can change them— assumes that the only valid reason to pay attention to local people is to find ways to sweep certain of their behaviors or attitudes away. Notwithstanding the colonial nature of such a proposition, this perspective offers a simplistic and even self-defeating view of "how people work" because (1) no sociocultural context is monolithic or necessarily predictable, since not everybody shares the same knowledge or thinks and behaves in the same, or even consistent, way, and (2) social engineering based on a crude carrot-and-stick approach often fails because it is based on a misunderstanding of people's motivations, especially in cross-cultural circumstances. Thinking of culture as a mere tool to change behaviors may undermine the very reason we might want to bring it to bear in conservation, which is its ability to help focus attention on the highly specific and context-dependent processes and interactions that help determine why people relate with their natural surroundings in certain ways. The problem is further complicated by the shifting intellectual and political terrains of qualitative cultural theory, which have increasingly emphasized the partial and situated nature of social and cultural knowledges themselves, as well as the dangers of slipping from the representation *of* reality to representation *as* reality. For contemporary cultural anthropologists and sociologists, "culture" is less an object to grasp than it is a variety of multilayered and contingent processes of interaction and projected meanings that one's very involvement as re-searcher and analyst reflects, refracts, and defines.[6] Furthermore, in post-colonial contexts in which knowledge is recognized as inherently political, social and cultural representations are open to new scrutiny and critique by the people who are the objects of research.

In both theory and practice, the conservation mainstream continues to perceive its work as divided into "natural" and "social/cultural" sides, re-flecting the separation westerners make between people and nature "out there." But conservation is never simply about what kind of nature people imagine or know they want to preserve or restore; it is also an important arena in which they, explicitly or implicitly, project and reimagine social re-lationships and cultural institutions. Indeed, the two should be considered as co-constructed categories: through conservation itself, new and authori-tative visions of nature are derived and implemented, just as culture and social relations are scrutinized, redefined, and normalized, *as aspects of the same process.* In other words, to define the attributes of nature and strate-gies for saving it inscribes its boundaries with the realm of the social and cultural, implicitly contributing to the way we think of people's place in na-ture and prescribing certain normative interventions into their lives. This leads to a number of important questions that we must ask of all conserva-tion initiatives. What new social orders does conservation seek to validate and implement? What is its vision of acceptable cultural relationships, in-stitutions, and attitudes? Who defines these new realities, and for whom do they apply? What are the hierarchies of relevant knowledge in specific con-servation initiatives?

In Latin America, which provides the context for this chapter, the lan-guages of natural resource conservation and environmentalism are often deployed as part of an effort to challenge traditional structures of uneven economic development, political domination, and traditional authority.[7] In fact, the relationship between the concentration of lands in elite hands and the destruction of natural resources is often an explicit argument that ac-tivists employ to justify their claims for sociopolitical justice and grassroots democratic action.[8] As a result, environmental debates are often closely tied to struggles over democratization, rights, and, increasingly, cultural af-firmation. Northern conservation professionals have often viewed their work in largely technical or scientific terms—as "saving nature"—thereby avoiding linking their efforts to "local politics," efforts to rectify uneven land distribution, and cultural regeneration, and this has been the source of conflict and discontent for Southern activists and communities, who often take for granted the essentially social and political basis of their struggles. Wolfgang Sachs is correct in arguing that even with the rise of Agenda 21, which emphasizes the union of nature conservation with economic development, in the realm of sustainable development "justice" and "nature" often collide, and when they do, Northern elites and their allies promoting nature often prevail over Southern majorities desiring justice.[9]

It is for this reason that an increasingly important chorus of voices have contended that the political relevance of nature conservation is in question at the grassroots, especially (but not only) in non-Western contexts.[10] A key aspect of rethinking conservation is acknowledging these gaps and finding ways to join claims for nature to ongoing struggles over the social and political realities of rural and urban communities. Before we can do that, however, we must come to grips with, for lack of a better phrase, "conservationist social science" and ask what cultural theories are assumed and deployed in conservation. Even more important, how have conservationist projections and assumptions about people, culture, and social relations drawn from and contributed to inaccurate stereotypes of people? The tendency to rely on latent paradigms about human groups is reflected in the title of this chapter, the notion that the world is divided into genuine and spurious cultures. By choosing these terms, I am following anthropologist Edward Sapir, who wrote in a 1949 essay titled "Cultures, Genuine and Spurious" that there are basically two types of cultures in the world, "genuine" (traditional) and "spurious" (modern). The modern is quintessentially superficial, a shallow world of no meaningful or spiritual engagement among people, exemplified by, according to Sapir, "a readiness to imitation in its bearers that is not reassuring."[11] Modern people exhibit relationships with nature that reflect spiritual disconnection and utilitarianism. A genuine culture, on the other hand, is one that "gives its bearers a sense of inner satisfaction, a feeling of spiritual mastery."[12] It ensures harmony between an individual and the aims of the broader society as well as between the individual and nature. As I will argue in this chapter, conservation has tended to rely heavily on such a dichotomy, reflected in images of "ecologically noble savages" and destructive peasantries.

The authority of environmentalist claims for control over the stewardship of landscapes is based on the assumption that local peoples do not properly manage the landscape. Especially when they are based on simplistic cultural stereotypes, environmentalist claims can reduce considerable particularities and subtleties, missing the flexible and strategic ways in which people in specific situations and times interact with their natural surroundings. Recent archaeological, ethnohistoric, and ethnographic research has adequately proven that in important instances Western projections of unpeopled wilderness are in fact artifactual landscapes manipulated by the hands of people.[13] Questions naturally arise over whose interests are served by stereotypes of culture. For the "wilderness critique" often (but not solely) identified with the work of William Cronon, these essentializations apparently serve to get us back to "the wrong nature," a nature of unrealistic projections. But more is at stake than simply "nature." Social relationships are at stake as well, and in an era of (at least rhetorical) skepticism toward top-down conservation initiatives, to continue to unreflexively project stereotypes about local social relations makes for missed opportunities to develop custom-made conservation initiatives based on local particularities, strengths, and concerns.

This chapter examines two contexts of conservation: in the first case, considering the character and persistence of stereotypes, and in the second, exploring self-conscious efforts to move beyond the genuine–spurious cultures paradigm. In the first, I look at the power and persistence of the genuine–spurious cultures paradigm, specifically through the case of Monte Verde, Costa Rica, where conservationists projected the imagery of spurious culture and destructiveness on rural Costa Ricans in the process of establishing large wilderness preserves. But this approach, which effectively defined rural Costa Ricans as destroyers of nature, and therefore as actors to be acted upon and not collaborated with, has had important negative consequences for the way rural Costa Ricans view conservation activities. Conservation, of course, is not monolithic: even though narrow and unreflexive uses of culture persist, there are examples in which there is an ongoing and creative reconstruction of conservation politics and techniques. This is happening in the second case, in the southern Mexican state of Oaxaca, where activists working with indigenous communities have not fallen into the trap of believing they are working with genuine cultures but are actively engaged in indigenous processes of cultural regeneration. They consider their work not as based on the imposition of Western visions of nature and modernist social engineering onto indigenous peoples but as an intercultural space in which indigenous and Western perspectives exist in dialogue, constructing, in effect, what some are calling an alternative modernity.

Projecting Genuine and Spurious Cultures

In his recent work *Reconceptualizing the Peasantry,* anthropologist Michael Kearney argues that the traditional centrality of the peasant, the static and autonomous small-scale farmer, in understandings of the Latin American countryside is based on inaccurate projections of rural realities.[14] Reflecting ongoing transformations in Latin American nation-states, neoliberal economic policies, and transnational migrations, Kearney argues that rural peasantries—he calls them "post-peasants"—are less concerned with primordial linkages to land and agriculture and increasingly more concerned with globalized politics of migration, human rights, ethnicity, and ecology.[15] He concludes, "The point here is that students who wish to critically assess the position of *the peasants* in rural society must first come to terms with *the images* of them,"[16] including the images projected by social scientists and development efforts meant to improve the lives of peasants. It is important to extend Kearney's insight to the realm of nature conservation, and, in doing so, we find that images of genuine and spurious cultures play important roles in the construction of sustainable development policy and action.

One particularly powerful image in conservation discourse that has its basis in the genuine culture ideal is that of the "green primitive," or the ecologically noble savage, which is the idea that indigenous peoples live in a unique conformity with nature.[17] A version of this is found in the words of John Muir, who wrote, "Indians walked softly and hurt the land hardly more than the birds and squirrels, and their brush and bark huts last hardly longer than those of wood rats, while their enduring monuments, excepting those wrought on the forests by fires they made to improve their hunting grounds, vanish in a few centuries."[18] The updated version of this is reflected in claims that indigenous models of development are inherently more sustainable than modern development patterns.[19] As anthropologist Roy Ellen points out, the stereotype of indigenous peoples as inherently ecologically wise is double-edged: on the one hand, it idolizes indigenous peoples, but on the other, it sets them apart as natural savages.[20] The underlying assumption is that when it is closer to nature, life is somehow more virtuous and genuine than in the superficial environments man creates for himself.[21] There is a tendency, therefore, to place indigenous peoples inside nature and outside history, denying the now well-known findings of archaeologists, historians, and others unearthing contradictory evidence, whose proliferating insights include (for example) the fact that large areas of the Amazonian rain forest were shaped by pre-Hispanic cultivators; or that, as demonstrated by the current situation in the Maya tropical forest of southern Mexico, Guatemala, and Belize—a situation of rapid ecological deterioration due to the movement of indigenous groups into virgin territories—there is no necessary correlation between indigenous peoples and the tenet that they live harmoniously in their environments.[22]

At the heart of the imagery of the "green primitive" is the notion that humanity can be assigned to one side of the nature–culture divide, with groups of people placed in an evolutionary framework that begins in primitivity and ends with modernity.[23] It is thought that the engagement with modernity and westernization leads to a profound transformation in the relationship with nature that ruins a people's ability to sustainably manage a resource. This assumption seems to be at work in the recent conflict over the resumption of whaling by Makah Indians of the Pacific Northwest, which pitted environmental and animal rights activists against Makah cultural survival activists.[24] A key argument of whaling opponents has been to highlight the modernity of the Makah, emphasizing that their use of motorboats and large-bore guns, combined with the possibility that they might sell whale products, disqualifies their claims that they are resuming their "traditional" cultural activity of whaling. A representative of the Sea Shepherd Conservation Society argued: "This is the most expensive whale hunt in history, and for what? Fun. . . . We don't see any tradition in this."[25] The underlying assumption here is that "genuine" Native American culture must be separate from economic trade and modern technologies and that the Makah cannot be virtuous and sustainable green primitives if they undertake a whale hunt under modern market and technological conditions. The anti-whaling rhetoric effectively delegitimates the claims of all contemporary Indians on the assumption that their cultures have gone spurious and materialistic simply because they have changed, an idea that is anathema to indigenous peoples who believe that their traditions were forcibly undermined or destroyed by the dominant society. It also denies novel forms of indigenous self-organization as "inauthentic," suggesting that the only relevant indigenous society is frozen into a tradition that itself in fact may be transient.[26]

It has to be acknowledged that representations and self-presentations of authenticity can have their rewards in ecopolitics. Exotic peoples in traditional dress and body decoration offer keen visual material, marking indigenous difference and identity in ways that affirm their closeness to nature.[27] For example, Kayapó Indians from the Brazilian Amazon have gained international media celebrity by playing up the role of green primitive and noble savage in Western environmentalist discourse, which has enabled them to enjoy a new level of political opportunity and influence, including success in persuading the World Bank not to loan the Brazilian government funds for the Altamira dam.[28] Nevertheless, as the Kayapó and other marginalized groups have discovered, there are trade-offs involved in aiming such symbolic politics at international audiences, including the fact that they are ultimately playing roles that are being handed to them by dominant discourses and stereotypes. As one Kayapó leader discovered when the media revealed his apparently unacceptable tastes for "modern" consumer products, these discourses also prohibit variation from idealized imagery. Furthermore, the success of international campaigns can become a liability at the national level, where the claims of marginalized or minority peoples often represent a challenge to the very legitimacy and hegemony of the modern states that encompass them.

The other side of the green primitive coin is the imagery of the spurious culture of the destructive peasant. As Kearney notes, peasants have also been viewed in evolutionary terms, as existing in a cultural space somewhere between the primitivity of indigenous peoples and the modernity of urban peoples.[29] Semi-modern, yet also unable to fully modernize, these people have stalled on the path of progress and as a result have been the target of development schemes and agrarian policy agendas designed precisely to help them along. Much of the discourse of "sustainable development" draws from a similar logic in its treatment of rural peoples: because they are poor and lack a cultural appreciation for nature, they are unable to relate harmoniously to it. Hence, sustainable development focuses on trying to unite poverty alleviation and nature conservation, on the dubious assumption that middle-class incomes will generate a harmonious relationship with nature. Reflecting on nonindigenous rural peasantries, biologist Norman Myers grimly observes that "by far, the number one factor in disruption and destruction of tropical forests is the small-scale farmer."[30] This is because "the new forest farmers are altogether different from the shifting cultivators of tradition. They ["shifting cultivators of tradition"] practiced a form of forest exploitation that was clearly sustainable; otherwise they would not have been able to continue with it for centuries. . . . But today they are joined by many times as many of the displaced peasants, there is less forest left to move around in, and the newcomers have little ecological understanding of how to make a sustainable livelihood from the forests."[31]

Research on nonindigenous rural populations has demonstrated that such overarching statements obscure more subtle understandings of local cultural and political ecologies, as well as the structural conditions under which rural communities relate to their natural environments. Exceptions to Myers' statement are many, and vivid examples range from *campesinos* (small-scale peasants) who have adopted sustainable agricultural techniques in the Petén region of Guatemala by sharing knowledge with indigenous peoples to, in West Africa, the cultivation of biologically diverse forest islands in savanna lands for social purposes.[32] The point here is not to exhaustively catalogue exceptions to Myers' point but to make the argument that misreadings of a region's cultural and political ecologies are not inconsequential: they underestimate how much Western concepts of conservation are oriented toward a static landscape vision of closed-canopy forests, dismiss local knowledge and land-use practices, and risk emphasizing ill-adapted, inappropriate, or ineffective aid and conservation programs.

In rural Costa Rica, where since the middle of the twentieth century more than 50 percent of the primary forest coverage has been lost to encroaching agriculture and settlement, *campesinos* have been widely projected as the main culprits in the country's rapid deforestation. Using mainly foreign funds to finance their work, conservation activists have created a major system of formally protected areas that includes more than 25 percent of the national territory. It is arguable that a key aspect of conservationist claims for nature have emphasized rural Costa Rican cultural spuriousness. For example, prominent biologist and conservation activist Daniel Janzen has observed that Costa Ricans have not been able to develop an "understanding of the natural history around them that their grandparents had . . . [because these] people are now just as culturally-deprived as if they could no longer read, hear music, or see color."[33] Janzen's vision is based on a fundamental distinction between rural Costa Rican land management patterns and nature's sustainability, proposing that the recuperation of their culture (and nature) requires their ejection from the landscape and their participation in natural history seminars. This vision of conservation, as anthropologist Lori Ann Thrupp pointed out in her critique of Janzen's philosophy, offers a noncollaborative and top-down

approach in which local peoples' participation is predicated on their sub-
mission to the depoliticized expertise of scientifically trained administrators and educators.[34] Furthermore, it places blame on local ignorance and
cultural spuriousness, in effect denying the complex political, economic,
and structural causes of deforestation that are based on an export-depend-
ent growth pattern required by international banks, development agencies,
and elites.[35]

In Monte Verde, a famous site of tropical cloud forest conservation and
tourism, a similar model of conservation developed between the 1970s and
1990s based on the concentration of lands as wilderness preserves. There
were two important elements to this work, including a wilderness philosophy that places humans outside of nature and the consistent invocation of
images of *campesinos* whose main relationship to the land was inflexibly destructive and inadequate to allow them to appreciate the biodiversity of the
cloud forest. For example, a proposal to the World Wildlife Fund to fund
the purchase of lands invokes powerful imagery of *campesinos* whose "only
option" is the inevitable destruction of the Peñas Blancas watershed.[36] An
article in a popular Canadian magazine by a biologist working in Monte
Verde explains that the cloud forests are at risk from "poverty-stricken mi-
grant farmers [who] have cleared [once lush and verdant woodland] to
provide land and fuel."[37] In practice, a conservation land purchase agent
explained to me, conservation organizations would sometimes pay twice
for lands whose boundaries were in conflict: as he explained, "the point
was to close the deal and get the people out of there so they don't do any
more damage."

In fact, in more than forty areas of settlement in the area in question, 92
percent remained "pristine virgin forest" (according to the proposal to the
World Wildlife Fund), reflecting a more complicated story that was not
being told. Of approximately sixty landowners, only nine lived on their
lands, and by admission only several were actively cutting trees. The point
is not to romanticize rural Costa Ricans as innocent of forest conversion,
but it is important to try to understand why such a large area remained
forested in spite of the apparent avariciousness and spuriousness of peasant
culture. Part of the answer lies in the fact that most landowners in this particular area did not use their lands for subsistence purposes but considered
them to be long-term investments to be used flexibly in times of economic
need. Furthermore, those who were cutting trees were doing so as an active
way to provoke either the government or environmental groups to expro-

priate their lands, which were already frozen by the decree of the area as a watershed forest reserve.[38] Nevertheless, the imagery of Monte Verde's imminent destruction at the hands of poor Third World subjects circulated internationally and helped raise literally millions of dollars to fund adopt-an-acre programs and land purchases.

In Monte Verde, land purchases are the single most controversial mechanism conservationists have employed. Expressions of discontent over land purchases have included public demonstrations, general resentment, and acts of resistance, including those in the community of San Luis, where residents organized themselves to resist creation of a biological corridor as proposed by one of Monte Verde's major conservation organizations. One of the organizers, a farmer and landowner, stated: "They destroy communities. I don't need their help. Call it a biological corridor, call it a reserve, call it what you want. It simply means more control over the *campesino*." Underlying such negative convictions is the legacy of land purchase campaigns, which have tended to consider landowners and farmers as obstacles to conservation. One former member of a Monte Verde conservation group explained to me that this is because conservation activists did not typically take the care to acknowledge the subtle realities of rural life, especially existing local knowledge, concepts of property ownership, and the conflicting political, social, and economic interests of rural people. He observed: "Sadly, all this hard work to protect forests could be undermined by people who do not care about these forests and are willing to invade them, simply because conservation did not care to establish a communication and sharing of information, participation, and shared interests. And this is not because people are ignorant or do not know the value of forests." The point, certainly a polemical one, is that conservation has succeeded as a stopgap measure alone, and in fact it has generated hostility because conservationists approached rural peoples not as equals with whom to negotiate but as obstacles and destroyers to be removed from the landscape.[39] At its basis, as we have seen, are powerful images of spurious cultures that unfortunately obscure more complex political and cultural realities, as well as local cultural standards of conviviality. More important, we have to question what kind of social relationships are assumed to result from the creation and management of foreign-funded wilderness preserves, driven by administrative experts and dismissive of local autonomous and democratic decision-making processes.

Conservation and Cultural Regeneration

In the southern Mexican state of Oaxaca, the Costa Rican model of nature conservation—a model whose ideology emphasizes the illegitimacy of the notion that rural communities and rain forests can coexist and whose first steps consist of clearing these people from the landscape in order to create and manage protected areas—has a dubious reputation. Here the majority of lands are held communally by indigenous peoples, and notions of unpeopled or unmanaged wilderness represent an alien, even unwelcome, ideology. Nature conservation is an increasingly important theme of public discussion and policy in Oaxaca; however, it provides some interesting opportunities for moving beyond the essentializing genuine–spurious cultures paradigm and its top-down realities.

Oaxaca is a state of profound contradictions, symbolizing both the negative social and ecological consequences of traditional Western economic development patterns and the endurance of indigenous communities. A state of 3 million people, it has sixteen major indigenous cultural groups that make up 70 percent of the population. It is also a place of astonishing biodiversity, ranked first in Mexico, which is usually ranked fourth worldwide, and most of this biodiversity is in indigenous hands, given that 70 percent of the land is communally held. At the same time, a United Nations report described Oaxaca as one of the "most eroded landscapes on the planet," and Oaxaca is by standard economic indicators the second poorest state in Mexico, with extremely high rates of migration to Mexico City and the United States.[40] Since the 1980s, the social and economic well-being of large segments of the population has declined because of failures of the green revolution technologies for small farmers that have undermined already stressed soils, as well as the national debt crisis due to neoliberal reforms.[41] But economic globalization and neoliberalism have also weakened the ability of the Mexican state to continue centralized economic programs and *indigenista* policies (welfare-oriented programs of guardianship of indigenous peoples), leading to inconsistent effects on civil society.[42] On the one hand, a "culture of decentralization" has emerged, with its focus on the local as a site for fostering political and economic change.[43] On the other, elites have embraced "globalism" through multinational investment and free trade as the political and economic future of the country.

Indigenous communities and civil society institutions have responded to this situation in innovative ways, themselves becoming new sites of public authority and reflecting, according to Oaxaca-based intellectual Gustavo Esteva, "the florescence of a wider movement that until now has been gathering momentum beneath the surface of social awareness both in Mexico and elsewhere,"[44] which includes the Zapatista rebellion in neighboring Chiapas. Mexican biologist Victor Toledo refers to this florescence outside Chiapas as "el otro Zapatismo" (the other Zapatismo), which he identifies as self-consciously "post-development" forms of organizing based on the nonhierarchical political participation of indigenous peoples on regional and state levels.[45] This form of political participation, which brings together disparate cultures in an arena of public dialogue, is centered on the expression of each group's cultural values and worldviews, the maintenance and regeneration of community structure, and collective control over resources. As a result, it is challenging received meanings of nature, civil society, citizenship, and governance, and it is quite literally aiming to radically reconstruct Oaxacan social and legal structures. A vivid example of this is the 1998 passage in Oaxaca of the Ley de Usos y Costumbres (Law of Traditions and Customs), which reforms the state constitution to recognize for the first time the legal authority of indigenous juridical systems. The law contributes to the political autonomy of indigenous peoples and implies profound changes in the system of governance in Oaxaca toward greater cultural and juridical pluralism.[46]

In this context of vigorous indigenous politicization and dialogue across the boundaries of cultural difference, conservation activists find themselves employing the same kind of language used in the earlier quotation by Nick Salafsky—that social and cultural concerns are central to doing conservation—although with different pretensions, because after years of domination by Spanish colonial authorities, Mexican national governments, and international development agencies, indigenous peoples are searching for ways to work with environmental advocates on their own terms and in ways that regenerate their local economies and cultures. As a result, conservationists working in the midst of indigenous communities are making some rather unlikely claims about the means and goals of conservation. For example, in a brief analysis of the future of environmentalism that he calls "The Twilight of the Environmentalist Era," Juan José Consejo, a prominent Oaxaca conservation activist, argues that an important threat to Oaxaca's grassroots communities "will come in the seemingly benign form of protected natural areas."[47] This is based on a skepticism toward wilderness ideology, not only because of its role in eliminating indigenous activities in and management paradigms for forests but also because creating natural islands "will prevent us from realizing that the areas surrounding these islands will be increasingly degraded by a system which favours short-term economic gains at the cost of nature and society."[48] He concludes: "The task of the radicals in the twilight of the environmentalist era will be to oppose [the] disastrous pretense of blending the principle of scarcity with the laws of nature. For that it will be necessary to defend and reinstate the community structures and relationships that bureaucrats and businesspeople will try to deprive us of."[49]

At the heart of this critique is a rejection of nature conservation as "sustainable development," a worldview that legitimates Western economic rationality and positivistic sciences as the universal paradigms that rule people's lives and nature. For Oaxaca's indigenous communities, models of conservation based on creation of preserves and their management by ecological experts, which inherently define nature as scarce and therefore subject to the logic of the marketplace and needful of expert management, contribute to an ongoing delegitimation of their cultural knowledge and worldviews, traditional ecological knowledge, collective ownership and management of resources, and traditional forms of community authority and organization based on cultural values of sufficiency. Given the potential consequences of ceding authority over their lands, local communities are less inclined to serve an agenda of nature conservation set by Northern or elite experts and fund-raisers; instead, they argue that conservation must be defined in terms that strengthen community structures and relationships.

But it would be mistaken to assume that Oaxaca's indigenous communities promote a vision of conservation based on an uncritical genuine culture paradigm that assumes their cultural traditions alone hold the key to sustainability. Rather, they are engaged in a broader historical process of regenerating and reconstructing cultural and community autonomy and self-determination. This is evident in the project of a nongovernmental organization called the Instituto de la Naturaleza y la Sociedad de Oaxaca (INSO), whose Manialtepec Initiative, based in the coastal regions and the watershed of the Manialtepec lagoon, has been organized around local concerns for clean water and cultural and political autonomy for the Chatino people living in the watershed, not the conservation of resources through ejection of people from the landscape. A central goal of this project has been to facilitate technical assistance to indigenous and *campesino* communities desiring to install dry latrines and highly efficient (Lorena) stoves made with readily available and inexpensive local products. The ecological effects are immediately apparent: in the case of stoves, communities no longer need to cut large amounts of wood for fuel, which enables them to begin regenerating communal forests, and in the case of water, they neither require water to flush toilets nor pollute river and lagoon waters with human feces.

In such acts there is a deliberate cultural and political thrust, and it lies in, to put it rather bluntly, communities regaining control over their crap. In a direct sense, a community's dependence on centralized government, which has maintained its domination of indigenous peoples through often unfulfilled promises of infrastructure such as sewage and water treatment, is reduced. More important, soils battered by green revolution agricultural techniques and fertilizers are regenerated and communities regain control over their destiny.[50] This is not about applying a genuine culture paradigm to conservation and appeals to static traditions, since these technologies and practices are not autochthonous to the region, nor do communities invoke romanticized ideologies about the ecological degradation that has resulted from their participation in modern agriculture. Rather, there is an active and flexible combination of new ideas and practices with older traditions based on dialogic processes, including communal forms of labor (*tequio*) to help install dry latrines and stoves, as well as communal assembly wherein decisions are made about conservation actions. The point here is that the goals of conservation are just as much about reconstructing nature as they are deliberately about reconstructing a social community and cultural tradition that does not see itself as standing outside of nature.

Conclusion

For many peoples of the South, nature conservation exists at a crossroads. Will it represent domination by a new set of elites, in this case scientifically trained natural resource administrators united with government or nongovernmental interests external to rural communities, or will conservation activists find ways to unite their struggles for nature with local struggles for equity, justice, and autonomy at the community level? If conservationists do consider their work to be essentially "social" in nature, whose definition of social relationships, culture, and worldview will count? Is conservation really simply about changing people's behaviors, or is there some way in which conservation activists can create opportunities for intercultural dialogues about people's place in nature and building appropriate and customized conservation initiatives?

It is necessary to confront these difficult questions because, as Ellen argued in his critique of the "green primitive" concept, "no one human culture has the monopoly of environmental wisdom, and . . . it seems unlikely that we could ever escape the more profound dilemmas of human life."[51] Although Ellen levels his critique at those in the environmentalist community who would romanticize indigenous peoples for their supposed ecological wisdom, his point should also be applied in the other direction, to other paradigms of conservation, be they scientific, utilitarian, preservationist, and so on. Communication about environmental issues across worldviews is fraught with difficulty because, as international communication scholar Peter Raine has observed, "listening to another's view is a different matter to that of actually validating that view as an expression of reality comparable to one's own."[52] The tendency to caricature alternative worldviews as stereotypes of certain kinds of cultures, genuine or spurious, may not always be deliberate, but their use often remains unchallenged because conservation experts often base their authority not on dialogue with and learning from other cultures but on the premise of standing in and speaking for nature. This expertise often carries with it an inability to recognize the dynamic and shifting complexities of any social milieu, which is counterproductive to conservation's reconstruction. We need a conservationist culture based on dialogue—not domination—that is not about simply facilitating an exchange of wisdom in order to convert people to some predetermined expectations of what conservation "should be." This dialogue should also involve a process of mutual enrichment in which the means and ends of conservation themselves are open to new contingencies and intercultural negotiations.[53]

There is evidence that such concerns are being taken very seriously in Oaxaca, where indigenous communities are unsentimentally engaging conservationists in a new kind of dialogue about the place of people in nature and the necessity of conservation to participate in cultural regeneration, vastly enriching conservationist concepts of process and end goals. There seems little doubt that it can contribute to Oaxacan concerns for regenerating the historically battered capacity for local decision making and cultural reaffirmation in the face of national and globalizing economic and cultural forces. Perhaps even more important, conservationists and indigenous activists are engaged in a self-conscious process of constructing an alternative modernity in which nature and society are projected not as inherently separate and predetermined but as mutually constructed in organic ways.

Acknowledgments

This chapter draws upon one and one-half years of ethnographic research in Monte Verde, Costa Rica, as well as research and dialogues in Oaxaca, Mexico. My research in Costa Rica would not have been possible without generous assistance from the Wenner-Gren Foundation for Anthropological Research, The John D. and Catherine T. MacArthur Foundation, The Andrew W. Mellon Foundation, and the following Princeton University entities: the Center of International Studies, the Council on Regional Studies, the Program in Latin American Studies, and the Department of Anthropology. I am grateful for significant support of dissertation and post-dissertation write-up from the New England Board of Higher Education and the University of Vermont. In Oaxaca, I learned much from dialogues with Gustavo Esteva, Juan José Consejo, the staff at INSO, Gustavo Teran, and Corrine Glesne. My special thanks to Ben Minteer and Bob Manning for their continued interest in my work and their invitation to contribute to this volume.

Part III

Reweaving the Tradition

Expanding the Conservation Tradition: The Agrarian Vision

PAUL B. THOMPSON

Had a seminar on conservation been held a century ago, the agrarian vision would have been "what every schoolchild knows" about the relationship between humanity and the natural world. It is a worldview fixated on the manner in which human beings derive their subsistence through activities such as farming, husbandry, horticulture, and forestry, often augmented by hunting, fishing, and other means of harvesting uncultivated plants and animals. At the risk of oversimplifying a complex and diverse set of human practices, I will refer to all these subsistence activities as forms of agriculture. I will use the phrase "agrarian philosophy" to cover a wide array of relatively systematic and explicitly conceptualized ways of understanding the role of these subsistence activities that give prominence to them as features of social organization and human experience. Agrarian philosophy takes agriculture to be particularly influential in establishing political or cultural identity, patterns of human interdependence, and forms of social psychology that bear heavily on the development of moral character. Philosophers who held agrarian views simply assumed that agriculture—understood broadly as I have defined it—constitutes the most important domain of human interaction with what we today call the natural environment. This assumption was so obvious to them that it is not, in fact, something that received much articulation in agrarian texts.

The importance of agriculture is far from obvious today. The idea that the material practices of subsistence could be a source of philosophical insight into humanity's relationship with the natural environment is almost wholly foreign to many. To some degree, the reason for this is obvious. The daily lives of most people are far removed from agricultural practices in a post-industrial society, and the practices of farming, husbandry,

horticulture, and forestry are themselves radically changed through industrial technology. Yet it is also true that agrarian themes in the Western
canon have largely been neglected by philosophers and environmental scientists who have contemplated the imperatives of conservation. As J. Baird
Callicott says in his contribution to this volume, many environmental
philosophers have tended to discuss conservation exclusively in relation
to the preservation of wild landscapes and ecosystems. A great deal of environmental philosophy has a "western" bias, in Richard W. Judd's sense of
the term. As environmental history has been skewed by an overemphasis
on western land-use conflicts, environmental philosophy has focused in-
tently on the arguments that can be deployed to protect land *from* agriculture. Relatively little philosophical attention has been paid to the norms or
goals that guided the land settlement patterns of the eastern United States.
These were, as the great scholar of early American intellectual life Perry
Miller argued, deeply intertwined with sectarian religious beliefs, but
farm-oriented immigrants *did* tend to stress permanent and sustainable
communities rather than short-term gain. In fact, agrarian philosophy has
been so thoroughly neglected and forgotten that it is now possible to see it
as something new, as an expansion of conservation thought that can play
a significant role in its reconstruction. A renewed and revitalized agrarianism would provide the eastern counterpoint to western-style conservation
ethics.

In agrarian philosophy, human beings are hard at work within nature.
Their actions shape and transform it as surely as nature shapes and transforms them. In thinking that natural landscapes could also be human
products, agrarian philosophers appear to backing away from the strong
non-anthropocentrism characteristic of late-twentieth-century environmental ethics. Yet in seeing human values as a product of interaction with
the natural world, agrarian thought makes a more radical commitment to
the idea of nature as an originating source of value than even the deepest of
deep ecologists. Agrarianism proposes to conserve a primary and values-
originating relationship between humanity and nature. It opposes moral
psychology that interprets all human-enacted valuations as reactive, as if
the basis for an environmental ethics could be found in the human subject
idly contemplating natural landscapes as if they were cuts of meat or paint-
ings in a museum. In practice, neo-agrarian environmental ethics provides
a rationale for conserving many different forms of humanity at work in nature: working farms, certainly, but also historically, aesthetically, and educa-

tionally important monuments to the manner in which the agrarian life has been and can become manifest in human experience. In the remarks that follow, I will sketch the history and outline of agrarian philosophy in the briefest of terms. I will then move on to exposit a new agrarianism by indicating how some key themes must be reinterpreted for reconstructing conservation.

The Agrarian Tradition

Agrarian themes and doctrines are scattered throughout the writings of philosophers who are routinely taken to be the greatest thinkers of the Western tradition. There is a school of classicists who believe that Socrates, Plato, Aristotle, and, indeed, many of the Greeks were preoccupied with the problem of preserving an agrarian social order. Victor Davis Hanson, a representative of this school argues that Greek city-states took up the problems of democracy and philosophy because they evolved a unique sociopolitical structure in which military power, relative wealth, and political stability depended on a class of independent, landowning farmer-citizens. The Greek landscape was not amenable to larger plantation-style farming, and this had limited the growth of large, centrally managed agricultural economies such as those of Egypt and Mesopotamia. The *hoi mesoi* controlled relatively small landholdings planted in trees and vines. Although aided by slaves, they contributed a large portion of personal labor and were intimately familiar with the details of farming. Since tree and vine crops represent lifetime investments for farmers, the *hoi mesoi* had a clear stake in preserving the social order that, in turn, secured their title and access to improved lands. Thus, they could be relied upon for military service and were intensely dedicated to the stability and integrity of the polis. Beginning in the fifth century B.C., maritime technology was making sea trade an important source of wealth for Greek city-states. By the time of Socrates, Plato, and Aristotle, trading interests whose loyalty to the polis was not permanently affixed to any geographic location had spawned both the growth of the first Athenian empire and its collapse under the leadership of Alcibiades. Opportunities for trade and conquest created the temptation for imperialistic (rather than defensive) use of military power. Hanson reads Socrates and Plato as responding to this tension and Aristotle as looking back upon the aftermath. To the extent that Socrates, Plato, and

Aristotle can be interpreted against this backdrop, we can read them as addressing agrarian themes.[1]

It is not my purpose here to examine or evaluate ancient thought for the presence or influence of agrarian philosophy. Hanson's picture of the ancient world is useful because he argues that unique geographic and biological features of the subsistence economy gave rise to the Greek polis and, in turn, the unique flowering of art and philosophy characteristic of the Greek personality. Such societies do not arise where conditions are too meager to support farmers dedicated to diversified farming or so abundant that centralized plantations arise in their stead. This type of thinking led Enlightenment philosophers to develop complex theories about the type of environment that would be most conducive to settled agriculture and most likely to support the rise of social classes having both desire for economic advancement and loyalty to a particular place. These were the conditions thought to be prerequisite to the evolution of a nation-state and thought to produce citizens having the moral personality necessary for civil society. To one degree or another, such themes were either implicit or explicit in the thought of virtually all the eighteenth-century political economists and natural philosophers, including Charles Louis de Secondat Montesquieu, Georges Louis Leclerc Buffon, Adam Smith, David Hume, and even Immanuel Kant.[2]

Eighteenth-century agrarian philosophy is also awash with themes that we rightly regard with suspicion and disdain. Its environmental determinism paved the way for Charles Darwin but also for social Darwinists, who justified European domination of colonized people on the ground that having lived in a deprived environment, they had not developed the prerequisites for civilized behavior. In placing emphasis on the moral personality of cultural groups, and in insisting that land—the traditional term for what we now call the natural environment—is an originating force in forming the personality of a people, agrarian philosophers used a philosophical vocabulary that is today linked to a number of anti-rational social movements, including German National Socialism and the radical Islamic fundamentalism of Osama bin Laden.[3] In our time, agrarian philosophy has not merely been forgotten; it has been repressed. And justly so, if such results are its primary fruit. I believe there are ideas and values that should be recovered from agrarian thinking, but we must also bear in mind that there were good reasons why such thinking has been set aside. Rather than attempting a wholesale review of the eighteenth-century literature, I will examine four themes that I believe to be central to agrarian philosophy and most important in reconstructing conservation. The first is the assumption that productive work is humanity's most profound point of contact with the natural world. The second is that engaging nature through work forms individual and social personality. The third is human and biological diversity, and the fourth emphasizes the dependence of social reproduction on nature's feedback.

The Primacy of Work

The agrarian vision presumes that human beings and human societies encounter the natural world most fundamentally through their productive activity. Productive activity was, of course, understood primarily in terms of farming, husbandry, and the other subsistence activities I have lumped together under the general heading of agriculture. Prior to the nineteenth century, this must have seemed to be a completely obvious and wholly unexceptional presumption. This is so much the case that I am at a loss to produce citations that really document this claim. Of course, many westerners were living in cities and engaged in occupations of manufacture, trade, and the provision of services for several hundred years before 1800. Agriculture was, nevertheless, the most common vocation in most European countries (and their colonial settlements) well into the nineteenth century, and anyone addressing questions of environment and values would have scarcely thought it necessary to point this out.

In the agrarian orientation to nature, productive work becomes an obvious focal point for moral and philosophical inquiries of many kinds. As Max Weber argued in his classic work *The Protestant Ethic and the Spirit of Capitalism,* the ideologies of work became entangled in religious doctrines in very complicated and even paradoxical ways. Working hard was thought to be a central moral value and a route to self-improvement, as expressed in the adage "God helps those who help themselves." The Calvinist doctrine of the elect stipulated that heavenly reward could not be earned at the same time it reinforced the value of productive work.[4] Weber, of course, was interested in the way this mentality fostered the growth of capitalism by encouraging the virtue of industriousness among the bourgeoisie. Within an agrarian context, the rewards tied people to nature. God's chosen people would be rewarded with higher-yielding crops or larger and more fecund trees and animals. All this occurred within a garden where

God's stewards were hard at work transforming nature, and where allowing land to lie fallow was to commit the sin of wastefulness.

Weber's analysis notwithstanding, the nobility of work is a theme that underwent substantial erosion and revision throughout the nineteenth and twentieth centuries. Economic utilitarians presume that work is an evil that all rational people want to minimize: the economically rational individual attempts to maximize consumptive enjoyment of pleasures, and work is understood as a cost borne only so that we may have the means to consume. By the twentieth century, the goals of working for the weekend and early retirement became themes in popular culture. The notion that environmental amenities are consumption goods was thematized in environmental economics, in which travel costs and shadow prices are computed and surveys are run to determine how much people are willing to pay in order to conserve nature. Environmentally oriented economists such as Thomas Michael Power[5] and philosophers such as David A. Crocker[6] argue that we should be even more attentive to consumption, on the assumption that those who emphasize production will see conservation as a drain on productive activity. Even Aldo Leopold seemed resigned to a more consumption-oriented attitude toward nature conservation when he bemoaned those who could not rationalize conservation without an economic argument to support it. Although he was discussing songbirds and not land use when he made this observation, Leopold must have rightly seen that in presuming that uncultivated land is wasted, those who adopt an agrarian vision may be led to undertake practices that are inimical to an ecologically informed understanding of conservation.

Yet those who emphasize production have philosophical resources at their disposal that are unavailable to those who see conservation in terms providing amenity values for which people must be willing to pay. Agrarians work in order to subsist, to dwell at a given place, and the goal of agrarian work is to do this well so that one's descendants will also be able to do it. There is no ideal of retiring to Florida in the agrarian vision of work. Production of food, fiber, and building materials is necessary for subsistence, and the goal of subsistence is to live a life that can be reproduced again and again at the same site, generation after generation. This is not to say that one aims for bare subsistence, but to knowingly ruin or despoil the land is to render it inhospitable to the kind of work that makes one what one is. Even if this does not happen in one's own lifetime, productive practices that cannot be passed down from parent to child fail to represent a heritable way of life, which (for an agrarian) is to say that they are no way of life at all. To speak of work in this way is to *re*construct conservation in the sense of constructing conservation as it once *was* constructed. Conservation serves the production and reproduction of practice at a given place.

Now, to talk this way is to speak of traditional agricultural practices in extremely idealistic terms, for failure and despoliation have been all too frequent occurrences throughout human history. Yet part of the mentality behind human societies that truly had class structures is that these classes were thought to represent enduring, stable, and mutually supporting ways of life that could and should be handed down from one generation to the next. Although this was, from our perspective, a very stifling and even repressive way of understanding human potential, it did orient people toward an ethic of strong sustainability, articulated primarily through their understandings of productive work. In such visions, the teleology of personal and social fulfillment coincides with a strong ethic of sustainable practice. Equipped with knowledge of ecology or even an ecologically advantageous mythology of nature, people who order their lives according to an agrarian vision will see no tension between conservation of wild nature and the duties of the steward. Whether such an attitude can or even should be rehabilitated in our time must await some discussion of the three additional agrarian tenets.

Character, Personality, and Landscape

In discussing the prominence of work, I have already begun to emphasize the influence of productive work on the formation of personal and social character. This link is, to some degree, just common sense. What one does has a profound effect on what one is, from a moral point of view. Sound character has routinely been attributed to farming people, especially in comparison with those who derive their livelihood in other ways. Thomas Jefferson called farmers "the most virtuous citizens" and likened tradesmen and factory workers to sores on the body politic. Early in *A Sand County Almanac,* Leopold states: "There are two spiritual dangers in not owning a farm. One is the danger of supposing that breakfast comes from the grocery, and the other that heat comes from the furnace."[7] Wendell Berry is perhaps our greatest contemporary agrarian voice, and he bemoans the way work and leisure are disjoint activities in urban life. Berry believes that working apart from the family and away from home divides the personality, making it difficult for people to comprehend the consequences of working poorly and thereby creating tendencies toward irresponsibility and indolence. This is particularly catastrophic for children, who correctly perceive how little their work—attending school outside the home—contributes to the family's livelihood. On the farm, everyone has something to do, and everyone knows whether or not it is done well. The interdependence of tasks creates an environment in which the importance of working well and productively is reinforced with constant feedback. And in agriculture this feedback is, of course, a direct extension of ecological interactions that penetrate directly into family structure and daily life.[8]

Neither Berry nor I would suggest that agricultural work always and in every case produces sound character or ecologically sound feedback. Technology and policy can intervene in these feedback loops, and there are the persistent problems of ignorance and bad will as well. What is more, this kind of talk about family, work, and character suggests a number of socially conservative themes that make many people nervous. When we remember that the agrarian worldview sees this productive work occurring in specific places, this conservative theme takes on an even darker tone. The suggestion that working over time at a specific geographic locale produces people with a specific national or regional identity has been a handmaiden to exclusionary ideologies, violence, and even genocide. Here, the link between productive work and the particular place in which it occurs is alleged to reinforce habits of practice and forms of mentality that underpin the shared character of a people. These patterns are often attributed influence far beyond the actual experience of productive labor. Thus, Scots are thought to owe elements of their national character to the difficulty and independence characteristic of Highland agriculture, and Germans are said to draw strength and spirituality from the unique character of their forests.

These landscape myths are obviously overstated, but should they be debunked entirely? There is clearly something profoundly attractive to people about the alleged links between land and moral personality.[9] Here, I want to concentrate for a moment on the way this link has been characterized in two great periods of agrarian thought in America. The first is, of course, associated with the time of the founding fathers, and its most renowned spokesperson was Thomas Jefferson. The second is the transcendentalist movement of the nineteenth century. The transcendentalists included poets, painters, and preachers, and they expressed their views through artworks and social experiments as well as more conventional texts. I will focus on the most philosophical of them, Ralph Waldo Emerson and Henry David Thoreau.

Jefferson's views on the link between land and character were quite similar to those that Hanson associates with the ancient Greeks. Jefferson saw the agricultural life as resolving a basic tension between citizenship and private economic interest. Those who own land and derive their living from working it will have an interest in defending it and will not support frivolous governments. Those who trade or manufacture can do so anywhere, and their capital is transportable. Hence, there is no check on their desire to vote themselves benefits and to shirk the responsibilities of defending their land and paying taxes. Democracy is possible only when such responsibilities are taken seriously.[10] Emerson and Thoreau, in contrast, emphasized a spiritual relationship with nature that occurs in lived experience, through experiences unmediated by the intellectualizations of science or literature. Secondhand representations of nature are generalizable and transportable, but the authentic experience of nature is had only by being in nature. Thus, one is never "in" the nature that is captured by a theory or a text. A natural relationship with nature arises most readily when one is doing what comes naturally, which is to say when one is deriving a subsistence living at a place. This is, in fact, the only authentic form of experience that can actually be had by human beings, and character traits formed out of living mediated and intellectualized lives are likely to be artificial and brittle.[11]

Of course, we, as did Emerson and Thoreau, live in a time when fewer and fewer people have ready access to an authentic experience of nature. If one follows their line of thinking, it is our lot to live highly mediated lives and to bear the risks of artificiality and alienation. We also bear the risks feared by Jefferson. Having no stake in our land, why should we sacrifice our lives or our wealth to secure it? It is, I submit, in these diagnostic terms that we should interpret the agrarian rhetoric of someone like Wendell Berry. The agrarian vision of how work and character intertwine suggests a diagnosis of the conservation problem quite unlike that of an environmental ethic that begins with the question of why and how we should value nature. This is not to suggest that the cure to our problem could possibly be found in regression to a mythical past or through rituals of purification intended to eliminate those who are not "our kind." The lessons of diversity explain why.

Nature and Diversity

Implicit within agrarian themes already described is the idea that the differences among individuals and among peoples are at least in part due to the different natural environments in which they live. I have already suggested that some of the great evils we associate with nationalist movements and exclusionary ideologies derive from the misguided thought that these principles of difference are sources of impurity and corruption. Agrarian visions turn sour when the people who hold agrarian beliefs embark on totalizing quests of domination or purification bent on the elimination or repression of difference. I can see nothing intrinsic to agrarian thinking that supports this turn of mind. In fact, everything we know about good farming and good ecology suggests quite the opposite. It is when practices and populations become too uniform that they are at greatest risk of collapse.

Agrarian philosophy anticipated ideas that have become more fully developed since Darwin and the growth of modern ecology and genetics. Environments—for the eighteenth-century agrarian philosophers, it was climate and landscape—reinforce the acquisition of both biological traits and cultural practices. But when a population, be it a biological population of organisms or a population of cultural practices, becomes homogenous, the population as a whole is more vulnerable to specific threats or forms of predation than is a population with more varied ways to address functional needs. The types of diversity that are relevant here are incredibly numerous. There is genetic diversity and species diversity, of course, but there are also diversified farming practices, crop mixes, and combinations of husbandry, horticulture, and forestry, as well as complex labor and distribution regimes. A discussion of how all these types of diversity are important would fill volumes, so a single example must suffice.

In 1972, the United States' corn (maize) crop suffered a devastating virus that destroyed upward of three-quarters of the acreage planted. Some experts believe that this event came close to triggering widespread food shortages, and it did indeed result in feed shortages and a subsequent hike in the price of meat. It was discovered that this virus attacked a locus on the corn genome where a single allele, Texas T-cytoplasm, was present in virtually all the major corn varieties being planted in the United States. Varieties containing Texas T-cytoplasm were particularly susceptible to the virus. If corn breeders had used (as they now do) a genetically more diverse seed stock, losses would have been more limited. The emergence of viral diseases is a threat to any population having a narrow genetic base. In this way, diversity is critical to good farming. Crop breeders relearned a lesson known by peasant farmers, who always plant multiple varieties of multiple crops in order to minimize the chance of total crop loss.[12]

Whether we are talking about genetic evolution within a species, the shifting mix of organisms within a particular ecosystem, or the mix of human practices extant throughout a given social group, environmental feedback will cull less optimal or effective specimens. There will be a regression toward the norm that reflects local environmental conditions. But when the range of variation becomes too narrow, the population as a whole becomes vulnerable to an extinction event. In this sense, populations can be *too* responsive to environmental conditions. Hence, stability or sustainability depends on diversity and novelty as much as on the responsiveness to localized optima. Diversity is often maintained because the boundaries or barriers between both biological and cultural ecotones are semipermeable. The boundaries are sufficiently strong to allow separate and hence distinct evolutionary mechanisms to do their work at culling, but open enough to allow the constant entry of novel genes, organisms, or cultural practices.[13]

Modern industrial agriculture often substitutes financial mechanisms for biological ones in limiting farmers' risk. Today, farmers use futures markets and crop insurance to hedge against crop loss. Ecological risks are largely addressed at the level of agricultural research and technology development, in which diversity continues to be important. In the agrarian world, diverse farming practices were more closely tied to the idea of agrarian virtue. Agriculture is never a case of operating in the same way year after year; it is always an art of mixing the novel with the tried and true, constantly experimenting with one corner of the field and, as a result, remaining open to diversity at the same time one's core practices are responsive to the particular needs of very localized soil types and other ecological conditions. Yet the examples of ethnic cleansing testify to the fact that people have often failed to generalize this wisdom beyond their farming practice.

Human beings have neglected the role of diversity because it is, frankly, an obscure bit of wisdom easily lost on someone engaged in daily pursuits. The temptations of conquest and ascetic practices of purification alike may have conspired to turn agrarian thinking away from the wisdom of diversity. Today we do not have that excuse, yet surely we must also acknowledge that elevating our collective appreciation of the way human practices depend on both biological and cultural diversity remains one of our great-est challenges. Any attempt to rehabilitate the agrarian vision must guard against its regressive tendencies. Cultivating a widespread appreciation of diversity and learning to understand the requirements of novelty must cer-tainly be foremost among the strategies for reconstructing conservation.

Social Reproduction, Institutions, and Habits of Mind

In their belief that political economy and moral personality are functional adaptations to climate and geography, the agrarian philosophers saw both individual and sociocultural practices as embodying a form of evolutionary wisdom. They were, thus, often no great fans of radical social change. The agrarian elements in the philosophy of someone like Montesquieu or Hume support a profound distrust of theory-driven reforms advocated by philosophers such as Jeremy Bentham and Denis Diderot. Within the framework of eighteenth-century thought, the idea here was perhaps best expressed by Edmund Burke in his *Reflections on the Revolution in France.* We should be suspicious of theories that predict great social benefits fol-lowing on institutional change, given that our existing institutions are the result of a long process of evolutionary adjustment. They reflect the kind of local optimum alluded to earlier, and, as such, they are likely to be more stable than reformed institutions predicated on the basis of theory. As such, be wary of conceits such as the utilitarian calculus or the rights of man, and stick with the forms of practice that are tried and true.[14]

What is insightful here is the recognition that human practices and so-cial institutions are themselves evolutionary products embedded in a com-plex nexus of social and biological forces that bring about their reproduction over time. What is problematic is the aforementioned lack of appreciation of the need for novelty and variety, and also a form of deafness to compelling arguments for moral reform. In this context, however, what needs emphasis is the way that any approach to conservation demands a sophisticated understanding of the embeddedness that characterizes human institutions and practices. One cannot motivate or bring about a change in human practice by simply *predicting* that bad outcomes are on the horizon. What we do as individuals and as groups is simply not ra-tional in the sense of consciously and straightforwardly selecting a course of action that leads to the best results. Instead, we are caught in webs of practice that are rational in the sense that they have gotten us this far. Mak-ing social reforms aimed at conservation cannot, thus, simply be a matter of figuring out where we need to go and then recommending the course of action that will get us there the quickest. Rather, it must be thought of as tweaking and nudging the multiplicity of factors that influence the reproduction of our social practices, in hopes that the next generation will be more adaptive.

Expanding the repertoire of conservation strategies along neo-agrarian lines is, thus, necessarily a horrendously complex business. The rehabilitation of agrarian philosophy will, I think, create a more sophisticated, which is to say a more ecological and evolutionary, understanding of human institutions than has hitherto been common. Environmental scientists have too frequently been deluded by the hope that good predictions would be sufficient to motivate changes in policy, if only they could get the information to key decision makers. The agrarian vision would suggest that policy decision making is only a very small part of where conservation needs to take place. Rather, it must be part of the feedback mechanisms that reproduce all our social forms, our workplace, our schools, our home place, and our recreation alike. We must be thinking about how these activities produce people having one type of moral character rather than another, and we must be looking for every opportunity to reinforce the object lessons that nature is trying to teach us.[15]

This general philosophical vision of human practice and its potential for reform must be placed in comparison with one that constructs conservation activities as justifiable in terms of their value for humans or wild nature. Here, we come full circle and return to the emphasis on productive work. Even environmental philosophers who have wished to break with resource economics and utilitarian ethics have not adequately broken with a philosophical tradition that sees the problem in what I have called consumption terms. On this view, conservation is undervalued, perhaps because people have been too narrowly focused on human interests. But this move simply constructs nature itself as a forgotten subject, a "consumer" of conservation, and the problem is to come up with ecological, economic, or ethical rationales that help us value conservation activities properly. Conservation activities are still thought to derive their justification from the value their consequences have for consuming subjects; it is just that this value is now computed by asking how these activities serve nature's interests as well as those of present and future human beings. The presumption behind this kind of environmental ethics is that decision makers will choose actions and policies rationally calculated to result in the most

valued outcome. In this respect, it does not break with the moral psychology of Bentham and John Stuart Mill.

The agrarian vision is certainly not opposed to rationality, yet it sees
both individual and social character as evolutionary products of the work
we do as conditioned by environmental forces. Practices and institutions
can be thought of as having a certain momentum that reflects the environmental conditioning of the past. To the extent that this is so, they are not
necessarily responsive to predictions of what is to become. It is even a good
thing that we are *not* strictly rational in simple instrumentalist terms, for
that would make our social practices less diverse, less resilient under
changed conditions. One practical problem with calculative optimization is
that it settles too quickly on the single, optimal strategy. Making nature a
consumer of conservation activities does not fully address this problem.
For example, conservationists slavishly following the recommendation of a
policy model that incorporates the predicted value of a strategy for endangered species preservation (as well as or instead of economic value to humans) into its optimizing equations will converge on a relatively uniform
set of practices. Arguably, we would be better off with a diverse set of
strategies being followed because we would be less vulnerable to flaws in
the model.

The philosophical problem resides in a particular characterization of the
human being as a moral subject. Extending this characterization to nonhuman subjects such as wildlife, wilderness, or nature itself is no help. Both
neo-Kantians and consequentialists seem content with a conceptualization
of the moral subject derived from a highly attenuated and idealized account of choice. What is ethics? It is the study of what we ought to do, of
how we should act, of making the right choices. The decision maker surveys her options and deliberates on them. According to a neo-Kantian
ethics, one must discern which options are consistent with principles of
universality and autonomy for all. According to a consequentialist, we base
our choice on our prediction of the value we expect to accrue from each of
the available options. In either case, the moral subject is a decision maker
that, in a moment of quietude suspended in time, "applies values" to the
various options in the same way a shopper compares breakfast cereals or
automobiles. Modern moral philosophy demands that this decision maker
sees others as experiencing value as well, and in this it becomes possible to
reconstruct nature itself as "applying values" to the options or outcome that
any decision maker faces. It is in rather unreflectively adopting this con-

ception of the moral subject as a master shopper that environmental philosophy has committed itself to a paradigm of consumption. It should not be surprising that many real-life environmentalists understand their cause in terms of lifestyle decisions that involve the purchase and consumption of sporting goods, homes, foods, transportation, and vacation holidays.

There are, I believe, many problems here. One is that the master eco-shopper is still at some psychic distance from nature's feedback and fails to realize the fullness and inseparability of ecosystem and daily praxis. One could also make a similar point as an existential critique. One could say that the problem here is the unreality of the subject and the denial of the body.[16] We are too deep into the chapter to give such themes their due. My larger point is that an Emersonian or Thoreauvian agrarian will not be tempted by such errors. Praxis is the presumption, the context, and even the product of moral action. Whatever we produce in the world, we produce ourselves through our acts, which, we must always recall, are *interactions* with the environing circumstances and co-produced by them. Emerson came to believe that those who produce their subsistence in the presence of nature have a firmer grasp of this truth than any poet or philosopher. Thoreau's experiment at Walden Pond illustrates this commitment to lived experience. Farming is more likely to produce worthy character traits because productive work in the presence of nature produces people who cannot easily think of themselves in the attenuated terms of the neo-Kantian or utilitarian moral subject. Agrarianism—whether of an Emersonian or other stripe—will need mighty rehabilitation and amendment to work as a philosophy that might reconstruct conservation practice and policy, but it has an enormous head start over any view that begins by telling us we should strive to be better shoppers.

Conclusion

The good news is that agrarian philosophy holds great promise for the reconstruction of conservation and an empowering environmental philosophy emphasizing community-based practice. Conservation is deeply interwoven in the agrarian vision. There is little chance that conservation would be undervalued by people living lives according to rehabilitated agrarian philosophies. We can be seriously misled about what conservation actually is, of course, but this is where environmental science can help. The bad news is that we live in a time when agrarian philosophy has been deconstructed and discredited so thoroughly that rehabilitation may not even be a serious possibility. What every schoolchild once knew about the relationship between humanity and nature is far from obvious now. We are, I fear, victims of the spiritual dangers Leopold attributed to not owning a farm, and whether a new agrarianism has any place in an expanded conservation tradition that must play to a predominantly urban audience is an entirely open question.

We can, perhaps, begin to resuscitate agrarian ideals within environmental philosophy by turning to Leopold himself. Whatever sense philosophers have made of key passages in *A Sand County Almanac,* Leopold's broader essays leave no doubt that he thought of the farm community as a source of implicit environmental values. He saw that farmers and conservationists would not always see eye to eye. A farm has to pay, after all. Yet Leopold does not seem to have thought that the farmer's attentiveness to the problems of farm survival amounted to the kind of thinking that he criticized so sharply in his scathing remarks on studies designed to show the economic value of songbirds. Farm survival was a dimension of sustainable practice. No farm: no farmer. No farmer: no steward, no person committed to the land. Leopold devised many plans to work with farmers in pursuit of his game management goals, and he did not object to the idea that game could be usefully seen as another crop.[17]

More broadly and more immediately, agrarian philosophy provides a rationale for conserving farms and farmland. An agrarian would endorse parks and museums that memorialize farms and farming ways of particular note but would find it ultimately of greater importance to bring working farms into the conservation ideal. Activities such as farmer's markets and community-supported agriculture, which connect those who do not farm with those who do, could come to be understood as productive conservation activities. These might go along with fairly mundane goals such as eating in season. In such ways are both our sustenance and our continuing linkage to the land produced. In such ways does the land have its way in producing our progeny and ourselves. To think of these simple acts of embodied praxis as having philosophical depth, as grounding us in a philosophical tradition, would be a continuation and a regeneration of the agrarian way to conservation. In comparison with policies built on the model of resource economics and instrumental rationality, it would contribute to the reconstruction of conservation thought and practice.

Chapter 7

Regional Planning as Pragmatic Conservationism

BEN A. MINTEER

When philosophers offer accounts of the development of American environmental thought, they usually depict the conservation movement as the story of the institutionalization of Gifford Pinchot–style utilitarianism in natural resource administration and policy. As a conceptual foundation for modern environmentalism, however, Pinchot's project is roundly criticized for its inappropriately narrow instrumentalist view of nature and its reliance on an efficiency-oriented, "wise use" model of resource development. John Muir, Pinchot's antagonist in the tradition, fares much better in philosophers' treatments, mostly because his aesthetic-spiritual preservationism resonates more soundly with the commitments of the field's historically dominant nonanthropocentrists. The "professional" conservation movement, however, is thought to offer only an ecologically uninformed and morally suspect philosophy of "resourcism" to the development of American environmental values and ethics. According to this plot line, we would have to wait for Aldo Leopold to push environmentalist thinking beyond these paltry philosophical foundations with his groundbreaking land ethic in the 1930s and 1940s.[1]

Historians have provided much of the justification for this view of the conservation tradition among environmental philosophers, most notably in the work of influential commentators such as Samuel Hays, Roderick Nash, and Stephen Fox.[2] But in recent years, a new wave of historical scholarship has begun to steadily challenge this conservationist orthodoxy. In various ways, these new contributions have offered a more contextual and ethically nuanced interpretation of the tradition's public conservation norms and practices.[3] In parallel fashion, intellectually sympathetic revisions of the philosophical commitments and policy attitudes of conservation principals such as Pinchot and Muir have sharpened our understanding of the political and moral motivations driving conservation advocacy at the national level.[4] Yet despite these important efforts, it is still true that most philosophers, and most academic observers of the history of American environmental thought, continue to paint early and interwar period conservation philosophy only in (traditionally understood) Pinchot-style utilitarian colors.

In the spirit of reconstruction, in this chapter I would like to broaden the conventional philosophical view of the conservation tradition to include a few significant thinkers other than the usual suspects (i.e., Pinchot, Muir, Leopold). I believe that doing so produces two general consequences for understanding the shape and content of conservation thought during the classic period. The first is that conservation goals beyond the traditional policy targets (i.e., wildlife management, forest conservation, park preservation) will come into sharper historical focus. The second is that alternative conceptual foundations for conservation philosophy will be revealed, if only in a necessarily abbreviated form in the present chapter. Specifically, I will examine two neglected and, I will suggest, intertwining philosophical threads that provide the grounds for rethinking the intellectual moorings of conservation during the interwar period. One is the "communitarian" regional planning movement active during the 1920s and 1930s, particularly the ideas of its intellectual and literary leader, Lewis Mumford (1895–1990). Mumford and this regionalist project are rarely mentioned in the intellectual histories of conservation and environmental thought, even though another of the movement's most important thinkers, conservationist and planner Benton MacKaye, was very active in conservation circles during this time. The other thread is American pragmatism, a loose and diverse philosophical school led during this period by John Dewey. As I will discuss in this chapter, I believe that the regional planning approach advocated by Mumford was significantly influenced by Dewey's pragmatism, particularly Dewey's unified method of inquiry and his strong social democratic vision. In addition to these intriguing philosophical underpinnings, Mumford's regionalist project also represents a novel attempt to expand the foundations of conservationist thinking beyond its narrow single-resource focus and its more well-known utilitarian commitments during this period. The resulting program is what might be called a "pragmatic conservationism": pragmatic in its embrace of the full sweep of the various contexts of human environmental experience, and pragmatic in its methodological approach and Deweyan democratic agenda.

By linking Mumford's attempt to reconstruct conservationism through regional planning with Dewey's pragmatism in the development of environmental thought, I hope to outline, in a preliminary and suggestive way, the elements of an alternative intellectual history for environmental philosophy.[5] I think this reading challenges the aforementioned view that environmental thought during the interwar period was limited to a morally unidimensional utilitarianism. It also calls into question the presumption, alluded to earlier, that the development of conservation/environmental philosophy is best thought of as narrative about the inevitable rise of nonanthropocentrism, a moral outlook on nature said to be expressed in its early form by nineteenth-century romantics such as Henry David Thoreau and John Muir and later given a more scientifically sophisticated and philosophically palatable articulation in Aldo Leopold's land ethic in the 1930s and 1940s.

My discussion in this chapter is organized into three sections. In the first, I provide a brief overview of the vision of the communitarian regional planning movement of the 1920s and 1930s, particularly the approach of the Regional Planning Association of America and its philosophical leader, Lewis Mumford. After examining the intellectual precursors of this movement and Mumford's provocative attempt to reconstruct conservation along regionalist lines, I briefly consider how his approach was informed by a pragmatic logic and Deweyan philosophy of democracy and social learning. I conclude by reflecting on some of the implications of Mumford's project for rethinking the conceptual presuppositions and intellectual agenda of environmental philosophy, and I then offer some suggestions for future work in the field.

Regional Planning and Lewis Mumford's "New Conservationism"

Although the regional planning vision of Mumford and his colleagues was in many ways a novel philosophical enterprise and implied an innovative policy program, it also drew from several earlier sources, including the work of two giants in the history of planning: Ebenezer Howard and Patrick Geddes. Howard and Geddes rarely appear in discussions of U.S. conservation history; their names are even less known in environmental philosophy. Some of this scholarly invisibility is probably due to the fact that neither was an American—Howard was British and Geddes was a Scot—but a more likely explanation is that their work, like Mumford's after them, was too intellectually precocious and geographically expansive (focused as it was on cities and regions as well as natural resources) to have fit neatly within the confines of the more traditional conservation movement during the same period.

Ebenezer Howard (1850–1928) preferred to think of himself as an "inventor" rather than a planner.[6] A shorthand clerk in London and not a design or planning professional, Howard was also an ardent urban reformer who saw in town and city planning the tools for directing social and moral progress in late-nineteenth-century England. This commitment to improving the lot of citizens, especially the economically and physically distressed urban dweller, led him to author his groundbreaking "garden city" proposal in the 1890s. In doing so, he advanced a design philosophy that would influence town planning in England and the United States well into the second half of the twentieth century. In his 1898 book *Tomorrow: A Peaceful Path to Real Reform* (republished in 1902 as *Garden Cities of Tomorrow*), Howard unveiled an intriguing vision for the construction of cooperative, small-scale urban commonwealths that would weld the social and environmental virtues of the country with those of the town while avoiding the vices of excess and deficiency associated with both settings.

Howard's garden city would be relatively small in size, even by late-nineteenth-century standards: its population would be capped off at 32,000 inhabitants over a land area of 6,000 acres. Yet it would be a fully functional urban form with residential, commercial, and industrial elements carefully planned and spatially distributed to promote a healthy and balanced biophysical environment. Heavy industries would be located away from the residential sector and placed at the city's edge. Beyond this zone would be a rural greenbelt of forests, parks, and farms extending over several thousand acres. These lands would supply agricultural goods to the city and provide a natural barrier to keep the cities from sprawling farther into the countryside: an early version of an urban growth boundary. When a garden city swelled to its predetermined limits, the population would split off and form a new, planned garden city settlement. Eventually, multiple garden cities would be linked through high-speed transportation networks to form a "social city": a polycentric chain of garden cities that would collectively provide the opportunities and benefits of a large metropolitan center while possessing none of the social, economic, and environmental drawbacks that Howard viewed as hallmarks of the Victorian city.[7]

As planning historian Robert Fishman points out, Howard was in many respects a product of late-nineteenth-century British radicalism, the views of a group of primarily middle-class, non-Marxist communitarians who advocated a decentralized, egalitarian social order supported by dramatic reforms in landownership, housing, and urban planning. Howard's garden city proposal was clearly driven by a social philosophy and a politics that sought to promote cooperative, noncompetitive relationships among citizens through urban planning and architectural design:

> These crowded cities have done their work; they were the best which a society largely based on selfishness and rapacity could construct, but they are in the nature of things entirely unadapted for a society in which the social side of our nature is demanding a larger share of recognition—a society where even the very love of self leads us to insist upon a greater regard for the well-being of our fellows. The large cities of today are scarcely better adapted for the expression of the fraternal spirit than would a work on astronomy which taught that the earth was the centre of the universe be capable of adaptation for use in our schools. Each generation should build to suit its own needs.[8]

Even if Howard was somewhat fuzzy on the more technical details of the garden city, as Mumford observed in his 1945 introduction to a later edition of *Garden Cities,* his contributions were not in technical planning. Rather, Howard's genius was in understanding and depicting "the nature of a balanced community and [showing] what steps were necessary, in an ill-organized and disoriented society, to bring it into existence."[9]

The other major influence on the interwar regional planning movement was Patrick Geddes (1854–1932), one of the more brilliant and eccentric figures in the history of environmental thought. An idiosyncratic thinker and polymath, Geddes studied evolutionary theory under Thomas Huxley—Darwin's "bulldog"—and later went on to apply an organic evolutionary model to social forms, including the development of cities. Specifically, Geddes developed a regionalist framework for understanding the influence of the physical environment on human settlement and cultural life, a relationship he would operationalize with his diagrammatic model of the "valley section." In this effort, Geddes was greatly influenced by

German-trained French geographer Jean Jacques Élisée Reclus, whose work taught the Scotsman the fundamental importance of the natural region in shaping social organization. To advance his regionalist investigations, Geddes proposed that an interdisciplinary survey method be employed to study regional geography and social life in preparation for town and city planning. Determined that the study of the human and natural conditions of the region proceed on solid scientific footing, Geddes borrowed Pierre Guillaume Frédéric Le Play's social survey model and transformed it into the core planning tool for landscape and community exploration. For Geddes, the survey would be the primary method for incorporating the natural and social features of the region into the planning of settlements and communities.[10]

One of the most intriguing aspects of Geddes' conceptualization of the survey method was its political justification. In his view, the regional survey was to be a highly scientific and systematic activity, but it was also intended to be a thoroughly democratic endeavor. The general public, working alongside professional planners, would explore and compile an inventory of the historical, geographic, and economic circumstances of their community and its regional setting.[11] By taking part in this critical stage in the planning process, individuals would gain a greater awareness of their community's history and its current sociobiophysical conditions, including the structure and significance of its built and natural environment. This environmental sociological knowledge would in turn transform the inhabitants of a community into enlightened and civic-minded "regional selves." Indeed, Geddes saw the regional survey as a tool for a new and progressive form of democratic citizenship:

> Our experience already shows that in this inspiring task of surveying, usually for the first time, the whole situation and life of the community in past and present, and of thus preparing for the planning scheme which is to forecast, indeed largely decide, its material future, we have the beginnings of a new movement—one already characterized by an arousal of civic feeling, and a corresponding awakening of more enlightened and more generous citizenship.[12]

Like Howard, Geddes was occasionally weak on the details of his project. Perhaps this is due to the fact that he was, also like Howard, more of an "inventor" and visionary than a planning technician (even though he wrote dozens of plans over the years for town and city projects, from Edinburgh to Tel Aviv).[13] As historian Helen Meller notes, if Geddes was never very precise about the scientific criteria for delineating natural regions, for example, it was because he was more concerned with advocating the activity of the regional survey, especially for schoolchildren, than he was with devoting his time to the formalistic "boundary question."[14] And if the environmental determinism on display in his valley section diagram and his late-nineteenth-century brand of social evolutionism would fall out of fashion as the twentieth century rolled on, Geddes' regional outlook and methodological innovations would have a powerful influence on subsequent generations of planners and environmental thinkers.

Among those inspired by Geddes' work was Lewis Mumford. Indeed, both Howard's garden city and Geddes' regionalism would exert a profound influence on Mumford and his colleagues in the 1920s and 1930s, an inspiration that would take wing with the formation of the Regional Planning Association of America (RPAA). Founded in 1923, the RPAA was a loose-knit group of planners, architects, and social reformers that, in addition to Mumford and Benton MacKaye, included architects Clarence Stein and Charles Whitaker, planner Henry Wright, and economist Stuart Chase, among others. The RPAA was an organizational reaction to a complex of social forces and environmental conditions that emerged in late-nineteenth- and early-twentieth-century America. These include, not unexpectedly, many of the same conditions that gave rise to the period's better-known conservation impulse, such as the growing recognition of the social and economic effects of the overexploitation and destruction of natural resources. But the RPAA was also concerned with a range of social and urban issues, among them the negative environmental and cultural costs of accelerating metropolitan growth and unplanned industrialization. The group saw these forces as only sharpening economic inequalities that had already taken their toll on citizens and their prospects for securing the "good life," a goal that included open access to decent and affordable housing.

Despite their varied professional backgrounds and interests, which naturally led to some differences regarding the association's philosophical bent and policy agenda, the contributors to the RPAA were united in their concern over the accelerating degradation of natural, built, and social communities by the steamrolling "metropolitan" forces of twentieth-century industrial capitalism. Their response to these forces drew creatively from both Howard's garden city model and Geddes' regionalism. The RPAA sought a reconfigured and rescaled relationship between metropolitan forms and the surrounding natural region, one characterized by a carefully visualized functional and spatial "balance" between urban, rural, and wild landscapes. The association's promotion of human-scaled "regional cities" as alternative urban forms would, in fact, reproduce many of the design elements of Howard's garden city, including the planned constraints on city size and the creation of an encompassing greenbelt to buffer growth and to provide food and outdoor recreation.[15]

The RPAA's regional cities would not represent a flight from urban life; rather, they would be decentralized, genuine urban forms planned in accordance with the natural context of the region and facilitated by the controlled diffusion of industry afforded by the rising availability of the automobile, construction of new transportation highways and hydroelectric dams, and establishment of widespread rural electrification. These technological developments—what Mumford, following Geddes, applauded as the hallmarks of the newly emerging "neotechnic" era—would allow for the controlled migration (as opposed to unplanned sprawl) of swelling metropolitan populations out of the overcrowded cities and into the smaller and more ecologically patterned regional forms.[16] The human scaling of the regional city would, the members hoped, encourage meaningful community building and allow for the development of what Mumford and MacKaye saw as organic, "indigenous" values: values authentic to locally diverse and vibrant regional cultures.[17]

The RPAA housing projects at Sunnyside Gardens in Queens and at Radburn in New Jersey are the most tangible examples of the RPAA's planning legacy on the built environment, even if neither project came close to full regional city proportions. The other enduring RPAA project is the Appalachian Trail, the 2,100-mile wilderness footpath running from Maine to Georgia, originally proposed by MacKaye in the *Journal of the American Institute of Architects* in 1921.[18] MacKaye's original vision for the trail—it was to be an instrument of regional and communal reconstruction and a defense of rural America against encroaching metropolitanism—is remarkable for its early linkage of traditional natural resource conservation with community and regional planning. Although the more communitarian elements of MacKaye's plan never materialized, the Appalachian Trail today is a highly valued public recreational resource, and MacKaye is finally achieving long overdue recognition as a significant and original environmental thinker.[19]

Lewis Mumford was the primary philosophical and literary force behind the RPAA's regionalism, an agenda that also found a strong supporter in his friend and colleague MacKaye. A self-proclaimed "child of the city" (New York), Mumford never took a college degree, even though he attended several universities and later held visiting appointments at Dartmouth College, Stanford University, and the Massachusetts Institute of Technology, among other august institutions. The quintessential "public intellectual," Mumford spent his career writing for an educated, yet general, audience, and over a seventy-year career he produced an impressive stream of books and countless articles and short pieces. His "Sky Line" column for the *New Yorker,* which ran from 1931 to 1963, quickly established him as one of the nation's top critics of architecture and urban planning.[20] It would be difficult to think of anyone, before or since, who has displayed a comparable grasp of Mumford's numerous fields of expertise: architecture, planning, literature, philosophy, art history, politics, sociology, and the history of technology.

Mumford's regionalism of the 1920s and 1930s was formed through early contact with the work of Patrick Geddes while the former was a student at City College.[21] This initial fascination with Geddes' ideas led to an active correspondence between the two men, and Geddes would soon become Mumford's most significant intellectual mentor. As urban historian Edward K. Spann wrote, the Scotsman "encouraged the development of what was central to Mumford's regionalism, the habit of viewing humankind in ecological perspective, emphasizing the dynamic relationship between human beings and their natural environment."[22] This ecological holism would set Mumford's (and, through his and MacKaye's influence, the RPAA's) approach to regional planning apart from other contemporaneous enterprises that operated under the same name, such as the planning approach of Thomas Adams and the "metropolitan" regional planners who produced the Regional Plan of New York and Its Environs in 1931.[23]

As Mumford worked through the substance and import of Geddes' regionalism and, later, in the 1920s, became involved in the RPAA, his writing often made explicit links between the approach he was forming with his planning colleagues and the natural resource conservationism of the interwar period. In doing so, he also significantly expanded the conservation agenda and strengthened its underlying philosophical justification. Mumford was, in effect, fashioning a completely new way to think about human influence and dependence on natural and built landscapes. Specifically, what I believe he was developing during this period (again, in tandem with Benton MacKaye) was a more philosophically and socially ambitious conservationism—and a potentially more comprehensive policy framework—than the era's prevailing utilitarian model of natural resource development. He was certainly developing a more holistic planning model, one that took its point of departure from the significance of the natural region and the limitations it imposed on development rather than from the assumed inevitability of metropolitan expansion.

This integrative project was therefore sympathetic to many of the commitments of the more conventional conservation movement, but Mumford pushed beyond the latter's often narrow utilitarianism and technocratic ethos by openly embracing the broader social and cultural values of the community within the context of the natural region. He put it as follows in 1925:

Regional planning is the *New Conservation*—the conservation of human values hand in hand with natural resources. Regional planning sees that the depopulated countryside and the congested city are intimately related; it sees that we waste vast quantities of time and energy by ignoring the potential resources of a region, that is, by forgetting all that lies between the terminal points and junctions of our great railroads. Permanent agriculture instead of land skinning, permanent forestry instead of timber mining, permanent human communities, dedicated to life, liberty, and the pursuit of happiness, instead of camps and squatter-settlements, and to stable building, instead of the scantling and falsework of our "go-ahead" communities—all this is embodied in regional planning.[24]

For Mumford, "conservation" implied much more than Pinchot-style "sustained yield" of natural resources for economic development, at least economic development as narrowly understood. Instead, it was the practice of sustaining genuine communal values, social organization, and environmental health in the face of invasive and destructive industrial and metropolitan forces. It was clear, too, that his proposals were not simply an attempt to reform current metropolitan planning by nibbling at the edges. "Regional planning asks not how wide an area can be brought under the aegis of the metropolis," Mumford wrote, "but how the population and civic facilities can be distributed so as to promote and stimulate a vivid, *creative life* throughout the whole region."[25]

The task of regional planning, according to Mumford, was thus more culturally and ecologically grounded than the approach taken by conservationists, which in his view merely attempted to protect wilderness areas from intrusion and sought to avoid the wasteful development of natural resources. Although he thought such a strategy was to be praised for protecting the rare and spectacular environments of the continent and for injecting efficiency measures into resource exploitation, he feared it was too limited in scope to serve as a guide for a true environmental ethic:

> If the culture of the environment had yet entered deeply into our consciousness, our esthetic appreciations would not stop short with stupendous geological formations like the Grand Canyon of Arizona: we should have an equal regard for every nook and corner of the earth, and we should not be indifferent to the fate of less romantic areas.[26]

Here Mumford anticipates the arguments of contemporary scholars, such as William Cronon, who have criticized the long-standing "wilderness bias" in modern environmentalism. Indeed, Mumford's conclusion is also Cronon's: that we must adopt a broader and more humanized environmentalism, one capable of instilling solicitude for human communities as well as natural ones—and one recognizing the value of the rural and the urban along with the wild.[27] Mumford's reconstruction of conservation to embrace the context of the larger region over the single resource, his attention to the built environment as well as the natural, and his commitment to securing the long-term sustainability of community values through regional planning, was thus a profound expansion of early-twentieth-century conservation philosophy. "If the conservation of a single resource is important," Mumford wrote, "the conservation of the region, as an economic and social whole, is even more important."[28]

Like Geddes, Mumford viewed the regional survey as a key tool in advancing the regionalist project. And, like Geddes, Mumford believed the act of regional planning possessed a great civic potential: it was not simply a narrow technical activity to be undertaken by experts. But Mumford also brought an additional justification and methodological underpinning to the planning discussion, especially in his fuller reflections in the 1930s. These contributions were, I believe, a pragmatist-inspired logic of inquiry and a more explicit theory of social learning, commitments I will suggest owe much to Mumford's contact with the work of American pragmatist philosopher John Dewey. If I am correct in these claims, Mumford's approach to regional planning by the 1930s had developed into an overtly pragmatic endeavor—so much so, in fact, that Mumford's reconstruction of conservation as regional planning and his Deweyan conceptualization of the planning method combined to form a new environmental philosophical project: a holistic, pragmatic variant of interwar period conservationism.

Regional Planning as Pragmatic Conservationism

Mumford recognized and openly acknowledged the influence of John Dewey's pragmatism on regional planning, though I believe he underestimated the significance of this particular intellectual debt. Looking back on the RPAA's philosophical outlook in 1957, for example, Mumford described the group's agenda as an amalgam of several sources, including

> the civic ideas of Geddes and Howard, the economic analyses of Thorstein Veblen, the sociology of Charles Horton Cooley, and the educational philosophy of John Dewey, to say nothing of the new ideas in conservation [and] ecology.[29]

As we shall see, Dewey's influence on the RPAA's philosophy, particularly his contribution to Mumford's own mature views on the method and justification of regional planning, was quite distinctive. But although a Deweyan educational ethos certainly can be read in the RPAA's and Mumford's emphasis on the transformative potential of regional surveys and the planning process itself, it is clear that Dewey's pragmatism—especially his theory of inquiry—was embedded in the very method of regional planning.

As a student at City College before World War I, Mumford had been exposed to an early form of pragmatism through the teachings of John Pickett Turner, a "self-professed pragmatist" who Mumford credited with turning him into a "loyal" devotee of the philosophy for a time.[30] But soon Mumford's immersion in the work of Geddes and his budding Neoplatonism would find him moving in a different direction. This shift was perhaps most pronounced in Mumford's cultural criticism of the 1920s, which suggested a growing preoccupation with an aesthetic transcendentalism and a greater emphasis on the symbolic elements of cultural life than the American pragmatists had demonstrated to that point.[31] Yet I believe the evidence supports the view that Mumford would never completely jettison the pragmatic deposits in his thinking, even if his ambivalence toward these strains tended to come across more in print in the 1920s.[32] His pragmatic commitments would clearly show through in his later writing on regional planning in the 1930s.

In his 1938 book *The Culture of Cities,* for example, Mumford staked out what I believe is a strong Deweyan position on the necessity of bringing the scientific outlook into human experience through regional planning. In particular, Mumford believed the instrument of the regional survey held great potential for advancing individual and collective moral development:

> The scientific approach, the method of intellectual co-operation, embodied in the regional survey, are moralizing forces, and it is only when science becomes an integral part of daily experience, not a mere coating of superficial habit over a deep layer of uncriticized authority, that the foundations for a common collective discipline can be laid.[33]

This sentence could easily have been written by Dewey had he taken an interest in regional planning. Indeed, this and other textual evidence suggests that by the late 1930s, Mumford had adopted an explicit pragmatic justification for the practice of regional planning. Before we move forward any further, however, it is helpful to briefly examine Dewey's instrumentalist project, since my claim is that Mumford employed a strikingly similar logic in his discussion of the method of regional planning.

Dewey's instrumentalism was advanced through his unified method of inquiry into the problems of human experience. This method applied to ends as well as means: beliefs and articulated values and ends were to be viewed as experimental tools—instruments—for solving the myriad and thorny social, moral, and technological dilemmas confronting the public. This argument for a continuum of means and ends within an instrumentalist framework was perhaps one of the philosopher's most radical proposals. According to Dewey, moral principles were not fixed, absolute, or transcendental beliefs floating above the fray of human experience. They were instead "ends-in-view": action-guiding hypotheses that, by means of intelligent social inquiry, could be appraised in terms of their ability to transform disrupted, unsettled "problematic" social situations into a more secure and stable condition.[34] To tackle these problematic situations, Dewey proposed a method of inquiry that was directly modeled after the logic of problem solving in the natural and technical sciences. This "unified method of inquiry" began with the initial recognition that a situation as experienced was, indeed, "problematic"—and thus inquiry was required because of the real deficiencies of the situation. The second step involved analysis of the problem context and creative generation of hypothetical solutions that might work to resolve the situation. This was followed by the appraisal, in the imagination, of each proposed solution's ability to effectively and efficiently resolve the vexing situation at hand. The final stage was the act of judgment: selecting a course of action from a set of alternatives and carrying it out in practice (including subsequent reflection and monitoring of performance).[35]

I believe Mumford came to embrace this Deweyan instrumentalist approach in his mature conceptualization of regional planning. As mentioned earlier, it was in his landmark book in urban studies, *The Culture of Cities,* that Mumford provided his clearest and most sustained discussion of the regional planning method. It is revealing to consider in some detail just how he infused his discussion with pragmatic elements and arguments. In *Culture,* Mumford described the activity of regional planning as following a general four-stage pattern:

> The first stage is that of survey. This means disclosing, by first-hand visual exploration and by systematic fact-gathering, all the relevant data on the regional complex. . . . The second stage in planning is the critical outline of needs and activities in terms of social ideals and purposes. . . . The third stage in planning is that of imaginative reconstruction and projection. On the basis of known facts, observed trends, estimated needs, critically formulated purposes, a new picture of regional life is now developed. . . . Now these three main aspects of planning—survey, evaluation, and the plan proper—are only preliminary: a final stage must follow, which involves the intelligent absorption of the plan by the community and its translation into action through the appropriate political and economic agencies.[36]

This description of the method of regional planning was essentially a Deweyan pattern of inquiry, right down to the "imaginative reconstruction and projection" of a desired future state of affairs (what Dewey referred to as "dramatic rehearsal"). And, like Dewey, who suggested that the values of prior experience must "become the servants and instruments of new desires and aims" through the method of social intelligence,[37] Mumford argued for the judicious union of tradition and invention in the planning process:

> Such plans, however, are instrumental, not final: what is planned is not simply a location or area; what is planned is an activity-in-an-area, or an area-through-an-activity . . . new combinations of old elements, and fresh additions from new sources, make their appearance.[38]

This "organic" character of regional plans would, according to Mumford, allow communities to respond to changing social and biophysical conditions, altering and revising their planning goals to meet new demands and novel circumstances. Here, Mumford's commitment to experimentalism and his adaptive view of the regional plan directly evoke Dewey's epistemological arguments and the iterative design of the philosopher's theory of inquiry. And his statements regarding the fallible and contingent character of regional planning also anticipate the late-twentieth-century development of "adaptive management" models within ecosystem ecology and the resource sciences.[39] Consider the following:

> Regional plans must provide in their very constitution the means of future adjustments. The plan that does not leave the way open to change is scarcely less disorderly than the aimless empiricism that rejects plan. *Renewal: flexibility: adjustment: these are essential attributes of all organic plans.*[40]

Mumford's observations about the experimental, dynamic quality of the regional plan were directly tied to his conviction that regional planning must be a robustly democratic activity. It was not the purview only of professional planners and designers; rather, it was a critical public enterprise that required active and widespread participation by such "nonexperts." Through this opening of the planning process to the broader democratic community, the self-corrective, intelligent character of public deliberation could come out:

> It is naïve to think that geographers, sociologists, or engineers can by themselves formulate the social needs and purposes that underlie a good

regional plan: the work of the philosopher, the educator, the artist, the common man, is no less essential; and unless they are actively brought into the process of planning, as both critics and creators, the values that will be imported into the plan, when it is finally made, will be merely those that have been carried over from past situations and past needs, without critical revision: old dominants, not fresh emergents.[41]

Mumford's conclusion here rehearses Dewey's well-known warning about the democratic and epistemological costs of social reliance on experts: "The man who wears the shoe knows best that it pinches and where it pinches."[42] It also affirms Dewey's epistemological justification for democracy, which suggested that intelligence could most effectively operate, and social problems could be most effectively addressed, through deliberative democratic institutions in which all citizens participate.[43] According to Dewey, this kind of broad-based public participation in reflective dialogue over social goals would work to root out error and counterproductive bias in an individual's beliefs and values: a view of public discourse Dewey shared with one of liberalism's founding fathers, John Stuart Mill.[44] Dewey summarized this argument in his 1935 book *Liberalism and Social Action:* "The method of democracy—inasfar as it is that of organized intelligence—is to bring [social] conflicts out into the open where their special claims can be seen and appraised, where they can be discussed and judged in light of more inclusive interests."[45]

In addition to the methodological and epistemological similarities between Dewey's pragmatism and Mumford's view of regional planning, there is the direct educational correspondence between the two projects mentioned earlier. Since Dewey's theory of knowledge hinged on his claim that all knowing flows from lived experience, it follows that by acting in (and on) the world, we learn about our environments—both natural and social. The knowledge gained in this activity then allows us to more effectively transform the outer world to meet our constantly changing social needs and interests. But it also allows us to intelligently revise and adapt these needs and interests in ways that are more suitable (and therefore more sustainable) for our supporting environment. Such educational transformation was for Dewey also the key to creating democratic citizens, democracy being in his view "the idea of community life itself."[46] He wrote in 1927:

We are born organic beings associated with others, but we are not born members of a community. The young have to be brought within the traditions, outlook and interests which characterize a community by means of education: by unremitting instruction and by learning in connection with the phenomena of overt association.[47]

Like Dewey, Mumford stressed the importance of experiential education for building an awareness of one's membership in the democratic community, and he believed that hands-on participation in regional planning activities could play an important role in this educative process. "Regional plans are instruments of communal education," Mumford wrote, adding that without such education, citizens could "look forward only to partial achievement."[48] The regional survey would therefore be a particularly important tool for bringing the younger generations into mature public and political life.[49] Indeed, following Geddes, Mumford wrote that one of the primary roles of the regional survey was to "educate citizens."[50] By taking part in the survey process (i.e., by cooperatively gathering soil, climate, geologic, industrial, and historical data relevant to their community and its surrounding natural region), individuals would become engaged, morally invested members of the community and would develop a sympathetic regard for their local environment and culture:

> These people will know in detail where they live and how they live: they will be united by a common feeling for their landscape, their literature and language, their local ways, and out of their own self-respect they will have a sympathetic understanding with other regions and different local peculiarities. They will be actively interested in the form and culture of their locality which means their community and their own personalities. . . . Without them, planning is a barren externalism.[51]

For Mumford, meaningful public participation in the planning process thus promised to enlighten and transform individuals on a number of levels: social, political, and environmental. It could teach individuals to see themselves as having a shared, common stake in the health and sustainability of their own community and its biophysical context. Viewed in this manner, citizen involvement in regional planning had the potential to deliver what Dewey was so urgently calling for in his landmark work in political theory, *The Public and Its Problems:* the retrieval of enduring community self-awareness. Dewey saw this civic awareness as providing a critical foundation for future democratic social action. "Unless local communal life can be restored," he concluded, "the public cannot adequately resolve its most urgent problem: to find and identify itself."[52] Therefore, involvement of the public in the practice of regional planning, whether by means of regional surveys or through participation in open deliberation about community goals and values, could stimulate civic self-organization and consequently lead to better and more intelligent social problem solving. Mumford was, in effect, providing Dewey with a necessary political technology—regional planning—by which the philosopher's cherished democratic publics might be effectively realized.

To summarize my claims of the previous two sections, I would suggest that Mumford's mature work on regional planning reflects a Deweyan influence in three respects. First, Dewey's project may be seen in the instrumental logic of Mumford's planning methodology and the adaptive character of intelligent inquiry. Second, Mumford's justification of regional planning placed a Deweyan-style emphasis on social learning and the educative potential of public participation in the survey and planning process. Third, there is Mumford's belief that the regional survey would create fully engaged democratic citizens able to recognize their common membership in an interlocking political and geographic community—what Dewey identified as a vital goal in solving the "problem of the public." Many of the roots of Mumford's approach to regional planning were thus planted in a Deweyan pragmatic soil.[53]

Mumford's Deweyan approach to regional planning, combined with his expansion of the conservation agenda to embrace urban and rural landscapes and communal ends beyond utility maximization, represents an intriguing, pragmatic form of interwar period conservationism. For Mumford, the regional planning method had great potential to help citizens and planners make progressive, pragmatic adjustments and improvements in a community's relationship to its surrounding environment, and to bolster its civic life in the process. A retrieval of this pioneering approach not only brings Mumford and regional planning into discussions of the intellectual history of conservation—this is important enough—but also raises several questions about the assumptions and practices of current environmental philosophy, as I mentioned at the beginning of my discussion. I would therefore like to end this chapter by briefly considering these questions.

Conclusion

One conclusion I hope will be drawn from the preceding pages is that the foundations of environmental philosophy are more diverse than typically thought. Environmental philosophy is not intellectually monolithic; rather, it is multi-foundational. There are significant alternatives to the conventional nonanthropocentric narrative told in contemporary environmental ethics, such as Mumford's pragmatic conservationism discussed in this chapter. Mumford's broad humanism and concern for the revitalization of cultural life through regional planning is not consumed with the question of establishing the independent "moral standing" of nonhuman nature, nor does it ask citizens to look askance at the values flowing out of lived human experience—two activities that seem to have become defining features of contemporary nonanthropocentric environmental philosophy. Whether or not it makes any sense to describe Mumford's project as "anthropocentric" (this term is now so shopworn that it should be retired), his philosophical outlook is clearly not nonanthropocentric, at least in the sense understood by environmental philosophers. And his approach was certainly a profound departure from the conventional utilitarianism and atomism that underwrote the classic conservation movement.

A second point is that Mumford's project reveals the roots of "environmental pragmatism" to be historically deep and to fan out more widely than previously thought. Recognizably pragmatic elements in environmental philosophy were in place long before the emergence of academic "environmental pragmatists" (and academic environmental philosophers) in the late 1980s and early 1990s. As I have suggested here, early forms of environmental pragmatism were articulated in the 1920s and 1930s by Mumford. I have written elsewhere about the quasi-pragmatic elements in Benton MacKaye's work.[54] If I am correct in making these arguments, Aldo Leopold (once again) thus stands in a very interesting position with respect to the tradition. For example, Bryan Norton, dissenting from the majority opinion that Leopold was a nonanthropocentrist, has suggested that the great author of the land ethic actually held a fairly explicit pragmatic theory of truth and that his vaunted ecological holism was more "managerial" than metaphysical.[55] If Norton is correct about this (I believe his case is quite compelling), and if my reading of Mumford is accurate, Leopold was therefore part of a larger pragmatic movement within environmental thought and the management and planning community during the inter-war period—a movement that also included "proto-environmental pragma-tists" such as Mumford and MacKaye. Leopold's pragmatism is thus not an isolated or unusual intellectual commitment during this time; it is an ex-pression of an emerging, wider pragmatic environmental philosophy in the 1920s and 1930s. What is more, recent scholarship has indicated that dis-cernible pragmatic elements may be found even earlier in the conservation tradition. Donald Worster, in his appropriately epic new biography of John Wesley Powell, writes that the great nineteenth-century explorer and con-servationist adopted an experimental, fallibilistic theory of truth in his later writings, a view Worster describes as thoroughly pragmatic, even if Powell did not explicitly engage the work of the pragmatists at the turn of the cen-tury.[56] The upshot is that pragmatism in environmental thought is not something developed by environmental philosophers in the late twentieth century; rather, it is found in the very roots of the American conservation impulse.

Third, and following Mumford's lead, a reconstructed conservation phi-losophy needs to address the complex whole of human experience in the environment, including the urban, the rural, and the wild. Toward this end, philosophers would do well to explore potential linkages with the environ-mental planning and design fields, in addition to working within the realms of environmental policy and management. Influential developments and movements within the former, such as new urbanism, industrial ecology, and sustainable architecture, to name but a few, promise to direct human communities, development, and productive efforts into more ecologically hospitable channels (and often in ways Mumford and his colleagues antici-pated many decades before). These efforts are environmental pragmatism at work, and philosophers interested in making contributions to "intelligent practice" could do so by engaging these fields more systematically.

Fourth, I hope the preceding discussion has shown that environmental philosophy did not develop in isolation from broader intellectual move-ments: reflective environmental thinking has not matured independently from American social and philosophical thought more generally. Indeed, environmental philosophy is not and has never been a freestanding "ideol-ogy of nature," nor does it represent a fundamental break with the Western philosophical and political tradition. Rather, environmental philosophy is itself suspended by these deeper moral, political, and social currents. It fol-lows from this that, instead of breaking away from these foundations in search of a "new environmental ethic" that is celebrated for its degree of independence of the tradition, we should be probing this philosophical bequest in our efforts to understand our place and obligations within our various surrounding environments: cultural, built, technological, and natural.

Last, environmental philosophers need to think more critically about the intellectual history of environmental values and ethics. The received nonanthropocentric account, as interesting and even compelling as it might be in some places, borders on ideological triumphalism. The intellectual historical record is, in fact, much messier and more conceptually pluralistic than this account would suggest. When we relax the often constrained semantic domains of "conservation" and "environment," for example, a new intellectual landscape comes into relief, and the ideas of thinkers such as Mumford, Dewey, MacKaye, Geddes, and Howard can be seen to form an interconnected (and previously invisible) web of conservation thought during a very critical period in its development. I believe that any reconstructed conservation of today, especially one in search of a philosophical "usable past" to inform and guide future thought and practice, could not ask for a greater intellectual inheritance.

Building Conservation on the Land: Aldo Leopold and the Tensions of Professionalism and Citizenship

SUSAN FLADER

Aldo Leopold's career spanned the first half of the twentieth century, during which time he was intimately involved in shaping two new professions, forestry and wildlife management. When I began studying his work more than thirty years ago, his classic collection of natural history vignettes and philosophical essays, *A Sand County Almanac* (1949), was newly popular with people who had suddenly discovered the idea of "ecology" and were seeking to reconstruct conservation as environmentalism. Many mainstream professionals in wildlife ecology and, to an even greater extent, in forestry felt threatened by the popular upwelling and dismissed or even disparaged Leopold as an impractical idealist. In my book *Thinking Like a Mountain* (1974)—which began as a biography but turned into an analysis of the evolution of Leopold's thought through a focus on one of the central preoccupations of his career, deer management—I saw my task as reestablishing Aldo Leopold's professional stature in order to give credibility to his philosophical and policy ideas. Yes, he pushed his two professions—and several others as well—further and faster than they wanted to move, but he enjoyed the respect of leaders in those professions in his own day, and he deserves no less in ours.[1]

More recently, in the final decade of the twentieth century, Leopold experienced an extraordinary comeback in the professions that once disparaged him. He has been embraced by professionals in forestry and wildlife ecology and their trendier offshoots, conservation biology and restoration ecology, as well as by the agencies both federal and state that employ them, as they struggle to reconstruct themselves and find a new way in the new

115

century. For example, in his 1992 memorandum announcing ecosystem management as the new approach for the USDA Forest Service in the twenty-first century, the agency's chief, F. Dale Robertson, identified Leopold's land ethic philosophy as a guide, replacing Gifford Pinchot's conservation philosophy in the twentieth century.[2] At the same time, Aldo Leopold's significance in the new millennium has expanded vastly beyond the professions in which he pioneered.

Much of the action today is at the grassroots in our communities, and the practitioners are ordinary citizens as well as professionals. Our somewhat belated recognition of the vital role of citizens in community-based conservation may in part be a response to an outpouring of books and articles in the 1990s on the meaning of citizenship, many of them lamenting the weakening of civic bonds in America, in which scant attention has been paid to the role of citizenship with respect to the environment.[3] Environmentalists have long realized that citizen action was a hallmark of the "new environmental movement" from the time of the first Earth Day (1970), but much of that action was geared toward expanding the role of government, which in turn entailed more responsibilities for professionals. Only recently, as some have increasingly questioned the direction in which government agencies and their professional staffs have been leading us, have we begun to appreciate the vital role of ordinary people in restoring the integrity of their own communities.[4] If we were to view this phenomenon in deeper time perspective, we would realize the extent to which our citizenry has played a key role in the shaping of our environment and environmental policies ever since the origins of the nation.[5]

As citizens, we may look especially to the vignettes in the almanac section of Leopold's *Sand County Almanac,* drawing inspiration from the images of the Leopold family thoughtfully restoring the exhausted acres of their river-bottom farm. But was Leopold acting on his own acres as a citizen or as a professional? What did Leopold, the consummate professional, think about the role of ordinary citizens in conservation? Did he experience any tension in his own career between the two? This chapter will explore the evolution of Leopold's thought about professionalism and citizenship and the tensions of the two in his life in an effort to understand the implications of his land ethic philosophy for both professionals and citizens as we seek to construct principles to guide our conservation practice in the twenty-first century.

The Consummate Professional

Aldo Leopold (1887–1948) began his career in the fledgling Forest Service, which has been regarded by scholars as the quintessential professional agency in the Progressive Era, a period in American history identified with the rise of the professions and their role in developing the administrative capacity of the modern state.[6] Gifford Pinchot, the first chief of the Forest Service, sought to place technically trained experts—professional foresters such as Leopold, who had earned his master's degree in 1909 from the elite Yale School of Forestry—in charge of developing specific policies and practices for managing resources in the newly established national forests. This was a model of governance that elevated the values of order, efficiency, and control, values closely associated with the Progressive Era. Pinchot once said, "The first duty of the human race is to control the earth it lives upon," and there is some evidence that Leopold himself believed that.[7] From the perspective of a later day, however, we may note that the Progressive model, in elevating the virtues of professionalism and technical expertise, tended to crowd out the citizenry and also their elected representatives.

Aldo Leopold throughout his career was a consummate professional, extremely efficiency oriented during his years in the Forest Service and fascinated by the intricacies of administrative procedures and standards.[8] And yet we get a sense from one of his earliest publications that he was not wholly satisfied with the Forest Service model of government administration. Shortly after he became supervisor of the Carson National Forest in New Mexico at age twenty-five, he was stricken with an illness that nearly led to his death and required more than a year of recuperation. From his home in Iowa, he addressed a letter "to the forest officers of the Carson" reflecting on their responsibilities. The problem that concerned him was how to measure success in forest administration. Was success simply a matter of efficiently following prescribed policies and procedures, as spelled out in the Forest Service manual, or was there something else? "My measure," Leopold wrote, "is *the effect on the forest*." Even at the start of his career, he was concerned about the *ends* of administration, what was happening to the land, not only the procedures, or *means*.[9]

It was a preoccupation he would continue to pursue into the early 1920s, when he was chief of operations in charge of roads, trails, fire control, personnel, and finance on 20 million acres of national forest in the Southwest. In order to improve the efficiency of administration while focusing attention on "the effect on the forest," he developed an intricate system of tally sheets for a new system of forest inspection that would enable foresters to diagnose local problems and monitor the effectiveness of management solutions on the ground. Leopold regarded this elaborate system of inspection as one of his points of greatest pride during his career in the Southwest. And, indeed, his lifelong fascination with tracking the dynamics of change and the efficacy of management for the total biotic system, begun during his inspection forays in the Southwest, would lead him in our own day to be acknowledged as the exemplar of the new philosophy of ecosystem management recently adopted by the Forest Service, the National Park Service, and other land management agencies.[10]

Clearly, Leopold was enlarging the responsibilities of professional land managers by extending the boundaries of the community of concern to include the entire biota—soils, waters, plants, and animals, as well as people. But there seems to have been scant room for ordinary citizens in Leopold's model of public land management. Although he recognized the difficulty of determining the *objectives* of management—the "desired future conditions" that so bedevil ecosystem management today—he concluded that these decisions should be made by "only the highest authority." Yet the handwritten essay in which he dealt most directly with what he called "standards of conservation" trails off in midsentence and remained unpublished, suggesting that Leopold may have realized he was caught in an unresolved problem of authority: who decides the objectives and on what basis? A kind of "superinspector" would crop up in his writing from time to time over the years, but I am not sure he was ever really comfortable with this appeal to authority. In another unpublished essay written about the same time as the "standards" piece, he acknowledged that certain individuals, often with no professional training whatever, seemed to have "intuitive judgement" or "natural skill" at reading the land, and he ruminated as to how the Forest Service might detect and utilize such abilities.[11]

Aldo Leopold and the American Civic Tradition

Despite Leopold's commitment to professional expertise in resource management, he also saw roles for citizens in related endeavors. Indeed, when his illness prevented him from resuming the strenuous post of forest supervisor, he began developing a new line of activity in the Forest Service, game management, in conjunction with which he traveled all across Arizona and New Mexico organizing local sportsmen, ranchers, and townspeople into game protective associations. These citizen conservation organizations were grassroots action groups in a long-standing American tradition. But in advocating such reforms as nonpolitical game wardens, predator control, and a system of refuges, they were also, we should note, seeking to put professionally trained people in charge.

As the United States was drawn into World War I, Leopold addressed the subject of citizenship in a number of lectures, including one titled "Home Gardens and Citizenship," delivered to students at the University of New Mexico in 1917. Cultivation of a home garden, he argued, was one mark of a useful citizen; nobility is won by soiling one's hands with useful labor, by building something. Leopold was always one for building something; indeed, he had developed an elaborate garden in his own backyard, complete with a series of carefully drawn garden plans. If your job doesn't allow enough play for creativity, you can be creative by working the ground, he told the students, whereupon he went into a soliloquy about how to raise spectacular tomatoes in your Albuquerque backyard. In a world threatened with food shortage, he argued, we ought to be good citizens and turn our yards into gardens.[12]

A year later, having left the Forest Service to become secretary of the Albuquerque Chamber of Commerce, he spoke to the women's club on the civic life of Albuquerque. "What has the 20th-century American city contributed to human progress?" he asked. His answer was public spirit, which he defined as "year-round patriotism in action; . . . intelligent unselfishness in practice." He tried to trace the idea historically, contrasting Confucius, whom he saw as more interested in personal virtues and family ties than in obligations to others, with Socrates, who knew that citizens had a moral obligation to support and improve their government. But then he lost the thread, explaining that "it would require a better scholar than I am to even attempt to trace the idea of public spirit through the era of individualism and the political revolutions of the 18th and 19th centuries."[13]

From Leopold's formulation, we realize he was assuming that in the era of the American Revolution, citizens had been dedicated to individualism; he had lost the thread of public spirit, though he sensed it must have been there somewhere. And in fact historians would not rediscover it until the late 1960s, two decades after his death, when a number of leading scholars of the American Revolution, after rereading numerous tracts of the time, would conclude that the era had been steeped in what they termed a republican ideology. What they found were people who thought of themselves as citizens of a republic in which the greatest virtue was civic consciousness, a willingness to subordinate one's self-interest to the good of the community—not, as has been so widely assumed, a citizenry in pursuit of individual rights. "Civic virtue," they called it, or "civic republicanism," referring to the participatory civic values of a republic like that of ancient Athens.[14] A case can be made that even the vaunted freedoms of speech, of the press, and of assembly enshrined in the first article of the Bill of Rights pertain to communities as well as to individuals; they protect the opportunity for ordinary citizens to organize and communicate with one another outside the formal channels of government to shape the environment of their communities or the policies of their governments.[15]

The foremost interpreter of the era of the American Revolution, Gordon Wood, has termed the phenomenon of revolutionary citizen action "the people out of doors." Although he most likely was not thinking environmentally, but rather was portraying citizens acting outside the channels of government, it is worthy of note how often citizens acted on environmental issues—to prevent new dams from blocking the passage of salmon upstream, for example, seeking to defend the community's customary right to fish against interference by new industrial mills.[16] The complex of republican values so pervasive in revolutionary America was largely overwhelmed, scholars agree, by democratic egalitarianism, liberal individualism, and capitalist development in the early nineteenth century, which ushered in the liberal democratic state we celebrate today. But the tradition of civic organizing persisted in American history. It was not mandated by law but done through voluntary associations, as Alexis de Tocqueville noted with qualified admiration.[17] It is the tradition out of which much of our American conservation movement grew, including Aldo Leopold's efforts to organize game protective associations and encourage civic betterment in Albuquerque.

Leopold, not knowing what historians would be saying half a century hence, went on in his speech to the Albuquerque Women's Club to define the "modern idea"—modern as of 1918—of public spirit: "It means that a democratic community and its citizens have certain reciprocal rights and obligations." Not only rights but also obligations—this was a theme to which he would return again and again during the course of his career. "The man who cheerfully and habitually tries to meet this responsibility," he told his female audience, "we call public-spirited." He then offered a critical assessment of the public spirit of Albuquerque, confiding his dream that the chamber of commerce he headed might serve as the "common center" to organize the "democratic welter" of professional societies, women's groups, and religious, political, labor, and other voluntary associations of citizens toward accomplishment of common goals for the betterment of Albuquerque. But he also admitted to some frustration—businessmen unwilling to welcome representation in the chamber by labor and craft organizations, for example.

After little more than a year, Leopold left the chamber of commerce to rejoin the Forest Service. A few years later, still feeling the effects of his experience in the chamber, he delivered a scathing criticism of the "booster spirit" to an Albuquerque civic society, in which he excoriated "the philosophy of boost." Boost was premised on growth by unearned increment rather than investment in basic resources, he charged, using as an example the recent demand for a national park for New Mexico by boosters concerned solely with attracting tourists.[18] By contrast, in his quest for fundamental improvement in the resource base, Leopold began looking to enforced responsibility of landowners. In "Pioneers and Gullies," for example, he described numerous valleys of the Southwest torn out by erosion and he predicted, for the first time in print, that one day proper land use would be a responsibility of citizens: "The day will come when the ownership of land will carry with it the obligation to so use and protect it with respect to erosion that it is not a menace to other landowners and the public."[19]

Leopold left the Southwest in 1924 to accept a job in Madison, Wisconsin, as director of the Forest Products Laboratory. Although the laboratory's focus on industrial products after the tree was cut proved ultimately frustrating for one so committed to the growing forest (he would leave the job after only four years), he did manage to extract from the experience a lesson for citizens. In an article titled "The Homebuilder Conserves," he admonished people to think, before castigating the "wasteful lumberman," about how their own arbitrary demands as consumers and home builders caused waste. The thinking citizen, he pointed out, has power not only in his vote but also in his daily thoughts and actions, and especially in his habits as a buyer and user of wood. "Good citizenship is the only effective patriotism," he concluded, "and patriotism requires less and less of making the eagle scream, but more and more of making him think." This theme of the responsibility of the citizen as intelligent consumer is one Leopold would return to from time to time, most notably during World War II, in an article on "Land-Use and Democracy."[20]

Tensions of Professionalism and Citizenship

In Wisconsin, Leopold became involved with the state chapter of the Izaak Walton League of America, the most vibrant citizen conservation organization in the United States in the 1920s. He worked with the league to promote a nonpartisan conservation commission and a forestry policy for Wisconsin. Still hewing to his professional orientation as a forester, however, he warned members to eschew the tendency to actually *write* policy: "It is a pretty safe rule to remember that while groups of men can insist on and criticize plans, only individuals can create them."[21] He meant, of course, professionals such as himself. Leopold was an inveterate writer of policies, having written policies for fire control, watershed management, wilderness, and inspection while in the Forest Service. After he left the service in 1928 to conduct game surveys in the north-central states, he drafted an "American Game Policy," which was adopted by the American Game Conference in 1930, and then in 1931 he helped write a "Twenty-Five Year Conservation Plan" for his home state, Iowa.

In Iowa, Leopold was tremendously impressed by the citizen commitment to conservation, and he was genuinely proud of the plan for integration of all aspects of conservation—parks, forests, wildlife, fish, water quality, soil conservation—that his team of nationally recognized experts wrote. Iowa was clearly a leader among the states in conservation thought and practice in these years. But buried in Leopold's correspondence are intimations of foreboding. He warned his colleagues in Iowa that they needed to make a special effort to educate the public about what was in the plan, lest people buy into it without personally engaging with it. He was concerned especially about the protection-minded women so active in the parks movement who might become upset if they were suddenly to discover that the plan aimed to produce game to shoot. "There is grave danger," he said, "that the conservationists will blow it up before they even understand what it is."[22]

In 1933, shortly after he accepted a newly created chair of game management at the University of Wisconsin, Leopold proposed to the dean of agriculture the development of a conservation plan for Wisconsin farms somewhat similar to the Iowa plan. The purpose, as in Iowa, would be to get all the government agencies working together to encourage farmers and other landowners to care for their lands in a more conservative way—or, as he put it, to "integrate economic with esthetic land use." But the means would differ. In Iowa, the plan was produced by imported experts who did not participate in its execution, an arrangement that clearly left Leopold uneasy, whereas in Wisconsin he proposed to "evolve" a plan from the ground up "rather than to *write* one out-of-hand."[23]

Leopold's emphasis on evolving a plan from the grassroots was prophetic—not only of the emerging emphasis on public involvement in resource planning in our own day but also of the situation in Iowa at the time. By 1935, the Iowa conservation plan had disintegrated, at least in Leopold's view. After Iowa merged all relevant agencies into a single department, as recommended in the plan, the new Iowa Conservation Commission bypassed the man whom Leopold saw as the obvious director, and most of the people Leopold most admired resigned or were fired. The issue apparently had to do with the commission's insistence on an immediate showing of quick results by government through professionally administered public works rather than, as Leopold and his colleagues preferred, a long-term emphasis on building a new conservation consciousness in the citizenry, especially among landowners.[24]

In the wake of the Iowa debacle, Leopold commented to a friend that the only state conservation effort to survive was in Michigan, "strangely enough, by a process of internal disharmony. I am tempted to draw the conclusion that complete unanimity within a state [such as in Iowa] is a symptom of approaching dissolution."[25] In other correspondence and articles in the 1930s, he addressed the problem of factions within the conservation community, especially the shotgunners versus the field-glass hunters, arguing for tolerance, a capacity for self-criticism, and an institutional structure within which factions could argue out their conflicts. "It is a question of applying the democratic process to conservation," he concluded.[26]

Individualism and the Community

Leopold's thoughts on democracy and conservation were further stimulated by travel in Germany in 1935, where he observed an elaborate system of law, public administration, ethics, and customs that was "incredibly complete and internally harmonious." Although he could observe no real distinction between the government, acting hierarchically from the top down, and popular acceptance from below, he recognized that the German system, with its strong central government authority, was "manifestly a surrender of individualism to the community."[27] Although he could admire it in Germany (before he understood its connection with the Nazi movement), he knew that it wouldn't work in America.

Leopold addressed the tension between the claims of the community and the rights of the individual in America in a number of other essays in the 1930s in which he dealt with the role of government. How can we get conservation? he often asked. His answer: we can legislate it, we can buy it, or we can build it. Government's initial efforts at conservation had been through laws prohibiting hunting, fishing, or cutting, a first step but inadequate. The second step, augmented by the open moneybags of the New Deal, was to buy land for conservation, but that could be carried only "as far as the tax-string on our leg will reach." In a classic essay, "Conservation Economics," Leopold mounted a trenchant critique of the New Deal's tendency to relegate conservation to public lands run by single-track government agencies, each with its specialized "scientific technology," arguing that the solution had to be found in integration of uses and public interests on private land.[28]

By the time he wrote "Land Pathology" under the menacing clouds of the dust bowl in 1935, he saw only two possible forces that could effect change in private land use. One was the development of institutional mechanisms for protecting the public interest in private land—a quest he had been on for more than a decade, especially after his new chair of game management was lodged in the University of Wisconsin's famed Department of Agricultural Economics, with its institutional bent. The other was his new preoccupation with "the revival of land esthetics in rural culture." Out of these forces he hoped might eventually emerge what he was even then beginning to term a "land ethic."[29] After his friend Jay "Ding" Darling cautioned him that his search for institutional controls could lead to socialization of property,[30] Leopold seemed increasingly to emphasize development of a personal sense of obligation to the land community, what he called a sense of husbandry.

During the 1930s, Leopold searched for and experimented with various forms of community-based organization to encourage the practice of husbandry on private lands. One venture, the Coon Valley Erosion Project near

La Crosse, Wisconsin, involved cooperation of local landowners with an array of professionals in a number of government agencies in a pathbreaking demonstration of erosion control and integrated land use on a watershed scale. This grassroots "adventure in conservation," in which two of Leopold's sons were also involved, was a pioneering effort in what we would today call a watershed partnership.[31]

Other efforts functioned entirely outside the formal channels of government, including farmer-sportsman cooperatives he was instrumental in establishing at the Riley and Faville Grove areas in Wisconsin, to encourage conservation of wildlife habitat and landscape beauty. He assigned various graduate students in succession to live in these or other project areas to work on the ground with landowners in the course of their research—in effect, building conservation on the land. Leopold described these experiments in community conservation as *vertical* rather than horizontal planning, focusing a battery of minds simultaneously on one spot. "It may take a long time to cover the country spot by spot," he admitted, "but that is preferable to a smear."[32] He even proposed public–private cooperation in the inventorying and planning for conservation of threatened species, with local conservationists or associations entrusted with custodianship of particular remnants.[33]

But most important of all in the evolution of Leopold's thinking about the husbandry of private lands was his family's experience on the exhausted acres they acquired in 1935 along the Wisconsin River. "On this sand farm in Wisconsin, first worn out and then abandoned by our bigger-and-better society," he explained in the preface to *Sand County Almanac,* "we try to rebuild, with shovel and axe, what we are losing elsewhere." For Leopold, the experience was a lesson in humility. For all his vaunted professional expertise, he still lost more than 90 percent of the pines the family planted in the early years, and he became acutely conscious of the innumerable, often inscrutable factors involved in life and death, growth and decay, and the inherent subjectivity of the decisions he was making as he wielded shovel and axe. From this intense personal participation in the life of the land, Leopold came to the central insight of his evolving land ethic philosophy: "In short, a land ethic changes the role of *Homo sapiens* from conqueror of the land-community to plain member and citizen of it. It implies respect for his fellow-members, and also respect for the community as such."[34]

Aldo Leopold's Concept of Citizenship

As I began paging through *Sand County Almanac* some years ago in an effort to discern more of Leopold's concept of citizenship, it struck me that the citizens one meets in the first two sections of the book, the almanac and the "sketches here and there," are nonhuman members of the land community, beginning with the very first essay, "January Thaw": "The mouse is a sober citizen who knows that grass grows in order that mice may store it as underground haystacks, and that snow falls in order that mice may build subways from stack to stack: supply, demand, and transport all neatly organized." The mouse engages in the most basic form of citizenship, going about his own business and pursuing his own interests. We have many such in our communities. Skipping perhaps a few citizens, we come to "Pines above the Snow": "Each species of pine," Leopold tells us, "has its own constitution, which prescribes a term of office for needles appropriate to its way of life." He continues with his analogy between human constitutions and the regimens of various pine trees, the white pine retaining its needles for a year and a half, red pines and jackpines for two and a half years. "Incoming needles take office in June, and outgoing needles write farewell addresses in October." These pines are participating in the legal process of citizenship, acting according to their constitutions, even taking office in a perfunctory way.[35]

Then we meet the thick-billed parrots of Chihuahua, who "wheel and spiral, loudly debating with each other the question . . . whether this new day which creeps slowly over the canyons is bluer and golder than its predecessors, or less so." They are debating the criteria of the good life, which in Aristotelian thought is an activity of citizenship more fundamental even than that of developing legal constitutions. The vote being a draw, Leopold observes, they head to the high mesas for breakfast. In "Clandeboye," the great prairie marsh of Manitoba, we find the grebe, a species of ancient evolutionary lineage impelled, Leopold believes, by "pride of continuity." The grebe's is the call that dominates and unifies the marshland chorus: "Perhaps, by some immemorial authority, he wields the baton for the whole biota." Here is the grebe as ethical citizen, a leader directing the chorus of the marsh for the long-term betterment of the whole community.[36]

Not until the more philosophical essays in the "upshot" section of the book do we meet *human* citizens. In "Conservation Esthetic," Leopold discusses the various components of the recreational process, beginning with

the most basic motivation of trophy seeking, common to professional conservationists as well as to gun and field-glass hunters; he goes on at length
about the essential preoccupation of professional managers with providing
trophies. He then discusses the search for a feeling of isolation in nature,
change of scene, and perception of natural processes before reaching what
to him is the most highly evolved component, a sense of husbandry. This
component, he tells us, "is unknown to the outdoorsman who works for
conservation with his vote rather than with his hands. It is realized only
when some art of management is applied to land by some person of perception."[37] So, to Leopold, husbandry is the highest form of citizenship—
not just going about one's business, or seeking trophies, or voting, or even
debating the criteria of the good life, but actually working with one's
hands, participating actively to build or maintain the land community.

And that brings us to "The Land Ethic," in which Leopold more pointedly offers us a concept of citizenship in a community larger than humankind; we are plain member and citizen of a community that embraces
the land and all the plants and animals that are a part of it. The usual formula for conservation, "obey the law, vote right, join some organizations,
and practice what conservation is profitable on your own land; the government will do the rest," he tells us, is too easy. "It defines no right and
wrong, assigns no obligation."[38] Leopold's formula implies a personal responsibility to participate actively as an ordinary citizen in maintaining or
restoring the health of the biotic community.

The Limits of Professional Expertise

As Leopold became more humble about the limits of professional expertise
and more committed to the role of ordinary citizens in the practice of husbandry, especially through his experience on his own land, he restructured
his teaching at the university, cutting back a bit on professional training in
game management in order to develop a new course for undergraduates
campus-wide called Wildlife Ecology 118. He was in effect answering his
own call for "a general cultural course in conservation" aimed at students
"who may want to understand the conservation movement simply as one of
the qualifications for effective citizenship." The new course, which he taught
for the first time in 1939, was intended "to develop the ability to read landscape, i.e., to discern and interpret ecological forces in terms of land-use

history and conservation." He would do this through a series of case histories—of a prairie coulee, an Ozark farm, a ragweed patch at Faville Grove, a tussock marsh, and the like—that he intended eventually to draw together in a new textbook that would serve as a more general counterpart to his professional textbook *Game Management* (1933). Although he never got around to writing the book, he articulated his new, more ecosystemic approach in a major speech to professional foresters and ecologists titled "A Biotic View of Land," and he encouraged other resource professionals to reach out to the whole campus "and thus eventually the whole community" in a speech he called "The Role of Wildlife in a Liberal Education."[39]

As war clouds darkened the horizon in the early 1940s and called into question Leopold's earlier admiration for Germany's tightly regimented if highly professionalized system of resource administration, he lectured to his Wildlife Ecology 118 students about "Ecology and Politics," presenting the case for an evolutionary mandate for individualism. Individual deviations from societal norms in land management, like individual evolutionary variations, he suggested, might enable certain individuals to survive catastrophe even when most members of a species were eliminated.[40] This was an individualism not of economic self-interest but of creative experimentation, in the sense of solutions generated from the bottom up by individual citizens or communities rather than mandated by government or professional orthodoxy on all alike. It was in this spirit that Leopold looked to the evolution of a land ethic, which defined general principles but operated through a sense of personal responsibility to the community.

American entry into World War II further defined the issue: "We must prove that democracy can use its land decently," Leopold argued in his seminal essay "Land-Use and Democracy." Here, he called again for conservation from the bottom up instead of from the top down. Vicarious conservation through government's professional managers simply could not do the job alone, as he illustrated through the inability of national parks and other sanctuaries to protect wildlife: "It seems to me that sanctuaries are akin to monasticism in the dark ages. The world was so wicked it was better to have islands of decency than none at all. Hence decent citizens retired to monasteries and convents. Once established, these islands became an alibi for lack of private reform." True conservation, he argued, had to begin with "that combination of solicitude, foresight, and skill which we call husbandry," practiced by landowners on their own land. But nonlandowning citizens also had responsibilities in their roles as consumers.

They could refuse to buy "exploitation milk" from cows pastured on steep slopes and insist on "honest boards" from properly managed forests. There was an indispensable role for government as "tester of fact vs. fiction" or guardian of standards, Leopold acknowledged, but farmers could scrutinize their own practices through courageous use of their self-governing Soil Conservation Districts, and there were opportunities also for self-scrutiny by industrial or citizen groups.[41] More than half a century later, the Forest Stewardship Council's independent third-party certification of forest products and other examples of the movement for "green" production and consumption standards would attest to the validity of Leopold's visionary argument.

Tensions of Professionalism and Citizenship: The Deer Debates

Aldo Leopold's ideas about the roles of government, professional managers, and citizens in the shaping of environmental policy were tested in the last decade of his life as never before by his involvement in the traumatic deer debates of the 1940s in Wisconsin. After being hunted nearly to extirpation in the early decades of the century and its habitat decimated by fire in the aftermath of the logging era, the state's deer herd had rebounded with protection and fire control to such an extent that, by the early 1940s, it needed to be reduced for the good of both deer and forest. Leopold sought to work with professionals in the conservation department to build a case for an antlerless deer season, shifting the emphasis from trophy bucks to does and young. But their call for herd reduction stirred disbelief and resentment among both hunters and the general public, to whom conservation of deer was a good thing. In an effort to deal with the imbroglio, the Wisconsin Conservation Commission organized a Citizens' Deer Committee, appointing Aldo Leopold as chairman.[42]

Leopold's committee had a cross section of citizens, mostly from northern Wisconsin, most of them distrustful of the herd reduction policy the professionals were urging on the commission. For the first meeting, he prepared maps and charts to provide a historical review of deer irruptions nationwide. But he was upstaged by a citizen member of the committee, Joyce Larkin, editor of the *Vilas County News Review,* published in the heart of deer country. Larkin didn't think there were too many deer, and she arrived at the meeting armed with a printed booklet of history and local opinion about the deer situation in her county. We don't know how Leopold reacted to Larkin that day, but we do know that he decided to take the committee and several newspaper reporters on a three-day tour of deer yards, to let them discuss what they were actually seeing on the ground. Joyce Larkin, among others, was impressed. She went back to Vilas, got the county board to accept Leopold's challenge to bring clashing interests together to look at the problems locally, and came to a subsequent meeting of the committee with a new report in favor of an antlerless season.[43]

However successful Leopold proved at creating an environment in which members of his Citizens' Deer Committee could change their attitudes through a process of arguing out their views with respect to conditions on the ground, the deer problem proved too widespread and public attitudes too entrenched for him to make much headway in the state as a whole. A new newspaper, *Save Wisconsin's Deer,* ridiculed and castigated him in virtually every issue and offered fuel to those who opposed his reasoning. Yet he never gave up on his effort to educate the citizenry, individually and collectively. It is likely that the unremitting stress of dealing with the deer issue in the public arena during the 1940s helped send Leopold to an early grave. But he had been appointed to a six-year term on the conservation commission, and he believed it was his responsibility as a citizen to serve.[44]

In analyzing Leopold's attitudes toward Wisconsin's deer problem, it has seemed to me, ironically, that his perceptions as a citizen serving on the commission were somewhat constrained by his stance as a professional. As a wildlife expert who had been analyzing deer and habitat relationships within certain professional paradigms since the 1920s—paradigms he himself had developed—and who had taken some highly public positions regarding deer policy in Wisconsin, Leopold seemed riveted on the idea of too many deer. He was somehow less able to integrate his observations of changing conditions into a comprehensive ecological analysis than he had been on similar issues in which he had not been so deeply involved professionally, such as soil erosion on southwestern watersheds or the role of fire in maintaining prairie. As a result, Leopold seems to have thought he was being sold out by his fellow commissioners who adopted a more pragmatic approach to the problem, as well as checkmated by recalcitrant public opinion.[45]

During the years of unremitting deer debates, he took solace in the exercise of another type of citizenship that he had advocated since the days of his backyard garden in Albuquerque: he practiced husbandry, as plain member and citizen of the land community, at the sand farm his family called "the shack." He expressed this form of citizenship—citizenship as creative individualism, building conservation on the land—perhaps most poignantly in his essay "Axe-in-Hand," which includes a definition of a conservationist that could as easily be read as his definition of a citizen:

> I have read many definitions of what is a conservationist [citizen], and written not a few myself, but I suspect that the best one is written not with a pen, but with an axe. It is a matter of what a man thinks about while chopping, or while deciding what to chop. A conservationist [citizen] is one who is humbly aware that with each stroke he is writing his signature on the face of his land. Signatures of course differ, whether written with axe or pen, and this is as it should be.[46]

Conclusion

Aldo Leopold never ceased being fully professional or an advocate for science-based solutions to conservation problems, but as the years went on he gained considerably more humility about the limits of professional expertise and became more committed than ever to the potentials and obligations of citizenship. However imbued he might have been with the progressive search for managerial control and efficiency, as embodied in the Forest Service, he responded also to the "natural skill" and "intuitive judgment" of certain untutored woodsmen and he came to appreciate the reality of uncertainty and indeterminacy, especially in ecological matters. However impressed he may have been with the orderly integration of land policies and uses in Germany, he believed deeply in the American democratic tradition, with its relatively low legal requirements of citizenship but its tradition, through voluntary associations, of vibrant ethical participation in the life of the community. Leopold sought ways to bring clashing interests together locally to discuss problems on the land, and he challenged local citizens to take responsibility for proposing reasonable policies responsive to local concerns.

In our day, Aldo Leopold would quite likely applaud community-based collaborative processes such as that of the Quincy Library Group, which came together voluntarily to work out a solution to the stalemated

planning effort for the Plumas, Lassen, and Tahoe National Forests in California, or that of the Community Conservation Coalition for the Sauk
Prairie, near his own Wisconsin River shack, but he would have been
under no illusions as to the difficulty of the task.[47] As an inveterate organizer of local farmer-sportsman groups and other grassroots efforts at land
restoration, he would be heartened by the myriad watershed partnerships,
community farms and forests, land trusts, urban wilderness projects, and
other community-based efforts that have been thriving in recent years.[48]
He would be particularly receptive to public–private partnerships of the
sort he fostered at Coon Valley, such as a successful effort by local
landowners, elected officials, and conservation organizations to develop a
"Farming and Conservation Together" alternative for the proposed Aldo
Leopold National Wildlife Refuge in the Fairfield Marsh, near his shack.[49]
As a believer in the responsibility of citizens to exercise discretion in their
roles as consumers, he would cheer the movement for independent certification of "green" production.[50]

One senses that Aldo Leopold, with his unusually open mind, would be
an advocate of what is today called adaptive ecosystem management, with
its acceptance of complexity and uncertainty, its commitment to humility
and inductive thinking, and its insistence on collaboration—not only
among professionals but also with citizen stakeholders. As one who
came—through hard-won humility—to appreciate something of the limits
of professional expertise, whether in the deer debates or as a husbandman
of pines at his shack, he would probably agree with those in our day who
argue that professionals are citizens, too, and are best understood as drawing their authority not from their profession or their position in the bureaucratic hierarchy but from their role as informed citizens in a
participatory democracy.[51] He would remind us, as he did in "The Land
Ethic," that all members of the land community are worthy of respect. And
he would insist, as he did throughout his life, that the true mark of environmental citizenship is building conservation on the land.

Chapter 9

Scott Nearing and the American Conservation Tradition

BOB PEPPERMAN TAYLOR

In 1993, when Robert Gottlieb wrote *Forcing the Spring,* his study of American environmentalism, he wanted to expand the way we look at the environmental movement. Environmentalism, he contended, must be viewed in the context of the wide universe of social and political movements that grew and developed over the course of the twentieth century. He offered "a broader, more inclusive way to interpret the environmentalism of the past as well as the nature of the contemporary movement. This interpretation situates environmentalism as a core concept of a complex of social movements that first appeared in response to the urban and industrial changes accelerating with the rapid urbanization, industrialization, and closing of the frontier that launched the Progressive Era in the 1890's."[1] Gottlieb investigated the environmental movement as one moment or element within "the new ideas and movements that arose to challenge . . . the 'organized society' and the search of these 1960s movements for environmental alternatives in the midst of social rebellion."[2]

On a much more modest scale but in a similar spirit, in this chapter I will use the example of Scott Nearing to suggest that we might expand the way we think about the conservation movement. Specifically, I would like to suggest that there is an "alternative" or "oppositional" strain of conservationism that is very much a product of the same historical moment as the conventional environmental movement, and that this movement is well represented by Scott Nearing. No one did more to promote subsistence homesteading and organic gardening than Scott Nearing, and late in his life, during the 1970s, he and his wife reported between 2,000 and 2,500 visitors per year to their Forest Farm in Maine—so many visitors, in fact, that by 1975 they had to limit them to special hours each day, and in 1978 they had to take a sabbatical from visitors altogether in order to get their work done.³ These elderly homesteaders were heroes and role models to huge numbers of young people during this time, and their work and examples continue to resonate within American culture today.

I will argue in what follows, however, that this oppositional strain of conservationism, as developed and promoted by Nearing and then adapted by the youth movement of the 1960s and 1970s, was seriously handicapped in its ability to promote a strong progressive political vision and practice. In large measure because of Nearing's own weaknesses as a political thinker and activist, what was originally intended as a radical critique of and alternative to conventional American society has lost its radical promise. In fact, what is left of this project has been successfully incorporated into the private consumer choices of our own time. The nature of Nearing's radical dream prevented his oppositional conservationism from promoting the serious political alternative to American economic and political institutions it aspired to. Any future attempt to develop such a tradition must come to terms with this failure.

Progressive Homesteading

In 1954, Nearing and his wife, Helen, published *Living the Good Life,* an account of their twenty-year experiment in homesteading in southern Vermont. They described the "venture as a personal search for a simple, satisfying life on the land, to be devoted to mutual aid and harmlessness, and with an ample margin of leisure in which to do personally constructive and creative work."⁴ Over this twenty-year period, the Nearings built a number of stone buildings, including a beautiful house; generated a modest cash income from maple sugaring; and became expert organic farmers who were able to satisfy nearly all their year-round (vegetarian) dietary needs from their remarkably productive gardens. Scott was almost fifty years old at the beginning of this adventure; Helen was twenty years younger. The Vermont experiment came to an end, however, not because of failure or exhaustion but because the Nearings were disgusted by the development of the ski and tourist economy at nearby Stratton Mountain, and they also believed they were losing their privacy to the long stream of tourists in their valley and visitors to Forest Farm. In response, they picked up and moved to even more remote coastal Maine and established a new

Forest Farm, where they lived the rest of their long lives (Scott died in 1983 at the age of 100, Helen in 1995 at 91). *Living the Good Life* is one of a number of accounts they wrote about their homesteading experiences, but it is the central and most widely recognized of these.[5]

Living the Good Life is littered with references to *Walden,* and Scott Nearing's most recent biographer, John Saltmarsh, tells us that the parallels between the two books and their authors were stressed by reviewers.[6] Indeed, the parallels between the books are obvious, and it is tempting to highlight them. Both authors promote a kind of asceticism, in lifestyle generally and in food, drink, clothing, and lodging more particularly, insisting that a strong distinction be made between livelihood and wealth, necessities and luxuries, needs and unsustainable wants.[7] Both offer their personal experience as a serious alternative to the conventional way Americans choose to live, and both, from time to time, had sharp criticisms of their neighbors.[8] Even though the Nearings were a married couple, and Henry David Thoreau's experiment at Walden Pond was, of course, an experiment only for himself, neither book describes the economy of a conventional household, at least to the degree that such a household would include dependent children.[9] Both books emphasize the cultivation of a kind of independence and freedom that requires a certain distance from entanglements in a full-blown market economy, and both include strikingly moralistic pronouncements and claims.[10] *Living the Good Life,* like *Walden,* promotes simple rural agrarian life as an alternative to the complexities, inequalities, injustices, and dissatisfactions of modern urban industrial capitalism.

These similarities between the two books, however, are superficial overall. Although there are certainly those who find *Walden* a preachy book,[11] it is essential to remember that Thoreau presented himself as a "representative man," no different in essentials from his neighbors, just as subject to human frailties and failings and possibilities as they were.[12] Such a sensibility is nowhere to be found in *Living the Good Life.* There is no self-doubt here, no sense of commonality with fellow citizens, no humility about the authors' own weaknesses and needs and temptations. The Nearings exude a profound self-confidence, indeed, a self-righteousness, about their own abilities, moral purity, and distinctiveness. And this quality informs another: *Living the Good Life* is an overtly ideological political tract, at one with a larger (communist) political program and sensibility, wildly at odds with Thoreau's individualism and distrust of organized political movements. Whereas Thoreau wished to march to his own drummer, the

Nearings were disgusted with the unwillingness of their rural neighbors to form agricultural collectives.[13] This modern socialistic sensibility is profoundly unromantic and scientific, emphasizing rational planning and meticulous record keeping.[14] When Thoreau plumbed the depths of Walden Pond, his science was an act of romantic self-discovery, all a part of the moral awakening documented throughout *Walden*.[15] There is no moral awakening dramatized in the Nearings' book, given that their own moral sensibilities are never troubled by serious doubt—their homes in Vermont and, later, in Maine grew from their moral certainty rather than providing them with an opportunity for moral investigation. Perhaps this difference helps to explain one final obvious and essential difference between the texts: *Walden* is, first and foremost, a work of art, designed to take the reader on a moral exploration; *Living the Good Life* is a manual, whose most effective passages give technical information about how to build a house or plant a garden. If Thoreau was primarily an artist, the Nearings were primarily technicians of what they presented as a kind of morally purified rural life.

This last distinction helps us see that the roots of the Nearings' project were actually in very different soil from Thoreau's. If Thoreau was a preconservation pastoralist in the romantic and Jeffersonian traditions, Scott Nearing was very much the product of the Progressive Era. In fact, Nearing's biography prior to the move to Vermont suggests that he was in many ways a very conventional representative of the Progressive generation. Born in Morris Run, Pennsylvania, in 1883 to a locally powerful old-stock American family (his father and grandfather managed a coal-mining operation), Nearing grew up with a strong sense of his own elite social position and obligations. As Stephen Whitfield observes, in his early life Nearing "fused curiosity with moral passion and identified himself with the most idealistic energies of Progressivism."[16] He earned a doctorate in economics and embarked on a teaching career. His politics became increasingly socialist just when American politics was becoming increasingly intolerant of such views. He was fired from teaching positions at the Wharton School of the University of Pennsylvania and then at the University of Toledo, and he was tried under the Espionage Act during World War I for an anti-war pamphlet he had written, "The Great Madness" (he was acquitted after a celebrated trial). Although he was called the "greatest teacher in the United States" by socialist leader Eugene Debs,[17] Scott Nearing found that his left-wing politics made it impossible for him to make his living in his chosen profession. In 1932, he and Helen purchased their worked-out farm in Jamaica, Vermont, and abandoned the urban life in New York City for good.[18] Although he was an alienated and self-exiled member of the Progressive generation, his early writings are classic Progressive performances: a civics textbook and a book on Progressive education, articles on the role of women in humanizing contemporary politics, the "scientific attitude" toward "the facts of social life," the idea that religious ideals are within the reach of earthly life, and the promotion of a vague democratic socialism.[19]

There is, then, no trace in Nearing's work of Thoreauvian transcendentalism or the romantic hope that nature will reflect and tutor our better natures. Late in his life, Nearing bowed slightly to these elements in the modern environmental movement, but these appear to have been gestures of goodwill toward allies more than expressions of real conviction. The most striking thing about them is how awkwardly they came to him and how perfunctory they sound coming from his pen.[20] Overall, Nearing's intellectual forebears were the technocrats and social engineers who represented a powerful strain of the Progressive movement,[21] and despite his socialist politics, he never lost these basic commitments and sensibilities.

If Nearing was less a child of Thoreau than of the Progressive generation, it is also true that he was far from a subtle representative of this Progressivism. It is not only in his early writings that we see as pure and simple an expression of a Progressive interest and hope in social science and political expertise as we could hope to find. In one of his many autobiographies, *The Conscience of a Radical*, for example, he wrote: "As modern technology spreads to the four corners of the earth it becomes more and more necessary to place the future of humanity in the hands of trained, skilled, experienced, wise men and women who are fully aware of the forces at work and the issues at stake; who understand their duties to themselves and the future, and are willing and eager to live up to their responsibilities."[22] In another late book, he stated: "Sooner or later social scientists and social engineers will develop a technique that will make it possible, by orderly procedure, to modify or eliminate an outmoded social apparatus in the same way that a modern community eliminates a fire, health or safety hazard embodied in an outmoded building."[23] This sensibility clearly inspired the Vermont experiment in homesteading. Although Nearing lived long after the Progressive Era and removed himself far from the urban context of the Progressive movement, it was this generation's interest in planning, social experimentation, science, and social progress that informed the entirety of his work as a homesteader.[24]

In this sense, then, Nearing's project as a homesteader represents an alternative conservationism. Inspired as much by the "rational" and "scientific" management of resources as the mainstream conservationism invented by Gifford Pinchot, Nearing provided a model not for government agencies and nongovernmental organizations but, most important, for those (especially young people in the 1960s and 1970s) looking to live simple, rural lives outside the mainstream of American society. Surprisingly, however, although the locus of his attention was clearly different from Pinchot's (Nearing carefully cultivated his position as a social and political outsider, whereas Pinchot, of course, was the consummate political insider), he was just as committed as any mainstream conservationist to viewing nature as a resource to be properly managed for the promotion and maintenance of what he thought was a desirable social order.[25]

The Nearings' retreat to Vermont in 1932 was very much intended, then, not as an experiment in self-discovery and social criticism (such as we find in *Walden*) but as an experiment in the construction of an alternative social order. The move to "nature," to Forest Farm, was designed to demonstrate three essential elements of this project:

1. That it is possible to build a rational, nonmarket productive process, for, as the Nearings wrote, they "[looked] upon profits and the profit system as iniquitous."[26] Later in life, they explained their intention in this way: "Our general aim was to set up a use economy for ourselves independent of the established market economy and for the most part under our own control, thereby freeing ourselves from undue dependence on the Establishment."[27]

2. That the key to this process is moral integrity (i.e., personal discipline and the ability to resist the temptation of profits and luxury) and proper engineering and planning. The Nearings noted that "after due consideration and in the spirit of the times, we drew up a ten year plan,"[28] and they proceeded to plan and record their activities almost to the minute. It was this discipline, they contended, that set them apart from their neighbors.[29]

3. That once it is proven that such a household economy can succeed and prosper, it is to be expected that the Nearings' neighbors, and then others more widely, would join the experiment. In this way, an alternative socialist economy would emerge from the countryside to challenge the injustices and decadence of the urban centers. This

ambition is obliquely alluded to in the introduction to *Living the Good Life:* "With the passage of time and the accumulation of experience we came to regard our valley in Vermont as a laboratory in which we were testing out certain principles and procedures of more general application and concern."[30] Like his Puritan forebears, Nearing wished his social experiment to be a "city on a hill" for all the world to see and emulate. The hostility of their neighbors to their project, discussed in more detail later, was the greatest disappointment the Nearings experienced in their career.

For the purpose of this chapter, there are three key points to recognize about this experiment's relationship to the land and nature. First, although Nearing had sentimental feelings about animals (he was committed, on humane grounds, to vegetarianism, and had to leave the woods every fall so that he would not see any deer killed),[31] his general view of nature was straightforwardly utilitarian—he held, very simply, that nature would provide the natural resources necessary for a proper and just social order if (and only if) it were correctly managed. For example, consider this passage written late in his life: "We have done what we could to conserve and improve the natural environment and to make its facilities available for social advancement."[32] Consider, too, this comment from another work: "Take seriously your assignment to use the part of the earth with which you are in contact intelligently, economically, and wisely."[33] It would be hard to find a more conventional statement of a utilitarian Progressive conservation sensibility.

Second, Nearing's development of what he took to be the proper management of nature (that is, his organic and labor-intensive agriculture) was informed much more by his hatred and distrust of profit-oriented production than it was by a concern for protection of the earth per se. The more alienated Nearing became from American society as a result of his own rejection by the academic and other established communities, the more he came to view the morality of industrial capitalism in extreme terms and the more he came to view the rural economy as potentially the only morally pure economy.[34] The "artificiality" Nearing rejected in the industrial economy was not the artificiality of engineering and planning and science, properly understood. It was the artificiality that promoted profit maximization over the quality of goods. Organic agriculture was his answer to this, discovered more as a result of his belief that all things profit oriented must be poison than through a rigorous agricultural and biological science.

Third, on his own terms, Nearing's experiments in Vermont and then in Maine were clearly failures. Although he was able to build relatively (and remarkably) self-sufficient households, he was not able to interest his neighbors in his alternative economy. This produced tremendous bitterness and, unsurprisingly, harsh claims about the corrupt and false ideological hegemony of advanced capitalism. He wrote of his neighbors, for example: "Perhaps the most significant lesson of the experience is that human beings, conditioned from birth by the professions and practices of a private enterprise, [and] individualistic patterns have little more chance to cooperate effectively than a leopard has to change his spots."[35] He recognized that the planning, the subsistence economy, the eating habits, the engineering, all of which he offered as models to his neighbors, were viewed at best as curiosities and eccentricities (and at worst as arrogant pretensions) by those who lived near him. The only explanation Nearing could imagine for why the locals continued to submit to a wage system, continued to live privately and individualistically, and continued to pursue what he considered to be frivolities and vices in their lives, was their deep moral corruption at the hands of the dominant social order. How else to explain their resistance to his own successful economic and social experiments?

> Atomism, separatism and consequent isolation have increasingly played havoc with rural life in the United States as the family has decreased in size while the household has shed some of its most essential functions. . . . The resulting absence of group spirit and neighborhood discipline, the chaos and confusion of perpetual movement to and from work, to and from school, and to and from the shows and dances, has destroyed the remnants of rural solidarity and left a shattered, purposeless, functionless, ineffective, unworkable community. . . . We are not writing this by way of self defense or self justification. Rather we are attempting to explain and to understand the determined, stubborn resistance of Green Mountain dwellers, in and near our valley, to every attempt at community and collective action.[36]

Although never one to blame himself for his failures, Nearing did recognize the reality of these failures by the end of his life. In the decade before he died, Saltmarsh reports, Nearing "realized that his ideas were no longer being taken seriously. He admitted at the age of ninety-five that 'my friends tell me what I have to say is less interesting than it used to be. I regret this deeply.'"[37]

Conclusion

There is an irony here, however: Nearing was expropriated by the youth culture of the 1960s and 1970s. Although sales of *Living the Good Life* never amounted to much in the 1950s and 1960s, they increased dramatically after 1970.[38] This success both pleased and disturbed him, and it is clear that he was unable to fully relate to his new constituency.[39] Nearing was glad to have allies among the young, even to the point of occasionally modifying the structure of his rhetoric to accommodate the youth movement.[40] But as welcome as these allies were, Nearing was never fully sympathetic to or comfortable with the counterculture of his later years.[41] He noticed, for example, that there were no African American youth and no sons or daughters of coal miners among all the thousands of young people traveling to Maine to visit his homestead.[42] It was clear that his example was not inspiring a useful politics for the African American and working-class constituencies he hoped to speak to. In addition, his own lifelong commitment to living a rational, well-planned, deeply disciplined and morally puritanical life fit poorly with the political, social, and moral anarchism of the youth movements.[43] Nonetheless, he found himself in the position of being among the greatest inspirations and models for their youthful antiurban rebelliousness.

By way of this youth movement, and its subsequent influence on American society as the baby boomers have aged, Scott Nearing continues to influence American culture. When young people flocked to him late in his life, they adopted him for the sake of "alternative lifestyles" that promised to promote personal health and a higher quality of life than that found in more conventional American society. Organically grown food, exercise, healthful country living—all these became more or less divorced from the old-fashioned socialist vision Nearing had always defended. What began for Nearing as a political project of the most ambitious kind (a vision for the actual transformation of industrial capitalism) became instead a set of personal choices that, paradoxically, over time became well served by market capitalism itself. What began as a Progressive plan for the building of an alternative social order has in our time been channeled in large part into individualistic market choices concerning health food, alternative healing, and so forth.

How is it that Nearing's political project could have failed so miserably (and, on his own terms, so perversely) even while his influence has been so great? The answer, perhaps, is found in the deepest weakness of Nearing's political ideas. Political theorist Wilson Carey McWilliams observed that it was common among Progressive intellectuals to assume a kind of human "species being." For these thinkers, as for Karl Marx, it was often assumed that if only unjust social and political institutions would disappear, people would no longer experience a conflict or tension between their wants and needs as individuals and the demands of the human community at large.[44] Although it is not my concern to evaluate the accuracy of McWilliams' claim about the Progressive generation in general, it is certainly the case that Nearing suffered from this illusion with a vengeance. In fact, one of the most striking elements of Nearing's thought is his profound disinterest in, or even contempt for, conventional democratic politics. Nearing was bored and disgusted by the most democratic political institution in American history—the Vermont town meeting.[45] And, as we saw earlier, he was unable to imagine any explanation for his neighbors' rejection of his social experiment other than their moral perversity and corruption. For all his talk of being a social scientist,[46] Nearing never critically investigated his own democratic theory or assumptions.[47] Democracy could simply be expected to emerge if and when capitalism were destroyed: get rid of social injustice, and democracy would naturally and spontaneously take care of itself. "Humanity can and will be united when exploitation is abolished and cooperation is substituted for competition as the basic principle of group relations."[48] That being the case, there was no ground to be gained by participating in the give-and-take and the morally difficult compromises of conventional democratic politics in the world in which we find ourselves at present.

It was this uncritical utopianism that allowed Nearing to conflate his public and private lives so dramatically and, in what is the flip side of the same coin, to withdraw from the real world of democratic politics so completely. Quite simply, Nearing's overt politics were inhumane[49] because they were disengaged from reality,[50] and they became unimportant to his overall project for precisely the same reason. It was because of the very unreality and irrelevance of these politics that Nearing's private household could become not only his primary focus of attention but also the key attraction for his admirers. This life and experience, divorced from an engaged and thoughtful democratic politics, could give the illusion of a committed and radical politics while in reality inspiring individuals to little more than personally gratifying lifestyle choices. Despite whatever illusion they may present to the contrary, these choices have no necessary or obvious political content. As a result, what began as a plan for an alternative social order has been easily transformed into our current preoccupation with "natural" foods and all the rest. This is a rather strange end to what began as a kind of oppositional conservation tradition, although it is an understandable, even predictable, one, given Nearing's failure to develop a serious democratic theory and practice.[51]

John Saltmarsh claims that "Scott Nearing's life is . . . emblematic; it illuminates twentieth-century America itself."[52] Although this comment exaggerates Nearing's life and influence, I have tried to demonstrate in this chapter that Nearing is a significant figure both on the American left and in the American conservation tradition, if only for the way his life and writings illuminate key qualities of particular strains of these traditions and their intersection. In fact, Nearing's life and legacy really do tell us something about the relationship between conservation and Progressive politics, and this something is not always what he intended to tell us. The story has a certain kind of perverse or ironic quality to it, as we have seen. Nearing's "good life" has become a force in American life precisely as a result of its having lost all meaningful political content.

The lesson of Nearing's life and example is that any "reconstructed" conservationism, especially within this oppositional form, needs to avoid the two fundamental elements of Nearing's Progressive inheritance that led him away from democratic engagement and commitments: his view that issues about nature are principally technical in character and therefore best solved by experts, and his (usually unselfconscious) assumption that political conflict and disagreement and compromise are signs of corruption and injustice, rather than being the natural stuff of democratic politics. The American left of the most recent generations is more tempted by the second of these vices, although some environmentalists and conservationists continue to be tempted by both.[53] These undemocratic tendencies grow out of traditions within Progressivism that represent the worst, rather than the best, of that historical moment and movement. A reconstructed oppositional conservationism, if such is to be found, must embrace the imperfections, even the modesty, of democratic political life. Such a movement must struggle for what that much more democratic representative of the Progressive Era, Jane Addams, called "sympathetic understanding," not only in its relationship to nature but also in its relationship to political opponents.[54] Only if and when this oppositional conservationism makes such a commitment will it be able to find a clear voice and a real politics beyond personal choice and the marketplace.

Chapter 10

Conservation and the Four Faces of Resistance

ERIC T. FREYFOGLE

In one of his several essays lamenting the decline of his home countryside and farm communities like it, Wendell Berry comments pointedly on what he perceives as the fading away of old political alignments. Long-standing dichotomies, Berry asserts, have become meaningless and hence confusing. Communists and capitalists, Democrats and Republicans, liberals and conservatives, all have bowed down to supranational corporations and to the juggernaut of the global economy. None takes interest in food quality, land health, or the plight of sagging communities, urban or rural. All show contempt for country life and country places. For a person worried about land and land-based cultures, old political camps are hard to tell apart.[1]

Although he is hardly a man filled with hope, Berry sees signs that a more honest political order is emerging. On one side is a political party that views local communities as valueless and hence dispensable: the party of the global economy, as Berry terms it, the party now plainly in charge. Opposing this party is one that sees the world in a far different light, one that seeks to preserve land and culture and that views neighborhoods and local communities as "the proper place and frame of reference for responsible work." This is the party of the local community, and it is only now, Berry relates, becoming aware of itself. Even though it remains weak and widely scattered, its resources are real and its potential is vast.[2]

Berry's observations are good ones for conservationists to weigh as they take stock of where they are and what lies ahead. The world is indeed a place of conflict, one where powerful resistance awaits those who labor to save, restore, connect, and heal. What Berry describes as clashing parties others might describe in less institutional terms, as opposing ideologies perhaps, or as alternative value schemes. But the conflict, however phrased, is as real as it is grave: those who would stoke the market inferno with anything that burns stand face to face with those alarmed by the mounting costs.

Useful as it is, however, one wonders whether Berry's dichotomy fully cuts to the root of current conflicts over lands and communities. People may willingly serve the global economy, but how many applaud it as an intrinsic good? How many campaigns are openly fought under its transnational banner? If the global economy were the only foe, conservationists ought to have more to show for their work. Without powerful allies, that is, Berry's party of the global economy ought not be enjoying anything like its current success.

If the conservation movement is to chart a successful path in coming decades, it needs to know clearly what it is up against. Berry is right, no doubt, in putting the community and its fate at the center of things. But the force pressing against communities is not the global economy so much as it is the ideology that undergirds it, the ideology of radical individualism: the constellation of values that exalts people as individuals and seeks to liberate them from restraint. Sound communities can exist at all levels, from local to global. Indeed, communities need to exist at levels well above the local, to deal with problems that can be handled only at larger scales. What corrodes all such communities is not global thought per se but rather the ethos of the selfish individual, the person who insists on the right to grab and consume with little regard for neighbors, future generations, and other forms of life.

A sound conservation ethic is, fundamentally, an ethic of community, given the realities of interconnection and interdependence. What pushes against such an ethic is not a single opponent but rather a suite of cultural opponents. And they are all the more influential because of the friendly faces they commonly present. Each of them has a good side, for each has helped the American nation to flourish. Yet like all good things, these cultural elements are good only in moderation. They are good when kept in their proper place.

Environmental degradation is a symptom of a flawed culture, as historians such as Donald Worster have explained.[3] To halt that degradation, conservationists need to confront the underlying flaws. In the case of the United States, the cultural flaws, ironically, largely take the form of excesses of virtue. They take the form of cultural beliefs and practices that honor the individual human and individual rights but do so in ways that threaten the well-being of the communal whole.

In recent decades, the conservation movement seems to have lost sight of its necessary role as cultural critic. Too often it forgets that it is, at root, a champion of the community as such, a defender of nature's interconnected entirety. As it moves ahead, conservation needs to regain its communitarian grounding, along with its intellectual clarity and rigor.

Leopold's Legacy

Perhaps the best way to come to terms with where conservation now stands is to back up to the mature thought of the leading conservationist of the past century, Aldo Leopold.

As a lover of the entire land community, Leopold belonged to a minority strand of American culture. As he so famously put it in his *Sand County Almanac,* he was one of those who could not live without things "natural, wild, and free," one who viewed "the chance to find a pasque-flower" as inalienable a right as that of free speech.[4]

Leopold is remembered chiefly for his often quoted land ethic, summed up in his essay of that name: "A thing is right when it tends to preserve the integrity, stability, and beauty of the biotic community. It is wrong when it tends otherwise."[5] So familiar are these sentences that it is easy to overlook the complexity of them, and to forget that the land ethic was merely one part—albeit a central one—of Leopold's finely argued, wide-ranging critique of the modern age.

From the ample written legacy that Leopold left behind it is possible to tease out four elements of his thought, useful for conservationists charting the path ahead. As the four elements make clear, conservation for Leopold focused on the totality of nature as an interconnected whole and on the need to counteract the chief forces—market economics and private property—that fostered individualistic, self-centered decision making.

The Land Community

Early in his professional career, Leopold gained a strong sense of the interconnection of all life. His experiences in the Southwest, where overgrazing caused harm that rippled throughout the landscape, led him to see how managers needed to address land as an integrated system, not as a collection of resources.[6] Reading in philosophy led him down a similar path, toward a sense of the organismic characteristics of natural systems. Soon, Leopold's expanding ecological wisdom provided an empirical and theoretical base for this intuitive sentiment.[7] The land was a community, he sensed. Its parts were interrelated in ways that reminded him of complex machines. They were interrelated, too, in ways similar to the organs of a body and the cells within an organ. These analogies were not exact, Leopold knew, just as it was not precisely right to equate the biota and a human community. But metaphors were effective tools, and Leopold used them often to bring home the basic truths of interconnection and interdependence.

The Goal of Land Health

A recurring complaint of Leopold's had to do with the fragmentation that characterized conservation in his day. The workers were many, but they pushed in different ways. Conservation was a "house divided," Leopold protested;[8] it lacked a philosophy and would not get far without one.[9] The result often was that conservationists worked at cross purposes, one promoting productive forests, another soil conservation, another the efficient use of waterways, still another the protection of wildlife habitat, in the process employing means that could and did clash. Leopold illustrated the danger:

> I cite in evidence the C.C.C. crew which chopped down one of the few remaining eagle's nests in northern Wisconsin, in the name of "timber stand improvement." To be sure, the tree was dead, and according to the rules, constituted a fire risk.[10]

Conflict in the field had secondary effects as well, for as long as conservationists promoted varied agendas, public action could stall. "The divided counsels of conservationists," Leopold complained, "give governments ample alibi for doing little."[11]

Leopold's worries about conflicts within conservation would soon merge with his ideas about land as community. To coordinate efforts, conservation needed an overall goal. It needed a common target at which all conservationists could aim. Given that land worked as an integrated system, the logical aim was one linked to the ability of the system as such to function over time. For Leopold, there was "only one soil, one flora, one fauna, and one people," which was to say "only one conservation problem."[12] A single problem called for a single resolution, however diverse the implementing means.

In an important essay in 1935, Leopold explored the principal signs of a land community beset with disease.[13] Soon he would assemble those signs into affirmative if vague statements of what it meant for land to possess health. The land was a community, Leopold realized, and communities could be more or less healthy. Conservation was properly aimed at promoting that health. Land health, then, was the much-needed conservation goal.[14]

"Land health," Leopold wrote in 1944, "is the capacity for self-renewal in the soils, waters, plants, and animals that collectively comprise the land."[15] "Health expresses the cooperation of the interdependent parts: soil, water, plants, animals, and people," he added two years later. "It implies collective self-renewal and collective self-maintenance."[16] Central to Leopold's goal was the ability of land to retain its font of fertility—its soil. Fertility was preserved only when sufficient types and numbers of species were present to keep basic nutrients cycling through the system efficiently. Land was healthy "when its food chains are so organized as to be able to circulate the same food an indefinite number of times."[17] Only when this happened would the soil—"the repository of food between its successive trips through the chains"—retain its fertility and produce abundant, nutritious yields.[18]

Conservation Economics

A third element of Leopold's conservation thought had to do with the economic realities of conserving land, particularly private land.[19] How private owners used land materially affected the surrounding land community. Because of that, and because communities endured far beyond any owner's life span, the public had a weighty interest in how landowners behaved.

As Leopold assessed the economics of sound land use, he was quick to see that conservation paid dividends, but the dividends were largely ones that landowners acting alone could not capture. Benefits spread to the entire community, of which the landowner was only a part. When all landowners conserved, each might gain. But conservation by an isolated owner rarely made economic sense.

For Leopold, these economic realities posed a challenge worthy of careful research. Repeatedly he would propose it as a topic: "the formulation of mechanisms for protecting the public interest in private land."[20] Existing institutions simply did not attend to the matter:

> The present legal and economic structure, having been evolved on a more resistant terrain (Europe) and before the machine age, contains no suitable ready-made mechanisms for protecting the public interest in private land. It evolved at a time when the public had no interest in land except to help tame it.[21]

Leopold worked hard on the challenge himself, identifying the tools available and assessing the relative merits of each. Economic incentives, education, legal restraints, boycotts, social ostracism, community-based conservation measures—Leopold considered them all, only to find in time that none would do the trick. "How can private landowners be induced to use their land conservatively?" Leopold would ask himself again and again:

> This question heretofore determined only the choice of method for executing a conservation program (for example, the choice between education, subsidy, compulsion, or public ownership). Now, it seems to me, it takes rank with technological unemployment as one of the critical tests of "The American Way."[22]

Images of Ownership

For Leopold, the leading conservation challenge of his day was starkly posed by the individual landowner, living on and using a single tract of land. For the land to become healthy, this owner had to act well. Achieving this outcome was challenging because economic factors were so unfavorable. Added to the economics was the whole matter of what it meant to own land. So long as ownership gave a person the right to ignore the common good, legally and culturally, conservation was doomed.

Leopold was no legal scholar, and he knew little about the history of private property as an institution. Had he known more, particularly about the many forms private ownership has taken in different times and places, he might have called even louder for institutional change. Yet his instincts were sound and he was prepared to act on them. Private ownership as commonly understood was itself a conservation problem, Leopold decided. Ownership gave landowners too much freedom to drag down the landscape. What was worse, landowners who did so were viewed as perfectly good citizens so long as they obeyed the law and paid their taxes. Ownership was a matter of individual rights and hardly at all about duties.

Early in his career, Leopold raised the possibility that laws in time might force owners to take better care of their lands. In a provocative passage, written as Leopold was departing the Southwest, he speculated that ownership one day would "carry with it the obligation to so use and protect [the land] with respect to erosion that it is not a menace to other landowners and the public." One day it would become illegal, he predicted, for landowners to allow erosion "to menace the public streams, reservoirs, irrigation projects" and neighboring lands.[23] Such "enforced responsibility of landowners," though, was "of the future." Until then and to make way for it, conservationists should push for cultural change.

These four points do little more than identify the main strands of Leopold's thought, leaving untouched much of its richness and subtlety. Yet perhaps they suffice to ground a point that conservationists might usefully keep fresh.

For Leopold, conservation posed a serious challenge to the practices and understandings of his day, and it would succeed only if it brought about major change. Minor adjustments would not suffice. To do that, conservation required a solid grounding in ecology and economics: when "devoid of critical understanding either of the land, or of economic land use,"[24] conservation could be "futile, or even dangerous." Conservation also required "an internal change in our intellectual emphases, loyalties, affections, and convictions."[25] People needed to "change their ideas about what land is for," and, in Leopold's view, "to change ideas about what land is for is to change ideas about what anything is for."[26]

Wendell Berry and the Social Community

If Aldo Leopold was the most important conservation figure of the first half of the twentieth century, his successor in the second half and beyond—in matters of private land, at least—has undoubtedly been Wendell Berry, who from his farm along the Kentucky River has written for four decades on the ways that people inhabit their homes.

Whether or not he set out to do it, Berry has added useful pieces to the conservation legacy amassed by Aldo Leopold. He has brought more of the social community into the picture and linked that community, more strongly than Leopold did, to past and future generations. He has expanded Leopold's critique of economic factors affecting land-use decision making while adding force and clarity to Leopold's call for a new vision of private property. And, like Leopold, Berry has put the community and its long-term health at the top of the conservation agenda. Yet Berry has met with similar frustration in his efforts to defend that community, against forces within as well as without. After decades of work and reflection, he, too, has fallen back on the need for people to better themselves, one by one, by embracing a sounder land ethic and by taking seriously the age-old call to love one another.

Wendell Berry grew up in the 1930s and 1940s under circumstances rare for Americans at any time.[27] He entered the world in the rural neighborhood not just where his parents were born but where all his grandparents were born and where his great-grandparents had lived. Drawn to his grandfather's farm at an early age, Berry learned to work fields with draft horses and to manage a diverse family homestead. His sensibilities were deeply agrarian before he even heard the word.[28]

Berry's observations about land and land use would build on his years spent conversing with respected farmers and wooing the soil. Experience and intuition forged a strong sense of land as a community, just as Leopold had declared. It also fostered a sense that land use was good only when it sustained the health of that community, including its human members. Land health was "the one value," the one "absolute good," that upheld the entire web of life.[29] When speaking on the subject, Berry has frequently borrowed a line from English reformer Sir Albert Howard, who urged readers to understand "the whole problem of health in soil, plant, and animal, and man as one great subject."[30] For Berry, the community as such is the smallest unit that might properly be called healthy. "To speak of the health of an isolated individual," given the individual's dependence on the whole, "is a contradiction in terms."[31]

Even more than Leopold did, Wendell Berry has regularly spoken about land use as an ethical issue, indeed a religious one. To abuse land is immoral as well as unwise, and the truth needs to be told. At the same time, Berry understands the complexity of good land use and how difficult it is for anyone to use a tract well. Mistakes are easily made. Lessons can come at high cost. Leopold portrayed the individual landowner as a member of the land community. Berry has gone further, linking the owner to the surrounding social order and explaining how an owner's success can depend on the existence of a shared body of local wisdom. Good land use is an art, and locally adapted skills take time to accumulate. In settled agrarian cultures, practical ways of using land are accumulated slowly and handed down, generation upon generation. An individual's success, then, can depend on the presence of a flourishing land-based culture.[32]

Even more than Leopold, Berry turned his mind to the challenge of farm economics, particularly the market forces that have debased communities such as his own. So competitive is farming that few owners earn more than modest incomes, especially on marginal lands. Free trade is an important element of the problem, particularly global trade, which forces owners to cut costs ruthlessly and to operate on ever bigger scales. Bigger scales, though, mean fewer farmers, which means fewer people to patronize community stores and fewer children in local schools. These in turn mean closed stores and schools, declining towns, and a landscape bled of people.

In his voluminous writing, Berry has added usefully to the wisdom of land conservation. He has spoken perceptively about the ways that one landowner's success is linked to the economic and social health of the surrounding community. He has probed the powerful economic forces that undercut shared life and that make good land use so difficult. Even when all community members are devoted stewards—a rare happenstance— local communities are buffeted by powerful outside forces. They can thrive only by developing tools of self-defense. Particularly in fictional works such as his masterful novel *Jayber Crow,* Berry has illustrated the difficulties that such communities confront. In practice they struggle, and largely fail, in their attempts to hold on.

In the end, Berry has found himself stalled in ways much as Leopold was. Economic and social forces push hard against landowners, and they respond as agribusiness companies and university scientists tell them to respond: by embracing practices that slowly sap local lands and economies. Advocates of the local community need effective ways to fight back. Yet the tools Berry has identified, like the tools of Leopold, are simply not up to the task. Berry criticizes government for failing to protect communities from outside forces, but he sees no clear way for that to happen that is consistent with America's cultural traditions.[33] Although he perceives clearly the ill effects of global trade, he knows no way to mitigate them, other than to call on people as individuals to resist.

Fighting for Community

When Aldo Leopold began his professional career, conservation was mostly a matter of protecting discrete resource flows, particularly wildlife, timber, and clean water, along with the human economies dependent on them. Wild areas, preserved for their recreational and spiritual benefits, were valued more as distinct enclaves than as vital parts of larger, integrated landscapes. By the time he died, in 1948, Leopold had considerably enriched this base, intellectually, ethically, and aesthetically. For readers paying attention, he had bridged the conservation–preservation split in ways that rendered it artificial, just as he had successfully mixed utility and beauty, ethics, and aesthetics.

Leopold understood, as many others did not and still do not, that to promote conservation is to stand up for community and to fight against fragmentation. The key battleground was the privately owned farm or other private tract, lived on and used by ordinary people. It was there that conservation would stand or fall. Private land was declining because of bad decisions by individuals as such, especially landowners. Landowners in turn acted as they did because of unfavorable land-use economics, poor ecological understanding, immature ethical and aesthetic ideals, and misguided propaganda coming from businesses and universities. Real change needed to address these deficiencies.

Wendell Berry usefully built on Leopold's work by embedding Leopold's ill-behaving landowner in a social community and a local economy. As he did so, Berry shifted part of the blame for poor land use to the communal level. Without healthy communities, even well-meaning owners could often do little. Bad land use had structural causes, Berry observed; until they were solved, conservation would remain cosmetic. Yet having clarified the challenges, Berry found himself unsure of how to respond to them, particularly to the domineering global economy. Farm towns such as his own had become pawns of outside forces.

Conservationists taking stock of things might usefully draw on this conservation wisdom, particularly Wendell Berry's portrayal of conflict. The dominant force at work today is undoubtedly the market. With every decade, it wields greater influence on the ways landscapes are occupied. To build on Berry's work, as Berry has built on Leopold's, it is vital for conservationists to probe these economic forces.

Markets operate on the principle of competition. Free trade widens that competition, intensifying it and imposing even stronger pressures on market participants to cut costs. Markets also work by means of fragmentation, by treating people as individual consumers and producers and by dividing nature into its parts, some assigned market values, most afforded none. In the worldview of the market, neighborhoods, communities, and ecological systems all count for nothing, save as individuals take them into account. Fueling it all is the inclination of people to look after themselves and to promote their own interests apart from the concerns of others.

In the world shaped by the market, almost everything is up for sale or negotiation. A person's ability to influence resource decisions is determined in the first instance by cash on hand. Natural systems count for nothing, save as market participants decide to recognize them. As for the future, individuals are nominally free to weigh it as they like. But competition imposes a stern discipline. Those who ignore the future can often outcompete those who act with restraint. Then there are the problems that come from the high specialization the market requires. Low-cost production is commonly achievable only by those filling a specific market niche. Market specialists often have only modest control over what they do and how they do it, and no power to change the larger system. If the system itself is destructive, of lands or people, the specialist's only choice might be either to participate or to drop out.

Many forms of land destruction arise as detrimental "externalities"—that is, as harms that a market participant generates, imposes on others, and then ignores.[34] The more fragmented a landscape and the stronger the competitive pressures, the greater this problem can be.[35] Although Aldo Leopold never used the term "externalities," the idea guided his thoughts about private land. To divide an integrated landscape into private shares was to skew the economics of good land use. Along with the problem of externalities were the many factors that led landowners to act unwisely even within the bounds of their tracts—the cognitive, ethical, and economic shortcomings that Leopold addressed so often in his writings.

The bane of communities at all levels is the forces that promote fragmentation, socially, politically, and naturally, the forces that elevate the parts while undervaluing the whole. Often, communal health requires wise concerted action to sustain it. When lands and people are fragmented, joint action can prove elusive. To divide a landscape into separate parcels, affording landowners full liberty to act as they choose, is to open the door to widespread degradation. Market forces push landowners to do whatever it

takes to stay afloat: erode soil, derange water flows, bulldoze wildlife habitat, allow exotic species to proliferate, replace complex biotic communities
with monocultures, and more. Shielding landowners from criticism is the
institution of private property, which like the market offers benefits that
can come at high cost. As much as the market, private ownership is a potent fragmenting force, affecting the ways people see land and make judg-
ments about its rightful management.

When the fragmentation of lands is matched by fragmentation of social
and political realms, matters worsen. Citizens can lose all means of getting
together, in person or through representatives, to talk about their landscapes. Deliberative decision making can atrophy, with government displaced almost entirely by the market as the organ that translates individual
choices into overall allocations. For conservationists, this shift can only be
disheartening.

In operation, the market is a powerful engine of fragmentation, at all
spatial scales. It stimulates and is in turn fueled by dissatisfaction, selfish-
ness, restlessness, and a striving to compete. To the extent it dictates land-
use decisions, the market undercuts decision-making processes that can
assign value more broadly, to the unvalued parts of nature, to ecological
processes, to aesthetics, and to the long term. These days, the market has
vocal, influential advocates, legions of them, who praise it lavishly as a
method of ordering affairs, who defend it ardently (often with obfuscating
language), and who applaud it for great accomplishments on dubious evidence, all the while downplaying or ignoring its limitations. Their enthusiasm, at times starkly uncritical, is both an obstacle on the path to land
conservation and a revealing sign of where American culture now stands.

For communities to be healthy, their defenders need to find effective ways
to contain these forces. The market needs firm boundaries if it is to respect
lands and people. Particularly as technology advances and populations rise,
citizen governance becomes all the more vital. Toward the crafting of effective
governance methods conservationists need to devote far more time.[36]

The Four Faces

One wonders, given the plentiful evidence of degradation, why conservationists face such resistance today. Why is it so hard to deal with the forces
of fragmentation? The term "community" conjures up good images for

most Americans. Public opinion polls show overwhelming support for environmental protection.[37] No one stands up to defend self-centered behavior; no one openly opposes the concept of caring well for land. Given this support, and given that markets as such—and advertisers and big industry in particular—enjoy at best mixed favor, why has conservation stalled (or worse) in so many places?

The answers are not hard to find, for they appear in the news media and in public speech nearly every day. They do not appear dressed as opponents of conservation. But when allowed to operate without control, they are.

First and foremost, there is the powerful cultural ideal of individual *liberty*, the bedrock of American culture. Liberty is the ability of a person in isolation to develop and implement a vision of the good life. Liberty means freedom from restraint as one goes about daily life. The difficulty with this ideal is that it contains no brake on its power. Liberty resists all restraint, however reasonable and necessary. Also absent within it is a principled way for determining when one person's liberty should yield to the liberty of another. Particularly in land-use settings, where actions on one parcel can spread wide ecologically, one owner can materially disrupt the lives of others. Where does one person's liberty end and another's begin? Then there is the critical matter of individuals who want to exercise their liberty by joining with neighbors to engage in communal lawmaking. Can a neighbor who objects to a legal restraint claim that it violates his liberty? If so, what happens to the liberty of those for whom the law is the only means of achieving their desired goal? Are they, in the name of liberty, foreclosed by law from achieving it?

Related to liberty is the familiar face of *democracy*—the power of ordinary people to govern their lives, free of kings, oligarchies, and other higher powers. In a democracy, sovereignty is exercised by the *demos*—the people—rather than by a monarch or ruling class.[38] But how do people exercise this power? Majority rule, one way of exercising it, commonly produces laws that some people oppose. From the perspective of opponents, majority governance can appear as an alien, intrusive power, controlled by special interests. Like liberty, democracy as popularly embraced is simply incoherent. It leaves open the critical question of majority rule versus individual choice. Incoherence, in turn, opens the way for image manipulation. Libertarians ask: Is not the market the most democratic of all institutions?

Is not the market the arena in which people can form their choices individually and act on them with little restraint?

Just as revered as these political ideals is the institution of *private property,* which has risen high in the pantheon of cultural icons since the fall of the Soviet Union.[39] Although the differences between the United States and the Soviet Union were countless—most conspicuously in the responsiveness of government to ordinary people—many Americans have pointed to private property ownership as the key division: the Soviet Union fell because it lacked private property; the United States has thrived and will thrive to the extent it respects private rights. The explanation convinces many, even though it is grossly incomplete. No doubt one reason for the story's popularity is that it taps into the unquestioned power of secure private property to foster economic enterprise. It also rests on the power of widespread ownership to add stability to a civil state. Private property ownership brings many good things, and the success of the United States is linked to it.

Yet private property, like liberty and democracy, loses its clarity as soon as one approaches it. Again, the land-use context offers evidence. The landowner who drains his or her land can cause flooding for the landowner downstream. In such a case, how does law protect private rights? Is property respected by allowing the upstream owner to drain or by protecting the downstream owner from flooding? In facile discussions of private property, the downstream owner is typically overlooked. The simple paradigm conflict pits the individual owner against the state, with no mention of neighbors and other community members.[40]

Private property shares defects with liberty and democracy, to which it is linked. Considered abstractly, private ownership includes no means of deciding where one person's property ends and another's begins. It includes no way to decide when the property rights of one landowner should be limited by the legitimate interests of other property-owning community members to enjoy a healthy, beautiful landscape.[41]

Finally, there is the friendly cultural ideal of *equality,* which stands alongside the other three even though strong tensions exist among them. Equality is the most incomplete of the four ideals in that it operates only when linked to independent understandings of fairness and human rights.[42] The truth is that no two people are identical. The question then becomes, when do we ignore the differences between two people, thus treating them as equal, and when do we take the differences into account? When it comes to voting, sex and race are irrelevant but age and citizenship are not. Again and again equality raises the question; in isolation, it never supplies an answer.

Equality is particularly troublesome in the context of land-use disputes, where it is linked to private property. Is equality fostered by a law that treats landowner A and landowner B the same, when each wants to build homes or graze cows or cut trees? Is it violated when a law allows A to proceed but stops B from doing so?

To answer such questions, one needs to distinguish between a law that views A and B differently as people and a law that treats A's land differently from B's land. To distinguish between A and B as people might well be improper. But land-use laws rarely do that; they deal with lands, and land parcels are never the same. If A's land is submerged and B's land is high and dry, a law might rightly distinguish between the two without violating any well-conceived notion of equality. In public discourse, though, attention focuses typically on the owners as people, and the cry of unfairness is raised.

One need only listen to the rhetoric of forces resisting land-use rules to see how these cultural symbols are deployed. In combination, they ably protect developers, home builders, mining companies, and agribusiness groups. Land-use laws restrict individual liberties, so it is claimed. When imposed by distant governments and particularly when fueled by the lobbying efforts of interest groups, such laws distort legitimate democratic processes. In all cases, restrictions diminish private property rights, unfairly forcing owners, without compensation, to use their lands to benefit other people. Laws that burden some landowners and not others—as nearly all do—also raise the specter of unequal treatment. All in all, land-use laws, it is urged, collide with cherished national ideals.

Taking Stock

To dwell upon the disheartening status of conservation today is to wonder whether the current predicament is not in important part self-induced. In the endless flurry of deals, lobbying, and litigation, have conservationists failed to attend to the intellectual and cultural sides of what they do? Have they driven ahead, confident of their bearings, only to find themselves ambushed in a culture war they are ill-prepared to fight?[43]

Opponents of conservation talk openly about this quartet of cultural and political ideals, which are, for them, very much on the public table. Where, though, is the conservation response? What does it mean, to conservationists, to own land privately? As industrial interests see matters, environmental rules interfere with core civil liberties. What do conservationists have to say in response?

Too often, they have nothing to say in response, at least not directly. Too often, they ignore the issue or accede implicitly to the accuracy of what opponents urge, arguing only that environmental benefits make costs worthwhile. More and more, conservationists turn away from the idea that there even is such a thing as a conservation perspective, proclaiming instead a plurality of views. But to endorse a plurality of views is to have no sensible response to opposing claims. In the sound-bite world, in the world of two-sided journalistic stories, a movement lacking coherence becomes easy prey.

More than conservationists realize, the battle over land is being waged in the realm of public rhetoric as well as on the land. And, as in most rhetorical battles, the tools of choice are the ideals that Americans have long used to frame disputes.

Given the pluralism that does characterize conservation, it is difficult to generalize about where conservation thought now stands, save to point out, as must be done, that conservation does not present a coherent message to average citizens. The rhetorical deficiencies are many, particularly when today's rhetoric is put side by side with the core ideas of Leopold and Berry.

First, although conservationists feel comfortable talking about emotional attachments to land, they have largely discarded Leopold's language of ecological connection and ecosystem processes. Few talk about land as community—the centerpiece of Leopold's thought. Exceptions do exist, important ones. But to the average listener, conservation deals with particular parcels of land that are protected from human use.

The dangers of single-parcel conservation are particularly acute when the parcels being protected have no people living on them. A familiar criticism is that conservationists care about wild things and not about people. The charge is easily disproved, yet it rarely is, at least not well. The charge would carry less weight in the first instance if conservationists employed a different rhetoric, if they talked regularly about the health of entire landscapes, including people. To talk about land solely in terms of parcels and parts is to accept a fragmented worldview.

A second rhetorical deficiency is that conservationists tend to ignore lands used to meet basic human needs or, if they address them, implicitly portray users as inherently bad. Leopold focused his mature work almost entirely on working lands; Wendell Berry, from his farm, has paid little attention to anything else. As Leopold put it, the conservation challenge is "co-extensive with the map of the United States."[44] The message deserves prominence.

A third deficiency of conservation rhetoric is that it rarely engages with the economic analyses of opponents, save to weigh in from to time on cost–benefit analyses. Indeed, the field of economics has largely been abandoned to universities and to the staffs of libertarian and free-market advocacy groups, whose position papers flow forth without restraint. Conservation is nowhere near as costly as the public assumes. Indeed, one would hardly realize, given the shape of public discourse, that environmental laws generate economic benefits that exceed their costs. To listen to public officials, mimicking the rhetoric of opposing groups, environmental protection is a luxury when the economy is weak. Better than they have done, conservationists need to rise to this challenge.

Just as disturbing as this inattention to economics is the near silence from conservationists regarding private property and what it means to own land. There is no need to guess what libertarians think about the subject, for they trumpet their views. Conservation groups, with few exceptions, keep their thoughts to themselves. Leopold, again, is feted but not followed.

This near silence on private property is linked to the reluctance of conservationists to talk about their work in moral terms, except on the issue of endangered species. Moral language, of course, requires careful use. But moral criticism can address ideas and practices rather than people. It can accentuate the moral good of healthy lands and intact communities without dwelling on the bad. Opponents of conservation hardly hesitate in framing liberties and property rights as moral claims. For conservationists, to avoid the terminology is to concede the high ground.

Finally, there is the plain fact that, outside the academy, conservation thought has largely dispensed with all talk of an overall goal. On few issues was the mature Leopold more adamant. Land health for Leopold was the antidote for many ills. It helped coordinate efforts. It helped instill an ecological perspective. It explained to the world what conservation was all about and identified its moral base. Slogans such as "jobs versus owls" would persuade far fewer people if the conservation movement were attending adequately to its overall rhetoric.

Reconstruction

In the common understanding, environmentalism is a liberal cause. Classically defined, liberalism is a political and cultural perspective that honors the individual human and seeks to free him or her from unfair restraint.[45] Its original opponent was the feudal system, which contained people within layered social orders and enmeshed them in status rules. So powerful has liberalism in this sense become, in both its welfare and its libertarian forms, that it defines American culture.

Is conservation by this definition a liberal cause?[46]

Were Leopold alive today, he would have a clear answer. As he perceived things, humans inevitably are members of biotic communities. They did not and could not thrive in isolation. Although they were free to throw off all shackles and pursue self-selected goals, they would, if thinking only of themselves assuredly harm the land. Leopold exalted individuals in that he respected their free will and believed that they could lead honorable, ethical lives. The individual did count, and it was to the individual that Leopold addressed his now famous ethic. At the same time, Leopold openly condemned versions of individualism that dignified narrow pursuits of self-interest: "bogus individualism," he termed it.[47] Ecologically and ethically, humans were integrated into larger systems, whether they knew it or not. Conservation was about mending the communal fabric, not enhancing freedoms.

Writing in the same vein, Wendell Berry also honors the individual, but only when the individual stands tall as a responsible community member. In Berry's world, humans living today need linking to past and future generations to tend the land well. Health comes from respecting natural limits, not from casting them off.

Despite this communitarian heritage, conservation is showing more and more signs of embracing classic liberalism. In the name of pluralism, it invites people as individuals to develop their own ideas about land and to embrace moral views of their own choosing. In doing so, it implicitly denies Leopold's and Berry's beliefs in intrinsic moral values. In its resistance to top-down thinking and its enthusiasm for community-based processes, it rejects any overriding goal put together by conservation's leading intellectuals. Classic liberalism is uncomfortable with objective visions of the common good, imposed on individuals. For conservation to embrace such relativity, abandoning its ecologically informed morality, would be to turn sharply away from core teachings of its intellects.

Conservation is losing ground—or at least failing to advance as it might, given public opinion—because it shies away from the culture war. It says too little about the moral and civic ideals that opponents have strewn on the path. If conservation really conflicted with these ideals, the impasse might make sense. But conflict arises only because of the ways libertarian and pro-industry groups have reshaped and distorted them. Conservation needs to rise to the challenge. It can do so best by drawing lessons from its past:

- Conservation needs to speak openly about the conflict in American culture, pitting those who stand up for the communal whole against those who are content to let people do as they please. American audiences do not shy away from conflict; some seem to relish it. Friendly faces and respectful language can remain. It is the underlying clash that needs a clear label: the battle for community.

- Conservation also needs better ways to talk about the tragic consequences of fragmenting lands and people. Fragmentation takes many forms: landscapes divided into parcels; states divided into small jurisdictions; human communities divided into consumers and producers. All pose problems for conservation efforts.

- Even more urgent is the need for the conservation movement to develop a thoughtful critique of the market.[48] The market is at once a powerfully creative force and a powerfully destructive one; it is both good and bad, at least when it operates without restraint. So infatuated has America become with the market that it understands poorly what the institution can and cannot do. The common belief that the market gives people what they want is half true and half terribly false. Equally flawed is the claim that environmental laws disrupt the market in ways that reduce productivity. Some do, but many have the opposite effect: they remedy market failings and aid overall efficiency. On economic issues as on moral ones, conservationists need to do their homework and then, having done it, charge forward with their findings.

- Related to the market issue is the institution of private property, and here, too, conservationists today are sorely lacking. The concept of private property put forward by conservation opponents is seriously miscast.[49] It rests on bad law, bad history, and bad policy. As in the case of the market, conservationists should hardly be rejecting private property; it is a wonderfully useful institution. But it is an institution in need of reform.

- Similar work needs to be done in crafting messages that address the other ideals tossed in the path of conservation work. In the case of liberty, libertarian rhetoric conceals the fact that liberty has a positive side as well as a negative one; it is freedom *to* as well as freedom *from*. Liberty's positive side respects the power of people to join with others to make rules for their common governance. To maximize individual liberty—negative freedom—is not to afford liberty its greatest respect; it is to favor negative liberty at the expense of core forms of positive liberty. In like manner, democracy has its own various forms. One of the most venerable is the one that honors rule by the majority: one person, one vote. Strong individual rights restrain the majority, undercutting this democratic process. Ardent advocates of individual freedom would undercut it almost entirely. Libertarian thought proposes a sharp departure from the nation's democratic traditions. Conservationists should be among those resisting.

Acknowledgments

I would like to thank, for useful comments on drafts of this chapter, Chris Elmendorf, Julianne Newton, Scott Russell Sanders, and Todd Wildermuth.

Chapter 11

Conservation and the Progressive Movement: Growing from the Radical Center

CURT MEINE

The year 2001 marked the 100th anniversary of two signal events in the annals of American politics and conservation. On January 1, 1901, Robert M. "Fighting Bob" La Follette was inaugurated as the governor of Wisconsin. Later that year, on September 14, Theodore Roosevelt assumed the U.S. presidency following the assassination of William McKinley. These events marked the arrival of the Progressive Era, during which conservation first emerged as a coherent movement. For several decades, the voices for reform had been swelling: Grangers, Greenbackers, and Populists across the rural Midwest; socially conscious urbanites and anti-monopolist businessmen; civil service crusaders and progressive educators; suffragists and settlement workers; forest advocates, wilderness preservationists, concerned scientists, and conscientious sportsmen.[1] With the rise of Roosevelt and La Follette, reform moved to the center stage of politics. In the decade that ensued, conservation flourished.

Roosevelt's immense conservation legacy is well known: the proclamation of more than 200 million acres of national forests, monuments, parks, and wildlife refuges on the public domain; appointment of high-level commissions through which his administration shaped the nation's first coherent conservation policy; enactment of new laws "to preserve from destruction beautiful and wonderful creatures whose existence was threatened by greed and wantonness"; and the bolstering of federal agencies to carry out these policies and enforce these laws. We have never had, before nor since, a president more knowledgeable in the natural sciences, or one

165

who took closer to heart the conviction that, as concerns conservation, "the Executive is the steward of the public welfare."[2]

La Follette's conservation legacy is more diffuse. Although a committed supporter of conservation measures throughout his political career, La Follette is identified primarily with his uncompromising dedication to political reform. To appreciate his contribution to conservation, one must read it in the broader context of the times. Wisconsin's timber barons, who in 1901 were stripping off the last of the great stands of white pine, had dominated the state's politics for three decades. La Follette's rise to the governorship and later (in 1906) to the U.S. Senate marked the end of the pine-logging era as plainly as did the vast stump fields of the cutover North. Consumed by its own excess, the era of forest exploitation in the upper Great Lakes—and of the political influence and corruption that accompanied it—was bound to pass (as it did, to the South and the Pacific Northwest).[3]

Under La Follette and his followers, Wisconsin became a national leader in policy innovation in fields from education and labor law to public health and electoral reform. Roosevelt and La Follette clashed regularly as their political fortunes intersected—an ongoing battle of Progressive titans. During a moment of détente, Roosevelt praised "the movement for genuinely democratic popular government which Senator La Follette led to overwhelming victory in Wisconsin" and recognized Wisconsin as "literally a laboratory for wise experimental legislation aiming to secure the social and political betterment of the people as a whole."[4] For his part, La Follette judged the president's leadership in conservation as "the greatest thing Roosevelt did, undoubtedly. . . . Inspiring and actually beginning a world movement for staying terrestrial waste and saving for the human race the things upon which, and upon which alone, a great and peaceful and progressive and happy . . . life can be founded."[5]

The Roosevelt and La Follette anniversaries passed by with no fanfare, no high oratory. It is no surprise, given the way our contemporary political constituencies line up. Few Republicans seem interested in emulating their party's Progressive forebears—Roosevelt and La Follette, of course, were both Republicans—and are content merely to invoke TR's legacy in surefire applause lines. Few Democrats, who rely on urban and suburban environmentalists as sure votes, seem aware that there was once a broad-based conservation movement that included rural America, without which environmentalism as we know it today would simply not exist. Few of the contemporary heirs to Progressivism seem to envision their place in politics as anything but pushing and pulling Democrats further toward the traditional left. Few libertarians seem to care as much about their public responsibilities as their private rights. All are bound by the tired mental image of a one-dimensional left-to-center-to-right political spectrum. All are inclined to render environmental issues into predictable politics.

By contrast, consider Wendell Berry's careful words: "Our environmental problems . . . are not, at root, political; they are cultural. . . . Our country is not being destroyed by bad politics; it is being destroyed by a bad way of life. Bad politics is merely another result. To see that the problem is far more than political is to return to reality."[6] The Progressive movement was indeed an intensely political response to a cultural problem. Roosevelt himself described the problem as a century-long "riot of individualistic materialism, under which complete freedom for the individual . . . turned out in practice to mean perfect freedom for the strong to wrong the weak."[7] In the arena of conservation, it meant unrestrained power to plunder a continent's natural wealth.

But, however political its means, the Progressive Era did not arise from within a single political party, and it was not identified with one (at least not until the tumultuous presidential election of 1912). Progressive forces fought within and between and outside the Republican and Democratic parties. Difficult as it may be, we must somehow try to imagine a time when the spirit of reform, fairness, equity, public service, and the primacy of the public good defined and pervaded political debate.

The conservation movement was among the fruits of that time and spirit. The twentieth century would bring fundamental changes in our understanding of ecosystems, the ethical foundations of conservation, and the social and economic connections within our lives and landscapes. These changes would call into question the scientific assumptions and utilitarian slant of Progressive Era conservation policies regarding development of the country's forests, rangelands, minerals, and waterways. But the actions undertaken in the first decade of the 1900s ensured that there would in fact *be* a movement capable of evolving with time.

The Roosevelt and La Follette anniversaries did not pass without at least a modest nod. On September 23, 2001, on an evening somber with recent events, a group of us gathered in commemoration in Wisconsin's Sauk County to hear voices from the Progressive tradition. It was a fit setting. Sauk County, in the south-central part of the state, was a historic hotbed of Progressivism and gave the world Fighting Bob's remarkable wife, Belle

Case La Follette. Later on, Sauk County became the home place for Aldo Leopold's essays in *A Sand County Almanac*. That September night, we recited the words of Roosevelt:

> The true reformer must study hard and work patiently. . . . Reformers, if they are to do well, must look both backward and forward; must be bold and yet must exercise prudence and caution in all they do.[8]

Of Gifford Pinchot:

> Conservation is a moral issue because it involves the rights and the duties of our people—their rights to prosperity and happiness, and their duties to themselves, to their descendents, and to the whole future progress and welfare of this Nation.[9]

And of Wisconsin's own Charles Van Hise:

> The paramount duty remains to us to transmit to our descendants the resources which nature has bequeathed to us as nearly undiminished in amount as possible, consistent with living a national and frugal life. Now that we have imposed upon us the responsibility of knowledge, to do less than this would be a base communal crime.[10]

We stayed late into the evening, finding solace in the words of those from an earlier generation who worked, each in his or her own manner, for a healthier body politic and a healthier land.[11] In 1901, a revolution dawned in the United States of America. Among its other contributions, that revolution challenged the assumption that had dominated national development for generations: that the American land was a mere storehouse of inexhaustible resources, existing solely for the indulgence of the present generation of its most privileged species. We are still reeling from the revolution.

Seeing Our History Whole

There is much confusion and debate over the way that revolution has played out in the decades since. How did we get from 1910's "conservation as wise use" to the anti-environmental opportunism of the so-called wise use movement in the 1990s? From "sustained yield" to "multiple use" to "ecosystem management"? From "fish and game" to "wildlife" to "biodiversity"? The answers are murky, even for careful observers of the history of conservation and environmentalism.

Take, for example, Peter Sauer's 1999 lament in *Orion* magazine that the environmental movement had deteriorated into "a cacophony of bickering ideologies." What had "happened to its unity and idealism," he wondered, "and when did it fall into disarray?" In Sauer's experience, the movement was once characterized by seamless connections between our concern for human rights and our concern for nature. Sauer recalled a golden moment in the late 1940s when, amid postwar chaos, we began to recognize our joint obligations to the human community and the biotic community. He cast a worried (and nostalgic) look upon a movement that had "[lost] its grip on the principles declared by [Rachel] Carson and Aldo Leopold." That hold, he suggested, had begun to slip with the death of Carson in 1964—two years before *A Sand County Almanac* became available in paperback, six years before Earth Day put environmentalism on the political map. Younger generations, Sauer feared, would never really know what the environmental movement "once stood for."[12]

Take, too, the caricature of environmentalists, popular in postmodernist critiques, as deluded naïfs, dismissive of human concerns, neglectful of local landscapes, seeking escape from history, denying people a place in nature, and waxing sentimental for a North American wilderness that never existed in the first place. This view, rising through the 1990s, underlay the "great new wilderness debate," at the core of which rests the contention that environmentalism, if it is to right itself, must be purged of its false and romantic fixation on an unpeopled wilderness.[13] Proponents of this view posit (in a too typical statement) "an emerging environmentalism that moves beyond merely preserving pristine wilderness and also calls for clean air and water as human rights as well as environmental necessities."[14] By this reading, the environmental movement never "stood for" any kind of broad conception of social obligation or justice. It never had anything like a unifying ideology, except perhaps a false one premised on securing opportunities for privileged white folks to contemplate and recreate in the great outdoors. It implies that protectors of the wild and defenders of human justice have never had, and could not have had, much of anything to say to each other.

These opposing takes reflect a broader confusion. They indicate that something is amiss in our reading of conservation and environmental history. We can lay out evidence both for and against their interpretations. We can point out the lax and often anachronistic use of the terms "conservation" and "environmentalism." (Neither Carson nor Leopold, for example, would have recognized the term "environmentalism." Leopold used the word "environment" no more than a handful of times in his entire corpus.) We could note that neither position adequately accounts for the complex interplay between social justice and conservation through the twentieth century. We could cite lesser-known verses from conservation's texts to both prove and disprove their premises—and to enrich the dialogue. (One of my favorites: the 1954 statement by the great wildlife biologist and wilderness defender Olaus Murie comparing conservation's modest ethical development to "our heavy-footed progress in toleration of 'other' races of men" and calling for "tolerance for the views and desires of many people.")[15]

The point is that in the rush to criticize, deconstruct, salvage, advance, and reform "the movement," those who care about such things have not yet achieved a satisfactory story. For all the work and writings of a generation of environmental scientists, advocates, historians, journalists, and critics, our narrative still has major holes, still misses the mark. The difficulty derives in part from the massive challenge of covering all the relevant bases. We have no comprehensive history of conservation—much less one that captures both the continuity and the disparity between conservation and environmentalism.

Ironically, this may reflect the fact that environmental history as a field achieved definition even as the baby boomer, Earth Day–inspired, counterculture-tinted, increasingly politicized, ever more globalized environmental movement grew through the 1970s, 1980s, and 1990s. Historians and other observers in this N_1 generation could be expected to view the past through the lens of the environmentalism they grew up in and with, to overlook or underemphasize important aspects of earlier conservation history, and to see plainly the conspicuous flaws in their own generation's environmental worldview. The effect, moreover, is not confined to environmentalists per se; "conservative" skeptics and outright anti-environmentalists see through the same lens, just from the other side.

In short, before we can "reconstruct" conservation, we need to lift the lens and see conservation and environmentalism with fresh eyes: as a dynamic amalgam of science, philosophy, policy, and practice, built upon antecedents in the United States and in cultures and traditions throughout the world, but responding to conditions unique in human and natural history.[16] During the Progressive Era, these constituent elements of conservation came into alignment and a new movement materialized. That movement has continued to evolve ever since in response to expanded scientific knowledge, emerging ecological realities, shifting political pressures, and a constantly changing cultural context.

Resources and Responsibilities: Conservation's Original Tension

Conservation in the Progressive Era rested on utilitarian and anthropocentric premises. "The first principle of conservation is development, the use of the natural resources now existing on this continent for the benefit of the people who live here now," Gifford Pinchot wrote in his 1910 book *The Fight for Conservation*.[17] In order to provide (as the guiding philosophical mantra had it) "the greatest good to the greatest number for the longest time," natural resources were to be efficiently managed and developed in a manner informed by science. The "science" of the time was disciplinary, applied, production oriented, pre-ecological. It sought and provided raw numbers: tree growth rates for the forester, stocking rates for the range specialist, base flow rates for the water engineer, tonnage rates for the mining engineer. It did not seek or provide much insight into systemic social, cultural, economic, or environmental effects.

Policies were geared toward ensuring the orderly administration of resources and the prevention of waste. Such policies were to be adopted and applied "for the benefit of the many, and not merely the profit of a few."[18] The policies would be developed and carried out by professional civil servants working within government agencies responsible for particular resources. Removed from direct political influence and trained in the relevant science, government experts would discharge their administrative duties with impartial, businesslike efficiency. Pinchot oversaw the premier manifestation of Progressive Era conservation, the USDA Forest Service. The Forest Service quickly became, in the words of Pinchot biographer Char Miller, "the prime marker of the executive branch's consolidation of authority" and the standard by which other efficiency-driven federal agencies were judged.[19]

With their commitment to enlightened, honest, and restrained use of resources, the new conservationists stood in *opposition* to the rank exploiters
of public lands and water, forests and minerals, game and grass. With their
emphasis on long-term development and management of resources, they
stood in *contrast* to those who placed priority on the preservation of wild
nature. The preservationist impulse had grown through the 1800s, focusing on special landscape features, unique scenic sites, and dwindling game
populations. The rapid destruction of the Great Lakes pineries swelled the
preservationist call through the 1870s and 1880s (and, significantly, drew
attention not just to rarities such as the redwoods but forestlands more
generally). In the 1890s, the call was answered with the designation of the
country's first forest reserves.

The contrast between proponents of wilderness and proponents of rational resource use intensified during Roosevelt's presidential years and beyond, coming to a head in the celebrated battle between John Muir and
Gifford Pinchot over the damming of Hetch Hetchy Valley in Yosemite National Park. It is an episode, and an ideological fissure, deeply incised in
the history we have told ourselves. The very drama of the episode, however, has distorted our view of the broader Progressive conservation crusade, of the events leading up to it, and of the subsequent role of
wilderness protection vis-à-vis the conservation movement (and ultimately
environmentalism). Only recently have historians begun to look at the
Muir–Pinchot schism more carefully and to understand how it has colored
our understanding of the relationship between utilitarian conservationists
and wilderness preservationists.[20]

For those whose support for reform grew out of the direct experience of
rampant resource exploitation, the Progressive conservation crusade was an
appropriate response of national authority to private, corporate irresponsibility. The enhanced role of the federal government did not represent centralization, Theodore Roosevelt informed the United States Congress in
December 1908: "It represents merely the acknowledgment of the patent
fact that centralization has already come in business. If this irresponsible,
outside business power is to be controlled in the interest of the general
public, it can only be controlled in one way—by giving adequate power of
control to the one sovereignty capable of exercising such power—the National Government."[21] Roosevelt had a fine gift for being simultaneously
coy and convincing. Of course his policies strengthened centralized au-

·thority. Of course that centralization was evoked by decades of corporate collusion, unchecked resource exploitation, and government corruption.

And, of course, stronger federal authority was anathema to those still busily profiting from exploitation, those who had known nothing for decades but the doctrine of laissez-faire, those who were among the "locally powerful."[22] They tended not to reside (at least not in their former numbers) in the wasted pineries of the upper Great Lakes. They were legion in the wide-open West. As Daniel Kemmis has written, "At the heart of the burning (and still burning) western resentment [toward the Forest Service] . . . lay a repeated exercise of centralized authority, one that has always made large numbers of westerners feel abused—feel, in fact, colonized."[23] Roosevelt, Pinchot, secretary of agriculture James Garfield, and their supporters built conservation into a movement, and they built it by strengthening the hand of federal authority. It may be said that they *had* to build it. It must be said in the same breath that the tension between local and federal authority—and responsibility—was built into conservation from the get-go.

The tension was already long established in American history and identity. It pitted two great channels of American democratic commitment against each other. One channel issued forth from Thomas Jefferson's dictum that that government is best which governs least (not forgetting Thoreau's addendum from "Civil Disobedience" that "that government is best which governs not at all"). Flowing through colonial rebels, Jacksonian democrats, states' righters, freeholding farmers, westering homesteaders, and even Theodore Roosevelt's own hunting, ranching, and rough-riding compatriots, it was "decentralist, localist, agrarian," resistant to powerful government authority.[24] The second channel issued from Jefferson's other words: that "in order to secure certain unalienable Rights. . . . Governments are instituted among Men." Flowing again through the colonial rebels and then through abolitionists, prairie populists, Mugwumps, unionists, suffragists, and Teddy Roosevelt's own fellow conservationists and scientists, it turned to government authority to secure political rights, honest administration, and fair economic play.

The two channels were not separate or distinct. They had long intermingled within the American soul, on American land. During the Civil War, the tension between them became, literally, unbearable.

Conservation in the Progressive Era, however, gave a new twist to the old tension. It linked the condition of the body politic to the condition of the land itself. It demanded that Americans, having drawn so much of their political identity from the land, now recognize their responsibility *for* the land. The conservation movement may have been primarily utilitarian in its genesis, but it insisted that there was a connection between the ultimate sources of wealth and the morality of the means by which that wealth was secured, distributed, and used. That, in time, would make all the difference in the world.

Changing Times, Shifting Foundations

Before Theodore Roosevelt assumed the presidency, "conservation" was an obscure word and concept, barely linked to the idea of stewardship. By the time Roosevelt left the presidency, it was a national watchword, policy, and ethos. But it had only begun its career. Gifford Pinchot himself noted, "Times change, and the public needs change with them."[25] As Char Miller notes, the Progressives' definition of conservation posed problems: "Who defines what the greatest good is, and on what basis? How to measure its production and equitable distribution or, more trickily, how to weigh humanity's material needs against environmental conditions over time? And would it be possible for succeeding generations to redefine the greatest good?"[26] Beyond these questions of intent lay questions of *process*. Assuming that conservation's aims could and would continue to evolve, how would the practice of conservation be defined, pursued, and implemented?

This is where things get murky. Even many historians are prone to jump directly to the present, to see environmentalism as a linear extension of Progressive Era conservation, bearing all its heroic strengths, flaws, and discords. There is a tendency to extrapolate uncritically the dualism between wilderness preservation and utilitarian conservation, as if nothing much had changed since Muir and Pinchot parted company. There is a tendency as well to run through the conflict between federal authority and local interests in environmentalism as if nothing much had changed since Roosevelt and Pinchot created the "midnight reserves" in 1907.

But much has changed. From the moment the Progressive agenda began to play out on the ground, it was subject to adaptation and amendment. The conservation movement was continually reshaping itself long before Rachel Carson's *Silent Spring* or Aldo Leopold's *Sand County Almanac* appeared. To assume a static view of conservation's early decades is to miss the opportunity for a more nuanced account of its later relationship to environmentalism.

Over the next three decades, roughly 1910 to 1940, conservation's utilitarian philosophical foundations began to shift as practitioners and policy makers explored a broader range of values. The science underlying conservation received its first strong influx of more integrated, ecological approaches. Policies established to encourage conservation addressed an ever-broadening array of issues, including protection and management of wildlife, outdoor recreation, wilderness protection, water pollution, soil and water conservation, and urban planning. Conservation became the province not only of the federal agencies but also of state agencies, local governments, and a growing private and nonprofit sector. And perhaps most significantly, conservation became a matter of concern in terms of not only the country's public lands and resources but also its private lands.

The story of conservation in these years is not a simple one of ever-expanding federal power and control. Certainly that trend was evident in many key federal actions: passage of the Weeks Law (1911), which allowed the National Forest System to be extended to the eastern states; creation of the National Park Service (1916); approval of the construction of Hoover Dam on the Colorado River (1928); passage of the Flood Control Act of 1928, which gave the federal government primary responsibility for controlling flooding on the Mississippi and Sacramento Rivers; passage of the Migratory Bird Conservation Act (also known as the Norbeck-Anderson Act), which in 1929 authorized establishment of a national system of waterfowl refuges; passage of the Taylor Grazing Act (1934), which restricted the further disbursement of the country's public lands; and passage of the Wheeler-Howard Act (1934), which established the Bureau of Indian Affairs and provided for federal assistance in the management of tribal lands.[27] The Great Depression and the dust bowl brought forth Franklin Roosevelt's New Deal, with its "alphabet soup" of agencies, echoing the earlier Roosevelt's response to looming economic and environmental pressures.

These developments seemed to mark conservation indelibly with the imprint of federal paternalism. Yet there was a countervailing trend, also evident in new legislation: the Clarke-McNary Act (1924), which supported cooperative measures in federal, state, and private forestry; the provision in the Taylor Grazing Act establishing grazing districts with advisory boards of local stock growers; establishment of the state-based Cooperative

Wildlife Research Unit system (1935); passage of the Federal Aid in Wildlife Restoration Act, popularly known as the Pittman-Robertson Act (1937), allocating revenues from the sales of sporting arms and ammunition to the states for wildlife conservation purposes. All these measures dispersed resources and authority, expanding the role of landowners, state agencies, and local governing bodies. Meanwhile, state and local governments increasingly asserted their own conservation responsibilities by, for example, strengthening their resource management agencies, passing pollution control measures, and establishing protected forests, parks, and wildlife areas.

But it was the challenge of soil and water conservation in the 1930s that revealed most starkly the need for local conservation commitment and the limits of centralized government approaches. Extensive soil erosion, development of submarginal soils, siltation of water bodies, disruption of hydrologic cycles, and dislocation of farmers were growing national concerns long before the situation assumed crisis proportions in the 1930s. The federal government responded in the old Progressive way, with the creation of the Soil Conservation Service (SCS) in 1933, but it had to do so in a novel manner. The SCS was not a landowning agency, yet its mission involved every square inch of the American landscape. It was the only federal agency specifically directed to work with private landowners on conservation. By the very nature of its charge, it had to address the relationship between social conditions and watersheds. If it hoped to have a salutary effect on the land, it could not work through coercive means; it had to respect the needs and experience of local landowners and rural communities.

The agricultural crisis of the 1930s thus prompted—at least for some—a basic reconsideration of the federal role in conservation, and hence conservation generally. As Randal Beeman and James Pritchard note in their book *A Green and Permanent Land: Ecology and Agriculture in the Twentieth Century,* the need to address root causes of land degradation in the 1930s helps to "explain the shift from conservation to environmentalism." Permanent agriculture (their preferred term for the antecedents of today's sustainable agriculture) "was an idea conceived by individuals born in the Progressive Era, when conservation was generally viewed as the managing of resources for human use, and a task to be pursued mainly by extractive technocrats. . . . Despite, or perhaps because of, their solid indoctrination in conservation values, members of the permanent agriculture cadre were susceptible to nascent ecological ideas that dictated a far more complex set of values than did mainstream conservation, including interdependence and a heightened reverence for all life-forms."[28] Conservation on agricultural lands required adjustments not only in the movement's philosophical stance but also in its implementation. Specifically, enactment of the New Deal conservation programs, while expanding the role of the federal government in the short term, also revealed the ultimate limits of centralized approaches.

As much as any figure of the time, Aldo Leopold appreciated the need for conservation to change to deal with new realities. As a boy, he had witnessed the results of unfettered markets in the deforested North Woods, the disappearing prairies of Iowa, the decimated waterfowl populations of the Mississippi River Valley. As a young Progressive Era forester, he was a carrier of national authority to the newly established national forests of the American Southwest. It was his abiding concern over the degradation of watersheds, first in the Southwest and then in the Midwest, that brought him to the crux of the conservation problem: its *universality.*

> The government cannot buy "everywhere." The private landowner *must* enter the picture. It is easy to side-step the issue of getting lumbermen to practice forestry, or the farmer to crop game or conserve soil, and to pass these functions along to government. *But it won't work.* I assert this, not as a political opinion, but as a geographical fact. The basic problem is to *induce the private landowner to conserve on his own land,* and no conceivable millions or billions for public land purchase can alter that fact, nor the fact that he hasn't done it.[29]

Conservation, in short, was coextensive with the landscape, and new methods of delivering and encouraging conservation had to recognize and adapt to that fact.

Under the New Deal, the federal role in conservation expanded lavishly. But, by that time, Leopold had developed a firm sense of what government agencies at any level could and could not accomplish. He had come to distinguish between what he called "bogus individualism" and responsible citizenship.[30] His effort to calibrate the proper relationship between the public and private sectors—and private and public responsibility— would continue to the end of his life, finding its final expression in "The Land Ethic":

Government ownership, operation, subsidy, or regulation is now widely prevalent in forestry, range management, soil and watershed management, park and wilderness conservation, fisheries management, and migratory bird management, with more to come. Most of this growth in governmental conservation is proper and logical, some of it is inevitable. That I imply no disapproval of it is implicit in the fact that I have spent most of my life working for it. Nevertheless the question arises: What is the ultimate magnitude of the enterprise? Will the tax base carry its eventual ramifications? At what point will governmental conservation, like the mastodon, become handicapped by its own dimensions? The answer, if there is any, seems to be in a land ethic, or some other force which assigns more obligation to the private landowner.[31]

In essence, Leopold's land ethic served simultaneously as a rebuke to irresponsible private, local, and individual behavior on the land (Jefferson's yeoman farmers notwithstanding) and as an open admission of the limits of the Progressive conservation mandate and methods (Pinchot's agency experts notwithstanding). We still struggle to navigate these political and ideological currents—with variable winds blowing hard from the right and left.

Conservation in Transition, Environmentalism Rising

World War II imposed a momentary calm before the winds picked up again. A renewed challenge to jurisdiction over the western public lands in the late 1940s and early 1950s failed to wrest control from the federal agencies but succeeded in inflaming the old tension between centralized and decentralized authority. Latent dissatisfaction with the 1934 Taylor Grazing Act ("federalism in the extreme," in one congressman's words) reasserted itself. Bernard De Voto, native westerner and pro-conservation partisan, derided the "many-sided effort to discredit all conservation bureaus of the government, to discredit conservation itself."[32]

Conservation groups, meanwhile, had rallied in response to growing threats to the nation's wildlands. The premier battleground in the late 1940s and early 1950s was Dinosaur National Monument in Colorado and Utah, where the U.S. Bureau of Reclamation had proposed to build two dams as part of a massive plan for developing the upper Colorado River basin (one of the planned dams, at Echo Park, gave its name to the struggle). Regional supporters of the project were arrayed across the political spectrum and across party lines. The dams—eventually stopped through a compromise between dam proponents and wilderness advocates—symbolized more than just the growing postwar threats to wildlands; they exposed the fundamental fault line under conservation's political landscape. The dams' sponsoring agency was first established as the Reclamation Service by Theodore Roosevelt's pen-stroke, through the National Reclamation Act of 1902. In effect, at Dinosaur National Monument, heirs to one part of the Progressive Era conservation tradition had circled around to oppose the actions of another.

Much as the universality of soil erosion had brought home the limits of centralized authority in conserving private lands, the battle at Dinosaur signaled a larger "crisis of progressive faith" (to use economist Robert Nelson's phrase) in dealing with the nation's public lands: "Created in the name of efficiency, public land agencies in practice gave little heed to efficiency. Part of the reason was that public land management proved in the event not to be scientific management, but politicized management."[33] Echo Park demonstrated that "politicized management" could involve clashes not just between local and federal interests but between different *alliances* of local and federal interests. More was at stake, evidently, than ideological purity.

All these events still predated *Silent Spring,* the first Earth Day, the National Environmental Policy Act of 1969, and the rise of environmentalism as a self-conscious movement. One way to understand environmentalism is as a response to private and public *irresponsibility* during the economic boom years between 1945 and 1965. Roosevelt's "riot of individualistic materialism" was enjoying a long and unprecedented reprise. Leopold's land ethic seemed to have gained little currency. Although the nonprofit side of the conservation movement found temporary solidarity in wilderness advocacy, the movement as a whole was increasingly fragmented. Some conservationists were willing to explore the broader social, political, and philosophical dimensions of wilderness loss, pollution, land degradation, species extinction, and resource depletion. Others, however, were unprepared or unwilling. As Leopold had noted earlier, "in our effort to make conservation easy," we had "made it trivial."[34] Under the strain of postwar economic expansion, social and demographic change, philosophical

disquiet, political realignment, and increasingly reductionistic and specialized science, conservation was cut loose from its old Progressive moorings.

Environmentalism arose as conservation drifted. Environmentalism reconfigured the substance of, and relationships among, conservation science, philosophy, and policy. Environmental science, building on ecology's
insights, was essentially integrative and systems-oriented. Environmental
philosophy was more accommodating of varied values and belief systems.
Environmental policies contended with issues that conservation as such
had not adequately addressed or anticipated: atmospheric and water pollution, nuclear and toxic waste, human population growth, energy production, land use and urban sprawl, endangered species, the global threats of
ozone depletion, climate change, degradation of the oceans. Conservation
suddenly found itself in a greatly enlarged political arena, and many older
conservationists were overwhelmed. Younger environmentalists rushed in
to fill the expanded space. And the new ranks of environmental activists,
drawing lessons from their contemporaries in the civil rights and women's
movements, relied on federal authority as a necessary tool to confront entrenched private interests and political power.

This is where we need to take time out to define our historiographic
problem.

Let us be painfully circumspect.

Let us say it this way: *When the modern environmental movement super-
seded the older American conservation movement and tradition, we gained a
great deal, and we lost a great deal; we have yet to understand fully those losses
and gains, and we are still reckoning with them.*[35]

In the transition, we gained, among other things, a global, more integrated view of humankind and the earth's ecosystems; appreciation of the
full diversity of life and the importance of ecosystem functions; a more coherent critique of heedless industrial and technological development; a
greater appreciation of interdisciplinary science as a tool for solving problems; a greater appreciation, nonetheless, of the limits of science in solving
problems; a broader and better-informed constituency that now included
urban and suburban dwellers; and a more thorough understanding of the
social and economic causes and consequences of environmental degradation. In short, we gained perspective on the full dimensions of humankind's environmental dilemma, as well as a broader base of support for
actions to address it.

But we also lost much in the transition to environmentalism, including the attitude of stewardship that formerly bound conservationists, hunters, farmers, ranchers, and other landowners more closely together; the heightened attention to private land conservation; a respect for the realities of rural life and the structural constraints facing rural economies; the connection, explicit in the 1930s and 1940s, between wilderness protection and other aspects of land conservation; the sense that this movement—call it what we will—was about more than honing legal tools to "protect the environment" (to use the lazy politician's shorthand); and the vision of conservation as a commitment binding people and places together across ideological divides, across landscapes, and across generations. As the institutional memory of "traditional" conservation faded, the very word itself seemed fated to slip into oblivion. It carried less and less weight with the new generation of environmentalists.

As the transition continued through the years following Earth Day, the historical tension between centralized and decentralized authority in American conservation and environmental policy reasserted itself. It did so now along multiple, overlapping fault lines: federalism versus localism in managing the country's public lands; regulatory versus free-market approaches in controlling pollution; the carrot of policy incentives versus the stick of enforcement in protecting endangered species; enthusiasm versus reluctance in supporting international environmental treaties and protocols. In these and other arenas, there was still room for lively policy debate; on at least some issues, creative solutions were hammered out and real gains were made.

At the same time, however, environmentalism became a combat zone in the culture wars. The environmental politics of the 1970s begat U.S. Secretary of the Interior James Watt and the sagebrush rebellion, which begat an ever closer alliance of Democrats and environmentalists, which begat the "wise use" movement of the 1990s, which begat the opportunism of the early presidency of Bill Clinton, which begat the "Contract with America" and the Newt Gingrich revolution, which mystified mainstream environmentalists but galvanized action by (among other culturally conservative environmentalists) the Evangelical Environmental Network, which took both conservative and liberal think tanks aback, which in turn left things in a complete muddle that neither George W. Bush, Al Gore, Ralph Nader, nor their dedicated camp followers could clarify as the new millennium arrived.

Every turn in the cycle further polarized the contestants. Partisan operatives drove the political wedges in ever deeper. As the sound bites flew, it became increasingly difficult to work out a coherent story.

We still don't appreciate fully just what we have lost and what we have gained.

Reintegrating Conservation

Remarkably, however, conservation did not simply wither away. Environmentalism had grown up fast, overshadowing its venerable predecessor. Yet, hunkered down under the canopy of environmentalism, conservation proved to be deep-rooted and shade tolerant. Written off, nearly forgotten, it surprised perhaps even itself by continuing, slowly and quietly, to lay on new rings of growth.

Gradually, from the late 1970s on, conservation began to reinvent itself. Conservation biologists, building initially on new concepts in island biogeography, sought to unite multiple disciplines in the effort to understand, protect, and maintain biodiversity. Conservation of the marine environment and biota established itself as a new arena for research and action. At least some wilderness advocates revisited their premises, retooled their science (including their anthropology), and returned to the necessary work of protecting wild places. Watershed advocates and community-based conservation organizations gave a positive focus to the "decentralist, localist, agrarian" strain of American democracy. Landscape ecologists and conservation-savvy planners, architects, designers, and builders lent their expertise to the effort to better integrate human land use and resource management at various spatial scales. Practitioners of sustainable agriculture reinvigorated the tradition of "permanent agriculture" that had tapered off after World War II. The movement for environmental justice arose to address an entire suite of neglected concerns and to involve communities that neither environmentalism nor conservation had effectively engaged.

A friend once observed that "we environmentalists are pretty effective at fighting against things; we are not so effective at creating solutions." Since the 1970s, ecological restoration has provided a new outlet for affirmative, hands-on action. Seeking to enhance the ecological integrity of local landscapes, from the wild to the urban, restoration has offered many a battle-weary environmentalist something to work *for* and *at,* not just something to *stop.* The restoration movement, as much as any development in recent decades, stood as evidence of a resurgent land ethic. Kenneth Brower, introducing a new edition of Leopold's *Sand County Almanac* in 2001, predicted that "the century or two of the Preservation Era will prove to be prologue, an introductory chapter, noble but brief. Almost all the wilderness that can be saved has been saved. For the duration of our time on the planet—for whatever piece of eternity we have left here—restoration will be the great task."[36]

In all these fields, people from varied backgrounds have been seeking ways to depolarize environmental issues (at least to some degree), reintegrate conservation, and build a new consensus for action. The common denominator is a commitment to land health on the part of individuals, neighborhoods, watersheds, organizations, agencies, and businesses, and a desire to achieve tangible results, whether on private, public, or community lands.[37] These trends suggest the possibility of an emerging "cross-landscape" constituency that can address the harmful feedback loops that encourage continued degradation of urban, suburban, exurban, rural, and wild lands alike. They reflect the emergence of a "radical center" where people who care about land and communities and wild things and places, whatever their political stripe, may meet to make common cause.[38] They point toward a new conception of economic freedom—one that realizes there can be no freedom without responsibility, and no definition of sustainability that does not embed the circle of human economics within the greater sphere of nature. They show that the desire to build better relationships between people and land is tenacious. It will not go away.

Always, the conversation must return to the core concept of responsibility. The latest "riot of individualistic materialism" and corporate avarice cannot last forever; the peak of Enron's stock price may have served as its high-water mark (or so we can hope). In any case, a renewed commitment to conservation values must, sooner or later, find a home once again in our civic life, under a form of political leadership that does not yet exist. Where might we find it? How might we encourage it? As historian Donald Worster has suggested, "a history that is more alert to the landscape around us, looking for clues there about our past behavior and acknowledging the agency of nature in human life, is . . . a good place to start. It can help overcome one-generation thinking. It may even promote a wider area of responsibility, which is all that conservation asks."[39]

Conservation emerged in the Progressive Era, effectively broadening the "area of responsibility" in American life. It has evolved continually ever since, one dominant strain having mutated to help create what is now a global environmental movement. Changes in science and in ethics, in society and in the world, continue to prompt us to reconsider our responsibilities: not merely in terms of long-term economic self-interest but in terms of our obligations to our neighbors, our communities, future generations, and nonhuman nature. In the long run, our own well-being is wound up in these broader responsibilities in intricate and inescapable ways.

The Progressives of the early 1900s could not foresee the utter transformation of the world that the ensuing century would bring. Nor, for that matter, could the stalwarts and plutocrats and reactionaries they fought. In three generations, we have built a world that their generation would not recognize. The solutions the Progressives devised to meet the problems of their time will not suffice for us to meet ours. However, the basis upon which they acted is of the essence. They saw the need, as we must again, for public responsibilities to keep pace with private privilege. To that end they made democracy work, as we must again, "to secure the social and political betterment of the people as a whole."

Part IV

New Methods and Models

Conservation: Moral Crusade or Environmental Public Policy?

BRYAN NORTON

The environmental movement was born in great rhetoric. At the height of the decade-long battle to save Hetch Hetchy Valley, John Muir relied most heavily on religious and spiritual appeal in reaction to the forces of utilitarianism and rising economic materialism. Framing the question of whether the beautiful Hetch Hetchy Valley should be a "water tank" for the city of San Francisco or a "cathedral" as it was meant by the Almighty to be, Muir referred to advocates of the dam as "selfish seekers of immediate Mammon," and San Francisco became "Satan and Company."[1] Muir was escalating the moral rhetoric he had introduced decades earlier in the fight to save the forest reserves, especially from grazing, which he characterized as the eternal battle between right and wrong, good and evil. In the battle to save Hetch Hetchy, it was natural to appeal to higher principles—since all the practical and economic arguments seemed to be arrayed against him. Muir's rhetoric was met from the other side by Gifford Pinchot, who loudly advocated a materialist approach of using utilitarianism to decide all questions of conservation policy. Pinchot, for example, said, "There are two things on this material earth—people and natural resources," and he fought consistently to use natural resource systems to maximize economic wealth and development of resources for human use.[2]

Since those days, American conservation thought has evolved ideologically as a battle between good and evil, between moral exhortations to save nature set in opposition to wanton economic excess. By referring to such commitments and exchanges as ideological, I mean to say that conservation thought has been aligned according to pre-experiential commitments to general principles—in Muir's case, a religious obligation to respect nature both for and as God—that polarize environmental problems, treating

187

them as either-or, right-or-wrong problems. Today we are learning that
Muir's poignant rhetoric has its costs, as federal environmental policy
whiplashes back and forth between benign neglect by Democrats and tendencies of Republicans to appoint economic zealots who want to dismantle
the system of environmental protections and turn resource management
over to the private sector. In most changes of administration in recent
decades, environmental policy has been held hostage to ideology, to "right
versus left" and "environment versus free-marketeering" shifts at the whim
of electoral politics.

Academically, ideology has also created dichotomies and polarization.
Environmental ethics, a recent addition to the realm of conservation
thought, has essentially embodied this opposition in its concepts and value
formulation, since many environmental ethicists develop theories that nature has intrinsic value as an antidote to economically based environmental
policy. Environmental ethics has thus defined itself as a field in opposition
to environmental economics, and both have virtually ignored the (noneco-
nomic) social sciences as a source of information.

As we ask, in this book, how conservation can be reformed, it is interesting to speculate whether its history might have been different. Might
the battle lines over conservation policy have been drawn in less black-
and-white terms? Could conservation policy be contested along a continuum of more-or-less choices rather than according to all-or-nothing
slogans? I begin by examining a case study in polarization: the development of the field of academic environmental ethics, which has evolved in
theoretical opposition to the idea of anthropocentrism—so poignantly
stated by Pinchot's classification of all things as persons or resources—
and its direct challenge to economists' human-centered analysis of resource use. I then explore the alternatives to polarization by examining
another way of thinking of environmental problems, not as a battle between moral evil and economic excess but as involving competition
among multiple goods and legitimate interests. This argument establishes
the importance of public, iterative, deliberative *processes* as a response to
problem complexity and difficulty in agreeing on the problem formulation. Finally, I suggest a new approach to articulating and implementing
environmental values, one based not on polarized opposition between
good and evil but on community-based, democratic procedures designed
to achieve a reasonable balance among multiple competing human values
derived from, and attributed to, nature. If we are to "reconstruct" conser-

vation for the twenty-first century, I intend to argue, we would do well to put public discourse about conservation policy on a less ideological basis, a basis that emphasizes experience and experimentally based management rather than pre-experiential commitments.

Environmental Ethics in the Age of Extensionism

Before asking where we should go from here, it helps to ask where we are, a question that in turn leads us to ask where we have been. I will argue that, if the conflict between academic environmental ethicists and economists can be thought of as a microcosm of the ideological battles that have characterized environmental discourse and policy formation, a broader, less ideological look at the possibilities for analyzing and interpreting environmental values may point the way to a more productive approach to environmental discourse and policy formation.

When one thinks about environmental values and theories for understanding these values, one might ask four questions, each of these leading to four different theories of environmental evaluation: (1) What is the nature of environmental value? Answers to this question can be called *onto-logical* theories of environmental value. (2) How can one measure environmental values? This question is to be answered by a theory of *measurement*. (3) How can or should environmental values be employed in justifying proposed environmental policies? Answers to this question can be called *epistemological* theories of environmental value. (4) How should we, given disagreements about environmental values, proceed toward satisfactory policies? Answers to this question might provide a theory of the *process* of policy formation based on environmental values.

Given this classification, environmental ethics has concentrated mainly on questions of the ontology of environmental values, focusing mainly on specifying the *nature* of environmental values and on determining which objects in the world possess such values. Given that ontology is a core area of philosophical study, it is perhaps not surprising that ontological theories of value were among the earliest topics addressed by environmental ethicists. One effect of this concentration on ontology and the true nature of environmental value has been to enshrine the either-or ideology of Muir and Pinchot in a more secular rhetoric of intrinsic versus instrumental values, thus ensuring that environmental discourse will be polarized between economic goods and moral good. The goal of this chapter is to reconsider these ideologically motivated approaches to environmental values and policy. Perhaps it is time for environmental ethicists, environmental economists, and environmental activists to consider alternative problem formulations and new approaches to environmental valuation.

The specialized and contingent nature of philosophers' concerns can be appreciated if we look in detail at the intellectual seeds that sprouted and became the subdiscipline of environmental ethics; to do so, we must look back to a 1967 article written by a historian and published in *Science* magazine. This article, by Lynn White Jr., was called "The Historical Roots of Our Ecologic Crisis."[3] This paper has an ongoing life as one of the most anthologized pieces in environmental thought. I believe this short paper—and especially a particular interpretation of it—shaped the subject matter of environmental ethics and has given environmental philosophy a rather unidimensional quality so far.

White offered a broad-brush historical account of the ideas and social forces—science, technology, and, especially, the melding of the two—that have shaped Western culture's view of the human relationship to nature, and suggested that these features may be responsible for the degradation of modern environments in the West. White offered several criticisms of Western ideas and culture, including, for example, a brief reference to the conception of time as directional—a Christian idea, absorbed from the Hebraic tradition, that saw creation as a beginning of history, which had also an end. White suggested that this linear conception of time, which differs from the Greek conception of nature as cyclical, with no beginning or ending, has instilled in Western consciousness a directionality and a sense of purpose—and also a form of unjustified optimism—that treats all technological change as progress. Westerners, he seemed to be saying, are poor critics of technological proposals because we tend to be technological optimists by default. If developed, this line of reasoning might have led environmental ethicists more toward the analysis of proposed technologies and their long-term and unintended effects on social values; had this happened, environmental ethics might today have been a specialized form of the philosophy of technology, one that addressed important questions of human value but did so in the more practical context of evaluating technologically induced environmental change and its effect on core moral and social values.

This line of reasoning, however, has not been very important in environmental ethics in the years since White wrote. Instead, environmental ethi-cists responded to another line of criticism, White's statement that Western Christianity "is the most anthropocentric religion the world has seen."[4] White was, of course, referring to the creation story in Genesis I, which is clear because he notes especially the claim that humans are made in the image of God and in an important sense are separate from nature, accord-ing to the creation story. It was the charge that Western culture is anthro-pocentric that provoked the first dozen or so papers and books that are clearly within the professional philosophical tradition. Indeed, most early environmental ethicists took White's criticism to be valid and compelling and proceeded to respond by proposing "nonanthropocentric" ethical posi-tions, which argued that nonhuman elements of the environment— elements of many different types, from individual animals to species and ecosystems—had intrinsic value and hence these elements should be con-sidered morally worthy of consideration in human decision making.[5] Mi-nority forces, in particular Australian philosopher John Passmore, argued, to the contrary, that the Western tradition has adequate intellectual and moral resources to criticize and reform environmental practices, that there are good human reasons to change current destructive practices, and that introduction of non-Western and nonanthropocentric ethical principles is unnecessary to correct environmentally damaging behaviors.[6] Passmore therefore rejected nonanthropocentrist ethical theory as inconsistent with central moral principles of Western social thought and unnecessary to sup-port improved environmental policies. Much of the writing on environ-mental ethics since those early days has addressed this issue of anthropocentrism in one way or another. Indeed, some leading advocates of nonanthropocentrism *define* environmental ethics as simply the study of intrinsic value in nature.[7]

Was this polarization and corresponding lack of communication in-evitable? Perhaps not. Environmental ethicists, as noted earlier, might have explored White's concerns about our technological optimism and failure to develop a sense of fairness to the distant future because of this optimism. Was the polarization inevitable once White had introduced the label "an-thropocentric" and made his charge of anthropocentrism against Western culture? No. With hindsight, we can see that White's general critique, espe-cially the charge of anthropocentrism, can be given two rather different in-terpretations. White might have meant, as environmental ethicists have taken him to mean, (a) that anthropocentrism is an *ontological theory of*

environmental value—the theory that all human beings and only human beings have intrinsic value and that only humans are morally considerable.
But White never explicitly states this theoretical interpretation of the target
of his criticism; in fact, the only explanation he gives of the term is in reference to the doctrine that humans are made in the image of God. White
could as well be interpreted as simply (b) criticizing an *attitude* of human-
centeredness, a kind of hubris about the importance of humans in the
larger scheme of things. This charge of hubris ties nicely to White's other
concerns about our optimism about technology and cultural progress, and
it requires no positing of intrinsic, ontological values in nature. The ancient
Greeks, clearly anthropocentric in their beliefs and evaluations of nature,
found the moral resources—in epic poetry, in theatrical tragedies, and in
Aristotle's ethics—to criticize overweening pride, hubris, the temptation of
humans to act on behalf of the gods. They did so without broadening
moral citizenship or radically changing their ontology of values, as they
saw no need to appeal to a moral anchor beyond the idea of living a worthy human life. Note that if one interprets White in the second way, no
particular antidote, theoretical or otherwise, is predetermined; and under
this reading, agreement with him requires acceptance of no particular ontological theory of environmental value. Anthropocentrism, in this attitudi-
nal sense, can be rejected without embracing an ontological theory that
opposes it.

Environmental ethicists, having embraced Muir's moralism but without
the religious justification he embraced, analyzed the problem not as one of
religiously defined evil—moral depravity according to a given code—but
rather as a failure in moral theory. Western society threatens nature, environmental ethicists seem to imply, because it believes in a false moral theory. Nonanthropocentrism, then, becomes an ontological antidote and
establishes the philosophers' role in the goal of saving nature. Nonanthropocentric environmental ethicists seek to articulate a replacement value
theory that is adequate to support Muir's moralism, without fully embracing his evangelism and deification of nature.

Moreover, White might have been understood to be expressing an explicit *political* concern about the environmental implications of a modern,
democratized culture—one in which greater and greater numbers of citizens have increasingly powerful and ecologically pernicious technologies at
their fingertips—rather than a narrowly philosophical argument for the
distinct moral status of nonhuman nature. Had this interpretation taken

hold, we would have found ourselves asking very different questions in the field—questions more accurately described as ones of "environmental political theory," perhaps, than of environmental ethics. This, too, might have turned philosophical attention toward more productive institutional and procedural issues rather than tendentious ontological questions about the moral standing of nature. And, if the value explorations of environmental ethicists had extended beyond an ontology inimical to ecological economics, there might have been far more opportunities for collaboration and development of shared concepts and measures of environmental value. This analysis, however, seems apt—from an activist perspective—only if one assumes that the problem with Western civilization is that it is based on a false theory of value, the theory that (all and) only human beings have intrinsic value. Having assumed that White's analysis had uncovered a theoretical problem in the ontology of values, environmental ethicists considered whether traditional moral theories—such as rights theories or utilitarianism—could be "extended" to allow the moral consideration of nonhumans.

Early extensionism simply addressed the question, is it intelligible—and perhaps true—to say that some elements of nature have intrinsic value?[8] And the related question, what does it mean to say that a natural object has intrinsic value? On the question of interpretation, it turned out under analysis that intrinsic value theorists were split roughly down the middle, between "strong" and "weak" nonanthropocentrists. Strong nonanthropocentrists, represented by Holmes Rolston III, Tom Regan, and Paul Taylor, argued that the intrinsic value found in nature exists entirely independently of humans, human judgment, or human consciousness. For example, Rolston once said that natural objects "generate" their own intrinsic value.[9] Weak intrinsic value theory, on the other hand, espoused by J. Baird Callicott and a number of other ethicists, has explicitly recognized the need for a valuer to attribute value. Callicott therefore treats intrinsic value "adverbially"—as a way in which humans value nature—a way that is analogous to the way a parent values a child, "for" itself, based on characteristics of the object, or the child, rather than according to selfish needs of the valuer.[10]

It is not clear what difference this difference should make in policies advocated, but, speaking theoretically and epistemologically, the difference is huge. Theoretically, strong intrinsic value would exist even if humans had never existed. It is a discoverable feature of natural objects that exists entirely independently of human cognition; it is therefore independent of human cultural differences and exists within nature itself. Strong intrinsic value is attractive to environmental ethicists because, if proved to exist, it would provide culturally independent arguments for environmental policies, arguments that would be persuasive even across cultures and worldviews. Intrinsic values would thus function, in policy formation, as "trumps," shifting the moral burden of proof against economic forces of development. Weak intrinsic value, on the other hand, is attributed by human beings, and these attributions cannot help but be affected by differences across cultures. Whereas strong intrinsic value is said to be "discovered" in nature—a characteristic of nature overlooked by anthropocentric cultures and theorists—weak intrinsic value is in an important sense creative and dynamic. Callicott, for example, argued that this kind of value was perceptible only once the science of ecology allowed us to expand our sense of what could be a "whole," worthy of moral consideration.

Epistemologically, both of these theories are problematic. Rolston's strong intrinsic value apparently achieves considerable moral authority because of its universality and apparent independence of actual human experience. But at the same time, this authority demands that Rolston embrace a most difficult epistemological task—to provide evidence of intrinsic value beyond any particular human experiences (which are all, of course, particular cognitive events, occurring within a context and highly charged with cultural and other background meanings).[11] Callicott, on the other hand, treats attributions of intrinsic value to nature as relative to culture and worldview. Appeals to weak intrinsic values as premises in protectionist arguments therefore lack scope. Arguments to appeal to those who adopt a different worldview or cultural understanding cannot be *based on* claims of intrinsic value understood in this weaker sense: the appeal of these arguments is restricted to those who accept the premise asserting intrinsic value. Lacking cross-cultural validity, intrinsic value theorists are limited to explicating the worldviews people already accept. They can offer no culture- or worldview-independent reasons to act to protect nature and natural objects; their theories, understood in this way, provide only an *explication,* not an independent *justification,* of nonanthropocentric principles.[12] Nonanthropocentrism, then, if taken to include thinkers as diverse as Rolston and Callicott, is not really a single ontological theory of environmental value; it represents, rather, a label that in fact comprehends a variety of kinds of value and a variety of methods of value analysis. They share an ontological focus, but they lack an epistemological method for identifying intrinsic values in nature or any means of measurement.

Cutting across this puzzling ambiguity about the nature of the independence that is asserted for natural intrinsic value is another question: what types of beings can have intrinsic value? Because of the speculative and exploratory tone of early work on nonanthropocentrism, little attention was paid to the *exact* nature of the natural objects that could be said to have intrinsic value, and there was no definitive understanding of whether only individual organisms could have intrinsic value (an analogy to intrinsic value as usually attributed to human beings), or whether some composites, such as species or ecosystems, might have or be attributed intrinsic value. In these early days, then, the literature of environmental ethics was not sharply separated from the growing and somewhat complementary— at least in their arguments critical of anthropocentrism's moral theory— literature on animal rights and animal liberation.[13] At first, the use of a common label, "nonanthropocentrists" or "biocentrists," papered over important differences; eventually, however, differences regarding what kinds of objects might have intrinsic value led to open schisms among academic environmental ethicists, who became divided into biocentrists, such as Taylor, and ecocentrists, such as Rolston and Callicott.

In 1980, Callicott published an influential essay on animal liberation and environmental ethics in the two-year-old journal *Environmental Ethics*.[14] This article first noted the attack on anthropocentrism mounted by animal liberationists, who he called "humane moralists" and characterized as expanding moral considerability to include nonhuman organisms, especially animals, and often domestic animals. Then, articulating a version of Aldo Leopold's land ethic, Callicott argued that fully capturing the concerns of environmentalists such as Leopold would require attribution of moral standing not to individual animals—certainly not to domestic animals—but rather to species, ecosystems, and communities. Callicott, casting his lot with Leopold and declaring individualism inadequate to the task of building a distinctively environmental ethic, endorsed a robust holism claiming that "the separate interests of the parts [are] acknowledge[d] to be subordinate to the health and well-being of the whole." In response, the staunch individualist Tom Regan declared Callicott and Leopold to be "environmental fascists," advocates of running roughshod over the welfare of individual humans and animals in pursuit of a higher, corporate good lodged in composite entities such as ecological communities.[15]

Actually, Callicott's famous triangle represents a truncated quadrangle—by considering anthropocentric individualism, nonanthropocentric individualism, and nonanthropocentric holism, Callicott apparently missed the possibility of an anthropocentric holism, a theory that the broader good of the human species is so dependent on whole systems of nature that we should seek policies that protect species and systems as a broad strategy for protecting present and future human interests in an effort to live sustainably. This fourth viewpoint may prove the most productive because it inoculates environmental ethics from the unfortunate implication that policy makers must always choose *between* human and nonhuman interests, allowing the creative search for convergent policies that serve both broad human interests for the present and future and also serve the "interests" of natural systems that support those human interests.[16]

Today, many environmental ethicists—disturbed by the apparent intractability and unclear policy implications of extensionism—have begun to wonder whether the experiment of simply extending standard ethical concepts such as welfare and rights to broader classes of entities, and the associated question of identifying beings who are morally considerable, represents the best formulation of questions concerning environmental values. These environmental ethicists, sometimes calling themselves environmental pragmatists, attempt to avoid simplistic and shortsighted interpretations of human values and seek to develop processes that will result in social learning about both values and the environment. These pragmatist philosophers often appeal to the principles of the American pragmatist movement (especially those of Charles S. Peirce and John Dewey) as a philosophical rallying point for a new, more contextual and problem-based philosophy of the environment.[17]

To illustrate the choice as I have come to see it, I begin with an anecdote, an experience I had in 1982, when I was first beginning to study federal endangered species and biodiversity policies. I was doing research at the University of Maryland's Institute for Philosophy and Public Policy, and I had a grant to study the rationale for having an endangered species act, such as the Endangered Species Act of 1973, and to explore the little-discussed topic of how to set conservation priorities (in the almost certain event that funding would fall short of doing everything desirable to protect biodiversity). I had decided to concentrate my philosophical efforts on environmental policies, and I was at least intrigued by the idea that there may be an obligation to protect biodiversity and wild species that was intrinsic to nature and extrinsic to human considerations of prudence or human well-being.

About that time, I began attending a regular lunchtime brown-bag meeting of a small group that called itself the Endangered Species Coalition, composed of bureaucrats from agencies such as the U.S. Fish and Wildlife Service and activists from various nongovernmental agencies. We met and discussed what various groups were doing, and not doing, in the effort to prevent extinctions and recover populations of endangered species. I remember that we often discussed gaps such as the woeful lack of protection for native plants and the weakness of marine conservation efforts at the time. One lunchtime when we had a light agenda, I raised the question of whether these activists had considered the possibility that nature has intrinsic value—a topic that had never arisen spontaneously in our discussions. The silence following my remarks was profound and lasting, embarrassingly so. We eventually went on to other topics. At first, I thought there must be something wrong with the activists and bureaucrats—how could they be uninterested in a topic so central to what they were doing? And yet I had to admit that, in decisions with regard to which policies to support or how to expend our efforts, the activists were never lacking in justifications for chosen actions, despite never mentioning an intrinsic value of species or their habitats.

Eventually, I came to see the incident differently, and I started asking not what was wrong with them but what was wrong with myself, and with environmental ethics. For a time, I became an irascible critic of my own field and its presuppositions. Since then, I have been called a traitor to philosophy and have been accused of trying to "silence" philosophers and spending too much time "inside the Beltway."[18] Here, I'd like to reexamine these questions by paying more attention to the policy context in which we ask questions about the value of species and ecosystems, and in which we propose policies and then evaluate them.

Beyond Ideology: Environmental Problems as "Wicked" Problems

Although I am hesitant to criticize John Muir—who is one of my personal heroes as well as a catalyst for environmental protectionism more generally—I hope it is not irreverent to point out that his rhetoric, so effective in motivating a broad-based effort to protect nature a century ago, may have outlived its usefulness. Because Muir lived in the age of economic expansionism, of timber barons, and of virtually unrestrained exploitationism, it was reasonable for him to articulate a strong moral reaction. But even Muir was, at times, more conciliatory. For example, before his celebrated falling-out with Pinchot over the question of grazing in the national forests, Muir explicitly expressed a respect for sustained use of the forests. He once said, "The forests must be, and will be, not only preserved, but used; and . . . like perennial fountains . . . be made to yield a sure harvest of timber, while at the same time all their far-reaching [aesthetic and spiritual] uses may be maintained unimpaired."[19]

But if the forests could be used for many and diverse human ends while still fulfilling their moral calling, there was an implicit recognition of a range of environmental values. These values—of varied use, of preservation, and of spiritual uplift—cannot easily be fit into the black-and-white categories of the ideology of right and wrong. So even Muir the rhetorician was implicitly cognizant that environmental problems are too subtle and many-faceted to yield to resolution by the cleaver of moral indignation.

In this section, I shift the focus of our questioning from trying to define a hard line between Environmental Right and Environmental Wrong to a second-level reexamination of the nature of environmental problems in all their complexity. This important shift, I believe, is best explained and supported by a classic paper in decision science, published in 1973, titled "Dilemmas in a General Theory of Planning."[20] Its authors, Horst Rittel and Melvin Webber, drew an illuminating distinction between two types of problems, which they dubbed "benign" and "wicked."

This pluralistic approach can be explained and justified by invoking the hypothesis that environmental problems are best understood as "wicked" problems as defined by Rittel and Webber. These authors contrasted wicked problems with the "benign" problems of mathematics and science. Benign problems have a unique solution, which is determinate—one knows when a benign problem is solved. Wicked problems, on the other hand, have no determinate solution; even the correct formulation of the problem is contested, and there is no "stopping rule." Rittel and Webber hypothesized that wicked problems have no definitive solution—and no agreed-upon formulation—because disagreements involve different and competing interests. For wicked problems, we cannot expect "optimal" and final solutions; rather, we can expect only a negotiated balance that will be acceptable for a time but will always be open to renegotiation and adjustment as context and power relations change in the society. If Rittel and Webber are right that most environmental problems are wicked problems, perhaps we should see these problems as a competition among multiple goods, such as economic development, avoidance of risks to human health, and maintenance of environmental quality.[21] Rather than trying to express all these values in a single measure, such as price or willingness to pay, it may be advantageous to accept pluralism and operationalize this aspect of environmental decision making by using a multi-criteria evaluation system.

Numerous studies of public values attributed to the environment have shown that most Americans value nature in many different ways.[22] Historically, leaders of the environmental movement, such as Muir, Leopold, and Rachel Carson, all used both human-centered arguments and life-centered arguments for changing policies.[23] As the environmental movement continues to diversify, we predict that environmental values will continue to be expressed in different vocabularies, by different voices coming from different viewpoints. We call this the fact of pluralism: Americans (perhaps all peoples) value nature in multiple ways, and, given presently available tools for analyzing these various expressions of values, these differing vocabularies and frameworks of value are in many cases incommensurable.

Faced with the fact of pluralism, most economists and environmental ethicists have nevertheless sought monism—the view that all moral quandaries can be resolved by a single moral principle, such as maximization of human welfare or protection of intrinsic value wherever it occurs.[24] Monists accomplish their reductions by heroic acts of defining one type of value in terms of another or, less accommodatingly, by denying the existence of a type of value that does not parse easily into their monistic definition of environmental good. Meanwhile, we face the fact of pluralism, and, although the competing monistic theories are interesting, they currently offer little concrete guidance to decision makers because the (first-order) methods they offer for actually evaluating specific objects are radically "incomplete." In this sense, they offer not so much *methods* of evaluation as *promissory notes for such methods.* A monistic calculation of which choices will protect valued objects will, except in the simplest cases, involve accounting for values not currently captured by the methods of the monistic approaches in question. For example, I noted earlier that intrinsic value theorists are nowhere near agreement on which objects in nature do in fact *have* intrinsic value. How could one begin to offer a complete accounting of which decisions protect the most intrinsic value until there is consensus on what things have it? Economists, on the other hand, have offered no convincing way to measure values such as biodiversity or healthy ecosystem function, as is readily admitted in A. Myrick Freeman III's authoritative survey of economic methods of environmental valuation. Freeman says, "The economic framework, with its focus on the welfare of humans, is inadequate to the task of valuing such things as biodiversity, the reduction of ecological risks, and the protection of basic eco-system function."[25] Because both of the grand monistic theories readily available are unable to offer comprehensive accountings of actual values, they usually end up offering examples, and promissory notes, with hand-waving substituting for the comprehensive measurement of values perceived and reported in real situations when communities face real choices. An incomplete accounting according to a unified system of counting values, however, is not obviously more useful to a decision maker than a more complete accounting of effects on incommensurate scales.

Toward a New Beginning in Understanding Environmental Values

Ideological environmentalism, with its dichotomous categories of good and evil, tends to see the problem as one of identifying and classifying environmental outcomes into two categories, which we could informally call "goods" and "bads." For economists, a "good" is any fulfillment of a human preference, and this unidimensional good leads inexorably to a logic of how much good, how much preference satisfaction, and how much economic growth—more is automatically better. For environmental ethicists, likewise, each "good" is the protection and thriving of some organism or object that is judged to be valuable in its own right. Once again, more is better. Ideology and polarized rhetoric emerges because of prior ontological commitment to a single kind of good. The result has been the development of two entirely opposed methods of counting value, and advocates of each of the methods have come to see their opponents as roadblocks standing in the way of maximizing the good as they see it. And roadblocks to maximizing good are easily labeled as "evil." Hence the polarization and failures of communication within the discourse of environmental valuation and policy assessment.

If, however, we follow Rittel and Webber in thinking of environmental problems more as a matter of multiple competing goods, and seek acceptable balances among goods rather than pursuing the maximization of a single kind of good, we can talk about and measure environmental effects in a new, less polarizing mode. In this final section, I will sketch—in very general terms—one possible approach to environmental valuation, an approach that is inspired by the insight of Rittel and Webber and that I believe holds open the possibility of a more effective way to evaluate environmental change and environmental policies.

The approach I have in mind is highly contextual because it is sensitive to the nature of environmental problems and the varied, sometimes conflicting, values that make such problems—as experienced in real situations—"wicked." Although it is difficult to talk in general terms about a process that is highly context dependent, my strategy for this sketch is to begin by stating crucial prerequisite conditions that must be in place before this approach to evaluation can be implemented. These conditions can be thought of as illustrating contextual requirements for a new approach to environmental valuation, an approach that could begin once these conditions are fulfilled. First, I assume an adaptive management process to be in place—an ongoing, iterative discourse that is located in a specific geographically defined "place"—for example, a watershed or an ecologically defined ecosystem such as the Greater Yellowstone Ecosystem. By "adaptive management" or "adaptive management partnership" I mean a public political process devoted to both cooperative action and strategic learning through controlled actions. Further, I assume that this adaptive management process will have some kind of forum for public deliberation, a forum that is open in the sense that all significant interest groups have a voice in it and all affected parties are welcomed as part of the deliberations.

Despite this openness, I also assume that the actual contributors will in fact be some smaller subset of the public—day-to-day participants can then be thought of as formal or informal representatives of stakeholder groups that participate in the process and in the deliberations. Next, I assume the participants—as evidenced by their participation—have signaled a commitment to seek cooperative solutions rather than resort to force or political stalemate. Finally, I assume at least a small amount of trust among the participants—trust, at least, that the other participants are bargaining in good faith and that, despite disagreements about the substance of what should be done to protect the place, the group shares a commitment to reach a cooperative solution acceptable to all participants.

Although this is a lot to assume, a large number of ongoing environmental management partnerships and adaptive processes fulfill this minimal set of assumptions;[26] and since there are a number of these, and more are being initiated all the time, it seems reasonable to design an evaluative method appropriate for use in them, despite the difficulties in specifying, in general terms for all cases, the shape of effective approaches. The goal of this exercise is to illustrate how a more pluralistic approach to evaluation might be appealing to participants in an adaptive management process, a process in which both scientific uncertainties and changing goals are up for discussion and debate within a process devoted to learning and cooperative problem solving.

Given these background assumptions, we can propose a new and less polarized—less ideological—way of addressing the problem of evaluating environmental change. First, we choose as the *object of evaluation* a set of "development paths." A single development path, as defined for a place under adaptive management, is a scenario—a future—that could be reached from where the place is now.[27] Each place can be thought of as having an open set of possible development paths, the set being limited by physical constraints ("you can't get there from here") and, at any given point in management time, by the imagination, creativity, and resources of the participants in the management process. It is then possible to evaluate and compare various proposed members of this open set of possible scenarios, or paths of development, for the future.

Within this process, participants will engage in an ongoing discussion of values and goals, articulating a set of values and associated indicators that are chosen to track the most important of these values. An indicator, then, is defined as a measurable variable characterizing the level or quality of a resource over time, and it must be a variable that tracks some feature of the environment that is of value to society. Treating indicators as representing features of environmental concern, we can operationalize pluralism by recognizing that success in environmental protection will be judged by multiple criteria, with each specific criterion being instantiated by an indicator. Following Rittel and Webber, we then treat the choice of which indicators to use, what management goals will be set with respect to them, and how to weight the criteria as open questions for deliberation. The varied viewpoints and concerns of the participants and stakeholders can then be articulated as advocacy for some particular indicators, goals, and weightings. These questions of choosing various indicators—and the process of deliberation involved in justifying them—can thus be made endogenous to the adaptive management process.

Given a pluralistic framework of competing values, it is still not impossible to hope for an integrated pluralism; the multiple criteria need not be applied willy-nilly. Rather, we can seek meta-level rational procedures by which to choose what rules to apply within particular contexts given particular, local, and distinguishing features of the decision context. Accordingly, we employ a two-tiered, or "two-phase," decision process.[28] Recognizing that these are not usually sharply separated in practice, we formally distinguish an "action phase" of policy, in which accepted rules are applied to a case at hand, from a "reflective phase" of deliberation, in which the question is which rule or set of rules is appropriate in a particular decision context. We can then think of questions in the reflective phase as meta-choices—they are choices regarding which rules to apply and how to determine the weight or priority to be given each applicable rule in a given decision context. We treat the two phases as "moments" in an ongoing process and, following Rittel and Webber, take the asking of these questions to be an iterative process, informed by applications in the active phase but open for renegotiation in the reflective phase based on new information from the active phase.

This multi-criteria, two-phase approach to evaluating development paths creates a fruitful connection between activist adaptive management and integrated assessment modeling, which is practiced by a group of scholars who use modeling techniques as a way of improving the understanding of choices facing a society.[29] They develop models—often by including stakeholders in the process—that will simulate various possible development paths for local places. One very effective technique is for groups of participants to go through a process of envisioning various possible scenarios, setting goals for some distant date, such as twenty-five or fifty years in the future, and then engaging in "back-casting." In back-casting, participants set out to determine what steps would have to be taken now, or in the near future, in order to achieve a given set of goals as represented in a scenario, or development path. This kind of modeling, especially when it is place-sensitive and when it incorporates the best science available about the possibility of scenarios, provides models that become tools for generating some scientific hypotheses about what is possible. These models also begin to connect behavior patterns of individuals, and policies of governments, as both causative factors and actors in the processes that will change their landscape.

The approach to valuation proposed here is well suited to application in situations in which modeling and back-casting are incorporated into planning and evaluation of proposed policies. By moving to a pluralistic framework of multiple values, it is possible for individuals and groups to articulate alternative indicators and measures and to cite the goals they have projected—not ideologies—as the basis for treating a given indicator as one worth monitoring because that indicator tracks an important social value, or set of values, they support. Surely, some will propose economic indicators as one of the criteria of good policy, but this will be one criterion among several, and the community will have to decide which criteria to adopt and how to weight them in various situations.

Once one passes beyond an ideologically determined vocabulary for expressing environmental values—and the either-or, polarized thinking that has gone with the monistic approaches—the study of environmental values can become more experimental, as multiple criteria will be proposed, tried, advocated, and criticized within a political process rather than through the interdisciplinary warfare of conflicting jargons. In this way, the conflicting ideologies and polarized rhetorics of the moralists and the free-marketeers may be made subservient to a new evaluative discourse, a discourse of action, not ontology. Under a pluralistic, multi-criteria system, good policies are marked by their robust performance over multiple criteria, which opens opportunities for win-win situations when one policy can support multiple values and goals, and negotiations in search of an acceptable balance among the multiple, competing, and intertwined goods of environmental quality and human thriving. Once such social and communal values become an integral part of public discourse, the foundation will be laid for reconstructing conservation in nonideological terms.

Acknowledgments

Some portions of this chapter have appeared in a paper by Bryan Norton and Ben Minteer, "From Environmental Ethics to Environmental Public Philosophy: Ethicists and Economists, 1973–Future," in *The International Yearbook of Environmental and Resource Economics 2002/2003*, edited by T. Tietenberg and H. Folmer (Cheltenham, UK and Northampton, Mass: Edward Elgar, 2002), pp. 373–407. I gratefully acknowledge their permission to include this material here.

Chapter 13

Social Climate Change: A Sociology of Environmental Philosophy

ROBERT E. MANNING

Democracy demands that public policy ultimately reflect evolving social thought. However, in the nonmarket realm of public land management, and environmental policy more broadly, where price signals that drive the free-market economy are generally lacking, this requires a concerted effort on the part of social science to measure and monitor societal values and related thinking in ways that will facilitate their integration into policy making. In fact, application of social science to environmental thought has been an ongoing project since the emergence of the environmental movement in the 1960s.

For example, economists have developed and applied methods to assign monetary values to environmentally related, nonmarket goods and services (see the chapter by David N. Bengston and David C. Iverson in this volume). Moreover, sociologists have measured public attitudes toward an array of environmental issues.[1] Geographers and others have studied the "sense of place" ascribed to significant environmental locations.[2]

Recent research by the author and others has become more interdisciplinary and has focused on more fundamental environmentally related values and ethics.[3] This research applies sociological methods to philosophical concepts and ideas—a "sociology of philosophy"—and is designed to measure public environmental values and ethics in ways that will monitor their distribution over space and time—"social climate change"—and that will ultimately inform public land management and environmental policy.

Study findings suggest that public environmental values and ethics can be widely *pluralistic,* manifesting a diverse array of environmental philosophies ranging from anthropocentric to ecocentric. However, these values and ethics tend to be ordered in ways that can *converge* on policies that support ecologically informed and farsighted public land management approaches and that enjoy broad public support. Moreover, evidence suggests that these pluralistic environmental values and ethics are applied to environmental policy in a *contextual* manner that recognizes and respects the ecological significance of place and the sociopolitical importance of community and related social institutions.

Study Methods

The data described in this chapter are derived from two surveys that focused on national forests in New England. The first survey examined the Green Mountain National Forest (GMNF) in Vermont and was administered by mail to a representative sample of 1,500 Vermont households randomly chosen from all telephone directories covering the state. The second survey focused on the White Mountain National Forest (WMNF) in New Hampshire and Maine and was administered to a representative sample of 1,000 households randomly chosen from all telephone directories covering the six New England states. In both cases, the surveys were administered following procedures recommended by Don A. Dillman (1978)[4]. Initial mailing of questionnaires and cover letters was followed one week later by a postcard reminding the recipients to complete and return the questionnaire. If completed questionnaires had not been returned within three weeks of the initial mailing, a second questionnaire and cover letter was sent.

In the GMNF study, 272 questionnaires were returned as undeliverable, reducing the sample size to 1,228. Six hundred twelve completed questionnaires were returned, yielding a response rate of 50 percent. In the WMNF study, 167 questionnaires were returned as undeliverable, reducing the sample size to 833. Three hundred forty-four completed questionnaires were returned, yielding a response rate of 41 percent. Both surveys included batteries of questions designed to measure environmental values, environmental ethics, and attitudes toward national forest management. A follow-up telephone survey of nonrespondents was conducted for both surveys, and few statistically significant differences were found between respondents and nonrespondents.

Environmental Values

As might be expected, human values have been the subject of considerable attention across a variety of academic disciplines.[5] Although several theoretical dimensions of value have been identified, the studies described in this chapter focus on preference-based held values. Held values have been defined as "an enduring conception of the preferable which influences choice and action."[6] In relation to forests, Bengston defines a held value more specifically as "an enduring concept of the good related to forests and forest ecosystems."[7] The preference-based component of this concept of value signifies that value is assigned through human preference as opposed to social obligation (e.g., societal norms that suggest what people should value) or physical or biological function (e.g., the ecological dependence of tree growth on soil nutrients). Recent commentary suggests that preference-based held values are the appropriate focus of research on forest values.[8]

Several classifications of forest and related environmental values have been proposed.[9] On the basis of this literature, eleven potential values of national forests were identified, as shown in table 13.1. This set of environmental values was designed to be as comprehensive as possible. Survey respondents were asked to rate the degree of importance they attached to the GMNF as a place to attain these values. A six-point response scale was used, ranging from "not at all important" to "extremely important."

Environmental Ethics

Ethics have likewise received considerable academic attention, particularly in the discipline of philosophy. Ethics can be defined as the "study or discipline which concerns itself with judgements of approval and disapproval, judgements as to the rightness or wrongness, goodness or badness, virtue or vice, desirability or wisdom of actions, disposition, ends, objects, or states of affairs."[10] Environmental ethics deal more specifically with human conduct toward the natural environment. It is inevitable that humans interact with the natural environment. But what ideas govern or structure this interaction? What is the appropriate relationship between humans and the natural environment? For the purposes of this study, environmental ethics are defined as the diversity of ideas that drive human relationships with the natural environment. Examples include stewardship of nature as a religious duty and intrinsic rights of nature. As used in this study, environmental

Table 13.1

Importance of Environmental Values of the Green Mountain National Forest

Value	Statement	Average Importance Rating[a]
Aesthetic	The opportunity to enjoy the beauty of nature	4.97a[b]
Ecological	The opportunity to protect nature in order to ensure human well-being and survival	4.95a
Recreational	The opportunity to camp, hike, and participate in other recreational activities in nature	4.83
Educational	The opportunity to learn more about nature	4.68c
Moral/ethical	The opportunity to exercise a moral and ethical obligation to respect and protect nature and other living things	4.53d
Historical/ cultural	The opportunity to see and experience nature as our ancestors did	4.40e
Therapeutic	The opportunity to maintain or regain physical health or mental well-being through contact with nature	4.35e
Scientific	The opportunity for scientists to study nature and ecology	4.30e
Intellectual	The opportunity to think creatively and be inspired by nature	3.93f
Spiritual	The opportunity to get closer to God or obtain other spiritual meaning through contact with nature	3.81g
Economic	The opportunity to get timber, minerals, and other natural resources from nature	2.98h

[a]The value 1 = "not at all important"; 6 = "extremely important."
[b]Letters indicate statistically significant difference using paired students' t-tests.

ethics are broader and more abstract constructs than values, and they apply to human relationships with the environment generally rather than with national forests specifically.

There is a rich literature in history, philosophy, and other environmentally related fields of study regarding environmental ethics, and much of this literature is reviewed in contemporary texts.[11] On the basis of this literature, seventeen environmental ethics were identified, as shown in table 13.2. This set of environmental ethics was designed to be as comprehensive as possible.

Table 13.2

Environmental Ethics

Category	Ethic	Representative Statement
Anti-environment	Physical threat	Nature is a threat to human survival.
	Spiritual evil	Nature is evil.
Benign indifference	Storehouse of raw materials	Nature is a valuable storehouse of raw materials.
	Religious dualism	Humans were created as fundamentally different from the rest of nature.
	Intellectual dualism	The ability to think makes humans fundamentally different from the rest of nature.
Utilitarian conservation	Old humanism	Human cruelty toward animals is wrong because it could lead to cruelty toward people.
	Efficiency	Humans should manage nature as efficiently as possible.
	Quality of life	Nature is important because it adds to the quality of our lives.

(Continued)

Table 13.2. Continued

Category	Ethic	Representative Statement
Utilitarian conservation	Ecological survival	Protecting ecological processes is important to human survival.
Stewardship	Religious/spiritual duty	It is our religious/spiritual duty to take care of nature.
	Future generations	Nature should be protected for future generations.
	God's creation	Humans should protect nature because it is God's creation.
	Mysticism	Nature should be protected because it is sacred.
Radical environmentalism	Humanitarianism	Humans should not cause needless pain and suffering to animals.
	Animism/organicism	Nature should be protected because all living things are interconnected.
	Pantheism	All living things have a spirit.
	Liberalism/ natural rights	Nature should be protected because all living things have a right to exist.

The seventeen environmental ethics were further classified into five broad categories based on conceptual similarities. Survey respondents were asked to rate the extent to which they agreed or disagreed with statements expressing the seventeen environmental ethics. An eleven-point response scale was used, anchored at "strongly agree" and "strongly disagree."

Attitudes toward National Forest Management

Research on attitudes has been a long-standing focus in sociology and psychology. In general terms, attitudes are measures of how people feel about issues. More specifically, an attitude can be defined as "an orientation toward certain objects or situations that is emotionally toned and relatively persistent. An attitude is learned and may be regarded as a more specific expression of a value or belief in that an attitude results from the application of a general value to concrete objects or situations."[12] A considerable amount of research has been conducted on attitudes toward environmental issues in general (a recent review of this research is presented by Riley Dunlap),[13] and some of these studies have focused on national forest management.[14] This study builds on this literature by focusing specifically on public attitudes toward the evolving concepts of sustainability and ecosystem management as applied to management of national forests.

Attitudes toward national forest management were measured by a battery of statements describing alternative national forest management policies. Twelve statements were adopted from an earlier study conducted by Bruce Shindler, Peter List, and Brent Steel,[15] and three statements were added that addressed issues more specific to the GMNF and the WMNF. These fifteen statements concerned a variety of national forest management issues, including single versus multiple uses, material versus nonmaterial values, holistic versus single-species management, use versus ecological protection, current versus future generations, and maintenance of biodiversity. These issues are broadly reflective of some of the basic principles or issues of the evolving concepts of ecosystem management and sustainability.[16] Respondents were asked the extent to which they agreed or disagreed with each statement. A five-point response scale was used, anchored at "strongly agree" and "strongly disagree." The fifteen statements are shown in table 13.3.

Table 13.3

Attitudes toward Management of the Green Mountain National Forest

Statement	Average Agreement Score[a]
1. Greater protection should be given to fish and wildlife habitats on the Green Mountain National Forest.	1.86
2. Greater efforts should be made to protect the remaining undisturbed forests on the Green Mountain National Forest.	1.83
3. Management of the Green Mountain National Forest should emphasize a wide range of benefits and issues rather than timber and wood products alone.	1.84

(Continued)

Table 13.3. Continued

Statement	Average Agreement Score[a]
4. Management of the Green Mountain National Forest should focus on the forest as a whole and not on its individual parts (such as bears and trees).	2.20
5. Logging on the Green Mountain National Forest should not be allowed to disrupt the habitat of animals such as bears.	2.18
6. The Green Mountain National Forest should be managed to protect basic ecological processes and not to favor individual plant or animal species.	2.52
7. The Green Mountain National Forest should be managed to meet human needs and desires as long as the basic ecological integrity of the forest is protected.	2.36
8. Human and economic uses of the Green Mountain National Forest should be managed so that they are sustainable over the long term.	1.86
9. The Green Mountain National Forest should be managed as a complete ecosystem and not as a series of towns or other political jurisdictions.	1.92
10. The Green Mountain National Forest should be managed to protect the natural diversity of plant and animal life.	1.79
11. The Green Mountain National Forest should be managed to meet the needs of this generation while maintaining the options for future generations to meet their needs.	2.02
12. Management of the Green Mountain National Forest should emphasize production of timber and lumber products	3.28
13. Clearcutting should be banned on the Green Mountain National Forest	1.77
14. Mineral exploration and extraction should be encouraged on the Green Mountain National Forest	3.76
15. Some existing wilderness areas on the Green Mountain National Forest should be open to logging	3.37

[a]The value 1 = "strongly agree"; 5 = "strongly disagree."

Study Findings

Findings from the two studies are highly comparable. Data from the study of the GMNF will be used to illustrate the issues of pluralism and convergence, and findings from the study of the WMNF will be used to illustrate the issue of contextualism.

Value and Ethical Pluralism

Study findings suggest that respondents embrace a wide diversity of environmentally related values and ethics. Table 13.1 shows that most potential values of the GMNF were judged as relatively important by respondents. In fact, eight of the eleven potential values received an average rating of at least "moderately" important. However, there were statistically significant differences among most of the values. For example, aesthetic and ecological values were rated as most important, and economic values were rated as least important.

Most environmental ethics also received some degree of support from respondents. Figure 13.1 shows that nearly all ethics elicited mean agreement responses on the positive end of the scale, and most drew at least "moderate" agreement ratings. Clearly, some environmental ethics enjoy especially high levels of support. All four environmental ethics in the "utilitarian conservation" category received high mean agreement ratings, particularly the "ecological survival" and "quality of life" ethics. Stewardship ethics were also widely embraced by respondents, with three of the four ethics in this category receiving strong support and the "future generations" ethic receiving the highest support of all ethics included in the study. A number of "radical environmentalism" ethics, which center on a set of arguments for the intrinsic value of nonhuman nature, were embraced by respondents, especially "animism/organicism," "humanitarianism," and "liberalism/natural rights." Environmental ethics in the "benign indifference" category, which represent views of the human–nature relationship that set nature apart from human moral and intellectual life, received an equivocal response from the study sample. Finally, "anti-environment" ethics, the most robustly anthropocentric of all categories, received the lowest agreement scores of all the ethics in the typology, suggesting that their currency among respondents is weak.

Further analysis suggests that there are relatively few differences in environmental values and ethics when tested by socioeconomic and cultural

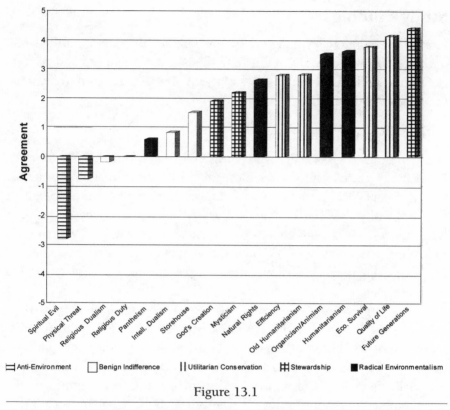

Figure 13.1

Support for Environmental Ethics

characteristics of respondents.[17] For example, when the New England sample was subdivided into residential (urban and rural) and racial (white and nonwhite) categories, statistically significant differences were found on only three of the eleven environmental values and six of the seventeen environmental ethics for residential subgroups, and on one of the eleven environmental values and three of the seventeen environmental ethics for racial subgroups.

Another analytic approach found statistically significant relationships between environmental values and ethics and attitudes toward alternative national forest management policies. Using regression analysis, environmental values and ethics explained nearly 60 percent of the variance in attitudes toward national forest management.

Convergence on Policy

The pluralistic nature of public environmental values and ethics might suggest that it would be difficult to reach consensus on resolution of environmental issues. However, Bryan Norton has suggested that both anthropocentrists (particularly those who rely on a sufficiently broad and temporally extended range of human values) and nonanthropocentrists (those who embrace a consistent notion of the intrinsic value of nature) may tend to endorse similar environmental policies in particular situations.[18] This overlapping of human and nonhuman concerns is to be expected, since in order to adequately sustain a broad range of human-oriented environmental values over time, the ecological contexts on which these values depend must also be sustained—a goal accomplished through the formulation of farsighted, multi-value environmental policy. Study data provide insights into the validity of Norton's "convergence hypothesis."

As described earlier, study questionnaires included a battery of questions about attitudes toward management policy of national forests. These questions focused on a variety of ecosystem-based goals and objectives. Study findings for the GMNF are shown in table 13.3. Taken as a whole, these data map out the sort of farsighted and multi-value environmental policies suggested by Norton. For example, the vast majority of respondents "agree" or "strongly agree" that (1) management of the GMNF should emphasize a wide range of benefits and issues rather than timber and wood products alone, (2) the GMNF should be managed to meet human needs and desires as long as the basic ecological integrity of the forest is protected, and (3) the GMNF should be managed to meet the needs of this generation while maintaining the options for future generations to meet their needs. Thus, despite the wide spectrum of environmental values and ethics embraced by the representative sample of Vermonters, there is overwhelming support for managing the GMNF to protect species diversity, wildlife habitat, and the overall ecological and social sustainability of this area. In other words, there is strong public support for the principles that underlie contemporary environmental paradigms such as sustainability and ecosystem management, and this support is drawn from a wide range of environmental values and ethics.

The Role of Contextualism

How can a community of people representing a wide range of environmental values and ethics converge on shared environmental policy? The answer may lie in the character or context of the environmental policy under study. That is, the problem at hand may suggest as much about its resolution as the range of environmental values and ethics that might be applied. The case of the GMNF, described earlier, may be suggestive. The GMNF is *public* land and represents the largest ownership of such land in Vermont. Moreover, much of this land is ecologically sensitive. The ecological and institutional character of this land may lead Vermonters to support management policies that emphasize maintenance of natural processes and that respect the need to protect this land for future generations.

To further explore this issue, the study of the WMNF included a battery of questions that posed three related scenarios, as follows:

This question asks your opinions about a potential management issue within the White Mountain National Forest and surrounding lands. The issue concerns beavers that live in this area. Beavers cut down trees and build dams. These dams cause local flooding, which can kill more trees. Should any action be taken to control the number of beavers and their actions? We would like you to answer this question as it applies to three different locations. The first location is an official "wilderness area" within the White Mountain National Forest. The second location is a "non-wilderness area" within the White Mountain National Forest. This area has been designated by Congress to provide for multiple uses, including sustainable timber production and outdoor recreation. The third location is "private land" outside the White Mountain National Forest. This land is owned by a commercial timber company. Please indicate the extent to which you think beavers should be managed in each of the three locations described above.

A five-point response scale was used, anchored at 1 ("the beavers should be left alone") and 5 ("the beavers should be eliminated or removed"). The midpoint of the scale, 3, was "beaver dams should be breached to minimize local flooding." Respondents were also asked to indicate the importance of each of the seventeen environmental ethics addressed in the study in influencing their answers to this question. A six-point re-

Table 13.4

Attitudes toward Management of Beavers

Land-Use Scenarios	Mean Scale Value[a]
Wilderness area	1.82
Non-wilderness area	2.66
Private land	2.86

[a]The value 1 = "the beavers should be left alone"; 5 = "the beavers should be eliminated or removed."

sponse scale was used, anchored at 1 ("not at all important") and 6 ("extremely important").

Study findings are suggestive of the role of context in resolving environmental problems. As shown in table 13.4, average scale values for the three management scenarios differed to a statistically significant degree. Respondents were more inclined to leave the beavers alone in the wilderness scenario and were more inclined to eliminate or remove the beavers in the private land scenario. Moreover, as shown in figure 13.2, respondents were remarkably consistent in their rating of particular environmental ethics as

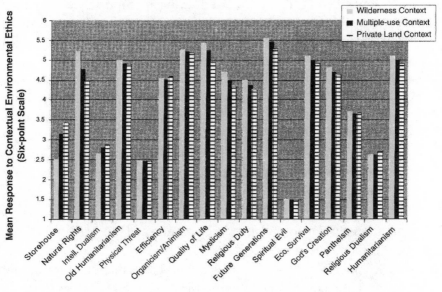

Figure 13.2

Environmental Ethics in Context

more or less important in influencing their decision-making process regarding the beaver dilemma. Thus, although respondents differed significantly in how beavers should (or should not) be managed in the three scenarios, they drew on the same wide-ranging set of environmental ethics. This suggests that respondents' environmental ethics underdetermined their specific management preferences. In other words, when respondents were presented with a real-world management scenario, they seemed to respond more to the empirical details of the problem (i.e., contextual matters such as land use and institutional status) than to the dictates of any universal moral principle.

Principles of Environmental Pragmatism

Study findings suggest that public environmental values and ethics are pluralistic but may converge on shared environmental policy, especially when the contextual details of environmental problems are considered. These findings, in turn, suggest a pragmatic approach to environmental philosophy and policy. Environmental pragmatism focuses on the contextual nature of environmental problems, respecting the ecological and institutional character of place and community and drawing appropriately on the diversity of public environmental values and ethics. Findings from this study are suggestive of an emerging set of principles of environmental pragmatism that might help build a framework for reconstructing conservation in the twenty-first century:

1. Environmental issues have important value and ethical components that must be addressed in the formulation of environmental policy. It is clear from the studies described in this chapter that there is a diversity of public environmental values and ethics and that these values and ethics can be related to alternative environmental policies. Information about public environmental values and ethics can be useful in guiding formulation of environmental policy that ultimately meets the needs of society.

2. Environmental values and ethics should be monitored over time and space. This can be done formally, through studies such as those described in this chapter, or informally, through political institutions

such as public meetings, referenda, and general elections. Research suggests that public environmental values and ethics have evolved over time to be more ecologically informed and more focused on holistic, future-oriented, and nonmaterial benefits, and this "social climate change" should ultimately be incorporated into environmental policy.[19]

3. The diversity of public environmental values and ethics must be respected in deliberations over environmental policy. Public environmental values and ethics range from anthropocentric to biocentric, and this range of values and ethics can be embraced even within an individual. Thus, it may not be productive to advocate any particular environmental value or ethic as a universal principle to be applied across a spectrum of people, places, or environmental problems. Environmental problem solving must be inclusive and democratic, not peremptory.

4. Pluralistic environmental values can converge on selected environmental policies as a function of ecological, cultural, or institutional context. Environmental pragmatism is as much an empirical, applied process as an abstract, philosophical one. Environmental problems have contexts that may shape their solutions as much as a priori philosophical positions. For example, ecological sensitivity, cultural significance, and institutional policy may signal the appropriateness of certain environmental values or ethics and their application to environmental policy.

5. A pragmatic approach to environmental policy suggests a diversity of environmental policies and conservation models. The inclusive, pluralistic, democratic, and contextual nature of environmental pragmatism suggests that environmentalism and conservation may take many forms. Variations in ecological conditions, cultural patterns, and institutional structure may lead to environmental policies and conservation models that vary across the natural and cultural landscape. Public lands in the United States offer a model of this policy structure, varying from the utilitarian philosophy of the national forests to the preservation philosophy of the national parks. Diverse environmental values and ethics offer empirical support for a correspondingly "patchy" natural and cultural landscape and a diverse mosaic of public lands.

Acknowledgments

Appreciation is expressed to the USDA Forest Service, North Central and Pacific Southwest Forest Experiment Stations, and The McIntire-Stennis Forestry Research Program for partial support of this research.

Reconstructing Conservation in an Age of Limits: An Ecological Economics Perspective

DAVID N. BENGSTON AND DAVID C. IVERSON

Throughout most of the twentieth century, natural resource management and economics shared a common moral philosophy (utilitarianism) and philosophy of science (positivism). The "gospel of efficiency"[1] that was so deeply rooted in natural resource management agencies, educational institutions, and management paradigms fit well with the gospel of economic efficiency preached by economists. As a result, economic thinking has had a significant influence on conservation thought and practice, much as economic rationality has colonized many other spheres of social life.[2] Driven by the goal of providing the greatest good to the greatest number over the long run, natural resource managers and policy makers have been strongly influenced by the reductionist theory of value and the optimization techniques of economics, often attempting to reduce multiple-use management to a mathematical problem.[3]

The influence of economic thought once served the natural resource management community well. Utilitarian rationality reflected the nation's prevailing cultural climate and belief system, and economic analyses have lent credibility to and helped justify natural resource management plans and policies in the eyes of high-level policy makers and politicians. But the emergence of global environmental problems, growing concern about the sustainability and environmental effects of economic growth, and major shifts in environmental attitudes and values in recent decades have raised serious questions about the relevance and sufficiency of mainstream economic approaches to dealing with conservation issues. The traditional economic paradigm is inadequate to inform conservation thought and practice in the face of the changed social and ecological contexts of the twenty-first century. Some observers go much further, arguing that environmental policies based on traditional economic analysis and social organization based on economic specialization and exchange are in fact among the main forces driving global environmental degradation today.[4] An ecologically informed approach to conceiving the value of nature and the relationship between economic and ecological systems is needed, based on a broader and pluralist theory of value.

This chapter traces the evolution of thinking about natural resources and the environment in economics, including the classical school, the neoclassical school, and the emergence of environmental and natural resource economics as subdisciplines within the neoclassical school. The changed social and ecological contexts for conservation are then described, as well as the search for sustainability prompted by the changed contexts. Important milestones in the search for sustainability include the emerging paradigms of ecosystem management and ecological economics. These alternative management and economic paradigms provide guidance for reconstructing conservation in an age of limits.

The Evolution of Conservation Thought in Economics

From the beginnings of economics as a field of scholarly inquiry, a minority of economists have focused on the central role played by natural resources in economic activities and the linkages between economic systems and ecological systems.[5] The first school of economic theorists was the Physiocrats, a group of French social philosophers writing in the mid-eighteenth century. Named for their belief that the universal laws of physics extend their rule to social systems, the Physiocrats emphasized the productive power of agriculture and land. As characterized in 1901 by economist Hannah Robie Sewall, "The fundamental economic postulate of the Physiocrats was that the cultivation of the soil is the sole source of new wealth."[6] Their land-based—or, more broadly, natural resource–based— economic theory identified the environment as the foundation of the economy and the ultimate source of national wealth.

Other classical economists were concerned with the earth's carrying capacity and long-term limits to economic growth. Best known of the classical economists were cleric-turned-economist Thomas Malthus (1766–1834) and businessman-turned-economist David Ricardo (1772–1823). The limits to carrying capacity suggested in Malthus' model and the limits to economic growth implied by the lower quality of the next available resources in Ricardo's model were in contrast to the widespread belief in progress in the nineteenth century. Long-term prospects for economic growth were not sanguine, according to the early practitioners of the dismal science. Ecological economist Herman Daly noted, "Classical economists thought that, over the long run, population growth and diminishing returns would unavoidably channel the entire economic surplus into rent, thus reducing profit to zero and terminating economic growth."[7] John Stuart Mill, who helped move economic theory away from the classical model and into the neoclassical era, was nevertheless influenced by classical economic thinking and wrote of the "impossibility of ultimately avoiding the stationary state" in his 1848 essay "Of the Stationary State." In the same essay, Mill also wrote eloquently of the undesirability of endless economic growth if it meant the obliteration of natural systems and natural beauty.

Subsequent economic thinkers downplayed the importance of population growth and resource constraints as driving forces as they developed the neoclassical, or marginalist, approach to economics. British economist Alfred Marshall (1842–1924) is often described as the father of neoclassical economics, although he was one of several economists who made key contributions in the late nineteenth century, including Carl von Menger and Léon Walras. The core concept of neoclassical economics is the role of the market system in optimally allocating scarce resources to their "highest-value" uses. The fact that markets and hence prices do not exist for most life-supporting environmental services undoubtedly contributed to the lack of attention to environmental issues in neoclassical economics. In addition, the world was relatively sparsely populated when much of the neoclassical theory was developed; it was a world in which the scale of the economy was small relative to the scale of ecological systems. Most economic textbooks throughout the twentieth century scarcely acknowledged the existence of the environment and said nothing about its role as the foundation of all economic activity. Instead, economists focused on the theory of utility-maximizing consumers, profit-maximizing producers, the process of market exchange and price formation, and, at the macro level, growth in national economies.

Another reason for the economists' lack of attention to environmental and conservation concerns relates to broader developments in the scientific community. The late nineteenth century witnessed a trend of increasing specialization in science, and by the early years of the twentieth century the economics profession was rapidly gaining ground as a distinct discipline and separate department within the structure of universities.[8] The separation and professionalization of economics quickly led to less interaction and communication with colleagues in other disciplines and incentive systems that rewarded only work within the field of economics. The result was isolation from the natural sciences and continued weakening of the link between natural resources and the economy in economic theory.

In light of these developments, the first half of the twentieth century is often regarded as a period in which economists showed little or no interest in conservation or environmental issues. But a small group of economists wrote about natural resource problems as conservation issues during this time. Some of these economists critiqued mainstream thinking and exposed its flaws, as in L. C. Gray's 1914 contribution to the theory of nonrenewable resources in which he explicitly recognized—in contrast to mainstream economic thought—that the intergenerational allocation of resources was an ethical issue rather than an efficiency issue.[9] These and other early contributions were largely ignored, however, by mainstream economics, which neglected the role of natural resources while focusing on refinements to its model of how the price system allocates scarce resources. Boundless faith in the price system, technological progress, and the substitutability of manufactured capital for natural capital led most economists to believe that the market could easily deal with any scarcity of natural resources.

The subdisciplines of natural resource economics and environmental economics began to emerge following World War II. Natural resource economists concentrated on renewable and nonrenewable natural resources as factors of production (forestry, fisheries, mining, energy, and land use) and regarded the environment as a source of materials that required special management because of their distinguishing characteristics. The rise of natural resource economics was stimulated in part by the booming postwar economy and the rapidly growing demand for raw materials, as well as concerns about dependence on foreign sources of nonrenewable resources. Along with this rapid and dramatic increase in the extraction of natural resources came the need for efficiency in production and utilization: both technical efficiency, which concerns natural resource managers, and efficiency in exchange, which is the purview of economists.

Environmental economics developed a bit later than natural resource economics, and it came to be recognized as a subdiscipline in the 1960s and 1970s. Growing concern about pollution and the rise of the modern environmental movement stimulated the development of environmental economics, which focused on problems of air and water pollution control and on the environment as a source of nonmarket amenities. The pioneering work of Siegfried V. Ciriacy-Wantrup inspired many who worked to establish environmental economics as a subdiscipline.[10] The establishment of the Association of Environmental and Resource Economists and launching of its *Journal of Environmental Economics and Management* in the 1970s were milestones in the institutionalization of environmental and natural resource economics.

As these subdisciplines grew and matured, environmental and resource economists pointed out the problems caused by the neglect of the natural resource base and environmental concerns in economic models. But, as part of the neoclassical mainstream, they generally insisted that environmental problems could be solved by means of market corrections, such as internalizing environmental externalities, ensuring that the "true value" of environmental goods and services are reflected in prices, and determining "optimal" pollution levels and depletion rates. Attempting to take account of the shifting and expanding set of environmental values in society during the 1960s and 1970s, environmental economists added concepts such as existence value, bequest value, and option value. But these nonuse values of the environment, as conceived by economists, are still narrowly instrumental in nature, based on aggregations of individual preferences measured in monetary terms.

Environmental economists' tinkering with the neoclassical model to deal with its environmental shortcomings has been likened to the work of Ptolemaic astronomers who added epicycles to their earth-centered model of the universe in an attempt to shore up a fundamentally flawed model.[11] The central flaw in neoclassical economics is its view of the economy as a closed system of production and consumption, symbolized by the circular flow model of the economy contained in most economic textbooks. Environmental and natural resource economists added to this conceptualization in limited ways by including the environment as a separate system that provides inputs into production processes (natural resources), a sink for wastes of economic processes (pollution), and a source of nonmarket environmental amenities (e.g., scenic beauty). But the vision of the economy as somehow separate from and largely independent of its biophysical foundations has had a powerful influence even on environmental and resource economists, as revealed by the opening sentence in an early review of environmental economics: "Man has probably always worried about his environment because he was once totally dependent on it."[12] Humans were once totally dependent on the environment, but, according to mainstream economic thinking, this dependence has been broken. This view of the relationship between economic and ecological systems stands in sharp contrast to the perspective of the Physiocrats and other classical economists, who saw natural resources as the foundation of economic activity.

In recent years, many mainstream environmental and resource economists have been bewildered by the declining influence of their recommendations in policy circles. For example, economist Paul Portney asked, "Will environmental law evolve to include a more prominent role for economic considerations?" He continued: "Writing from the vantage point of 1989, the answer would appear to be no. If anything, the more recent environmental laws . . . move somewhat away from allowing economic considerations in standard-setting."[13] The main reason Portney gave for the declining influence of economic recommendations on environmental policy is that economists haven't done a convincing job of explaining to policy makers why the monetized cost–benefit approach to environmental policy is advantageous. Neoclassical environmental and natural resource economists seldom, if ever, ponder the possibility that waning interest from policy makers may be due to flaws and limitations of the economic paradigm from which their policy recommendations flow. Nor do they consider that the growing irrelevance of neoclassical prescriptions may be due to the changed context for conservation that we find ourselves in today. But the social and ecological contexts and the nature of environmental problems—now global in scale—have shifted dramatically, as discussed in the following section.

The Changed Context for Conservation

The social landscape of today would be unrecognizable to conservationists of a few generations ago, as a result of a wide range of social changes. Globally, most important is the fact that the earth's human population recently surpassed 6 billion and, according to projections from the United Nations Population Division, is headed toward 8 billion to 11 billion by the year 2050. In the United States—the most rapidly growing developed country—population has doubled since the 1960s and is projected to increase by another 50 percent by the year 2050. Economic growth and rapid urbanization have accompanied population growth, resulting in an increase in the demand for natural resources and increased strain on the ecological systems that produce these resources. Urban growth and sprawling development patterns have been identified as the most significant factor affecting forest ecosystems in the southern United States, and urbanization is the leading cause of habitat loss and species endangerment in the mainland United States.[14]

Other demographic changes include an increasingly multicultural and multi-ethnic society and a shift in place of residence from rural to urban areas, with more than 80 percent of Americans now living in metropolitan areas and more than 50 percent living in suburbs.[15] Both of these trends imply shifts in environmental attitudes and values, and social scientists have found strong evidence of fundamental change in environmental values in recent years. Environmental values have shifted, expanded, and gone mainstream since the beginnings of the modern environmental movement in the 1960s. Social scientists have found remarkable agreement on core environmental values among diverse social groups and have concluded that current environmental beliefs, values, and cultural models represent a major change in the way we conceive of our relationship with nature. As wilderness and undeveloped natural areas have become increasingly scarce, the ecological, moral, and aesthetic values of the environment have become increasingly important and economic or utilitarian values have become relatively less important.[16] Polling data indicate that environmental health and quality had been transformed from an issue of limited concern in the late 1960s and early 1970s to a settled issue of universal concern by the 1990s: "Large majorities of Americans across all classes and social groups are deeply committed to a safe and healthful environment."[17] Countless additional demographic, economic, cultural, political, and technological changes could be listed. But these few examples illustrate the nature of the changing social context for conservation and the magnitude of these changes.

Even more striking is the ecological context for conservation, which has been transformed by the growing influence of economic activities. Humans have extensively altered the natural landscape locally and regionally throughout history, sometimes unsustainably and with disastrous effects.[18] But the explosive growth in population and economic activity and the increased power of technology have greatly magnified our effects on natural systems, including consequences at the global scale. Some examples of the effects of economic activities on the global ecosystem make this point abundantly clear:[19]

- Logging and conversion of forests have shrunk the world's forest cover by about one-half, and remaining forests are being fragmented by roads, farms, residences, and urban growth.
- We are currently in an era of species extinctions that is unprecedented in human history.
- An estimated 75 percent of the world's major marine fish stocks either are depleted from overfishing or are being fished at their biological limit.
- Humans now use an estimated 54 percent of accessible surface freshwater; it is estimated that the rate of pumping of groundwater by the world's farmers exceeds natural recharge rates by at least 209 billion cubic yards each year.
- Sixty-five percent of the approximately 3.7 billion acres of cropland worldwide have experienced some degree of soil degradation.
- Between one-third and one-half of the earth's land surface has been transformed by human economic activity.
- Humans appropriate about 25 percent of potential total global net primary productivity and 40 percent of terrestrial net primary productivity.
- The concentration of carbon dioxide in the atmosphere has increased by about 30 percent since the industrial revolution, with almost half of that increase coming since 1959.
- Humans move more earth each year than all the traditional forces of nature—rivers, winds, and oceans—combined, and the rate is increasing.
- More than half of the original wetlands of the lower forty-eight states of the United States have been lost. The rate of loss is slowing, but loss of wetlands continues.

The list of momentous anthropogenic effects on the earth could go on and on: stratospheric ozone depletion, growing evidence of global climate change, and the like. But it is clear that the magnitude of human-induced environmental change is enormous.

Collectively, these unprecedented ecological and social changes imply a new relationship between humans and nature and a new context for conservation. The scale of human economic activity has increased dramatically relative to the scale of the earth's life support systems. We have rapidly made the transition from a relatively "empty world" in terms of humans and the human footprint on the landscape to a "full world" in which the consequences of economic activities are dominant.[20] This represents a watershed in the development of economic systems. Throughout human history, manufactured capital and labor have been the scarcest, or limiting, factors in economic growth. We have now entered an era in which increasingly scarce natural capital—the stock that yields the flow of natural resources and ecological services—is the limiting factor. But this turning point has gone largely unnoticed for a variety of reasons that allow us to ignore a wide range of social and environmental costs of economic activities, including the failure to account for depletion of natural capital in national income accounting.[21] As a result, the ecological systems on which all economic activity—and life itself—depends are undergoing rapid changes that threaten social and economic well-being and sustainability.

There are, therefore, limits to the growth of economic activity on a finite planet: the classical economists had it right. A point is reached at which economic growth becomes uneconomic—that is, the costs of aggregate economic activity outweigh the benefits. In 1992, the Union of Concerned Scientists issued its *World Scientists' Warning to Humanity*, signed by about 1,700 of the world's most prominent scientists, including the majority of Nobel laureates in the sciences. This declaration is a clear and forceful statement of the need to recognize environmental limits and the need for a changed relationship between society and nature:

> The earth is finite. Its ability to absorb wastes and destructive effluent is finite. Its ability to provide food and energy is finite. Its ability to provide for growing numbers of people is finite. And we are fast approaching many of the earth's limits. Current economic practices which damage the environment, in both developed and underdeveloped nations, cannot be continued without the risk that vital global systems will be damaged beyond repair.[22]

What is less clear is the *nature* of the limits to economic growth. As we approach limits to material and energy resources, waste absorption capacity, and so on, are we likely to experience catastrophic ecological collapse, as some have warned? Or are the limits to economic growth and related en-vironmental degradation more likely to be continuous and gradual?[23] Cer-tainly, there are many examples of localized ecological collapse, such as the collapse of a fishery, and the possibility exists of catastrophic thresholds at larger spatial scales. An example is the possibility of global warming bring-ing about abrupt, large-scale changes in ocean circulation patterns, which in turn could cause significant and rapid changes in world climate. But in general, most environmental degradation is more like a gradual fraying of the web of life, a slow but inexorable reduction of our options and erosion of possibilities for future generations. Yet more immediate than the bio-physical limits to growth may be the social limits as people are forced to confront the extent of loss of beauty, degradation of sacred space, and ero-sion of quality of life they are willing to withstand.

The Search for Sustainability in an Age of Limits

The changed context for conservation has prompted a worldwide search for policies, institutions, and ways of thinking that will move us toward sustainability. This search is manifested in many ways and at all spatial scales, including global efforts such as the Earth Summit (United Nations Conference on Environment and Development, or UNCED), held in Rio de Janeiro in 1992, and the "Rio+10" World Summit on Sustainable Develop-ment, held in Johannesburg in 2002; national efforts such as the President's Council on Sustainable Development in the United States; and thousands of local efforts around the world, such as the sustainable cities and com-munities movement. In natural resource management, concerns about sus-tainability have been central from the earliest days of modern resource management. But the meaning of sustainability has evolved considerably over time. Many notions of sustainability have been suggested, ranging from dominant product sustainability (reflecting a strongly anthropocentric perspective) to ecosystem benefit sustainability (reflecting a strongly bio-centric perspective).[24] Economists have tended to favor an anthropocentric approach to sustainability that focuses on nondecreasing human welfare over time, and they often adopt a "weak sustainability" concept that as-sumes the loss of natural capital can be compensated by the substitution of manufactured or human capital.[25] But notions of "strong sustainability" that assume limits to the extent to which natural capital can be substituted for other forms of capital and that emphasize the interdependencies between ecological and economic systems have gained favor in recent years.[26] This section discusses ecosystem management and ecological economics, both of which reflect the shift toward strong and ecologically informed approaches to sustainability.

The emergence of ecosystem management is a manifestation of the search for sustainability in response to the changed context for conservation. Natural resource management agencies in the United States began to adopt an ecosystem approach to the management of public lands in the late 1980s and early 1990s. By the mid-1990s, ecosystem management initiatives and activities were taking place in eighteen federal agencies and had been adopted or endorsed by a growing number of state agencies as well as private firms and associations.[27] Ecosystem management can be seen in part as a response to new goals for environmental and natural resource management that have arisen as a result of the changed context, including maintaining ecosystem health and ecological integrity, protecting biodiversity, and ensuring sustainability. Increasingly, adaptive management practitioners are adding systems resiliency to the list.

Despite the interest in and apparent growing acceptance of ecosystem management, a single, widely accepted definition has not emerged. The lack of consensus about a definition of ecosystem management is not surprising: a single definition of multiple-use natural resource management did not emerge during the decades in which this model was formulated and implemented.[28] A natural resource management model is too complex and dynamic—changing with new scientific understanding, professional experience, and social values—to be codified into a single definition that satisfies all stakeholders. As social scientist Thomas More observed, ecosystem management is a fuzzy concept "that contains practices, techniques, goals, and objectives that share overlapping attributes or characteristics. It is defined through these characteristics, any one of which may or may not be present in a particular project."[29] Ecosystem management is similar to the central but imprecisely defined concepts that guide other professions, such as the ideas of "health" for medicine and "justice" for law.

Several scholars have characterized the main elements in ecosystem management.[30] The following list is adapted from More's summary of the most widely discussed characteristics. The first three items are frequently mentioned goals, and the next two are important perspectives of ecosystem management:

1. Maintain ecosystem health (e.g., maintain and protect ecosystem integrity and functions; restore damaged ecosystems).
2. Protect and restore biodiversity (protect native genes, species, populations, ecosystems).
3. Ensure sustainability (e.g., incorporate long time horizons; consider the needs of future generations; include ecological, social, and economic sustainability).
4. Employ a systems perspective (e.g., take a broad, holistic approach to management; manage at multiple spatial scales and consider the connections between different scales; coordinate across administrative, political, and other boundaries to define and management ecosystems at appropriate scales).
5. Include human dimensions (e.g., incorporate social values and accommodate human uses within ecological constraints; view humans as embedded in nature).[31]

To this list we would add two additional characteristics that relate to the implementation of ecosystem management:

1. Adaptive management, in which management is conducted as a "continuous experiment where incorporating the results of previous actions allows managers to remain flexible and adapt to uncertainty."[32]
2. Collaboration, in which planning and management are joint decision-making processes that involve sharing power with stakeholders.

None of these seven interrelated characteristics alone defines ecosystem management, and all of them need not be present in a given project. But overall, these characteristics in many ways reflect responsiveness to the changing social and environmental contexts, and they provide clear guidance for reconstructing conservation in an age of limits.

Another manifestation of the search for sustainability is the emergence of ecological economics as a response and alternative to the neoclassical economic model. Ecological economics has been defined as "a transdisciplinary field of study that addresses the relationships between ecosystems and economic systems in the broadest sense, in order to develop a deep understanding of the entire system of humans and nature as a basis for effective policies for sustainability."[33] Essentially, ecological economics is an ecologically informed approach to economics. Ecological economics represents a reintegration of economics and the other sciences (biophysical and social) and a return to some of the classical roots of economics, including the view that the scale of the economy cannot increase indefinitely and must eventually reach a "stationary state," as John Stuart Mill put it in 1848. Although its origins can be traced far back in history, the recent emergence of ecological economics as an alternative paradigm dates from the writings of seminal thinkers such as Kenneth Boulding, Herman Daly, and Nicholas Georgescu-Roegen.[34] The International Society for Ecological Economics (ISEE) was officially established in 1988, and the first issue of ISEE's journal, *Ecological Economics,* appeared in 1989. Interest in ecological economics has spread rapidly, as shown by the formation of national and regional societies affiliated with ISEE, including the Australia–New Zealand, Brazil, Canada, Europe, India, Russia, and United States regional societies.

Differences between ecological economics and neoclassical economics have been widely discussed.[35] The differences run deep, beginning with the preanalytic vision or basic conceptualization of the economy and running through a variety of other ontological assumptions and disparities in epistemological approaches to understanding relationships and interactions between economic and ecological systems. Given space limitations, we are unable to discuss in detail all these differences.[36] Instead, we focus on the key difference: the theory of value. As economic historian Joseph Schumpeter noted, the way in which the question of value is dealt with in economics holds the "pivotal position."[37]

At the heart of neoclassical economics (including neoclassical environmental and natural resource economics) is a reductionist and narrowly instrumental theory of value. Economists assume that the ways in which people value the environment instrumentally—as a means to an end—in their roles as individual consumers exhausts the ways they care about it.[38] Economic value is based on an aggregation of individual preferences and is measured in monetary terms. Value is measured as the sum of individual's willingness to pay (WTP) for some benefit or willingness to accept (WTA) compensation for the loss of some benefit. Despite the limitations of this notion of value, economists view it as a meta-value that comprehends all others, as revealed in the following statement by an environmental economist: "Economics takes people as it finds them, and to the extent that such ethics [Leopold's land ethic] are present, they should express themselves as economic values."[39]

In contrast, ecological economics embraces value pluralism, which strives to include all the diverse values people hold for the environment, as well as the worth of life-supporting environmental services and functions that people may or may not be aware of. Ecological economists have proposed a wide range of approaches to environmental values and valuation, from nonanthropocentric approaches based on embodied energy or energy cost of production[40] to anthropocentric approaches that include traditional economic value based on people's WTP or WTA. Most ecological economists would agree, however, that no single theory of value or valuation approach can capture all the values of natural systems, which include both instrumental and noninstrumental, or intrinsic, values. The instrumental values of nature arise from the fact that "nature benefits us. Nature is useful: it serves a purpose, satisfies a preference, or meets a need."[41] Ecosystems are instrumentally valuable because of their utility as a means to achieve specific ends or from the realization of other values. Traditional economic value, based on human preferences, is one type of instrumental value. The economic value of an ecosystem is due to its utility in achieving human ends, where the ultimate end is maximizing preference satisfaction.

Ecological or life-support value is another broad concept of what is instrumentally good about ecosystems. Life-supporting environmental functions and services are good because human well-being depends on these functions and services. As with economic value, the basis of ecological value is certain tangible benefits that people receive. But unlike the case with economic value, people's preferences for these benefits play little or no role. Many people are unaware of the life-supporting benefits that ecosystems provide, such as atmospheric gas regulation, climate regulation, flood control, regulation of water characteristics and flows, erosion control, soil formation, nutrient recycling, waste treatment, pollination, and many others. Therefore, a simple aggregation of people's preferences or willingness to pay for life-supporting environmental services will not provide a meaningful measure of their importance. The benefits exist whether or not we are aware of the role of ecosystems in providing them. Life-supporting environmental functions and services are as essential to all economic activity and to life itself as the foundation of a building is to its structural integrity. The perception of life-support value requires an observer or valuer who understands why the foundation is essential—someone with some level of understanding of how ecosystems work and what life-supporting services they provide. Neoclassical economics cannot adequately incorporate ecological values in this sense because its theory of value reduces all values to human preferences.

As mentioned earlier, the value pluralism of ecological economics also recognizes noninstrumental, or intrinsic, values—valuing nature as an end in itself rather than a means to an end. We value our children and other humans in this way, in addition to valuing them instrumentally for the benefits we receive from them. They have "a good of their own"; they are not substitutable or replaceable. The majority of people today value the environment intrinsically, in ways that go beyond its contribution to self-interested goals.[42] A diversity of intrinsic environmental values may be distinguished, including moral, spiritual, cultural, and aesthetic values. Environmental philosopher Mark Sagoff has noted that our unwillingness to pay may be a better measure of the worth of these deeper values than willingness to pay: "It is fair to say that the worth of the things we love is better measured by our *unwillingness* to pay for them. . . . The things we are unwilling to pay for are not worthless to us. We simply think we ought not to pay for them."[43]

The idea of intrinsic value in this sense is alien to neoclassical economists because a fundamental principle of economics is that economic agents are motivated only by self-interest, not by broader ethical or social interests. Economists have, in effect, assumed intrinsic values—the most deeply held and meaningful of environmental values—out of existence. As it has been observed, "the purely economic man is indeed close to being a social moron."[44]

Conclusion

Adapting to change has long been the greatest challenge of conservation. The history of conservation in the United States is a history of responding to changing social, economic, political, technological, and environmental conditions. The Progressive Era conservation movement, for example, was in part a response to unregulated, destructive, and unsustainable exploitation of natural resources and opposition to that exploitation by a small group of conservation leaders.[45] Another example is the spate of major environmental legislation of the 1960s and 1970s, including the 1964 Wilderness Act, the National Environmental Policy Act of 1969, the Endangered Species Act of 1973, and the National Forest Management Act of

1976. These environmental laws were responses to growing perceptions of environmental decline and changing environmental attitudes and values.

Given this history of change and adaptation, we can expect that conservation thought and practice will continue to evolve in response to the changing social and ecological contexts outlined in this chapter. Part of this adaptation must be a rejection of the narrowly utilitarian gospel of economic efficiency of neoclassical economics, which had such a strong influence on conservation throughout most of the twentieth century. The economics of sustainability is fundamentally different from the economics of growth. The traditional economic paradigm is inadequate to inform conservation thought and practice in the face of the changed social and ecological contexts of the twenty-first century because it is unable to comprehend and incorporate all the diverse values people hold for the environment, especially noninstrumental moral and spiritual values and the value of life-supporting ecological services and functions. As a result, neoclassical economic thinking has led us to systematically undervalue our dwindling natural heritage. It has also exacerbated conflict in natural resource management by ignoring or marginalizing deeply held values that people care most passionately about. The changed context for conservation demands an approach that takes limits on the scale and effects of economic activities seriously and embraces a value pluralist approach that includes the full range of environmental values.

Without a broader, pluralist understanding of all the values associated with natural systems, natural resource planners, managers, and policy makers are a bit like the proverbial drunkard who looked for his lost keys under the lamppost because "that's where the light is." In the past, natural resource managers and policy makers have often looked to traditional economic analysis for guidance about difficult public policy issues. Traditional economics casts a bright light, and it has a role to play in the making of policy choices.[46] But economics illuminates only a small part of the overall picture, and the keys may be found elsewhere. Natural resource planners, managers, and policy makers need to grasp and incorporate the full range of environmental values and learn to manage for multiple values rather than multiple uses.

The Implication of the "Shifting Paradigm" in Ecology for Paradigm Shifts in the Philosophy of Conservation

J. Baird Callicott

For nearly half a century now, ecology has been shifting away from a "balance-of-nature" to a "flux-of-nature" paradigm.[1] By the mid-1970s, the latter had begun to eclipse the former in ecology, but non-ecologists remained, for the most part, clueless that such a sea change was occurring. In the early 1990s, the new, fluxy way of understanding associations of organisms and ecological processes began to dawn on the laity.[2] Not surprisingly, fields of endeavor that have been informed by ecology will have to take account of the paradigm shift in ecology that is now virtually complete. Here I suggest how the philosophy of conservation might be affected. I begin with a review of the dominant schools of twentieth-century thought about conservation, go on to review the shift from the balance-of-nature to the flux-of-nature paradigm in ecology, and, finally, suggest what the implications of that paradigm shift might be for an ecologically well-informed twenty-first-century philosophy of conservation.

Conservation *philosophy* has been primarily an American enterprise, precisely because the *practice* of conservation, traditional in many European and Asian societies and in pre-Columbian North American societies, was suspended after the conquest of the New World by the Old. The indigenous populations of the Western Hemisphere suffered a demographic disaster during the first century after European contact. Old World diseases such as smallpox and influenza wiped out an estimated 90 percent of the microbially inexperienced human populations of the New World.[3] With a

proportionate reduction of cultural predation (i.e., human hunting pressure), horticulture, and cultural fire, wildlife populations soared and forests
regenerated throughout the Nearctic.[4] When European settlers began gradually to spread across the North American continent during the seventeenth, eighteenth, and nineteenth centuries, they encountered a nouvelle
"wilderness condition" and superabundant plant and animal resources. As
long as more unharvested and unclaimed timber and game could be found
over the next hill or across the next river, no one gave a thought to conserving forests or wildlife. With the completion of a transcontinental railroad, the conquest of the Plains Indians, and the wholesale slaughter of the
vast herds of bison—all during the last quarter of the nineteenth century—
the midcontinental North American frontier palpably closed.[5] By the end
of the nineteenth century, wildlife had actually become scarce and deforestation rampant in the United States. Conservation was necessary, but for
nearly three centuries, no one had theorized it. The situation was ripe for
the birth of a philosophy of conservation.

Three Paradigms in the Philosophy of Conservation

From the mid-19th century to the mid-20th, three distinct paradigms
emerged in the philosophy of conservation: preservationism, resourcism,
and harmonization.

Preservationism

The first staunch protest against the unrestrained exploitation of American
forests and wildlife was articulated by Henry David Thoreau. Thoreau was
an associate of Ralph Waldo Emerson, a leading exponent of a religio-
philosophical movement called transcendentalism. In his essay *Nature,*
Emerson posited the existence of a noumenal reality that lies beyond the
phenomena disclosed by the senses.[6] One must leave "the streets of the
city," all "society," and even one's private "chamber" to find a genuine solitude; and alone in "Nature," more particularly in "the woods" and in "the
wilderness," a person might transcend the finitude of ordinary existence
and become one with the "Universal Being."[7] There, too, one might encounter the purest and most perfect forms of beauty.

These ideas had been vaguely anticipated half a century earlier by the
Puritan preacher Jonathan Edwards, who found "the images or shadows of

divine things" in nature.[8] Edwards was also a warm advocate of the extreme Calvinist doctrine of original sin, according to which all human beings are fallen and depraved. Historian Perry Miller argues that transcendentalism actually evolved from Puritanism.[9] The first generation of Puritans believed themselves to have been sent by God on "an errand into the wilderness," which they imagined to be the worldly stronghold of Satan, whose minions were the Indians. Taming and civilizing the wilderness was thus more than a utilitarian task for William Bradford, John Winthrop, Cotton Mather, and Michael Wigglesworth in the seventeenth century; it was a crusade.[10] By Edwards' time, a century after, the errand into the wilderness had been successfully run. In New England, shining cities on hills had been built, farm fields cleared and planted to crops, the Indians and the large predatory animals exterminated or driven away. Sin and the abode of the devil had moved to town, in the eighteenth-century Puritan imaginary. Nature in New England had become less an evil realm of violence, chaos, and undisciplined eros than an unfallen realm of innocence, peace, beauty, divine order, and truth.

All these currents of thought gather in the writings of Thoreau advocating preservation of Nature (always spelled with a capital "N" in the writings of Emerson, Thoreau, John Muir, and others of like mind). In *Walden*— subtitled *Or Life in the Woods*—Thoreau finds solitude, solace, perfect beauty, and higher laws and truths in Nature.[11] Although Thoreau was not a Puritan in doctrine, his lifestyle was certainly puritanical: he was celibate, a vegetarian, a teetotaler, and a scold. Thoreau was also borderline misanthropic. His attitude toward his fellow "citizens" was a secular equivalent of Edwards' attitude toward his fellow "sinners in the hands of an angry God." In "Walking," Thoreau richly and concretely retraces the movement from city streets to Nature as envisioned in Emerson's ruminations. In that essay, Thoreau produced the enigmatic slogan that is so often quoted, "In Wildness is the preservation of the World" (and misquoted as "In Wilderness is the preservation of the World").[12] In the posthumously published *Huckleberries*, written in 1861, a year before his death, Thoreau actually proposes wilderness preservation, albeit a scaled-down version of it in comparison with twentieth-century ideas about an appropriate size for wilderness areas: "I think that each town should have a park, or rather a primitive forest, of five hundred or a thousand acres, either in one body or several— where a stick should never be cut for fuel—nor for the navy, nor to make wagons, but to stand and decay for higher uses—a common possession forever, for instruction and recreation."[13]

In the late nineteenth and early twentieth centuries, John Muir popularized and politicized Thoreau's call for Nature preservation. Muir is best known for his rapturous celebration of the "glories" of Nature, especially in California's Sierra Nevada range.[14] But according to Donald Worster, "there was a harshly negative side to Muir's vision, a disgust for human pretensions and pride that ran very close to misanthropy. Lord man, the self-proclaimed master of creation, was for him an ugly blot on the face of the Earth."[15] Like Thoreau, Muir was greatly influenced by the writings of Emerson. The intimate, albeit counterintuitive, relationship between transcendentalism and Puritanism is confirmed in Muir's biography. He was born in Calvinist Scotland, raised a Presbyterian, and force-fed the Bible by his father, Daniel, who could without hyperbole be called a religious psychopath.

Reduced to its essential elements, the preservationist philosophy of conservation comes to this: first, dualism—man and Nature are separate. This dualism is highly value charged. Man is fallen, depraved, and sinful; Nature is innocent, pristine, and virgin. For the most part, the very presence of fallen man, to say nothing of his works, rapes and desecrates pure and virgin Nature. For some select (or "elect") sensitive souls, however, Nature has "higher uses"—for aesthetic experience and as the site for a monastic sojourn, whereupon the pilgrim gladly endures Nature's spiritually cleansing hardships, embraces its solitude, and retreats into it from a profane and fallen human society. The wilderness sojourner ideally becomes so enraptured and transcendent that he or she is barely present materially in Nature at all. Emerson described it thus: "Standing on the bare ground,—my head bathed by the blithe air, and uplifted into empty space, all mean egotism vanishes. I become a transparent eyeball. I become nothing. I see all. The currents of Universal being circulate through me."[16]

This Emersonian vanishing act is carried forward into the contemporary wilderness experience. Ecofeminist philosopher Val Plumwood notes:

The presence and impact of the modern adventure tourist is somehow "written out" of focus in much of the land called wilderness. . . . The modern subject somehow manages to be both in and out of this virginal fantasy, appearing by wilderness convention as a disembodied observer (perhaps as the camera eye [or Emersonian "transparent eyeball"]) in a landscape whose virginity is forever magically renewed.[17]

Maybe this explains the otherwise apparently hyperbolic and overwrought rule requiring transcendental tourists to pack out—rather than thoroughly and discreetly burn or bury—all material traces of their presence in designated wilderness areas, even their feces.

The principal policy supported by preservationism is the cordoning off of national parks and designated wilderness areas, primarily for the "instruction and recreation" of the elite segment of the public capable of putting Nature to these "higher uses" identified and lionized by Emerson, Thoreau, and Muir. Such organizations as the Sierra Club (of which Muir was the founding president) and The Wilderness Society are the principal political manifestations of the preservationist philosophy of conservation.

Resourcism

Resourcism is more democratic than preservationism. The problem with the way hunters, loggers, farmers, and miners used American natural resources was not that such uses were consumptive and vulgar—as Thoreau and Muir insinuated—but that they were inefficient and destructive, from the resourcist point of view.

The first American thinker to make this case was George Perkins Marsh, in 1864. Two years before the word "ecology" would be coined by Ernst Haeckel and a quarter century before a distinct science known by that name would crystallize, Marsh's observations were essentially ecological. Marsh served as United States ambassador to Turkey from 1849 to 1854 and to Italy from 1861 to 1882.[18] He attributed the eroded and desiccated landscapes he found in the Asian and European countries around the Mediterranean Sea to the deforestation of the region that occurred in the ancient Persian, Greek, and Roman empires. Marsh argued that ancient anthropogenic deforestation caused soil erosion, flashy streams and rivers, and, eventually, regional climate change and partial desertification. The deforestation then in process in North America could cause his country eventually to look (and ecologically malfunction) like contemporary Turkey, Greece, and Italy. That in turn could have severe economic and geopolitical consequences. The decline of empires, he believed, had more to do with anthropogenic environmental change than with social decadence. In addition to his economic and more generally pragmatic brief for conservation,

Marsh added a religio-ethical argument: "Man," he wrote, "has too long forgotten that the earth was given to him for usufruct alone, not for consumption, still less for profligate waste."[19]

In the concept of usufruct, Marsh got at one of the core ideas of resourcism. "Renewable" natural resources, such as trees and fish, can be consumed without depleting and eventually destroying them. But to do so successfully takes more than a concept. One must know the growth rates of various kinds of useful trees and the age at which their growth begins to slow, the reproductive rates of edible fishes and other wildlife, and thousands of other things about renewable natural resources to make them yield both plentifully and sustainably. Thus, to realize Marsh's idea of only skimming the interest off living natural capital requires the development, through research, of various applied sciences (such as forestry and fishery biology), the development of enforceable public policy regarding natural resources, and the creation of state and federal agencies to implement the findings of these sciences and enforce these public policies.

Further, public ownership of natural resources makes implementation of resource-related science and public policy a lot easier. Upon the assassination of his predecessor, William McKinley, Theodore Roosevelt—an outdoor enthusiast and nascent conservationist—became president of the United States in 1901. Among other signal accomplishments, he created the USDA Forest Service in 1904 and used his executive powers to add immensely to the federally owned national forests. He appointed Gifford Pinchot, who had been educated as a forester in Europe, as the first chief of the Forest Service.[20]

It fell to Pinchot to fully articulate the elements of the resourcist philosophy of conservation. He reversed the preservationists' virtual apotheosis of Nature. Their "Nature" became Pinchot's "natural resources"—a name that slyly implies the natural environment exists solely for human use. And in case one missed the point of that name change, Pinchot bluntly declared that "there are just two things on this material earth—people and natural resources."[21]

The dualism evident in preservationism was evidently intensified in resourcism, but the values charging the dualism were different. As the meme-line of thought ancestral to preservationism moved from seventeenth-century Calvinism to nineteenth-century transcendentalism, the Manichean value poles reversed in the way they charged the human–nature ontological dichotomy with good and evil. In resourcism, it was not that people were good and natural resources were evil; rather, people were privileged and natural resources were other-ized and objectified. They lost their identities as individuals, even as species, and became but raw material for human transformation into humanly useful commodities.[22] Pinchot deliberately assimilated resourcism into the broader utilitarian ethic then current in philosophy by echoing John Stuart Mill's summary moral maxim—"the greatest happiness for the greatest number"—with his own, "the greatest good of the greatest number for the longest time."[23]

Whereas preservationism is politically expressed primarily through often oppositional nongovernmental organizations, in the United States resourcism is institutionalized in federal and state agencies.[24] The Forest Service (housed, tellingly, in the U.S. Department of Agriculture) was the first and the organizational and philosophical model for most of the others, including the U.S. Fish and Wildlife Service, the Bureau of Land Management, and various state departments of natural resources. The National Park Service, more dedicated to nature preservation and higher uses, may represent an anomalous government institutionalization of preservationism in the United States, but as an agency it is the exception that proves the resourcist rule in the public sector.

Harmonization

Aldo Leopold single-handedly conceived a third philosophy of conservation. He began his lifelong career in conservation firmly in the resourcist camp. Leopold was educated at the Yale Forest School, which was founded by Gifford Pinchot, and joined the Forest Service immediately upon graduation in 1909, the penultimate year of Pinchot's tenure as chief. Leopold's passion for hunting inclined him to be interested in "secondary" forest resources, especially game animals. His earliest sketches of the science of game management, for which he eventually wrote the first textbook, were modeled squarely on forestry—a game population census was analogous to timber reconnaissance, the game farm was analogous to the tree nursery, predator control was analogous to fire suppression, and so on and so forth.[25]

Leopold's resourcist identity was obscured by his interest in wilderness preservation, for which he began to campaign within the Forest Service after about a decade in its employ. Leopold resigned from the agency in 1928.[26] And in 1935 he helped to found The Wilderness Society and even flirted with the prospect of serving as its first president, an honor that went to Robert Marshall instead, but only after Leopold demurred.[27] Given this trajectory, we are tempted to see Leopold as gradually moving out of the resourcist camp and into the preservationist camp. But that would be mistaken. Rather, Leopold rearticulated the preservationist agenda first in resourcist terms and then later in terms of his own novel philosophy of conservation.

While still with the Forest Service, Leopold argued that wilderness recreation was the "highest use" of certain areas of the national forests that were too rugged and remote to log, were too poor to farm, and had no mineral resources worth mining.[28] And by "highest use" he did not mean anything like what Thoreau meant by "higher uses." In the resourcist lexicon, "highest use" means, rather, the use of a piece of land that yields the most utility. For example, if a patch of old-growth forest is clear-cut, should it be replanted with trees that will, after seventy-five years, yield more timber; should it be allowed to quickly grow back on its own to early fast-growing successional trees useful only for pulp; or should it be burned periodically to create a grassland useful for grazing domestic sheep and cattle? Which of these is its highest use? In this sense, Leopold argued that the highest use of some Forest Service lands was wilderness recreation, and by "wilderness recreation" he mainly had in mind big game hunting and primitive modes of travel (by pack train and canoe)—his own preferred uses—not transcendental tourism.[29]

Leopold's confidence in resourcism was shaken by several experiences.[30] The first was a disastrous consequence of his forestry-inspired resourcist ideas about game management. In the mid-1920s on the Kaibab Plateau and again in the late 1920s in the Gila National Forest, after predators had been exterminated—in the latter case, at Leopold's own behest—deer populations irrupted and then, after overbrowsing and ruining their range, precipitously crashed. The second experience, in the mid-1930s, was a trip to Germany, where Leopold personally observed the untoward end point of intensive forestry. Generation after generation of even-aged spruce monocultures had sickened the German soil on which they stood, and artificial maintenance of deer populations had impoverished the understory of German forests. The third event was a hunting trip in the late 1930s to the Sierra Madre Occidental, where Leopold observed a robust but apparently stable population of deer in unmanaged forests coexisting with wolves and mountain lions.

That Marsh's proto-ecological insights lie at the fountainhead of resourcism is ironic, given that ecology was not among the sciences that resourcism inspired and that, in turn, informed it. For lack of anything better, we might term the suite of resourcist sciences "Newtonian biology." Resource management sciences focus on getting the maximum sustainable yield out of various species—ponderosa pine, rainbow trout, white-tailed deer—largely in isolation from one another. Leopold noted the futility of this conception of conservation in his plenary address to the joint meeting of the Society of American Foresters and the Ecological Society of America in 1939. "Conservation," he said, "introduced the idea that the more useful wild species could be managed as crops, . . . [but] utility attached to species rather than to any collective total of wild things. . . . The emergence of ecology has placed the economic biologist in a peculiar dilemma: with one hand he points out the accumulated findings of his search for utility, or lack of utility, in this or that species; with the other he lifts the veil from a biota so complex, so conditioned by interwoven cooperations and competitions, that no man can say where utility begins or ends."[31]

By the time Leopold had begun to view the world through the combined lenses of ecology and evolutionary biology, he had moved to Madison, Wisconsin, and joined the faculty of the state's flagship university.[32] A big part of his job—as professor of game management in the Department of Agricultural Economics in the College of Agriculture at a land-grant institution—was extension services. Leopold worked with Wisconsin farmers to grow wild game "crops" as an ancillary to domesticated crops.[33] In this middle landscape between the streets of the city and the wilderness, Leopold began to think of conservation as a harmony between people and land.

Both preservationism and resourcism were thoroughly infected with residues of the prescientific Judeo-Christian worldview. Preservationism is imbued with the Judeo-Christian idea of a fallen humanity and an Edenic nature. Resourcism assumes the Judeo-Christian idea of human privilege coupled with fiduciary responsibility—"stewardship," in a word. But both, however differently value charged, assert the radical human–nature dualism foundational to Judeo-Christian belief. Further, according to historian Brian Balogh, Pinchot's zeal for maximizing the utility and efficiency of natural resource exploitation was largely motivated by the "social gospel . . . [that] salvation lay in collective good works," which pervaded Anglo-American Protestant thought in the late nineteenth century.[34] From the point of view of evolutionary biology, however, people are a part of nature. Thus, in sharp contrast to both preservationism and resourcism, Leopold's harmonization philosophy of conservation was nondualistic and, more

generally, reflected a Darwinian scientific rather than Judeo-Christian religious worldview. Leopold conceived the human economy to be a subset of
the economy of nature. His basic idea was to reform the human economy
so that it complements and enhances the larger economy of nature in
which it is embedded, instead of disrupting and degrading it. He himself
worked to reform the smallhold agricultural economy of south-central
Wisconsin as a starting point.

From the preservationist point of view, the conservation norm, standard,
or ideal is wilderness, where, as David Brower once quipped, "the hand of
man had never set foot."[35] Such a standard, of course, is not an achievable
conservation goal in places, such as most of Wisconsin, that are humanly
inhabited and economically exploited—short of evicting the human population or exterminating it, as happened to the Indians all over the continent. Alternatively, Leopold posited an essentially functional ecological
norm for conservation that he called "land health."[36] Conservation—that
is, a harmony between people and land—could be achieved when human
use of land did not negatively affect such natural ecological functions as
soil building and retention; water retention, water purification, and streamflow modulation; nutrient retention and cycling; damping of the amplitude
of animal population cycles; exclusion of invasive exotic species; and retention of native biodiversity.

Wilderness, in Leopold's harmonization philosophy, was assigned two
new roles. First, not all wild animals can coexist with human beings, and
among these are the most charismatic—the big, fierce predators. Wilderness serves conservation as the vital habitat of "threatened species."[37] Second, it can provide "a base-datum of normality" for land health.[38] How do
we know what are the normal ecological functions of an ecosystem that is
humanly inhabited and economically exploited? By studying the same
functions in a similar area that is not so inhabited and exploited, Leopold
answered. As a resourcist, he had once argued that every state should have
a designated "wilderness playground," for the convenience of impecunious
wilderness recreationists.[39] As a harmonist, he argued that every sort of
ecosystem should have a representative wilderness set aside. These wilderness ecosystems could serve as scientific controls in comparison with
which ecologists could measure the departure from normal function—
ostensively defined by reference to control ecosystems, that is ecosystems
similar to those that were humanly inhabited and economically exploited.
In reference to such controls, conservationists could also measure their

own success in restoring ecosystem processes and functions to normality.[40] Leopold proposed the very place of his epiphany, the Sierra Madre hunting grounds he had visited in Mexico, as a base datum of normality against which to measure the ecological dysfunctionality of the ecologically similar but manhandled U.S. Southwest after it had experienced three-quarters of a century of logging, grazing, dam building, and irrigated agriculture.[41]

The Paradigm Shift in Ecology

Historically, ecology has been a contentious science, rich in competing paradigms—the superorganisms, the biotic community, the ecosystem, salient among them. But a deeper-running shift from a conception of nature in a state of equilibrium, undisturbed by humans, to a conception of nature constantly changing and disturbed by many natural forces is now largely complete.

The Balance of Nature

Early-twentieth-century ecology was almost as metaphysical as it was scientific. Frederic E. Clements, the most influential ecologist of his era, believed that "plant associations" were actually organisms of the third kind. He suggested, in other words, that the earliest organisms to evolve were single-celled and that after many generations of close symbiotic association, some single-celled organisms of different species had evolved into multi-celled organisms. Finally, he posited, these two levels of biological organization had in turn formed close symbiotic associations and eventually become components of a third level of biological organization— "superorganisms"—which were the proper objects of ecological study. As cells are to multi-celled organisms, so multi-celled organisms are to superorganisms; and as organs are to multi-celled organisms, so species populations are to superorganisms.[42] Consequently, ecology was often characterized as a branch of physiology.[43] Whereas traditional physiologists study the function and coordination of the various organs in organisms, the new ecological physiologists studied the function and coordination of the components (species populations) of superorganisms. Clements' own specialty was plant succession, which he conceived to be the developmental biology—the ontogeny—of superorganisms.

Serious discussion of superorganisms in ecology was accompanied by serious discussion of another putative ecological entity, the biotic community. Species perform roles or even have "professions," Charles Elton suggested in 1927, in the "economy of nature."[44] Just as in the human economy there are butchers, bakers, candlestick makers, doctors, lawyers, and college professors, so in the metaphorical economy of nature some organisms are producers (plants), others are consumers (animals), and still others are decomposers (fungi and bacteria). Each of these great guilds is divided into myriad specialists: various herbaceous, aquatic, and woody plants; herbivorous, omnivorous, and carnivorous animals coming in all sizes and shapes (or taxa). And just as human socioeconomic communities can be sorted into types (and subtypes)—hunting-and-gathering communities (adapted to tropical forests, temperate savannas, or arctic tundras), rural/agrarian communities (practicing horticulture, hydraulic agriculture, or aquiculture), industrial/manufacturing communities (making textiles, paper, or heavy machinery)—so biotic communities can be sorted into types: forests (tropical rain forests, mixed temperate hardwoods, boreal softwoods), grasslands (tallgrass prairies, short-grass prairies, steppes), wetlands (swamps, marshes, bogs).

Exasperated by both the metaphysical and metaphorical tendencies of his discipline, Arthur Tansley suggested a nonmetaphorical organizing concept for ecology. He argued that the proper objects of ecological study should be entities he called "ecosystems."[45] He was sharply critical of Clements' superorganism concept, especially as it was mannerized by John Phillips, a South African ecologist enthralled with the holistic speculations of his statesman-philosopher countryman Jan Smuts.[46] However nonmetaphorical it may have been, Tansley's ecosystem concept was almost as metaphysical as Clements' superorganism concept. He denied that ecosystems were third-order organisms but conceded that "mature well-integrated . . . plant associations had enough of the characters of organisms to be considered as quasi-organisms [and that] a mature complex plant association is a very real thing."[47] These very real quasi-organismic ecosystems were "relatively stable," had "a more or less definite structure," and exhibited "dynamic equilibrium," according to Tansley; in them could be found an "inter-relation of parts adjusted to exist in the given habitat and to coexist with one another."[48]

The ecosystem concept was greatly developed by Raymond Lindeman, who measured the amount of solar energy captured by the primary producers of an aquatic ecosystem and by the organisms at each succeeding trophic level (herbivorous, omnivorous, and carnivorous).[49] Soon thereafter, the primary fields of ecosystem studies came to be how energy flows through and nutrients cycle within ecosystems. But even in these quantitative thermodynamic and chemical ecosystem studies, Clements' organismic idea was latently present. Lindeman's mentor, G. E. Hutchinson, for example, characterized the study of energy flows through ecosystems as the study of their "metabolism."[50]

The ecosystem concept was further greatly developed by Eugene Odum. Like Tansley, Odum accepted Clements' belief that ecological succession proceeds through an orderly and predictable series of steps to a "climax" community.[51] For example, in well-watered temperate climates, opportunistic, invasive, herbaceous grasses and weeds are followed by woody bushes and shrubs, which are followed by sun-loving, fast-growing, short-lived trees, which are followed finally by shade-tolerant, long-lived trees that reproduce themselves in perpetuity. He then argued that as succession proceeds to climax, photosynthetic energy is increasingly allocated away from production of biomass and toward "maintenance" of the ecosystem— "namely, increased control of, or homeostasis with, the physical environment in the sense of achieving maximum protection from its perturbations."[52] Odum in fact revived Clements' original superorganism concept, but in a much more scientifically sophisticated guise.

The balance-of-nature paradigm in ecology is characterized by both typology and teleology. As are individual members of a species, each superorganism or ecosystem is a member of a type—a juniper–ponderosa pine forest, a tallgrass prairie, a tamarack–sphagnum moss bog. Daniel Simberloff critically traces this mode of ecological thought through Linnaeus and Newton all the way back to Plato.[53] As to teleology, an ecosystem will exhibit linear development through the same successional seres as other members of its type toward a single equilibrial end point, the climax. Tansley, Hutchinson, and Odum even believed ecosystems to be sufficiently robust as biological entities to have evolved by natural selection—which favored ecosystems that could achieve homeostasis, resistance to perturbation, "symbiosis, nutrient conservation, stability, a decrease in entropy, and an increase in information."[54] Hutchinson's evolutionary theory of ecosystems was intimately connected to the then prevailing belief that stability was proportional to diversity. Because biotic communities with the greatest diversity are the most stable, Hutchinson reasoned, they would outcompete less stable ones in the struggle for existence.[55] He thought this explained the great diversity of life. In the balance-of-nature paradigm, moreover, ecosystems are conceived as "closed"—open only to sunlight, rainfall, and air currents—otherwise, they are supposed to be resistant to invasion by outside organisms and to be internally self-regulating through such thermostat-like negative feedback relationships as predator–prey population dynamics and production–respiration equilibria. Further, in the balance-of-nature ecological paradigm, natural disturbances are regarded as exceptional events that are external to ecosystems. And, finally, human beings are regarded as disturbing agents external to ecosystems. Thus, the proper objects of ecological study are ecosystems that are substantially free of anthropogenic effects.

The Flux of Nature

Henry Gleason was an early critic of Clementsian ecology.[56] He argued that although various examples of a putative type of plant community often looked alike, on closer, quantitative inspection, the composition of each example differed so greatly from other examples of the same putative type as to confound organization by means of such a typology. Moreover, Gleason noted, the spatial boundaries between putative types of communities were often so fuzzy that it was difficult to declare where one began and the other ended, and the same was true of the temporal boundaries between successional seres. Thus, Gleason asked rhetorically, "Are we not justified in coming to the general conclusion, far removed from the prevailing opinion, that an association is not an organism, scarcely even a vegetational unit, but merely a *coincidence*?"[57] Gleason offered his own alternative explanation of vegetational associations. Each species is individually adapted to a suite of environmental parameters or gradients—soil acidity or alkalinity and nutrients, temperature, moisture, light intensity and duration, herbivory, and so on. Plants that are frequently found together in the same association are those that are individually adapted to similar suites of environmental parameters. The unique—that is, type-defying—mix of species in a given association is attributable to several factors. First, the peculiar combination of environmental parameters at various generally similar sites will often differ. For example, even though the temperature and moisture regimes of two generally similar sites may be nearly the same, the soils may differ. Second, plants living at the margins of their climatic, edaphic, or other environmental parameters may be present but more vulnerable to competitive exclusion by those for whom the same conditions are optimal. Third, the plants found at a given site will be those whose "propagules" (seeds or spores) chanced to have found their way there.

Gleason was virtually ignored in his own day, but by midcentury his observations began to be confirmed and his theory of stochastic propagation and coincidental individualistic adaptation to environmental gradients began to be believed.[58] Gleason's individualistic model of vegetational groupings was reinforced by a growing consensus in evolutionary biology that rejected "group selection."[59] Lacking inheritable DNA, typological biotic communities and ecosystems are not the sort of entities that can evolve by natural selection toward greater and greater internal "symbiosis, nutrient conservation, stability, a decrease in entropy, and an increase in information."[60] Decisive support for the individualistic view came from palynology. As Tansley graphically put it, "if a continental ice sheet slowly and continuously advances or recedes over a considerable period of time all the zoned climaxes which are subjected to decreasing or increasing temperature will, according to Clement's conception, move across the continent 'as if they were strung on a string.'"[61] But an analysis of pollens preserved in pond sediments indicates that the forest communities now existing were assembled recently—no more than 5,000 years ago—and that the trees that compose them migrated from different Pleistocene refugia, in different directions, and at different rates.[62]

A better appreciation of disturbance in ecology complemented the latter-day triumph of Gleason over Clements. Disturbance of biotic communities and ecosystems by such forces as fire, flood, wind, disease, and pestilence has come to be regarded as frequent and routine—so much so that ecologists began to recognize the existence of "disturbance regimes."[63] Disturbances at smaller temporal and spatial scales are often abnormal, external, and destructive, but at larger scales they become "incorporated"—periodic, internal, and benign. Thus, at a spatial scale of 250 acres and a temporal scale of 10 years, fire in a ponderosa pine forest is abnormal, external, and destructive, but at a spatial scale of 25,000 acres and a temporal scale of 100 years, periodic fire is itself as much a necessary and beneficial internalized ecological process as succession or nutrient cycling.

The ecological myth that diversity and stability are positively correlated was thoroughly debunked by Daniel Goodman.[64] Ecosystem processes are carried out by a relatively few "driver" species and the rest are more or less expendable "passengers," although ecology is not so exact a science that ecologists can know for sure which are which, and passengers become drivers and vice versa under changed circumstances.[65] Moreover, actual populations of predators and their prey do not obey the mathematical laws that they were believed to obey in the balance-of-nature representation, such that their populations fluctuate only slightly around a point of equilibrium.[66] They might even exhibit mathematically chaotic behavior.[67]

As open, ill-bounded, disturbance-ridden, directionlessly dynamic quasi-entities, ecosystems are hardly stable, that is, in any state of equilibrium whatsoever. Rather, they may temporarily settle into a "domain of ecological attraction" and then suddenly "flip" to another domain in response to the vagaries of the disturbances and invasions to which they are continually subjected.[68] For example, in response to anthropogenic fire suppression and grazing by domestic livestock, the arid Southwest region of the United States flipped from a mosaic of grasslands at lower elevations and forests at higher elevations to one in which the herbaceous grasses were replaced by woody brush and forests expanding downhill.[69] For another example, in response to heavy commercial fishing and the creation of the Welland and Erie Canals, which opened an invasion route from the Atlantic Ocean, the Laurentian Great Lakes flipped from biotic communities dominated by deepwater ciscoes and lake trout to ones dominated by alewife and sea lamprey invaders.[70]

Finally, the wilderness myth has been debunked.[71] *Homo sapiens* has been such a ubiquitous ecological presence for so many thousands of years that anthropogenic disturbances have been long incorporated into all the world's ecosystems (with the exception of those of Antarctica). For example, the great prairies covering the broad midlongitudes of North America were historically maintained by anthropogenic fires,[72] and the pre-Columbian ungulate populations of the intermountain West of North America were kept low by cultural predation.[73]

Ecologists S. T. A. Pickett and R. S. Ostfeld summarized the new, consolidated flux-of-nature paradigm in ecology:

> Ecological systems are never closed, but rather experience inputs such as light, water, nutrients, pollution, migrating genotypes, and migrating species. . . . Stable equilibria are rare, although some systems of sufficient size and duration may exhibit stable frequency distributions of states. For example, a landscape may be a shifting mosaic of patches or community types, and in some cases, the number of young and old communities can remain constant, even though specific spots change as a result of disturbance and succession. Successions are rarely deterministic, but are affected by specific histories, local seed sources, herbivores,

predators, and diseases. Disturbance is a common component of ecological systems, even though some sorts of disturbance are not frequent on a scale of human lifetimes. . . . And finally, landscapes that have not experienced important human influences have been the exception for hundreds if not thousands of years.[74]

Implications of the Flux-of-Nature Paradigm in Ecology for Reconstructing Conservation Philosophy

Because the philosophy of conservation is informed by ecology, the shift from the equilibrium to the non-equilibrium paradigm in ecology—from the balance of nature to the flux of nature—requires a thorough review and reorganization of conservation philosophy.

Caveats and Qualifications

First of all, we must be careful not to throw out the ecological baby with the ecological bathwater. Ecosystems may not be organisms or even quasi-organisms. And the problem of definitively determining an ecosystem's boundaries may be so intractable as to require a postmodern resolution—an ecosystem is ecologically constructed by the questions ecologists ask and will be differently reified by different questions.[75] Still, the ecosystem concept has not gone the way of phlogiston and the luminous ether in physics; it remains alive and well in ecology. Organisms may not be as tightly linked and functionally integrated in ecosystems as organs are in organisms, nor is every organism in an ecosystem strongly and equally connected to every other, but all are dependent on some others and none is wholly self-sufficient. Donald Worster, who helped popularize what he calls the new "ecology of chaos," asserts "the principle of interdependency: . . . No organism or species of organism has any chance of surviving without the aid of others."[76] And because actual predator–prey population dynamics may not be very accurately described by the Lotka-Volterra logistic equation,[77] and because in some cases such dynamics may exhibit mathematically chaotic behavior,[78] we should not leap to the conclusion that prey populations are not at all affected by predators and vice versa. The classical models may be too simplistic, but it is a question of developing more sophisticated descriptions, not of denying any predator-prey relationship at all because the classically posited relationship is not confirmed by observation or experiment. Finally, although ecological succession may not follow a deterministic path toward a fixed climax and the temporal boundaries between seres may be blurry, ecological succession, however stochastic and variable, does occur in nature.

Ecologist and historian of ecology Robert McIntosh, a leading neo-Gleasonian, offered the following caveat about too readily jumping to the conclusion that there is no ecological order in nature, however complex and disequilibrial it may appear to be:

> The implication of anarchy, or lack of any order, is a common misrepresentation of Gleason's individualistic concept, which some have erroneously said is a random assemblage of species lacking any relations among the species. Neither Gleason nor any of his successors ever said that. Not *all* things are possible in an individualistic community, only some. The resulting pattern is more elusive than in a purported organismic community, but it is certainly not anarchy or random. . . . It is doubtful . . . that any ecologist envisioned a community as a merely chance aggregation of organisms and environment lacking discernible pattern. Gleason and his successors recognized patterns of gradual change of species composition in space and time, in contrast with the putative patterns of change of integrated groups of organisms.[79]

Pickett and Ostfeld, the leading architects of the flux-of-nature ecological paradigm, offer a similar caveat:

> The balance-of-nature metaphor can stand for some valid scientific ideas. The fundamental truth about the natural world that the idea may relate to is the fact that natural systems persist, and they do so by differential response to various components. The idea also points toward the ecological principle that there are limitations in natural systems. No component of a natural ecological system grows without limit. . . . Examples are density-dependent processes (i.e., the tendency of populations to grow when small and shrink when large) and the existence of successional trajectories.[80]

These qualifications and caveats having been registered, what are the implications of the flux-of-nature paradigm in ecology for reconstructing conservation philosophy?

Implications of the Flux-of-Nature Paradigm for the Three Twentieth-Century Paradigms in the Philosophy of Conservation

The new flux-of-nature paradigm in ecology creates different problems for the three historical paradigms in conservation philosophy.

PRESERVATIONISM

Most obviously, the flux-of-nature paradigm forces a rethinking of preservationist policy. First, in an ever dynamic and nonteleological nature, what should we preserve? There are no "original" states of nature—no self-reproducing climax communities that will persist in perpetuity if only people do not disturb them—just multiple historical states of nature, temporarily persisting domains of ecological attraction. Nor are any ecologically recent historical states of nature free of anthropogenic influence; none are "pristine" any more than they are original. Preservationists therefore must consciously develop and defend criteria for determining which historical states of nature should be selected as worthy of preservation. And if they are to remain in the states that are selected, historical natural *and* anthropogenic disturbances will have be simulated. More generally, these inherently dynamic, ecologically open preserves will have to be actively and sometimes aggressively managed to hold back or redirect succession and to prevent invasion by weedy exotic species.

RESOURCISM

Resourcism may appear to be vindicated because nature is now thought to be less well integrated and organized than ecologists of Leopold's day believed. But, as just noted, the magnitude of the current paradigm shift in ecology can be exaggerated misleadingly. Single species of great utilitarian interest cannot be managed without regard to their relationships with other species and to the organization of the biotic communities and functionality of the ecosystems in which they exist.

HARMONIZATION

The virtual abandonment of the organismic model of ecosystems forces a rethinking of the harmonization conservation norm—land (or ecosystem) health—for only organisms can be said literally to be healthy. Frank recognition that land (or ecosystem) health is a metaphor combined with a clear articulation of the ecological conditions that the metaphor comprises might rescue this norm.[81]

Toward an Integrated Twenty-First-Century Philosophy of Conservation

The coincidence between the consolidation of the new flux-of-nature paradigm in ecology and the appearance of biodiversity as the norm for the new crisis transdisciplinary science of conservation biology in the mid-1980s is intriguing.[82] Obviously, the felt need to conserve biodiversity is a response to the realization, growing more acute over the last quarter of the twentieth century, of a global species-extinction crisis. But is there more to it than that? Perhaps the neo-Gleasonian aspect of the new paradigm in ecology shifted concern away from conserving problematic ecological entities such as biotic communities and ecosystems and focused it instead on conserving individual species, regardless of their utility as either resources or ecological functionaries.

Clearly—in view of the fact that the earth is fixing to endure only the sixth abrupt mass extinction event in its 3.5 billion year biography—the conservation of biodiversity should remain a central focus of conservation efforts and a cornerstone of any new, integrated conservation philosophy.[83] Biodiversity conservation may provide a means of integrating preservationism into a new twenty-first-century philosophy of conservation through an answer to the central question forced on preservationists by the flux-of-nature paradigm in ecology: What should we preserve? Habitat for threatened species is certainly a leading candidate for preservationist priority. Classic preservationism's beleaguered wilderness ideal might be replaced by the concept of a biodiversity reserve. Because of its long and tangled history and reversing value polarities, the very idea of wilderness preservation is confusing. Does wilderness exist for higher transcendental uses by elect, materially vaporous human beings; or for noisy, virile outdoor recreation by sportsmen and -women; or as land laboratories for ecological study; or as habitat for species (such as interior obligate species of birds) that cannot adapt to urban, suburban, and exurban human disturbances; or as habitats for big fierce predators (such as bears, wolves, and mountain lions) that do not coexist well with human habitations? Perhaps, in the "multiple-use" spirit of resourcism, wilderness might be preserved for all these reasons. But calling preserved areas "biodiversity reserves" makes their highest use clear and unambiguous—habitat for threatened species.

Other uses—transcendental, recreational, and scientific—might be made of them as well, but only to the extent that such uses are compatible with and subordinate to their highest use.

If directionless successional change characterizes nature, as fluxy ecology would have it, to keep habitat fit for threatened species in biodiversity reserves requires constant management. This is a point of focus for integrating resourcism into a new twenty-first-century philosophy of conservation. Resourcists traditionally focused on managing single species of great utilitarian value or interest. The lore of traditional forestry and wildlife and fishery management is being redirected to the conservation of threatened species irrespective of their utility as resources.[84] The only way to manage a species in situ is to manage its habitat, more particularly to try to preserve or restore the optimal environmental gradients in the habitat to which it is adapted. From the point of view of the new flux-of-nature paradigm, the principal way to do that is through judicious manipulation or fine-tuning of disturbance regimes.[85] For example, to conserve native fishes of the Colorado River, such as the Colorado squawfish and humpback chub, whose populations have been declining since Glen Canyon Dam was constructed in 1963, fishery managers, who are now familiar with the concept of disturbance regimes, believe it is necessary to simulate the annual Colorado River springtime flood by means of a pulsed high-volume release of water from the dam.[86] The first such simulated flood occurred in 1996, with successful results. The classic example is the conservation of Kirtland's warbler, which can nest only in immature stands of jack pine. But jack pine reproduction requires fire to open the tree's seeds. So only by simulating the historical fire regime in pine barrens can conservationists manage the vital habitat of Kirtland's warbler and thus conserve the species.[87]

The current emphasis in the field of ecology on disturbance regimes and on ecological processes in general has recently focused attention on ecosystem services—such as pollination, water purification, and regional climate modulation. Ecosystem services produce at least as much human utility as do traditional natural resources—such as lumber and pulp, sport and meat—which we may reconceive as ecosystem goods.[88] Thus, conserving them can be regarded as an updated resourcist project. Biodiversity reserves are necessary for maintaining viable minimal metapopulations of threatened species that do not coexist well with human habitations and landscape fragmentation. And they may be sufficient for doing so if they are many, large, connected, judiciously located, well designed, and well managed.[89] Such reserves are also necessary for maintaining ecosystem services, but they are not sufficient for doing so. Pollination, for example, is as needed in farmed and gardened rural and urban landscapes as in national parks and forests, and few biodiversity reserves will be large enough to maintain favorable regional climatic conditions or prevent soil erosion and flashy hydrodynamics. Conserving ecosystem services may thus be a point of focus for integrating classic harmonization into a new twenty-first-century conservation paradigm. We might begin to explore ways in which human economic activities can be reformed so as not to be disruptive of vital ecosystem services, such as the retention, modulation, and purification of surface water and groundwater. Indeed, conserving ecosystem services may so overlap or coincide with conserving land or ecosystem health that we can dispense with the latter, ecologically more problematic term altogether, without any substantive (or pragmatic) change in the harmonization philosophy of conservation.

Because Leopold believed that land health was positively correlated with native species diversity, his practical approach to harmonization did not match his conception. In fact, his practice was to scale down the neo-preservationist agenda. At best, the farmers with whom Leopold worked would, he supposed, continue to plow and plant, harvest and graze, as they always had done. He mainly asked farmers to resist the ever-escalating industrialization of agriculture; the use of chemical fertilizers, pesticides, and herbicides; and such efficiency-inspired and production-driven modifications of the rural landscape as stream straightening and wetland draining. And he also asked them to farm as mindfully of soil and water conservation as conventional farming methods would permit. Finally, and most important, he urged the farmers with whom he worked to dedicate portions of their smallhold lands—fencerows, roadsides, woodlots, stream corridors, ponds, marshes, and bogs—to wildlife habitat.[90] It was mostly in these "waste" lands (miniature biodiversity preserves) on the rural farmstead that native species would maintain land health or ecosystem services.

Leopold's vision of a traditional family farm oriented in these ways to conservation is still certainly laudable and beautiful.[91] But abandonment of the diversity–stability hypothesis in ecology frees us to think that ecosystem services may be maintained in ways supplementary to maintaining native species diversity. Wes Jackson, for example, envisions a radical shift in agricultural emphasis from annual monocultures (of wheat, maize, soy beans, and the like) to "perennial polycultures."[92] He and his associates are working to develop a mix of four groups of perennial plants—cool-season grasses, warm-season grasses, legumes, and sunflowers—bred to produce harvestable, edible, and processible seed. After the initial planting, no tillage will be necessary. In addition to contributing to the crop, the legumes will fix nitrogen from the air and make it available to the non-legumes as well, and the sunflowers will pull minerals and moisture from deep in the soil, thus reducing or eliminating the need for artificial fertilizers and irrigation. Because the soil is not to be tilled annually, use of perennial polycultures may conserve many of the most valuable elements of ecosystem health and services—soil retention, nutrient recruitment and cycling, water-flow modulation, and water purification, most obviously. Although Jackson's model for perennial polycultures is the structure of native prairie communities, the perennial polycultures themselves would be highly artificial, consisting of selected prairie plants (such as cut-leaf sylphium, big bluestem, and lupine) bred to produce edible, harvestable, and processible seed or traditional seed-bearing crops (such as maize, wheat, and soybeans) bred to be perennials.

In conclusion, then, a viable reconstructed twenty-first-century philosophy of conservation would consist of an integration of central features of the three twentieth-century schools of conservation, informed and transformed by the contemporary flux-of-nature paradigm in ecology. Consistent with the neo-Gleasonian focus on individual species, a viable twenty-first-century philosophy of conservation would put a premium on the preservation of biodiversity, even if diversity is not vital to stability (which is problematic in any case). Existing systems of national parks and wilderness areas—the legacy of twentieth-century preservationism—might be enlarged, supplemented, and connected by additions and reconceived as biodiversity preserves. Complementing these preserves, we might work—in the spirit of twentieth-century harmonization—to reform human habitation and economic exploitation of lands outside biodiversity preserves so as to degrade their ecosystem health and services as little as possible. Both biodiversity preserves and the lands outside them that are productive of both goods (resources) and ecosystem services will require active management—the legacy of twentieth-century resourcism—largely by means of simulating or fine-tuning historical disturbance regimes.

An Integrative Model for Landscape-Scale Conservation in the Twenty-First Century

STEPHEN C. TROMBULAK

Any discussion about where conservation should go in the twenty-first century has to first cast a critical eye on where it was in the twentieth century. What approaches did the United States take during the period when its population grew from 76 million to 280 million people, a time that also saw the spread of automobile transportation networks and industrial-scale agriculture, as well as the rise of both the suburb and megalopolis? And further, what do we think of the results of those approaches? Are we satisfied with how well we are dealing with conservation challenges as they are in the present time based on the legacy of these approaches? Although the history of conservation movements and policy in the twentieth century is complex,[1] approaches to conservation during that time can be fairly described by four general themes:

1. Society desired to maximize everyone's cooperation, approval, and happiness by designating, to the greatest extent possible, conservation lands as multiple-use lands. Recreation, resource extraction, and the protection of natural values were largely imagined to be conservable simultaneously on the same parcels of land. This is exemplified through the creation and management of a system of national forests. Much of the national forest land is managed to allow some combination of timber extraction, recreation, hunting, mining, grazing, watershed protection, and maintenance of ecological health. Other multiple-use lands include national grasslands, fish and wildlife refuges, and lands in the Bureau of Land Management system. The

philosophical basis for the management of such multiple-use lands was that if each use was practiced responsibly, the magnitude of all uses' effects on the health of the environment would be minimal, and uses would then be largely compatible with one another. Conflicts that emerged, such as the decline or loss of species that could not persist in the face of large-scale habitat modification, were often thought of, by the stakeholders affected by management philosophies, if not by management agencies themselves, as the unfortunate but necessary consequences of compromise.

2. Conservation organizations and agencies promoted entrenched, one-dimensional approaches to achieving conservation goals. Each approach was defended as a better alternative to all others and was promoted to the exclusion of all others. This has been mirrored recently in the international conservation arena by the polarity that developed in the 1980s and 1990s between the promotion of sustainable development initiatives and the promotion of parks and other ecological reserves. Some international conservation organizations supported one approach (e.g., rural development) in the belief that other approaches simply could not work. This theme is not without its counterexamples, of course, such as the eventual establishment of wilderness areas within conservation lands designated for extractive uses. But such exceptions were imposed from outside, rather than within, the managing agencies.

3. Conservation groups that worked in different domains of conservation rarely talked to one another. For example, there was little interaction among groups that worked in the areas of sustainable agriculture and forestry, wildlands protection, and urban redesign. This lack of dialogue was probably based on the belief that the groups' different goals (e.g., sustainable production or extraction of commodities, protection of nonhuman nature, prevention of sprawl) left them little common ground and made communication and cooperation unnecessary.

4. Many people had the expectation that a great deal of conservation could be achieved without the need for much direct action because (a) so much of the land in the United States was undeveloped, (b) American society created only a small environmental footprint, and (c) the magnitude of the conservation problem, at least in terms of the number of species at risk, was small. Complex approaches to

conservation, especially those that asked some people to forgo opportunities for settlement or economic development, were often believed to be unnecessary. It was thought that the few species at risk could just as easily be protected through regulation (or, rarely, proscription) of the actions that put them at risk (e.g., hunting) or through relocation to controlled environments such as zoos, aquariums, and botanical gardens. Species that could not be protected in this way were thought by some to represent an unfortunate but minor consequence of human development.[2]

As we look back now from the early twenty-first century, however, we can see that these approaches were insufficient for achieving conservation, for several reasons.

First Deficiency: Expansion of American Conservation Goals

The first reason these approaches failed is the dramatic expansion, over the last three decades of the twentieth century, of Americans' understanding of what the goals of conservation should be. In the late nineteenth and early twentieth centuries, conservation was focused narrowly on maintaining either the transcendental or the utilitarian values of nature, with different groups promoting one or the other of these goals.[3]

Yet, over the course of the twentieth century, biologists and natural resource managers came to realize more and more the nonanthropocentric values associated with nature. This view was earliest, and still perhaps best, articulated by Aldo Leopold in his "land ethic": "A thing is right when it tends to preserve the integrity, stability, and beauty of the biotic community. It is wrong when it tends otherwise."[4] Such philosophies expanded our vision of the true extent of the nature that we should try to conserve. This expansion first moved us beyond a concern for only a subset of species that had strong economic or emotional appeal to society to an embrace of all forms of life and all levels of biological organization, from genes through landscapes, or biodiversity.[5]

More recently, the conservation goal of protecting biodiversity was seen to be incomplete because it did not include consideration of ecological structure or processes and it was not intrinsically placed in the context of natural conditions. "Promoting biodiversity" was sometimes interpreted as "maximizing species number," regardless of whether those species would naturally be found in the area in the absence of the proposed conservation action. For example, clear-cutting was often promoted in forest management plans as a conservation action on the grounds that such silvicultural treatments increased habitat diversity (through enhancement of artificial edges) and often increased species richness.

Although the concept of "naturalness" presents an interesting philosophical challenge, it has both operational definitions and metrics for evaluation.[6] From the perspective of the practice of conservation, "natural" refers to conditions as they would exist if nature were allowed to operate in its own way in its own time.

Recognition of the importance of natural conditions as a standard led to development of the concept of biological integrity. First articulated as a conservation goal in the Federal Water Pollution Control Act Amendments of 1972 (33 USC §1251[a]), where it is stated that "the objective [of the amendments] is to restore and maintain the chemical, physical, and biological integrity of the Nation's waters," "biological integrity" refers to the ability of a community of organisms to maintain the same composition, structure, and function as it would under natural (i.e., nonanthropogenic) conditions.[7] What this means in operational terms is that conservation should seek to maintain all natural ecosystems, viable populations of all native species, and both ecological and evolutionary processes.[8] From an ecological perspective, any conservation strategy that aims for less is incomplete.

The development of biological integrity as a goal for conservation explicitly recognizes three important perspectives. First, species have at least some values that transcend their values to humans in aesthetic or economic terms.[9] For example, we recognize that all species alive today are the products of approximately 3.5 billion years of evolution, regardless of where on the evolutionary tree of life they fall relative to humans. Moreover, some communities of organisms are dependent on species that we in other times might have considered small, primitive, or unimportant. Yet, as George Perkins Marsh pointed out almost 140 years ago in *Man and Nature,* "Nature has no unit of magnitude by which she measures her works," and humanity should "learn to put a wiser estimate on the works of creation."[10]

Second, aggregates of species—called natural community types or ecosystems—have values that transcend the species themselves. For example, wetlands represent a distinct combination of species that can persist under a particular set of hydrologic, chemical, and even topographic conditions. The ability of wetlands to purify water, recharge groundwater, prevent flooding, and minimize erosion is a result not of the intrinsic properties of any one species in the community but of the emergent properties of the entire community and associated abiotic environment. So, too, with properties of mangrove forests, riparian forests, grasslands, rain forests, coral reefs, and kelp beds: all are based on the aggregate members, not merely on one or a few of their parts.

Third, nature is not static but dynamic. In fact, the persistence of many components of nature depends entirely on this dynamism. For example, intermittent fire is necessary for the short-term persistence of species such as the pitch pine (whose seeds can escape the cone only after it has been burned); long-term shifts in geographic ranges are vital for the persistence of natural community types in the face of climate change; and predation is often required for the persistence of species that are vulnerable to competitive exclusion by the animals on which the predator feeds.

Since the time of its inclusion in the regulatory framework for federal management of natural resources, the concept of biological integrity has come to play an increasingly important role in shaping federal management of the environment.[11] In contrast to the dominant views in the early years of the twentieth century, conservation biologists now recognize that the full scope of conservation requires attention to all species, all ecosystems, and the natural condition of their composition, structure, and function.

Second Deficiency: Growth in the Human Population and Its Consumption

The second problem with the approach to conservation taken during the twentieth century was the growth in the human population. The United States is no longer a nation of 76 million people. It is a nation of 280 million people who travel on 3.7 million miles of roads[12] that directly or indirectly affect one-fifth of the U.S. land area[13] and that uses, in total, about 3.4 trillion kilowatt-hours of electricity per year.[14] And now, whether we like it or not, whether we approve of it or not, the rest of the human race aspires to achieve that same level of consumption. It is, of course, a critical question of whether that is desirable, justifiable, or even possible in a world of more than 6 billion people who already appropriate nearly one-quarter of the world's primary production.[15] But it is pointless to pretend that global society is not going to make the attempt and that the pressure from both inside and outside the conservation community to facilitate that development is not going to increase.

There may have been a time when the human footprint on the landscape was a minor element of its character: agriculture was practiced in distinct areas surrounded by untouched grassland, isolated urban centers were separated by a greater expanse of wilderness, and patches of cleared forest were widely scattered among primary forests. But in the face of exponential growth, society's efforts to meet its needs for food and shelter and its efforts to fuel the social desire for ever-expanding economic growth and consumption have irrevocably put those days in the past.

However, the dominant approaches to conservation still seem to be predicated on the notions that these two deficiencies do not exist. As a result, the twentieth century ended with (1) a handful of species having gone extinct; (2) almost 2,000 species listed as federally threatened or endangered under the Endangered Species Act of 1973; (3) great loss of many natural communities, including wetlands (55 percent loss), old-growth forests (90 percent), and tallgrass prairie (98 percent); (4) an exponential proliferation of exotic species; and (5) yearly struggles to deal with the legacy of fire suppression, erosion, soil salinization, overgrazing, and sedimentation in streams and rivers.[16]

Our society has achieved many important successes during this time, both in terms of implementing visionary policies—such as creation of the National Park System, the 1964 Wilderness Act, and the Endangered Species Act—and in terms of the many species that because of these policies did not go extinct. But these successes can fairly be characterized as merely slowing the rate at which the erosion of the biosphere is occurring rather than reversing its trajectory. If conservation efforts in the future are to be anything more than an ultimately unsuccessful effort to hold back the tide of extinction, our society must do better than it did during the twentieth century.

An Integrative Model for Conservation

Fortunately, there is a way for our society to practice conservation better. Yet to actually do it will require that the conservation community (1) articulate explicit goals that include the full scope of what ought to be conserved in the biological world and (2) be willing to advocate for what is necessary to achieve those goals, regardless of whether it is politically expedient or traditionally acceptable. And further, the conservation community needs to advance these goals publicly, not just within the circles of academia or conservation organizations and agencies when out of the public eye.

To be successful, I believe that the central paradigm for conservation in the twenty-first century will have to be based on the following idea: dominant-use designations for specific locations across the entire landscape. This paradigm shift will require that society make decisions about what the dominant use for a given location ought to be and invest the funds necessary to help establish those uses in their designated places over time.

Dominant use implies that any given location would not be expected to maximize simultaneously all values or be expected to achieve multiple (and often conflicting) social and ecological goals. It is a spatially explicit approach to conservation in that it considers not only what conservation strategies (as well as what extractive uses of the landscape) will be promoted but also where on the landscape they will be promoted. It is, in some ways, an alternative to the policy of multiple-use designation common on many public lands, wherein a given location might be expected to provide for off-road vehicle recreation, grazing, and protection of endangered species. The term "dominant-use designation" is adapted from the work of William S. Alverson, Walter Kuhlmann, and Donald M. Waller,[17] who argue that national forests should be managed through the approach of dominant-use zoning.

This spatially explicit approach to conservation planning is not as idealistic as it might sound. The American public is already comfortable with the idea of dominant-use designation, even if it may not yet have thought about applying it across the entire landscape or to the extent that would be required to effectively achieve large-scale conservation goals. The continued existence and popularity of the National Park System indicates that society accepts the principle of designating lands and waters where the primary, and in some cases only, goal is preservation of ecological values. The recent public support in the United States for not opening the Arctic National Wildlife Refuge to oil drilling is another example of society's willingness to consider some uses of the land incompatible with—and subordinate to—conservation.

Further, many states protect soils that are of prime agricultural value from development, even if the development would be considered by everyone to provide a social good. For example, in Bennington, Vermont, the state's environmental board recently turned down a request for a much-needed expansion of a hospital to include facilities for elder care because the site of the proposed expansion would have been on prime agricultural soil.[18] Further still, society at large has staked claims to large portions of the landscape for major urban and industrial centers where there is virtually no expectation that those lands will also provide croplands, timberlands, clean water, or habitat for disturbance-sensitive species.

In short, society already designates dominant uses on the landscape. What it has not done is look broadly across the landscape to see whether the magnitude and spatial patterns of the designations are adequate to achieve all the articulated goals for conservation and to meet both social and cultural needs.

To develop a system of dominant-use designations, society would need to decide what kinds of uses it wants to plan for. It would be impossible for society to decide on this at too fine a scale, so the most useful conceptual model ought to be a simple one in which, at the coarsest level of planning, just three primary designations are considered:

1. *Stewardship lands,* where the primary designation category is the extraction of natural resources following best management practices, refined and improved over time, allowing for the sustainable use and extraction of such resources as food crops, animals, and timber. Land in this category could be thought of as sustainable agriculture and forestry land, although other sustainable uses could be imagined. Such lands might also include nonsustainable extractive activities, such as mining, to the extent that they do not degrade the landscape's ability to achieve its dominant use. In this context, the "stewardship" designation implies that it is land that experiences measurable human effects, but ones that are firmly moderated to provide for both human needs over the long term and the values of those aspects of nature that can persist in the face of such uses.

2. *Ecological lands,* where the primary goal is the conservation of wild nature, particularly those elements that cannot persist in the presence of a significant human presence. In the United States today, these are more commonly referred to as wilderness areas. Even

though it has recently been debated whether or not wilderness is a social construct and, therefore, is not an objective conservation goal,[19] this is largely irrelevant. William Cronon, in the essay that originally questioned the social basis for the wilderness concept, re-marked, "I hope by now it is clear that my criticism in this essay is not directed at wild nature per se, or even at efforts to set aside large tracts of wild land . . . for nonhuman nature and large tracts of the natural world do deserve protection."[20] By this, even Cronon ac-knowledges that, regardless of its philosophical origins, wilderness designation serves legitimate conservation goals. These goals include protection of species and natural communities that cannot persist in areas modified or disturbed by humans and whose existence is no longer supported by conditions outside wilderness areas, and they provide the best baselines for ecological normalcy present on the earth. Regardless of what one thinks about the social construction of the wilderness concept, one would be hard pressed to defend a com-prehensive conservation strategy that did not include wilderness areas as an integral part.

3. *Intensive-use lands,* where the primary use would be meeting those needs of society that cannot be met on stewardship lands, especially high-density occupancy, industry, and most, if not all, extractive ac-tivities that cannot be carried out sustainably. To some extent, intensive-use lands could also provide for goals intended for both stewardship and ecological lands because some elements of resource production and ecological protection can be congruent with inten-sive human use. For example, community gardens, urban parks, and greenbelts can provide for multiple goals, and their presence ac-tually improves the quality of life for the people who live there. However, it is important to recognize that not all stewardship and ecological goals could be satisfied there, so distinguishing these three separate categories for dominant-use designation is critical for achieving all the goals for conserving biological integrity as well as meeting social needs.

As stated earlier, society in fact already broadly conceives of these three designations. What has been missing in the approach to conservation that was dominant during the twentieth century, however, was careful and bal-anced consideration about how these three categories should be distributed across the landscape. By this it is meant precisely where on the landscape stewardship, ecological, and intensive-use lands would be designated. The "where" question needs to be driven by legitimate efforts to determine what is needed to achieve the goals for human and nonhuman occupancy on the land and by recognition that there are more valid goals than simply those any single person holds dear. Conservationists would need to acknowledge that people have needs and rights, and extractivists would need to recognize that wild nature has needs and rights as well.

The "where" question also needs to be addressed through defensible science and economics. This is dangerous territory because some have used the argument for "sound science" to hinder the understanding and application of legitimate science to a whole host of social issues, ranging from the health effects of tobacco to the environmental consequences of pesticides.[21] Nevertheless, the identification of ecological lands needs to involve a strong scientific understanding of what is required to achieve the goals of protecting and restoring biological integrity. It should not be based solely on acquiring lands that merely have high recreational value (e.g., classic "rock and ice" ecological reserves), are inexpensive, or are not controversial. Society has a legitimate expectation that this be true. This expectation of a strong scientific basis for identifying ecological lands needs to be coupled, in turn, with the expectation that a system of ecological lands sited across the landscape based on defensible science to achieve comprehensive ecological goals will be taken seriously by policy makers.

With respect to the science that underlies the procedures for answering the "where" question for ecological lands, the tools necessary to identify the specific locations on the landscape that, taken together, are necessary to protect and restore biological integrity are reasonably well developed. Mathematical approaches to identifying collections of sites that, taken together, optimize solutions for meeting specified conservation goals, such as achieving a minimum number of separate populations of a group of focal species or communities, are now commonplace.[22] Many of these analytic tools have been packaged in applications that run on personal computers (e.g., Sites[23] and MARXAN[24]) and that planners can use to identify critical sets of ecological lands over any area for which data are available. The quality of the identified set with respect to its ability to achieve comprehensive conservation goals is now limited only by the quality of the available data on the locations of such biological entities as species and communities. With the growing use of citizen-initiated biological inventories, remote sensing, and Global Positioning System (GPS) technology, the quality of these data is improving at lightning speed, leading to a great increase in confidence in the ability of proposed systems of ecological lands to achieve the conservation goals set for them.

Similar to the developments in the science that underlies the siting of ecological lands is the science that underlies policies for sustainable resource extraction, such as sustainable agriculture and sustainable forestry, and in the social sciences, particularly the economics of developing sustainable communities. Taken together, these approaches can lead to the development of an integrated plan for dominant-use designations that identifies where on the landscape areas ought to be designated for a balanced approach to conservation, sustainable extraction, and various forms of intensive use by humans.

This approach to integrating different desired uses of a landscape by allocating dominant uses to different areas across a landscape grows from approaches to siting ecological reserve systems first advocated in the 1970s by the United Nations Educational, Scientific and Cultural Organization (UNESCO) in its Man and the Biosphere Program[25] and later refined by such conservation advocacy groups as the Wildlands Project.[26] The difference here is one of extent rather than of kind; attention to the distributional patterns of each dominant use—stewardship, conservation, and intensive human use—is made explicit.

Such a model raises obvious questions. First, what is the spatial scale over which such planning would occur? Clearly, adopting an approach of dominant-use designation without considering the scale of planning potentially leads to abuses through the expectation that some regions of the country would primarily achieve some goals (e.g., meeting ecological needs) and other regions would achieve other goals (e.g., meeting social needs). This expectation is unrealistic, however, if for no other reason than that ecological goals for an area as large as the United States cannot be achieved by focusing efforts primarily in one or a few regions. Relatively few species have their natural distributions across the entire continent, and the tremendous climatological and geographic diversity seen in the United States demands that all parts of the country participate in achieving conservation goals. From an ecological perspective, such planning should take place at the scale of the ecoregion,[27] regions of the country that share common geographic and biological characteristics, with each ecoregion engaged in identifying stewardship, ecological, and intensive-use lands as appropriate.

Second, how would this planning be done? Such an effort could be carried out in a top-down manner that largely involved planners, scientists, and government employees. Similarly, it could be carried out from the bottom up, largely involving local citizen groups who use information provided by others to reach decisions on use designations within their region. Neither approach taken alone would succeed. Numerous examples of planning initiatives indicate that distrust among stakeholders, self-interest, and misunderstanding of the relevant issues would almost certainly lead ultimately to a lack of support for any plan developed without participation by stakeholders, managers, and planners. Even with widespread participation, such problems are not easily overcome,[28] but the best chance of success for this model is to improve the social tools for including multiple parties in planning initiatives rather than reducing the number of parties involved.

Third, how will all of this—both the planning and the acquisition of land that would be dedicated to public uses—be funded? I believe that this approach is the only one that will achieve conservation, given the twenty-first-century realities of the biosphere and the human race. Achieving the goals of conservation is of utmost importance not only for the health of the natural world but also for the quality of life for humans; thus, this approach ultimately needs to be deemed important enough to be funded by the public. Society cannot expect reallocation of the dominant uses of lands to happen solely through the altruism of the private landowner. Fortunately, such altruism, although desirable, is not required. Improvements in the management plans of existing ecological lands, the purchase of new ecological lands from willing sellers, economic incentives to promote sustainable practices on stewardship lands, and public investment in developing sustainable communities are all possible and can contribute to the bulk of the necessary change.

Finally, how long will it take to implement such an approach across the country? The correct answer to this is, clearly, a long time. This should not be a surprise. It took several decades to create the current situation. It will take several decades to implement this new model in full. Yet the model could be advanced in some regions of the country sooner than in others. Credible proposals for the siting of ecological lands have been developed in parts of the country, including the Coast Ranges of Oregon,[29] the Klamath and Siskiyou Mountains of southern Oregon and northern California,[30] the

Sky Islands region of Arizona and New Mexico,[31] and Florida.[32] Development of citizen-based groups to integrate such plans into larger, regionwide strategies to identify priorities for stewardship and intensive use could, in principle, be accomplished relatively quickly.

Barriers to the Proposed Model

Achieving this vision will, of course, not be easy. In fact, it will be more difficult than we can possibly imagine. The difficulty lies in our need to overcome several barriers caused by limitations in our thinking about the causes and consequences of the present conservation challenge.

First, we fundamentally have to accept the reality that conditions in the United States at the start of the twenty-first century are not the same as they were at the start of the twentieth century. Our opportunities for dealing with problems are now dramatically different from what they used to be because of the increased number of people, the increased use of technology, and the increased environmental effects of those technologies. To pretend that new solutions to conservation problems are not needed because they challenge our traditional approaches is, at best, naïve and myopic.

Second, we have to recognize that conservation requires more than simply protecting scenic landscapes and economically important species. The conservation community has made this shift, but society as a whole has not. In fact, it can be argued that we have lost ground in this regard, if one compares the high level of support given to the Endangered Species Act on its enactment in 1973 with the regular efforts in the United States Congress ever since to weaken the act and make conservation of noncharismatic and noncommercial species harder.

Third, we have to be willing to put lines on a map. Large-scale conservation planning processes often begin with everyone involved agreeing on goals and general principles, but in the end, when it comes to putting lines on a map to indicate where the lands important for conservation are, the perceived personal and professional risks seem too great and those involved back away. If the conservation community—scientists, managers, and advocates alike—is not willing to take a stand on where on the landscape conservation of wild nature should take place, then we have no reason to expect that the rest of society will do so, and comprehensive conservation then will not happen.

Fourth, we have to recognize that no single approach to conservation can provide the entire solution and, in fact, that any solution based on only one approach will fail. Redesigning the economy so that it is not structurally dependent on ever-increasing growth will fail, making agriculture and forestry sustainable will fail, designating a system of ecological reserves will fail, if any of these is the only thing we do. Each will be able to do its part for achieving comprehensive conservation goals only if it takes place in conjunction with the others.

The logical consequence of this, of course, is that advocates for various approaches to conservation and priorities in conservation are, in fact, natural allies rather than competitors. Those advocating increased societal emphasis on sustainable agriculture, for example, need not consider wildlands advocates as threats to agriculture. Rather, they should see them as promoters of a complementary conservation strategy, one that not only takes place in different locations from agriculture but also promotes natural characteristics of ecosystems, such as clean water and viable populations of pollinators, on which agriculture depends. Alliances between advocates for wildlands, sustainable agriculture, sustainable forestry, and sustainable communities then become not only possible but logical, as demonstrated by work on the part of such traditional conservation organizations as the Sierra Club with respect to the 1990 Farm Bill (officially the Food, Agriculture, Conservation, and Trade Act of 1990).[33]

This awareness points out the final barrier, which is that each person has to recognize that he or she can support a concept being applied in a specific location without advocating that it be applied in every location. By adopting an integrative model for conservation, one in which different goals and uses are explicitly promoted in specifically designated areas, any person should be able to support wilderness, high-intensity use, expansion of agricultural land, logging, or grazing in the appropriate location.

This list of barriers is daunting, and it would be understandable to feel discouraged about our society's ability actually to achieve such an integrative, spatially explicit approach to conservation writ large and inclusive. But what ought to provide us with the necessary incentive to keep on trying to improve this approach is the realization that the easier, nonthreatening approaches will be insufficient. Extinctions will accelerate and ecosystem loss will accumulate, and as conservationists we will have failed. By taking the harder road, however, we stand a chance of reconstructing conservation in a way that will succeed.

Part V

Reconstructing Conservation Practice

Community and the Future of Conservation Stewardship

Chapter 17

Community Values in Conservation

PATRICIA A. STOKOWSKI

The concept of conservation has undergone numerous transformations over the past 150 years in the United States. At a minimum, three general orientations can be identified. First, the idea of "conservation as preservation" emerged in the mid-1800s, along with westward expansion and the closing of the American frontier. At that time, scenery and resource scarcity combined to encourage leaders to set aside public reserves to protect extraordinary landscapes for park, wilderness, and heritage values. The late 1800s and early 1900s periods of national parks establishment illustrates this period. Second, an alternative notion of conservation is seen in the idea of "conservation as wise use"—a perspective developed by those concerned with managing competing uses of natural landscapes for settlement, resource extraction, and government and corporate projects. Establishment of the USDA Forest Service in 1905 (and other resource management agencies), as well as current public debates about gas and oil drilling in the Arctic National Wildlife Refuge and locations for siting hazardous nuclear waste, are examples of this perspective. A third perspective is the idea of "conservation as environmental responsibility," an idea that emerged when national social movements fostering ecological health, environmental sensitivity, and ethical human action toward all life on the earth captured public consciousness. Described as "reform environmentalism" by sociologist Robert J. Brulle,[1] this view is represented by the environmental movement of the 1960s–1970s and its legacy.

The three approaches just noted—conservation as preservation, as wise use, and as environmental responsibility—have drawn support from a pervasive American value: the use of science in resource and environmental management. Claims for more and better science and increased levels of "expert" analysis have accompanied most efforts to solve recalcitrant problems associated with nature and people's interactions with nature. The application of science has at its foundation the idea that humans can control or at least channel the forces of nature, as William R. Burch Jr., Hixon professor of natural resource management at Yale University, explained: "The earlier movements for the conservation and rationalization of natural resources . . . only demanded that we extend our faith in science and technological progress outward to expanding resource supply."[2] The apparent failures of science in this respect (newly created chemicals polluted the environment; agricultural engineering produced adverse consequences; improvements in technology allowed easier access to resource areas but also stimulated overcutting, overgrazing, and overuse by humans; and so on) demanded new ways of thinking about conservation. The solution seemed to be in developing a national environmental consciousness that sought moral, ethical, and behavioral social change. Burch wrote: "The environmental movement of the 1960's demanded fundamental changes in the image we had of ourselves as a civilization, required a global scale of actions and made the changing of personal values and behavior the most significant turn of fate."[3]

The revised notion of public environmentalism required science as a foundational element, and it also necessitated a sense of public-spiritedness and an effort at environmental education. These criteria were developed in legislative, economic, and community contexts, as Daniel A. Mazmanian and Michael E. Kraft illustrate.[4] They subdivided the third era of public environmentalism into three further epochs: the 1970–1990 period of legislating for environmental protection; the 1980–1990 period of efficiency-based economic regulatory reform; and the current period (1990 onward), characterized by work toward sustainable communities. Their analysis suggests that the history of conservation extends beyond simply a description of significant national events, primary pieces of legislation, key resource sites, memorable historic individuals, or visible government and nonprofit organizations that shaped the early years of conservation in America. Rather, American conservation must also include the work of average citizens, people who experience nature primarily in daily life, typically with family members and friends, and usually in their hometowns or in their travels for recreation. Karl Hess Jr. notes: "People are an inescapable and necessary part of their environments. . . . They are not (just) special interest constituencies who are properly managed and supervised by mammoth bureaucracies; and they are not, as Muir would have us believe, nondescript hordes of destroyers ravaging . . . forests."[5]

The three conceptions of conservation identified at the outset of this chapter form the foundations of a new vision of contemporary conservation that gives prominence to notions of *community.* Social scientists interested in contemporary conservation issues have a challenging task. Priorities in conservation have broadened to include local and regional as well as national issues and to consider public and private lands at their intersections. The range of topics of interest to conservation scholars has expanded to include land-use planning and ecosystem integrity, regional tourism development, and cultural landscapes. Traditional government and market-driven solutions to environmental problems are now being challenged by voluntary, collaborative, and negotiated arrangements. Values once taken for granted are now at issue, and while new methods of organizing for collaborative action at the local level have emerged, issues of agency and public accountability are now evident.

Moving away from top-down, bureaucratic planning models and toward social mobilization at local, grassroots levels, new community conservation practices are oriented toward protecting significant landscapes and important natural and cultural environments at local and regional levels.[6] The emphasis on community-based conservation focuses attention on people as well as on nature, assumes that natural landscapes will not be privileged over historical and cultural settings, and draws its power from collaboration by local leaders and citizens. National conservation problems retain public significance, but the newer participatory approaches reorient the work of conservation to local community settings and practices in which public resource protection and private development interests intersect.

Thus, this chapter focuses on the new community conservation approaches gaining currency in America. The theoretical basis for the new movements in community-based conservation are reviewed, an example is provided from community tourism development, and general principles for reconstructing conservation in the twenty-first century are discussed. The focus throughout is on rural communities (rather than urban), and examples from the context of rural community planning, particularly in the American West, take precedence.

Community in Conservation

Analysis of contemporary community conservation movements must begin with consideration of the concept of *community*. Although there are many ways to define community, most perspectives have in common some combination of geographic area, shared activities, and social interactions and relationships.[7] Sociologist Larry Lyon summarized these elements simply, suggesting that community be defined as "people living within a specific area, sharing common ties, and interacting with one another."[8] Community would thus be manifest in the collective actions of people living in a generally identifiable locale, and the roles, organizational forms, language, images and symbols, culture, and interpersonal interactions of those people made visible, as Thomas Bender, noted scholar of American cultural history suggested, within "a network of social relations marked by mutuality and emotional bonds."[9]

Community is not merely an objective, tangible, static entity, though; it is continually recreated and renewed by people participating in it. Social anthropologist Anthony P. Cohen pointed out that "people construct community symbolically, making it a resource and repository of meaning, and a referent of their identity."[10] Community identity arises from social interactions centered in locally meaningful places, and community identity is exhibited in the shared cultures of a people in place. As Cornelia Butler Flora (sociologist and former president of The Rural Sociological Society) and colleagues explained, community symbols represent the core values around which residents orient: "When members of the community have grown up within a common culture or have . . . accepted a common set of values and norms. . . . The community develops a set of sacred symbols that reflect its most strongly held values."[11]

The same symbolic and imaginative potential used in creating community is also applied in creating and understanding landscapes. Noted historian Simon Schama explained that "although we are accustomed to separate nature and human perception into two realms, they are, in fact, indivisible. Before it can ever be a repose for the senses, landscape is the work of the mind."[12] What he is suggesting is echoed by sociologists Thomas Greider and Lori Garkovich, who proposed that landscapes "are the symbolic environments created by human acts of conferring meaning to nature and the environment . . . through a special filter of values and beliefs. Every landscape is a symbolic environment."[13] Resource places, then, are not only objective sites existing in a landscape or a local community but also symbolic places of social construction, experience, and recollection made visible in the images, narratives, and myths of people.

The basic theory behind community-based conservation approaches is that people who know one another, have shared interests, and work collaboratively will simultaneously accomplish environmental stewardship and also improve community quality of life. In essence, conservation cannot be seen as only the work of protecting objectively identified natural or cultural resources. Rather, conservation must also be about building community, so that people will be more likely to value others as well as value places. These actions are part of forming and maintaining a "sense of place."

Several concepts from social science are relevant to the discussion of new community conservation approaches, and these are discussed in the following sections: social capital, sense of place, and discursive models of planning and democracy. The practical applications of these ideas are currently visible in the conservation activities of land trusts, watershed collaboratives, scenic byways management organizations, community farming groups, and other kinds of government and nongovernmental partnering efforts.

Social Capital

The term "social capital" gained increasing currency over the last several decades of the twentieth century. The concept emerged in several social science disciplines simultaneously, but one of the clearest descriptions was provided by Robert D. Putnam in his study of democratic traditions in Italy.[14] Putnam found that communities that had high levels of civic-mindedness—that is, that could draw from large stocks of social capital—were more effective in governance and development. He defined social capital as the levels of cooperation in community such that communities with high stocks of social capital had citizens who were active participants in public affairs, were linked in dense networks of reciprocal horizontal relationships, trusted and respected their neighbors and leaders, and were active in a variety of voluntary community associations that reinforced norms of public-spiritedness. The basic argument, according to rural sociologists Jeffrey C. Bridger and A. E. Luloff, is that "successful cooperation for long-term mutual benefit depends on cultivation of social capital."[15]

Daniel Kemmis, writer and former mayor of Missoula, Montana, wrote,

"What holds people together long enough to discover their power as citizens is their common inhabiting of a single place."[16] Current environmental literature suggests that communities with high levels of social capital are more adept than others at weaving the fabric of community actions around preservation and conservation of local nature, history, and culture. Snow observed about collaborative conservation efforts in the West that "when conservation interests can ally with other influential forces in society, the chances of having their combined goals officially ratified are raised substantially."[17] If human communities are sets of people linked in interdependent networks, supported by friendships, and offering one another civic cooperation, they are also likely to include people who have similar engagements with local landscapes and culture. Cornelia Butler Flora and Jan L. Flora suggested that "building social capital and social infrastructure provides an important avenue for becoming native to place."[18] An appreciation for the resources and processes of local nature weaves people intimately to place and to one another in the fabric of contemporary and historical community life.

Sense of Place

Communities are not only island-like geographic locales; they are also interconnected people who share identifiable settings characterized by historical, natural, and cultural features. For many people, it is in the immediacy of a local community, in settings where people live, work, and play, that a "sense of place" is formed. The concept of sense of place is emerging as a key orienting concept in today's world. Academics and popular writers have used the term to refer to the emotions people experience and the behaviors they enact when they develop special attachments to landscapes, settings, and communities.[19] One's sense of place may appear to be intangible, but it is expressed as observable emotions, attitudes, and behaviors.

Although individual encounters with landscapes can create a personal sense of place, much of what people know about places—as well as much of what people feel about places and do in places—is mediated by others. Sociologists Peter Berger and Hansfried Kellner wrote in 1964 that "the reality of the world is sustained through conversation with significant others."[20] Thus, communities of people identify and remember places as meaningful and also derive identity from their shared understandings. Geographer E. C. Relph observed that "the relationship between community and place is a very powerful one in which each reinforces the identity of the other, and in which the landscape is very much an expression of communally held beliefs and values and of interpersonal involvements."[21] Tom Greider and Lori Garkovich elaborated, "Our understandings of nature and of human relations with the environment are really cultural expressions used to define who *we* were, who *we* are, and who *we* hope to be at this place and in this space."[22]

People understand the meanings and functions of natural, cultural, and historical resources primarily through personal and collective attachments to local places. In fact, much of what people know and feel about places is mediated through conversation with others. As a result, places become socially created, shared, sustained ideas, bounded by personal attachments to local geography, and remembered in the stories, language, and history shared by members of a human community. When people share in community, their conservation values are expressed in the discourse and narratives and memories that arise from conversations about local natural and cultural places.

Discursive Models of Planning and Democracy

Because the significance of place emerges in conversation and interaction with others, language is central in the formation and persistence of community. As the great Western writer Wallace Stegner wrote, "no place is a place until things that have happened in it are remembered in history, ballads, yarns, legends, or monuments."[23]

The social and cultural values of significant resource places are expressed in the multiple languages and stories of place. Places exist in the discourse and narratives and imaginings of people who are participants in community, who are oriented toward a valued place, and who have emotional attachments to features of local environments. Linguist and English professor Barbara Johnstone explained: "Just as narrative structures our sense of self and our interactions with others, our sense of place and community is rooted in narration. A person is at home in a place when the place evokes stories, and conversely, stories can serve to create places."[24] Kent Ryden, folklorist and cultural geographer elaborated: "Places do not exist until they are verbalized, first in thought and memory and then through the spoken or written word."[25] If a sense of place is sustained through interpersonal interaction and participation in community, then symbols of place become etched in collective consciousness and memory,

and they become remembered in the narratives, symbols, and images associated with local history.

Drawing from the role of language in creating community as well as a
sense of place, discursive models of democracy have been introduced in
the academic literatures of planning, social policy, and critical theory. Many
of these authors draw from the work of influential critical theorist Jürgen
Habermas' theory of communicative action, a theory that conceptualizes
social action as emerging from the interpersonal agreements created in language practices.[26] The stable, situated, ritualized languages that arise are
called "discourses." Discourses reflect the cultural and organizational structures of the social worlds that produce them and offer a perspective for
evaluating what appear to be rational individual and institutional behaviors. The utility of the discursive model of democracy is that it can foster
new approaches toward collaborative learning, public participation in environmental conflicts, and social change.[27]

An Illustration: Gaming Tourism Development in Rural Communities

Even though grassroots social movements aimed at improving community
quality of life and fostering natural and cultural landscape appreciation are
inherently appealing, they sometimes fail to achieve their goals, even with
the best intentions. Even those that attempt to involve citizens, or that offer
many opportunities for participation in the planning process, or that claim
to be civic-minded, are sometimes flawed.

One example of a community-led effort that produced mixed results is
offered by the casino gaming developments in two former gold-mining
towns in Colorado. About an hour's drive from Denver, Central City and
Black Hawk—the latter two the only two incorporated towns in Gilpin
County—were boomtowns in the 1860s and 1870s, but they declined over
time as the gold mines played out. Seasonal tourism kept the towns afloat
after World War I, but by the 1980s, local leaders claimed that their towns
were dying. In 1989, the mayors and other community leaders proposed
limited-stakes gambling as a way to simultaneously improve the local economy and increase funding for historic preservation.

Early efforts to convince the Colorado state legislature of the merits of
the pro-gambling proposal were unsuccessful, and so, in the summer of

1990, a statewide signature campaign was used to obtain support for the gaming proposal. That grassroots effort was a success, and the initiative was placed on the state ballot in 1990. In November of that year, about 57 percent of the citizens of Colorado who voted on the measure cast their vote to approve gambling in the two towns (and in Cripple Creek, another former gold-mining town near Colorado Springs that was also part of the ballot initiative). The day after the amendment passed, signs proclaiming "The Boom Is Back!" were unfurled in the former mining towns.

Gaming began on October 1, 1991, with eleven casinos open in Central City and Black Hawk. Ten years later, there were twenty-five casinos in those two towns, employing about 4,850 people (only 13 percent of whom lived in Gilpin County) and offering about 10,400 gaming devices (table games and slot machines). In calendar year 2001, casinos in the two towns generated adjusted gross proceeds (AGP) of more than $538 million (AGP is defined as total wagers minus payouts to bettors) and paid more than $81.7 million in gaming taxes. The tax monies fund historic preservation projects around the state, with state and local governments to allay adverse environmental effects brought about by gaming as well as administration and regulation of the Colorado gaming industry.[28]

The gambling developments proved problematic from the very beginning. Properties that could not be sold prior to approval of gambling sold for millions of dollars when investors found them suitable for reconstruction as casinos. Shop owners lost their leases, local businesses moved away, and some residents were displaced. Although gambling was supposed to be located in existing buildings in the towns' commercial zones, many 100-year-old buildings were not up to code and could not accommodate the industry—and "renovation" often meant gutting buildings and saving only facades. The environmental effects were also apparent. A road was carved into a steep hillside to create a massive parking lot on the mesa at the top; tree cover was lost, wildlife habitat was affected, erosion became a problem, hazardous mine tailings were exposed, and the glare of casino and parking lot lights spilling over the hills enraged residents when the parking area was completed. Residents also complained during the construction, which took place in the summer of 1991, that the history of the towns was being carted away in dump trucks while external entrepreneurs constructed new casinos that were out of scale with local landscapes. "We trusted our leaders to keep things under control," said residents, but many town leaders were seen as complicit in the problem. As local businesspeople who also held town government positions, they were the residents most likely to open casinos or take jobs in the new industry.

The complaints were suggestive of a larger issue: economic development projects on this scale, especially those using community history, memory, and landscape as a stimulus for growth, tend not only to affect the restructuring of the built and natural environment but also to manipulate symbolic aspects of community and place. Residents saw their towns' special places disappearing and felt a sense of community loss, but those in the gaming industry believed that residents should have been grateful for the infusion of money into public coffers, which they saw as saving the town from a fate worse than reconstruction. A "boomtown mythology" was used to justify the new growth: if mining had changed the area in the past, gaming was simply history repeating itself—and so, the rationale went, the industry should not be blamed for unexpected community changes.

One example that demonstrates the manipulation of community symbols in the tourism development is that of the "Shady Ladies of the Motherlode," a troupe of performers who were designated in 1994, three years after gaming began, as the "city ambassadors" of Central City. Apparently modeled after the provocatively dressed casino greeters who represented "wild western" ladies of the evening, the troupe claimed to be an educational organization that celebrated "the successful business woman in the old West."[29] The obvious problem with their claims was that Central City—unlike wilder western boomtowns such as Denver—had been remarkably proper. Records show that the town had only a few houses of ill repute and a small red-light district, and the name of only one prostitute (Lou Bunch) is to be found in historical records. The Shady Ladies thus represented, through the power of local government designation, a contrived version of community history and culture—one that tantalized visitors with fantasy but trivialized and exploited local history.

Other social, economic, political, and environmental effects of the gaming development are discussed in my book *Riches and Regrets,* which analyzed the years building up to the opening of gaming and the first five years of its operation.[30] Many of the persistent natural and cultural resource conservation issues stimulated by the gaming development are still developing, though others were resolved with community participation. Proposed water diversions from a local stream were canceled after residents of Gilpin County adopted activist tactics and protested in front of the county courthouse; the Environmental Protection Agency required that hazardous mine tailings be paved over to reduce dust and drainage problems; and the sewage and water supply systems in the towns were upgraded with local bonds based on projected gaming revenues. But debate remains about public uses of the new Central City reservoir, air pollution from cars and buses remains a problem, and a massive new casino recently built in Black Hawk shocked many when town planners gave approval to dynamite the side of a mountain so that contractors could gain more land for construction.

Some of the most contentious issues in the gaming developments related to the visual quality of the environment. Should unoccupied historic homes located in the commercial zones of the towns be moved to a single site to be recreated as a "historic mountain village"? They were, but not without significant community dissention and lawsuits. To what extent is the rapid construction of new residential housing in the county and towns changing the social dynamics of the local community and the environmental qualities of the area? The need for long-term community planning is evident, but the political will still lags behind perceived economic values of expanded gaming opportunities. As evidence of the problems, though, the National Park Service—which had designated the entire Gilpin County mining area as a national historic landmark in 1961—placed all three of Colorado's gaming towns on their "most endangered landmarks" list in 1992.

Several conclusions about community and conservation can be drawn from the gaming developments of Central City and Black Hawk. First, economic development projects that attempt to protect community values must be on a scale appropriate to the community and should attempt to be faithful to community history and culture. Second, under conditions of rapid growth, local governments are likely to make incremental policy shifts that exceed their public mandates; that is, governments begin to serve the emerging industry rather than serving the publics who elected them.[31] Thus, residents must be vigilant about monitoring the development itself as well as the actions of local leaders. Third, public participation alone is not enough to keep a project on track: citizens may be vocal, but they also need power to challenge those who may have vested interests.

Gaming development may be an extreme form of community development, but it is not a unique form; many of its adverse effects, in fact, parallel those of other boomtown-type projects.[32] The failure of the Gilpin County gaming developments was in their focusing on individual gain while community languished. If, as I have noted elsewhere, "cooperation is at the heart of a 'good community,' a place where people respect and preserve what is meaningful and important from the past, resist what is detrimental or unnecessary, and choose to work together toward humanistic and civic goals," then economic returns cannot be the sole measure of community success.[33] The Colorado gaming developments offer a key lesson for other rural communities: social capital—the features of community organization such as norms of trust and networks of social relationships that can improve collective action—is not merely an inheritance but an ongoing process of community participation, organization, and action.

Issues in Community-Based Conservation

Community approaches to conservation have been hailed for their power to stimulate face-to-face public interaction and democratic participation that may help resolve long-standing resource conflicts.[34] Nevertheless, there are serious questions about this approach. In particular, community-based conservation movements have been accused of being elitist, of promoting special interests, and of operating outside the bounds of elected democratic mechanisms. The theory behind community-based conservation approaches—that people working collaboratively and with shared interest in a place will do good things for that community and that place—is rejected by some as fostering romantic notions about society. Social scientists observe that even social capital can have a dark side: revolutionary groups might have high internal social capital, but their methods of operation may not be fair or equitable.

Thus, community conservation approaches are not a panacea to traditional forms of elected rule, legislative action, and market functions. Additionally, one cannot simply assume that all members of a community share the same or similar visions, and one should not imagine that all individuals or social groups will be equally affected by changes in ways of conducting local business. The issue is illustrated by some of the "collaborative conservation" models now emerging in watershed planning. These have been defined by environmental policy experts Philip Brick and Sarah Van de Wetering as approaches that emphasize "the importance of local participation, sustainable natural and human communities, inclusion of disempowered voices, and voluntary consent and compliance rather than enforcement by legal and regulatory coercion."[35] But George Cameron Coggins, professor of law, asserts that "the all too frequent reference of the participants to vague concepts such as 'community' and 'lifestyle' indicate that collaboration is often intended as a means of status quo preservation," and "local collaborative solutions could impede or contravene national laws and policies."[36] In his view, issues of the breadth of local participation, the accountability of interest groups, and the value orientations inherent in community practices take on added importance under community conservation approaches, regardless of whether they focus on natural, historical, or cultural resources.

Community conservation has also taken root in other settings, notably in rural and international development projects. Policy researchers Bill Cooke and Uma Kothari acknowledge similar concerns about those projects, writing that "participatory development is conventionally represented as emerging out of the recognition of the shortcomings of top-down development approaches. . . . The ostensible aim of participatory approaches . . . was to make 'people' central to development by encouraging beneficiary involvement in interventions that affect them and over which they had previously had little control or influence." But, the authors continue, "proponents of participatory development have generally been naïve about the complexities of power and power relations."[37] The authors refer not only to power relations between the different groups of participating social actors (donors, facilitators, native residents) but also to the discursive elements of power inherent in local knowledge, social norms, and cultures.

The issue of funding is also relevant in this respect. If community conservation groups receive public funds (or partner with public agencies in their activities), to what extent are they accountable to the greater society? When boundaries between public and private interests are blurred, how does government fulfill its role of looking after the welfare of all citizens in community? Because collaborative approaches typically exist outside the bounds of elected democratic position, they have no mandate to be representative, fair, or equitable for all social interests and groups in a community.

Additionally, the role of science, especially social science, is also of issue in contemporary community conservation practice. Many proponents of the new community participation models are ecologists who focus their attention on the observable characteristics of local ecosystems. The tools of their trade—field identification methods, ecological inventory approaches, and historical review of human uses of landscapes—are generally inadequate for assessing social processes over time and for evaluating how social processes influence and are influenced by landscape decisions, management, and planning. To the extent that ecologists incorporate the study of human communities in their models, they tend to apply a simple definition of community as geographic locale rather than adopt a process approach that realizes the complexities of linked personal, collective, and institutional actions and the socially constructed nature of community realities. The marginalization of social science is a weakness of much of the current inventory practices that guide conservation efforts. Sociologist Nancy L. Peluso's observation that "the elimination of people from natural history changes the ways that resources are perceived, defined, valued, allocated, and used, and can ultimately undermine conservation" admonishes scientists of all types to develop more sophisticated understandings of community conservation that go well beyond simple inventories of historical landscape uses.[38]

Conclusion

At the heart of new community-based conservation approaches are two questions: What makes a good community? How can communities better protect and manage their significant natural, historic, and cultural places? The issues discussed in this chapter suggest several generalizations about community-based conservation that can provide a road map for the future:

1. *Conservation arises from community participation and engagement.* Conservation is about people in relation to place; it is not only about the inventory of objects in nature. The more social capital is available in a community, the more likely it is that people will devote their energies to valuing and working on behalf of local resources and environments. If people enjoy most of their experiences with nature in the local places where they live, work, and play, then the work of conservation is ultimately the work of maintaining local places that have meaning and relevance for community. Encouraging people to live fully as residents rather than as passers-by in their local places, and actively making communal choices that sustain the well-being of those places and their people, are the basic ingredients of sustainable living. A stellar example of these goals, taken from the arena of landscape design, was described by environmental planner Randolph T.

Hester Jr. in his analysis of how a small town chose to set aside community "sacred places" in planning for new economic development.[39]

2. *Community can be reinvigorated by the shared work of environmental stewardship.* Reciprocally, conservation work can generate community social capital. Working together on environmental projects establishes and reinforces patterns of civic behavior that spill over into other realms of community activity. To be successful and have permanence, community conservation practice must be able to link traditionally isolated concerns of life—work, leisure habits, natural environments, historical and cultural heritage, educational systems, religious and spiritual institutions, social services, economic opportunities, governments, and others. Wendell Berry, a noted poet, essayist, and farmer wrote, "If we want our communities to survive [we must build] a system of local or community economies . . . that would carry us far toward the ecological and cultural ideal of local adaptation" to nature.[40]

3. *Local leaders and citizens must work to broaden the discourses of community conservation.* Sociologists David R. Maines and Jeffrey C. Bridger wrote that community "is not only a form of social organization . . . but it also is a discursive representation. And when it is involved in rhetorical narratives, it can become part of the process through which futures are created."[41] Their analysis speaks to the value of encouraging alternative "imaginings" and vision making in community conservation practice. Rarely will all members of community agree about appropriate ideals or courses of action. Yet, if community members develop respect for one another and tolerance of alternative views, the trust engendered by increasing social capital should allow for some shared conservation practices to emerge among people with divergent interests and views.

4. *Successful community conservation requires a variety of models of organizing.* Current experiments in community-based conservation range across a variety of operational strategies. People meet in public discussion groups and planning meetings; they engage in community visioning processes; groups of stakeholders develop community indicators; environmental interest groups monitor local ecosystems; participatory research approaches that seek to incorporate local knowledge into agency-led planning efforts are employed; community-based projects (community gardening, for example) are carried out; land trusts and

other conservation groups enact landscape protection efforts; and so on. Many of these models attempt to reconnect people to place such that people come to live with care in the local landscapes that sustain both people and nature. Grassroots planning is intended to support ecologically sound, economically viable, and socially meaningful actions in place. In an essay titled "Coming into the Watershed," poet and author Gary Snyder referred to this work as the "practice of profound citizenship in both the natural and the social worlds."[42] In many cases, the structure of such organizations may be less important than their functions: if people participate together in good causes, they will improve their neighborly ties and will be more likely to collaborate on other local projects.

5. *Deliberative discourse models have drawbacks, but they may facilitate a more engaged citizenry.* Mazmanian and Kraft noted that "building sustainable communities is a formidable challenge. . . . In most locales, there will be substantial conflict over community goals—social, economic, and environmental—and it is not clear what form of public involvement or community process will help most in developing consensus on those goals, or the public policies that can bring a community closer to them."[43] Deliberative discourse models of planning and management have been promoted as a solution for conservation practice, and research shows that collective deliberation works best when participants are willing to listen carefully and fairly, when participants control their emotional reactions, when the "best available" information is brought to bear on decisions, when political power can be used to "coerce the recalcitrant," and in the absence of genuine opposition of interests.[44] Strategies are needed, though, to ensure that these criteria can evolve from shared participation in learning communities.

These five principles for reconstructing conservation as community-based phenomena provide a guide for the future. In fact, they are not independent of one another, as Hess illustrates in linking discourse with organizational forms. He proposes a method for solving environmental problems by creating a "market of landscape visions" in which "the land community would be rescued from the airy realm of utopian musings and brought down to earth. . . . Power and control in the land community would be withdrawn from the visionary state and returned to where they have rightfully belonged from the start—in the hearts, minds, and hands of visionary individuals and their communities."[45] Individual social action and institutionalized social structures are interlinked processes.

If communities wish to preserve resource places, or to wisely use and manage the special resource places that surround them, it is necessary to involve citizens in programs of sustainability at the local level, where sense of place is strongest—and where the collective influence of those local programs can stimulate wider regional utility and application. Institutional arrangements that support communal goals will be necessary, whatever forms those goals or systems may take. One deterrent to reconstructing conservation in this manner is social mobility: in today's world, people move so frequently that they might never begin to feel settled and part of a community. The challenge, then, may be to find ways to imagine community and place—that is, to help develop people's shared senses of place so they can experience a sense of membership in an ideal and a collective larger than themselves.

A "return to simpler times" may be one way of accomplishing this, but that phrase typically indicates a romantic, unrealistic, or even unappealing version of the past. A more appropriate strategy might be to begin with what people value in their communities and in their cultures. Beyond the formal state-provided agencies and environmental interest organizations of conservation administration are other approaches that are community driven, ritualistic, and highly symbolic. Examples of communal activities centered on ritual activities involving nature symbolism can be found in many societies and cultures. Group-based nature meditations, social activism for ecological protection, workshops focused on developing skills for living in harmony with nature, efforts to foster local folklore and culture, revival of nature-based rituals, and other examples of "spiritual ecology" are intended, as historian Carolyn Merchant observed, "to effect a transformation of values that in turn leads to action to heal the planet."[46] The sheer number and variety of these alternative approaches is evidence of their social and cultural importance in contemporary times. Moreover, these activities counter tendencies toward isolation and community dissolution. Their practice can help create and enrich the civic life of a community—thus increasing social capital and also contributing to community conservation.

Stewardship and Protected Areas in a Global Context: Coping with Change and Fostering Civil Society

BRENT MITCHELL AND JESSICA BROWN

Conservation practice today is a rapidly developing field, learning lessons from the past, incorporating new ecological understanding, and adjusting to increasingly dynamic political, economic, and cultural realities. Conservation approaches are also becoming more complex, requiring us to weave together the broad strands of culture and nature with a diversity of disciplines and to embrace broader social goals. We find more and more that institutional roles have been turned around, with communities rather than government agencies taking the lead.

Increasingly, conservationists in America are taking notice of the rich store of innovations to be found in other parts of the world, especially in countries with fewer financial resources, an array of institutional constraints, and differing cultural and social contexts. There is fertile ground for mutual learning and exchange.

This international perspective is offered in the tradition of George Perkins Marsh, the "prophet of conservation," who was one of the first American environmental writers to enrich today's conservation movement with lessons from abroad. David Lowenthal, Marsh's biographer, described him as follows:

> Vital for his alertness to human impacts, and the need to amend them, were the vivid parallels he drew: parities and disparities between ancient and modern environments, Old World and New World use and abuse of nature, Mediterranean and American reaction to degraded landscapes. Similar physical processes; differing cultural responses. The task Marsh

set for himself was first to account for the differences, and then to bridge them, in order to engender awareness and spur reform on both sides of the Atlantic.[1]

To simplify the discussion, we will focus on conservation in and around protected areas, very broadly defined as areas where management decisions are largely influenced by conservation or restoration objectives.

Trends in Conservation

Emerging global trends in conservation and protected areas management set the stage for new approaches that engage and support local people in the stewardship of their natural and cultural heritage.

There is among the conservation community a growing recognition that biodiversity conservation, ecosystem protection, and other goals can be met only by addressing resource management over large areas of land. Worldwide, conservation strategies are becoming increasingly bioregional, ecosystem based, or comprehensive in scope. The field of conservation biology has highlighted the pressing need to work on the scale of ecosystems and the wider landscape to conserve biodiversity. There is growing recognition that protected areas—as a major conservation tool—can no longer be treated as islands but must be seen in a larger context, with an emphasis on compatible management of surrounding lands and creation of linkages among reserves.[2] One conservation biologist expressed it as follows:

> For those committed to conserving the biodiversity of the world, it has become increasingly clear that parks and protected areas are only part of a more broadly based solution. Not only are the most protected areas not large enough to be ecologically self-sustaining, but even if they were, the fragile ecological shells that contain them are all too permeable to anthropogenic change. Effective in-situ biodiversity conservation, therefore, must entail consideration of the vast areas of land outside protected areas.[3]

This, in turn, can be achieved only by engaging local residents and communities in the protection and management of areas that are often privately or communally owned. Stewardship and the related field of community-based conservation provide a variety of tools for meeting these objectives and are widely viewed as central to the future of protected areas world-wide. Conservationists are finding they must adopt inclusive approaches that encourage local participation.

New Paradigms in Protected Areas

This strategic imperative is contributing to major changes in the way we view national parks and protected areas. The phenomenon of "paper parks"—areas protected in name only—has demonstrated forcefully that approaches relying solely on regulation and enforcement are costly and too often meet with failure. Managers of protected areas are turning instead to inclusive models, in which the interests of local communities are considered, resident populations are not displaced, and there is a high degree of local participation in planning and management of the protected area.[4]

Protected areas simply cannot be viewed in isolation from the communities within and near them. This is true of the broad spectrum of protected areas, including those established by governments during the twentieth century according to a "conventional" national park model. And this principle is, of course, inherent in the idea of "community-conserved areas," places not necessarily officially designated, yet socially codified, which communities have been creating for millennia to protect the natural and cultural resources of importance to them.

It is not simply that by ignoring local communities we imperil the security of existing protected areas. We also risk continuing a range of injustices that have been perpetuated on communities, in ways that include forced displacement, restrictions on access to livelihood resources, and cultural erosion. At the same time, those people closest to the resource can bring their rich experience to bear when they are encouraged or simply permitted to take responsibility for their stewardship. We need to tap the wealth of knowledge, traditional management systems, innovation, and love of place that so many communities could bring forth.[5]

Community involvement is central to an emerging new paradigm for protected areas worldwide. This new paradigm is based on inclusive approaches, partnerships, and linkages, in which protected areas are no longer planned against local people but instead are planned with them (see table 18.1).[6]

Corresponding to this trend is a global trend toward people demanding more control of management decisions regarding their resources, especially those immediate to them. In many countries and regions, authority is being

Table 18.1

Evolving Approaches to
Planning and Management of Protected Areas

As It Was—Protected Areas Were:	As It Is—Protected Areas Are:
• Planned and managed against local people	• Run with, for, and—in some cases—by local people
• Run by central government	• Run by many partners
• Set aside for conservation	• Run also with social and economic objectives
• Developed separately	• Planned as part of a national or international system
• Managed as "islands"	• Developed as networks (strictly protected areas buffered and linked by green corridors)
• Established mainly for scenic preservation	• Often set up for scientific, economic, and cultural reasons
• Managed for visitors and tourists	• Managed with local people more in mind
• About protection	
• Viewed exclusively as a national concern	• Also about restoration
	• Viewed as an international as well as a national concern

Source: M. Beresford and A. Phillips, "Protected Landscapes: A Conservation Model for the Twenty-First Century," *George Wright Forum* 17 (2000), p. 19.

devolved to the local level out of political or economic necessity. This devolution affects conservation as much as other areas of life and commerce. Increasingly, local communities are challenging protected area authorities to answer the questions "Protected from whom? Protected for what?" They are redefining that protection and often implementing it themselves.

Another important trend lies in our growing understanding of the link between nature and culture: that landscapes are shaped by human culture as well as the forces of nature and that rich biodiversity often coincides with cultural diversity. Ever since George Perkins Marsh posited that the earth is not immutable but is shaped by man, conservation has seen a growing recognition that all lands on the earth have been altered by human activity to various degrees. It follows that conservation cannot be undertaken without the involvement of people in some stewardship role, especially those closest to the resources or with the most likely influence—positive or negative—on those resources.

Stewardship

Stewardship means, simply, people taking care of places. In its broadest sense, it refers to the essential role individuals and communities play in the careful management of their natural and cultural wealth for present and future generations. More specifically, it can be defined, as we have noted elsewhere, as efforts to create, nurture, and enable responsibility in landowners and resource users to manage and protect land and its natural and cultural heritage.[7]

Stewardship taps our basic human impulse to care for our home and its surroundings—be it a parcel of land, a community garden, a neighborhood, a historic monument, or the larger area of a watershed, mountain range, or stretch of coastline. It builds on our sense of obligation to other people: our family, our community, and future generations.

The stewardship approach offers a means of cultivating local involvement and reaching beyond the boundaries of conventional protected areas. The stewardship concept draws on an array of tools to conserve natural and cultural values. Whatever the specific means, by fostering individual and community responsibility, the stewardship approach puts conservation in the hands of the people most affected by it.

Community-based conservation reverses top-down, center-driven conservation by focusing on the people who bear the costs of conservation. In the broadest sense, then, community-based conservation includes natural resources or biodiversity protection by, for, and with the local community.[8] Both community and individual levels are, of course, necessary for success, with community work impossible without a foundation of individual commitment, and individual effort alone diluted or obviated by those in any location who are fundamentally opposed to conservation. Like stewardship, community-based conservation ranges from exploiting tangible benefits to conservation to nurturing a conservation ethos, with the most successful examples embracing a large part of the spectrum. Both involve similar techniques and approaches, adapted to differing cultural and economic conditions, to give people rights and responsibilities for sound resource management.

Experience from the Field

How are these concepts of private stewardship and community-based conservation being implemented? In this section, we will provide a very brief "tour" of exemplary conservation projects that manifest the rich array of approaches to conservation in current practice. Some are old ideas adapted to new, changing circumstances; others are innovations born of necessity and invention. Drawn from diverse regions of the world, all provide insights into the potential for conservation based on equitable rights and responsibilities. Although we have space only to describe one or two cases briefly to illustrate a theme, there are, of course, many other equally interesting stories. Each case description includes only enough detail to make a thematic point and refer you to the literature for further description.

Private Initiatives, Private Reserves

Of particular interest is the growing importance of formal and semi-formal private conservation work. In an expanding number of countries, land is coming under protection through designated private reserves and through legal vehicles such as conservation easements negotiated by land trusts. For example, in the Czech Republic, in a few short years since land was reprivatized following the communist period, twenty-eight private land trusts have emerged.[9] Even though they "protect" fairly small areas, these tend to be very significant areas. Perhaps more important, they are a mechanism for people to be directly involved in conservation in a country where for a generation nature preservation was the exclusive domain of government specialists.[10]

Networks of private reserves have been established in recent years in virtually every country in Latin America. Although these vary in designation and purpose, they all represent landowner interest in stewardship. Land trusts are growing in this region, too. Conservationists have finalized the first conservation easements in many countries, including Mexico, Guatemala, and Belize, to name a few.[11] In Paraguay, the Natural Lands Trust is negotiating the first conservation easement with an indigenous community, the Ache people. In return for safeguarding other features of the land in question, they will legally secure subsistence hunting and other rights.

Private conservation and private reserves are powerful forms of stewardship because they formalize both rights and responsibilities for land management. They are attractive to individuals in many cultures because they represent a direct method of land protection, with less opportunity for political or other forces to detract from the primary conservation objective. On the other hand, because they are private, without a strong, carefully monitored legal framework, they are vulnerable to abuses, especially by powerful individuals.[12]

Participatory Planning

Increasingly, protected areas are being planned in a participatory manner, starting with the decision of whether a protected area is the appropriate management mechanism at all. The limits and zonation of the Port Honduras Marine Reserve in southern Belize were developed not simply in consultation with fishermen; instead, this reserve was delimited by the fishermen themselves, working with a facilitating nongovernmental organization. Local fishermen describe how fish stocks have increased in the extraction zones, enhancing local livelihoods. They serve as the de facto enforcement system for the reserve and play a leading role in developing management plans. Fishermen support management of the reserve because they were integral in setting it up.[13]

On the Caribbean island of St. Lucia, a participatory process that has included a broad range of local stakeholders has enhanced management effectiveness in the Soufriere Marine Management Area. An extensive consultative process involving representatives of the main interest groups resulted in an agreement and a zoning plan that laid the groundwork for designation of the marine management area. Fish stocks in areas adjacent to the reserve have increased in recent years, and this has enhanced the local community's commitment to the success of this protected area.[14] In the early 1990s, St. Lucia led the way in participatory planning on a national scale to develop the country's systematic plan for protected areas, an approach that has been followed by other countries in the insular Caribbean region.[15]

Customary Laws and Social Practices

Customary laws and social practices can complement legislation, and the resulting innovative governance offers tremendous potential to improve management of resources inside and outside protected areas. For example, in Zanzibar (Tanzania), the Commission for Natural Resources has tested the application of customary Islamic principles in the management of the

Misali Island Marine Conservation Area, an area rich in marine and terrestrial biodiversity and important as a fishing ground.[16] The process has resulted in designation within the conservation area of a *hima,* or strictly protected zone, in accordance with the customary *shariah* (Islamic law), which has been incorporated into the secular law of Zanzibar. In a paper reviewing this case study and two others (located at Silves, in Amazonian Brazil, and Kowanyama, in northeastern Australia), anthropologist Janet Chernela and her colleagues observed that traditional groups with high stakes in resource sustainability will invest creativity and effort, especially in the face of external threats. The resulting innovative governance can foster sustainable resource use and encourage local self-determination.[17]

In the South Pacific, a regionwide conservation program has built on customary landownership, long connections to the land, and traditional resource management practices. Created in response to the failure of past efforts to establish protected areas in the region, the South Pacific Biodiversity Conservation Programme works with customary owners and community leaders in twelve countries of the region. Communal lands constitute the majority of land in the region and support the lion's share of biodiversity. Under customary ownership, land and resources are managed by communities according to patterns that have been maintained over many generations. As a result, land is seen as heritage rather than commodity. Tapping this strong local stewardship ethic has been critical to the program's success.[18]

Community Self-Determination

Community self-determination is also pronounced in an initiative to create a community-conserved area in the ancient Incan valley of Pisac in the southern Peruvian Andes. This cultural landscape has been shaped by the traditional agricultural practices of its indigenous inhabitants over centuries and is rich in agro-biodiversity. Here, in an area believed to be one of the sites of the origin of the potato and home to the greatest variety of potatoes in the world (some 280 varieties have been documented), several communities are working to create a community-conserved area. The Parque de la Papa, or potato park project, will protect the area's rich agro-biodiversity, support local livelihoods, and enable the indigenous communities to document their knowledge of the practices that have created and sustained this landscape. Alejandro Argumedo of the Indigenous People's Biodiversity Network, which is working with these communities, writes,

"Landscape conservation based on traditional agro-biodiversity knowledge and practices is likely to have greater success in conserving the local landscape than those that rely solely on conventional conservation approaches."[19]

Combining Values

Often there are many values people hold for a landscape or resource. In the cultural landscapes of the White Carpathian Mountains, which straddle the border between the Czech Republic and Slovakia, important habitats for orchids and other species have long been created and maintained by meadow management for hay. Today there is no longer a significant market for the hay, and the meadows are filling in. Conservation groups that recognize the natural and cultural value of these meadows are working to keep them open. For some, the most important value is cultural, keeping alive a tradition that long defined their agrarian communities. Others stress the importance of biodiversity; species richness is reduced when the land is allowed to return to a "natural" forested state. Even though both are trying to keep the meadows open, these groups disagree somewhat about the means, some insisting on traditional hand tools, others on more efficient machines. But both draw on the variety of values that people attribute to the landscape.[20]

Civil Society

One of the most exciting elements of stewardship work is that it often leads to advances in other social areas. Stewardship helps to build civil society by giving people opportunities to participate in shaping their environment and, therefore, their lives. The sweeping political changes in central and eastern Europe that began in 1989 were precipitated largely by people's disgust with the state of the environment caused by the centralized economic and political systems, with a corresponding demand to participate in improving it. A wave of environmental leaders went into politics in the early 1990s, and as a result certain central European countries boast some of the best environmental legislation on the continent.

We see stewardship leading to civil society development all over the region. In the notorious "Black Triangle" found at the nexus of Germany, Poland, and the Czech Republic, egregious air pollution caused heavy forest damage during the communist period. In northern Bohemia (Czech Republic), a group that originally set out to restore the forests of the Jizera

Mountains now finds itself also engaged in leadership development in the surrounding communities. Its work is helping to create forums for communities to participate in improving the management of state-owned land and, in the long run, to have a voice in decisions regarding the future of the area where they live. These colleagues see clearly the link between this kind of community-based conservation and the fostering of civil society in emerging democracies of the region. Conservation approaches that are inclusive, participatory, and concerned with equity are inherently democratic.[21]

Stewardship versus Custodianship

Stewardship means people taking care of the land. However, it means their doing so in the context of normal social and economic life. In some economically developed countries, projects are under way (with many more being debated) that move "taking care of the land" to an extreme role that might better be termed "custodianship."

Although both stewardship and custodianship could mean taking care of the land for future generations, the latter implies more of a service for a contemporary or contemporaries (read society) and implies an expectation of remuneration. This has obvious policy implications: how much should society pay to have some people take care of the land, to be large-scale gardeners for the urban majority?

Although many countries already pay for custodianship in certain agricultural subsidy programs, in some (especially in Europe) they have, in many respects, gone even further in taking a fee-for-service approach to private land management. The prospect is alluring as many practitioners struggle with ways to find financial incentives for conservation. But the hazards are many, starting with the obvious problem of the money disappearing during the troughs of normal economic cycles. But more basically, it puts a distance between conservation and direct resource use. The issue is different from profit-sharing schemes such as those employed in southern Africa, of which the best known example is CAMPFIRE.[22] The latter ensure that the benefits of controlled resource extraction, such as managed big game hunting, are shared by people who support the wildlife populations (local people whose crops are trampled or eaten by the game). In custodianship, landscape management is supported by funds not directly derived from the resource, for example to maintain large landscapes in a certain form valued by the larger society.

Principles for Reconstructing Conservation

These and other examples of experience in the field suggest ways of thinking about conservation that are broader than conventional conservation practice, and in many ways new to its professionals. All of these principles will present challenges but, if taken up, will lead to greater conservation success.

Relationships to Land

Our first and primary principle for conservation in the twenty-first century is that we should focus on people's relationship to the land. People's relationship to the environment is where all conservation starts. Whether it is called a land ethic, a sense of place, a stewardship imperative, or simply a love of nature, conservation is lost without people connecting at a personal level to land and resources.

John Ogonowski understood this. A farmer in Dracut, Massachusetts, he was a founder of the Dracut Land Trust. Besides protecting his land with an agricultural easement, he shared some of it with Cambodian immigrants through the New Entry Sustainable Farming Project. As one of the project's first volunteers, he gave space to people from a vastly different culture, uprooted to the nearby urban center of Lowell, so that these farmers could also work the land. He rarely collected rent, and he helped the farmers with advice and with materials he provided himself. Across a huge cultural divide, he understood their need to be connected to the land.[23] Unfortunately, Ogonowski had another career as a pilot. He was captain of American Airlines flight 11 and perished with the World Trade Center towers.

Learn How to Work with Diverse Communities

Community-based approaches are practical, have multiple benefits, and often are more successful over time than efforts driven by other levels of organization. They offer perhaps the only antidote to increasing globalization. We must, however, be careful to define community carefully. Although we often tend to think in terms of the people living in or near a natural area, there are many kinds of communities, and these communities are not in themselves homogeneous. In a recent article on experience from the insular Caribbean, Tighe Geoghegan and Yves Renard challenge the common view that local communities are homogenous, stressing the need to understand and reconcile the interests, needs, and expectations of a

wide range of stakeholders as well as the complexity of their relationships
with the resource and one another. They also point out the importance of
institutional arrangements and transparent, negotiated processes for decision making.[24]

Refine and Redefine the Role of Government

Critics of community-based conservation point out that conservation at the
local level is blind to larger changes in the environment. A local conservation commission cannot detect global climate change or develop comprehensive responses. But the local approach does not argue against
conservation working at higher levels of organization. Rather, it provides a
mechanism for successfully implementing conservation strategies. The difference with community-based conservation is in how specific, local management changes are structured within a larger conservation agenda. Public
agencies still have a role; it is just different, concerned more with guiding
than with dictating, and it is especially concerned with carefully constructing institutional frameworks that grant genuine authority to appropriate
community groups while ensuring that conservation efforts succeed in
their primary objectives.

Cultural Diversity

On a global scale, human society is homogenizing. One need only look at
the astonishing rate of loss of language diversity to witness one indicator.
We're all familiar with the reasons—communication technology, enhanced
transportation, a single dominant economic system—but the implications
for conservation are less clear. Even though cultural diversity may be diminished, stewardship may be simplified by reduction of the variety of
value sets. As chilling as the thought is, more people around the world
share a common worldview than ever before. Does this make conservation
easier, allowing more focus on universal values, or does it make it more
perilous, reducing the margin for error in the way a larger, more homogeneous society responds to change?

Others, noting the relationship between high natural and cultural diversity (for example, in certain regions biodiversity coincides clearly with linguistic diversity) argue that natural conservation is eroded when cultural
diversity declines. Taghi Farvar, who has worked with local and indigenous

groups in many parts of the world, observed, "Cultural and biological diversity are natural, powerful allies and it is only this alliance that may eventually succeed in saving them both."[25]

Balance Social, Ecological, and Economic Perspectives

It is both practical and just that we address social, environmental, and economic needs in conservation to the fullest extent possible. This is not a call to be content with compromise but rather a caution that conservation cannot be fully divorced from commerce and society. Difficult as it is to address with specific programs or approaches, the greatest environmental effect comes from the cumulative small decisions each individual makes every day (what people eat, how they transport themselves, how they heat their homes, etc.), and these are greatly influenced by culture. We must give social considerations equal weight with ecological and economic determinants. David Western, chairman of The African Conservation Centre, and former head of Kenya Wildlife Service, put it well when he wrote, "If conservation is to become embedded in our daily activities, nature and society must be intimately linked in our minds."[26]

Equity

To the extent that conservation has always been concerned with what we pass on to our children, the idea of intergenerational equity is not new. Newer, perhaps, is the simple but radical idea, as expressed by the environmental justice movement, that everyone is entitled to clean air, clean water, and food, and that no population or group should bear unequally the adverse environmental effects of development. In many developing countries, where these concerns are paralleled, there is also growing debate over who bears the costs of conservation, particularly where people are denied access to traditional resources or territories and are asking, "Protected for what?" Globally, the issue of equity translates into concerns over glaring differences in consumption patterns and the uneven participation of nations in solving global problems.

Equitable participation in conservation requires that we pay attention to diversity and recognize that communities are never homogenous but include a diversity of actors on a playing field that is rarely level for reasons of gender, socioeconomic status, race, and ethnicity, to name a few.

Continued Expansion from Conservation to Restoration

Conservation has overwhelmingly focused on the protection of rare or endangered habitats, areas of high aesthetic value and usually high threat, and "saving the last great places," to quote The Nature Conservancy's slogan. Although this emphasis is useful for focusing attention and resources, if viewed in the extreme it tends to limit conservation to something society does on the fringes, allowing and perhaps even excusing degradation of the larger landscape. Conservation has sought to restore ecological functions and, where possible, semi-natural habitats to landscapes that have been abused by human activity, and it must continue to do so.

Think "Long Term" and Work the Demand Side

Stewardship is most difficult to achieve when threats are immediate, and it is especially challenging the farther the agent of change is from the resource. Convincing hunters to adjust or suspend their activities for the benefit of conservation would be of little use should a rapacious mining proposal come along, to give a simplistic example. The larger conservation community must continue to complement community-based approaches with society-wide changes in consumption patterns and excesses. So long as society demands resources, site-specific conservation efforts ultimately cannot protect resources demanded by a consumer society. The point is analogous to drug enforcement: ultimately, control of sources of drugs or interdiction of their transport to distant markets cannot be successful so long as demand for the products is high. Alternatives and reduction in demand are also required. Similarly, those of us working in conservation must consider how we can address the growing rate of consumption in our society.

Even in cases in which external influences are relatively contained, community-based conservation will not always result in incontestably positive results for both natural and human communities—and results will rarely come quickly. Specific frameworks must be monitored and modified over time, with expectations fitted to larger goals of sustainability. That said, community approaches to natural resource management represent great opportunities for more pluralistic, just, and ultimately successful conservation for the world today and into the near future. Beyond that, conservationists must be prepared to be flexible and adaptive.

Be Flexible and Adaptive; Emphasize Process

Social, economic, and environmental conditions are always in flux, not to mention our understanding of them, and conservationists must respond. Again, here are the words of David Lowenthal:

> Many today share Marsh's concern about environmental impacts and salute his pioneering efforts to comprehend and contain their malign effects. But how we define and tackle these issues is now utterly different. The problems we face, our confidence in resolving them, our views of progress, nature, ecology, human transcendence, culture and history— all have changed strikingly since Marsh's day, even since I first studied Marsh fifty years ago.[27]

Thus, in our efforts we should focus more on *process* than on specific, prescribed outcomes. This builds flexibility into our framework and opens opportunities that a design approach does not. Conservation evolves. We may reconstruct our personal or our organization's thinking on conservation, but beyond that it develops more organically. What's more, as has been pointed out in several earlier discussions of history, our ideas about the objectives and even the goals of conservation change as well. We will always be *practicing* conservation to get it right because what we believe to be "right" is a moving target.

Chapter 19

Reinventing Conservation: A Practitioner's View

ROLF DIAMANT, J. GLENN EUGSTER, AND NORA J. MITCHELL

"Timing is everything," says an old adage. From the perspective of conservation practice, it is a particularly important time to step back, reflect on recent trends, and begin to describe a new vision of conservation for the twenty-first century. The transition between centuries is a time of change and shifting paradigms. It is a time of tension between the old and new, the perceived and the imagined, wilderness and stewardship. It is also a time of confluence, of tributaries joining and widening, swelling into a broad stream and making connections with a broader landscape—the re-envisioned landscape of conservation. There are shifts in understanding and perception, in scholarship and practice, and among the larger public. This is also a time of challenge—but, more important, a time of opportunity—as conservation stewardship evolves from a historical emphasis on objectives dealing with efficiency, development of material resources, and preservation of selected wildlands, to an emphasis on objectives more closely tied to public amenity, quality of life, social equity, and civil society. There is also a concurrent devolution of centralized decision making, led by government, to a more pluralistic, community-based process, driven by private or multi-sector initiatives. This chapter explores these recent trends and examples of successful conservation practice and offers fundamental principles for reconstructing conservation in the twenty-first century.

Ways of Working: Contemporary Trends
in Conservation Practice

As conservation objectives have diversified and become embedded in a broader vision of sustainability, the nature of conservation work has changed. Participation in conservation is far more inclusive, being accomplished in new ways by new constituencies and collaboration across many sectors of society. The following list of trends is not intended to be comprehensive but provides examples of how conservation work is changing in fundamental ways.

Coalitions of Diverse Interests

Writer Rick Bass describes his neighbors on the Yaak Valley Forest Council in northwestern Montana as "hunting and fishing guides, bartenders, massage therapists, road builders, heavy construction operators, writers, seamstresses, painters, construction workers, nurses, teachers, loggers, photographers, electricians and carpenters."[1] Whereas once the diverse coalition working in the Yaak Valley was an unusual phenomenon, diversity is now more a rule than an exception. Community leaders don't want to choose between a healthy economy, culture, and environment—they want it all. The diverse coalitions that have formed reflect all the interests of society. Groups such as the United Auto Workers and the Delaware Nature Education Society are supporting the protection of the White Clay Creek watershed. In northern Virginia, the Arlington County Democratic Committee, patients from a Fairfax County hospital, and the Greater Washington chapter of the Jimmy Buffett "Parrot Heads" are cleaning up the Potomac River. Across the country, these diverse conservation networks are stepping forward to shape the future of their communities and the landscapes that surround them.

Local Initiatives for Quality of Life

Stuart Cowan and Sim Van der Ryn wrote in *Ecological Design,* "Everyone is a participant and a designer!"[2] More than in the past, people want to be involved in conservation efforts. "Don't do it to us. Don't do it for us. Do it with us" is a request that is heard over and over in communities across the land. More important, community leaders, such as those in Cape Charles, Virginia, are working with interdisciplinary teams of experts and conservation service providers to design sustainable strategies for the future.

The desire to conserve important values and have natural or cultural park-like qualities in all our communities—not just in Yellowstone National Park or the Everglades—seems to have converged with the nation's rediscovery of democracy. Quality of life has increasingly become an issue in the United States, and people realize that government alone is not capable of maintaining or restoring communities and landscapes, nor is it the appropriate force to attempt to do so.

Motivated by aspirations for a high quality of life and the realization that people can—and need to—influence their future, groups and individuals have taken responsibility for conservation efforts in huge numbers. Local initiative, occasionally in partnership with government, has taken the form of land trusts, small watershed associations, greenway and trail groups, friends of parks, "Main Street" organizations, and heritage area coalitions. These organizations have taken a hands-on approach to craft conservation plans and work to carry out specific actions, with a level of sophistication normally found only in consulting firms and government agencies.

Democracy and Civic Dialogue

Author and essayist John Elder wrote, "We must pursue stewardship not simply as the maintenance of valuable resources but also as a way of fostering a broader experience of democracy and community."[3] Certainly, the National Environmental Policy Act of 1969 and the National Historic Preservation Act in 1966 forever changed the landscape of public dialogue in environmental and historic preservation decision making. These landmark laws and many state and local derivatives vastly expanded opportunities for greater inclusiveness and public participation.

More recently, the concept of conservation as a "big tent" continues to broaden as the reach is increasing with the level of public engagement. The focus of conservation has also been extended beyond a traditional emphasis on natural resource issues such as air and water pollution so that the public environmental agenda embraces an expanding list of "quality of life" issues, including public health, sustainable practices, smart growth, energy conservation, public transportation, environmental justice, and cultural heritage.

In her landmark book *The Power of Place: Urban Landscapes as Public History,* Dolores Hayden explores places associated with history of women and people of color, illustrating the loss of many and the lack of value given to those that remain in our public memory. Hayden speaks of "memory rooted in places" and how "new kinds of professional roles and public processes may broaden the practice of public history, architectural preservation, environmental protection, and commemorative public art, when these are perceived as parts of wider urban landscape."[4]

Exploration of public history and memory is also opening up new venues for civic dialogue and making those conversations more inclusive. Several recent additions to the National Park System serve as illustrations, including Cane River Creole National Historical Park and its plantation slave quarters; Central High School National Historic Site in Little Rock, Arkansas; and Manzanar National Historic Site, the World War II internment camp for Japanese American citizens. "Our goal," wrote Dwight T. Pitcaithley, chief historian of the National Park Service, "is . . . understanding who we are, where we have been, and how we as a society, might approach the future. This collection of special places also allows us to examine our past—the contested along with the comfortable, the complex along with the simple, the controversial along with the inspirational."[5]

Recognition of Cultural Landscapes

Since the 1990s, recognition of the heritage value of cultural landscapes has grown in the United States and in other countries.[6] Adrian Phillips, former chair of the World Conservation Union's (IUCN's) World Commission on Protected Areas, called for "conservationists in many countries to focus their attention on . . . those inhabited landscapes where nature and culture are in some kind of balance [and where] talk of sustainable development can be more than rhetoric."[7]

Since the 1920s, the fields of cultural geography and, more recently, historic preservation, environmental history, and conservation biology have contributed to the concept of cultural landscapes.[8] This concept gives value and legitimacy to peopled places, a fundamentally different perspective from nature conservation's traditional focus on wild areas and historic preservation's focus on the built environment.

Cultural landscapes have value because they reflect history, beliefs, and ways of life. Consequently, traditional land use and associated management systems, as well as intangible cultural heritage, are given greater attention. In addition, a recent study of European landscapes documented examples of how humanized landscapes with traditions sustained over centuries have created environments rich in biodiversity.

Cultural landscapes are often large in scale and involve traditional management systems and multiple ownership. As such, they require conservation strategies that are locally based and work across boundaries, respect cultural and religious traditions and historical roots as well as ecological systems, and focus on sustainable economies.[9]

Measurement of Conservation Success

Robert Putnam, the widely read author of *Bowling Alone,* describes "social capital" as the "connections among individuals—social networks and the norms of reciprocity and trustworthiness that arise from them. . . . Civic virtue is most powerful when embedded in a dense network of reciprocal social relations."[10] It would be difficult to imagine successful conservation on any level in the twenty-first century that is not in large measure dependent on such social benefits. Fortunately, conservation activities often generate their own social capital. It is seen in grassroots organizing, fundraising, meetings, and all manner of volunteer activities.

Conservation practitioners are also seeing ethical reevaluation and enrichment of personal and public life through the processes of reconnection to place, social networking, and the act of conserving. This trend not only recognizes the centrality of place in people's lives but also suggests a fundamental rethinking of how success in conservation work, particularly land conservation, is measured. Reflecting on this transition, Gus Speth, dean of the Yale School of Forestry and Environmental Studies, said: "We broke things down to the component parts and laid out rational plans of attack, with deadlines, for tackling isolated problems. Now we know the most important resource is human motivation—hope, caring, our feelings about nature and our fellow human beings."[11]

Writer, photographer, and conservationist Peter Forbes has been an early and consistent voice for new measures of success. In a speech to a national gathering of the land trusts, he describes conservation as an engine for social cohesion:

> To save a piece of land, people rethink their future not in terms of what they could do for themselves but in terms of what they could do for others. They are building rootedness, based on their sense of service toward one another and the land. To act on such feelings is the essence of citizenship and moves us from isolation to community.[12]

"The act of conserving land," he goes on to observe, "has brought into people's moral universe a renewed sense of justice, meaning, respect, joy and love, and made people feel more complete."[13]

But there is more to this than personal self-fulfillment; it is also about community building. Land conservation and social capital are so interdependent that no action or benefit can be continued for any extended period outside the context of a healthy, stable, engaged community vested in conservation's success and continuity. Measurement of conservation's contribution to social capital is gradually becoming more sophisticated. The *Northern Forest Wealth Index,* a report of the Northern Forest Center (NFC), is one example. The NFC, a nonprofit organization established to strengthen citizen leadership and regional collaboration in the northeastern United States' Northern Forest region, based the *Wealth Index* on a community's self-assessment of core assets and values. These core assets and values, including culture, economy, educational systems, and environment, were measured to determine the overall wealth or well-being of Northern Forest communities.[14]

A Framework for Multiple Objectives

The idea of creating a framework for multi-objective planning and decision making was given national prominence in the conservation movement as a result of two somewhat parallel efforts. One effort, the Unified National Program for Floodplain Management, involved a redesign of the federal government's approach to flood loss reduction. This initiative attempted to make sense out of twenty-eight different federal agencies with forty-four different legislative authorities that were involved in flood control activity. As a result of this effort, long-term institutional, technical, and funding solutions to flood loss were created using a combination of structural and nonstructural controls.

In 1989, the second effort was led by Congressmen Joseph McDade of Pennsylvania and Morris Udall of Arizona, with the assistance of the National Park Service, in response to a growing public concern for river conservation. This initiative sought ideas and information from government and private sector leaders across the United States about ways to "recognize all of the legitimate beneficial public and private uses of river corridors and encourage coordinated decisions which result in the maximum public and private benefit with the least adverse impact on significant river values."

Although neither the floodplain management effort nor the McDade-Udall initiative met all the expectations of its supporters, both of these efforts had a major influence on conservation theory and practice. The multi-objective perspective began to be embraced by a significant part of the river conservation community and some parts of the federal bureaucracy. Since the National Park Service played a role in the river conservation initiative, the framework was replicated in other conservation projects and programs. These two efforts also began to redefine the traditional conservation role of government and resulted in a shift from centralized federal and state activities to a more decentralized approach.

Entrepreneurial Models of Conservation Economics

Experimentation with entrepreneurial models of conservation economics is encouraging new ways of working and new relationships that cultivate a more sustainable development path. "Conservation economics," a term coined by The Nature Conservancy's Center for Compatible Economic Development, represents a broad range of ventures in different parts of the country.

For example, alternative financing mechanisms for sustainable development are being tested in places such as Virginia's Clinch River valley. The Nature Conservancy has set up a "forest bank" for owners of small private woodlands. They permanently "deposit" their timber rights in return for a guaranteed annual income based on a program of sustainable forestry and the knowledge that their woodlands, which often have been in the family for many generations, will never have to be clear-cut or liquidated to meet debts. Another example is ShoreBank Pacific, a community development bank with an environmental focus, founded as a joint venture between Shorebank Corporation of Chicago (the nation's first community development bank) and Ecotrust (a nonprofit environmental organization). The bank is set up to provide financial and advisory support to individuals and community enterprises that combine conservation and economic development. Projects such as these enhance conservation and build social capital while generating new opportunities for employment and strengthening community self-determination and confidence.

More and more ventures involve food, a cultural common denominator that can build social capital in almost every corner of the world. The Nature Conservancy, for example, is now using the World Wide Web to market "conservation beef" from conserved ranches in Montana's Madison Valley. Ecotrust, in addition to its financial ventures, also partners with local fishermen on the Columbia River to market value-added seafood with the "Fresh from Young's Bay" label, a guarantee of both high quality and ecologically sensitive fishing practices. With the advent of the "slow food" movement, which began in Italy in the 1980s, careful stewardship and marketing of traditional food products, often cultivated or created by artisanal methods, is gaining international recognition and momentum. In many places around the world, food is bringing together people who are passionately committed to landscape and agricultural stewardship, cultural diversity and tradition, craftsmanship, public health, and general well-being—and good, healthy food.

Place-Based Education

Experts agree that a longer-range horizon for conservation change will include significant investments in schools, curricula, and lifelong learning opportunities. These investments reflect a priority on place-based education and life skills, including civic learning, service learning, and cooperative group work and problem solving. Place-based education, according to Jack Chin, codirector of the Funders' Forum on Environment and Education, "provides students with opportunities to connect with themselves, their community, and their local environment through hands-on, real-world learning experiences. This enables students to see that learning is relevant to their world, to take pride in where they live, to connect with the rest of the world, and to develop into concerned and contributing citizens."[15]

David Lacy, an archaeologist with the Green Mountain National Forest, runs a summer archaeology camp for middle-school students in Rutland, Vermont, called Relics and Ruins. Guiding students to cellar holes and remnant orchards on abandoned farmsteads with sheaths of historical maps in hand, Lacy takes a place-based approach to learning that focuses on the nature of change and its relevance for young people. "We look at artifacts and their stories but also look at the larger vision of change," says Lacy, "and the powerful influence people have had through history on land use, shaping all our landscapes, even places that today appear wild. We want students to realize that they too hold this power in their hands and they need to be very thoughtful about the change they put in motion."[16]

Cautionary Observations

Although the trends described here are generally favorable to conservation, a number of circumstances can create serious obstacles to successful conservation practice, particularly in the implementation and management of community-based efforts. It is important to understand how these circumstances arise and their potential consequences.

Tyranny of Small Solutions

Community-based efforts by nature are focused on a local scale, independent, diverse, and, frequently, geographically random. With the ever-increasing number of relatively small public or private conservation initiatives, it is harder to predict whether these efforts are efficient and effective and will accomplish anything beyond their project boundaries.

The scattershot approach of these efforts confronts conservation leaders with a phenomenon called "the tyranny of small solutions." Community-based efforts may result in small, apparently independent conservation decisions made by individual communities, groups, and local governments that may or may not achieve a predictable or desirable outcome.

Undervaluing the Relationship between People and Their Landscape

On the whole, the trend in conservation practice is toward inclusiveness, collaboration, and the valuing of local people's knowledge and experience. However, work is still being done in which people are treated as "the problem" or, worse, either are the object of condescension or are largely circumvented in the process. Many conservation practitioners and technical experts are not adequately trained or skilled in areas such as the building and maintaining of relationships, collaborative problem solving, human ecology, and use of social science tools and analysis.

Home Rule and Fragmentation

Land-use decision making remains the responsibility of local and state governments. Home rule and private property issues have made meaningful discussions of regionwide growth and the conservation of larger landscapes extremely sensitive and often controversial. Conservation organizations and agencies are in some instances reluctant to advance, or even discuss publicly, policies and alternatives that suggest any departure from a traditional emphasis on economic development or that might be perceived as infringing on private property rights. The inability of multiple ownerships and jurisdictions to work together to define common conservation goals—such as the protection of wildlife corridors—can result in the continued fragmentation of landscapes. Landscape fragmentation contributes to the loss of critical habitat, scenic and cultural character, and traditional land uses.

Principles for Reconstructing Conservation in the Twenty-First Century

The emergence of community-based conservation has shifted the center of gravity from top-down management strategies toward more decentralized, localized, place-based approaches. This emphasis on local solutions and place-based strategies is balanced with a greater sense of larger regional and global contexts.

Conservation practitioners are thinking at larger scales, looking at whole systems and landscapes. There is a growing emphasis on cross-boundary collaboration, interdisciplinary, and international perspectives. Conservation is often most effective when it is carried out across sectors. Today there is a more favorable environment for participatory activities and comanagement and a growing appreciation of the important role conservation can play in enhancing public life and long-term economic prosperity and sustainability.

The ethical framework for conservation is becoming more socially inclusive, focusing on broader community values and social equity. There is also a greater respect for the cultural relationships that have developed between human communities and the natural world, often based on traditional local land-use practices and a deep spiritual connection between people and place.[17]

In light of recent trends and constraints identified here, several principles emerge for reconstructing conservation in the twenty-first century. The following principles illustrate four characteristics of an evolving framework for conservation: people, dialogue, and civil society; place knowledge; leadership; and creativity.

People, Dialogue, and Civil Society

Conservation is about building and sustaining a network of relationships that creates the environment for common vision and common action. This is an inclusive process that encourages open communication and dialogue.

- *Conservation is always about people.* Conservation success is people-dependent, and the way the work is conducted is crucially important. The process needs to be fair, equitable, and open. Dialogue provides an exchange of ideas, reflecting the experience and point of view of all involved. Trust and credibility are critical and are established and maintained through actions, not just words. Successful strategies acknowledge that all conservation partners, both local and outside experts, are important. A vision for the future is built on special knowledge of the landscapes and communities.
- *Conservation requires good civics as well as good information.* The current generation of conservationists works to integrate good information with good civics. Conservation thought and practice require better understanding of the values of a community and its ecological, cultural, and economic contexts. The conservation process is locally led, open to public discourse, interdisciplinary, and inclusive. Dialogue, relying on story, skill, and experience, is used to exchange ideas and move the discussion beyond individual opinions and points of view.

  Deciding what action to take to conserve a community, a landscape, and specific sites within it requires a process—an equation—to decide what actions should be taken, why, by whom, and how. The process is consensus based, and agreement is secured both at the beginning and at every major decision point.
- *Conservation creates a framework for integrating programs, interests, and points of view.* Landscapes and the conservation business are extraordinarily complex. A framework to manage these places and activities involves cooperation with a complex array of stakeholders from all levels of government and the private sector; strong communication; the crossing of traditional areas of responsibility; respect for other values and perspectives; and the spirit of "getting to yes." Anne Swanson, Michael Haire, and Paul Schwartz, in "Chesapeake Bay: Managing an Ecosystem," wrote about the difficulties encountered in place-based efforts, including "defining management units, understanding the biological, physical, economic, and cultural factors at play, and structuring a management framework that properly integrates all the component parts."[18] Ultimately, integration of programs, interests, and points of view is essential to ensure the success of landscape conservation.

Place Knowledge

A comprehensive understanding of place requires a systems-thinking approach that probes relationships and connections. This approach considers the larger context and recognizes that the whole is greater than the sum of the parts.

- *Multidisciplinary approaches are used to understand landscapes and communities.* Geographic context is essential in understanding a region, watershed, or site and in gaining knowledge of the place, its inhabitants, and the area's physical, biological, and cultural history. It is essential in recognizing all environmental, community, and economic values.

  Conservationists use resource information and community visioning to answer the following "McHargian" questions for a place (e.g., a basin, physiographic region, or site): What are the environments? How did they come to be? What physical, biological, and social processes characterize them? What tendencies do they exhibit? What has been the effect of human use? What is their current status? What do we want for our future?[19]

- *Conservationists think one size larger.* Conservation leaders think one size larger than the scale at which they are working, to ensure that they understand the relationship of their actions to other values, efforts, and influences. Ecology—biological, physical, and human—demonstrates that the ecological, social, economic, and spatial context is important to consider in any conservation project or program. It's important to recognize the relationship of conservation work to the people, businesses, living resources, and values most directly affected.

Leadership

Collaborative leadership can build a common vision and sense of purpose to engage and energize communities of people to work together.

- *Conservation leadership is about collaboration.* Although most conservationists will agree that it is more important to be successful in conservation than it is to be in charge, many efforts are thwarted because of "organizational turf" and egos. Successful conservation leaders have collaborative skills, and share decision making and recognition in order to achieve positive results. Sharing conservation responsibility improves effectiveness, enhances equity, and builds organizational capacity.

- *Conservation action is never just about money.* Even though funding is typically a high priority with public and private conservation agencies and organizations, successful conservation work never depends totally on money. Whether a conservation effort succeeds always depends on whether various stakeholders can agree on what they hope to achieve together. If there is agreement on vision and on conservation action, money never seems to be a problem.

Creativity

Conservation is as much an art as a science. Effective conservation relies on imagination, resourcefulness, and adaptation to continually meet challenges in constantly changing circumstances.

- *Conservation is both design and discovery.* Each landscape, community, or site is unique, and the conservation process used to respond to an opportunity or a problem is hand-tailored to fit the unique set of circumstances. Conservation initiatives include a dynamic interplay of two salient features—a general emphasis on designed approaches and an openness to discovery—that work together to create progress.

Frances J. Seymour, director of the World Resources Institute's Institutions and Governance Program, wrote that "design" means the use of tools, templates, methods, or approaches that have been developed and proven outside a specific place and that are brought in to respond to specific concerns or issues. "Discovery" is the emergence of locally conceived and instituted actions developed to meet a particular need or demand that may have emerged or revealed itself during the conservation process.[20]

Conservation leaders who are open to the dynamic interplay of designed and discovered approaches are more effective at building on the successful traditions of a community and create more approaches to solving problems and seizing opportunities for conservation.

Conclusion

In response to nearly three decades of accelerating landscape change, disinvestment in urban areas, sprawling development, and biodiversity loss, a promising new direction in community-based conservation is emerging, based on the fundamental principles outlined here. It is important, however, to recognize that community-based conservation work in today's world can often be difficult, complicated, and challenging. Success requires time, patience, and perseverance. There are few shortcuts or alternatives to a way of working that carefully builds and sustains long-term relationships, respects a process that is fundamentally democratic and inclusive, and is guided by sound conservation principles.

The conservation community is challenged to continuously broaden its base and encourage an ongoing dialogue among people representing a wide variety of backgrounds and interests. This dialogue can include a sharing of conservation experiences in both wildlands and urban neighborhoods; public and private lands; tangible and intangible heritage; leisure and working landscapes; and the academy and practice.

Wendell Berry wrote that "people now are living on the far side of a broken connection, and . . . this is potentially catastrophic."[21] To reach across to the far side of that broken connection, we will need to strengthen the potent ties that bind people to places, to stories, and to one another. We will also need leadership and imagination to better define a language for conservation that is more inclusive than the paradigms of the nineteenth and twentieth centuries. We will need a conservation community that is ethical, democratic, and humanistic in the broadest sense as well as creative, entrepreneurial, and intergenerational. Conservation that both taps and invests in the next generation is conservation that will have social capital for its own sustainability.

Chapter 20

Conservation Stewardship: Legacies from Vermont's Marsh

DAVID LOWENTHAL

Mankind's greedy and ignorant abuse of the earth was first comprehensively chronicled by George Perkins Marsh in 1864, early in his twenty-one-year tenure as American ambassador to Italy. The long saga of Old World devastation led him to urge environmental reform so as to prevent like catastrophe in the New World. Marsh's *Man and Nature* limned a bleak portent:

> In parts of Asia Minor, of Northern Africa, of Greece, and even of Alpine Europe, the operation of causes set in action by man has brought the face of the earth to a desolation almost as complete as that of the moon. The earth is fast becoming an unfit home for its noblest inhabitant, and another era of equal human crime and human improvidence would reduce it to such a condition of impoverished productiveness, of shattered surface, of climatic excess, as to threaten the depravation, barbarism, and perhaps even extinction of the species.[1]

What gave rise to this apocalyptic warning, at the very peak of America's confidence in its conquest of bounteous nature? Up to then, that conquest had seemed almost wholly auspicious—a fruitful working of superabundant resources. Man's improvements accorded with divine intent; the wealth won by clearing and draining and cultivating showed God's approval. Where human influence was not benign, it was insignificant. In newly settled America, adverse environmental effects were easy to ignore: soils eroded or exhausted were simply vacated for lands farther west; forests logged or burned seemed insignificant next to the abundance of timber beyond the horizon. Meanwhile, buoyant nature would soon heal itself.

But confidence in nature's recuperative powers less and less matched

observed reality. In Marsh's native Vermont, optimism was sapped by deforestation, erosion, and land abandonment. A single lifetime had seen
tracts cleared, planted, and improved—and then worn out and laid waste.
Based on his own observations and extensive reading on both sides of the
Atlantic, Marsh reviewed the dire effects of technological progress on
woods and waters, soils and living species—the whole fabric of organic
and inorganic nature.

Nature thus misused did *not* heal itself; land exploited and then abandoned remained depleted for ages, if not forever. Confirming Marsh's warning, population growth, commodity needs, clear-cut lumbering, intensified
farming, engineering, mining, and building soon became acutely evident. By
the late nineteenth century, some worried that exploitation might not only
outrun existing resources but endanger the very fabric of productive nature.
By the late twentieth century, this fear had become received wisdom.[2]

Marsh's admonitions and proposed reforms are now so widely accepted
that it is hard to realize how pervasive confidence once was in man's benign
use of the earth, and how blind most were to their forebears' and their own
environmental damage. The tale of waste and greed chronicled in *Man and
Nature* appalls environmentalists today. Nonetheless, a substantial residue
of past purblind optimism still endures. Despite manifold proof of the extent and malignity of adverse human influence, many continue to cling to
two comforting myths: on the one hand, that mankind is impotent to seriously damage the earth; on the other, that human agency can easily mend
any damage done. Unlike Marsh, both the general public and policy makers discount the gravity of the injuries we inflict and overestimate our
restorative powers.

I do not advocate resurrecting Marsh's conservation philosophy; that
would be anachronistic folly. We now confront environmental menaces
unimaginable in his day, albeit with the aid of ecological expertise unknown to him. But the threats of his day seemed no less alarming to him
than ours appear to us. And Marsh's insights offer a useful template on
which to map our own parlous plight.

Hence, I focus here on five Marsh tenets salient for our own dealings
with nature: that human powers are uniquely formidable and human influence singularly intentional; that we cannot relinquish control of nature;
that we can never know enough to foretell all the effects of our interference; that notwithstanding our imperfect knowledge, we dare not post-
pone restorative action; and that stewardship, indispensable for the
common good now and in the future, needs to be ceaselessly nurtured.

Human Potency

That mankind's effect on the earth was uniquely swift, extensively ruinous, and long irreparable was Marsh's chief ecological insight. Memory and foresight, imagination and machinery equip the human tenure of earth with unmatched powers. Whereas animals act only instinctively and "with a view to single and direct purposes," humans aim consciously at preconceived and often remote objectives.[3] And new technology ever magnifies human potency; the effects of mankind's manipulations increasingly impinge on the earth, rivaling climatic, edaphic, and geologic processes.

The Necessity of Intervention

Human agency can never be revoked, nor can the management of nature be relaxed. Because our influence is incessant, perpetual meddling is required to rectify or mitigate damage done or likely to ensue. Man's impact is extensively ruinous and long lasting; "the wounds he inflicts . . . are not healed until he withdraws the arm that gave the blow," or, indeed, for long thereafter.[4] Land once subdued and then abandoned does not recover its previous plenitude. It remains impoverished until taken into human care.

Against humanity's massive derangements, Marsh saw nature as largely impotent. Species wiped out were never reborn. Domesticated creatures did not revert to the wild. Woodlands utterly denuded might never recover. Yet neither regret for past improvidence nor fear of future follies justified noninterference. Rather, men must manage nature with foresight and understanding, exerting not less but more control. We need to think like a mountain, in Aldo Leopold's phrase, but we do so not to *act* like a mountain but to learn how to mitigate the effects of torrents, avalanches, and other features of mountain behavior whose chaotic and intemperate excesses we try to tame and assuage. Civilized tenure of the earth is a history of largely successful efforts to alleviate the tempestuous extremes of natural processes, ensuring regular and reliable supplies of food and water, heat and fuel, by means of sowing and storing crops, building dams and reservoirs, laying out roads and conduits.

Acknowledging Ignorance

Marsh stressed that ecological uncertainty is our chronic condition. However much we may learn about nature and the ways we affect it, our environmental future is bound to be perilous. Ecological complexity is intrinsically unfathomable; every advance in knowledge generates new consequences whose end effects on nature outpace our understanding. Even more than Marsh, we are now fearsomely aware that the consequences of our acts are virtually without limit. The worst effect of the Chernobyl nuclear disaster, as Kai Erikson put it, is that most of its victims *have not yet even been born.* What good is it that the proposed nuclear waste burial disposal at Yucca Mountain in Nevada is certified to be safe against leakage for ten thousand years, when the by-products of its decay may lethally contaminate air and water for as long as a million years?[5]

Acting with Imperfect Knowledge

Marsh stressed that environmental protection ought not to be deferred until all the facts are in. To arrest decay and restore nature, he sought comprehensive surveys of terrain and soils, climate and vegetation. But such surveys would require decades, and "we are, even now, breaking up the floor and wainscoting and doors and window frames of our dwelling, for fuel to warm our bodies and seethe our pottage, and the world cannot afford to wait till the slow and sure progress of exact science has taught it a better economy."[6] The fact that environmental amelioration took a long time was no justification for postponing it. "The *improvement* of forest trees is the work of centuries," Marsh later noted; "so much the more reason for beginning *now.*"[7] "More research is needed," President George W. Bush's classic excuse for doing nothing about global warming, is a recipe for disaster. More research is always needed, but remedial action is so likely to be crucially essential that delay would be folly.

The Necessity of Stewardship

Environmental conservation requires concern for the interests of the future.[8] Such concern is sometimes unpopular because it is believed to come at the cost of present interests. Marsh was at pains to show that future concern in fact enhanced present worth. "It requires a very generous spirit in a landholder to plant a wood on a farm he expects to sell, or which he knows will pass out of the hands of his descendants," he wrote, "but the very fact of having begun a plantation would attach the proprietor more strongly to the soil" and, hence, reduce the "restlessness" and "instability" he saw as major defects of American life. In caring for the well-being of our heirs and successors, we enrich the purpose and meaning of our own brief span of life and enhance the longevity of our communal attachments.[9]

Yet environmental stewardship is far from innate, nor it is easily sustained; it must be inculcated into the values of each generation. As Marsh came sadly to realize, enlightened self-interest was no adequate safeguard for long-term resource management. Unlike Old World serfs, American yeomen owned the land they tilled and could reap the benefits of their improvements. But selfish individualism, the lure of instant profits, and the cancer of corporate monopoly dimmed Marsh's hopes. Unless it were "his pecuniary interest to preserve them, every proprietor will fell his woods." Freeborn Americans would stomach no effort to abridge "the sacred right of every man to do what he will with his own." Only public control could curb maltreatment of nature, protect national resources, conserve the common weal. To be sure, government power spawned official abuse. "But the corruption thus engendered, foul as it is, does not strike so deep as the rottenness of private corporations."[10]

Even more than in Marsh's time, the insistent demands of the immediate present drown out the needs of future generations. Bias toward what is wanted right now is ingrained in our social and political institutions. Individuals are too impotent, corporations too profit-bent, governments too dependent on instant results to take care for environmental well-being beyond the next election, let alone beyond our own lifetimes.

Viable environmental management demands collaborative effort over many generations. Any reform initiated or furthered by us will require the inputs and insights of our distant descendants to be effectual. We cannot commit future generations to carry on our plans. But whatever may be worth continuing is more apt to succeed if today's activists consciously attend to their descendants' interests. Environmental reform has, up to now, in the main been kindled by sorrow for prior mismanagement and contrition for past damage. But grief and regret alone are not enough to instill constructive and durable reform; also needed is pride based on sturdy confidence in the value of ongoing stewardship.

Coda on the Pace of Change

Writing in an era of radical transformation, Marsh sought to protect all manner of things—landscape, language, historical memory, national identity—from corrosive decay and oblivion. He knew that change was, to be sure, inevitable in all institutions, all environments, all lives. To embargo change, to seek to preserve the past in aspic, would be not only futile but also counterproductive. Rather, we must carefully weigh the benefits and losses of status and change, old and new. Given the prevalence of short-term bias, Marsh thought it generally wiser to keep than to transform. Rapid change was especially to be feared, for it sundered the present and the future from the past and deprived society of its collective inheritance. "Love of innovation is more dangerous [than] ultra-conservative attachment" to tradition, he wrote, "because the irreverent and thoughtless wantonness of an hour, may destroy that which only the slow and painful labor of years or of centuries can rebuild." He likened the physical benefits of environmental stability to the cultural benefits of linguistic continuity: because the English language had changed but slowly and retained so much, its early classic works remained a living source of creative inspiration. "Like the ultimately beneficial rains of heaven, social changes produce their best effect when neither very hastily precipitated, nor very frequently repeated."[11]

Of all the changes looming on the immediate horizon, Marsh saw the most ominous as mankind's conjoined slaughter of nature and of itself—a double suicide of ecology and of society. "The human race seems destined to become its own executioner," he mordantly forecast in Man and Nature, "on the one hand, [by] exhausting the capacity of the earth to furnish sustenance to her taskmaster; on the other, compensating diminished production by inventing more efficient methods of exterminating the consumer."[12]

Yet this very book by Marsh was cheered by a heroic Italian colleague who found it a prime antidote to destructive strife. In 1865, General Giuseppe Garibaldi thanked Marsh for sending him Man and Nature:

> You treat like a true master subjects which ought to be the favorite occupation of the eminent men of this century . . . instead of employing their genius in the invention of instruments of death. It is truly consoling to hear an authoritative voice arising from the very midst of that Diplomacy . . . of deception and despair, urging man forward towards . . . the study of nature, from which every fountain of prosperity flows.[13]

No more hopeful accolade to environmental stewardship could be conceived; no more constructive a prelude to reconstructing conservation could be desired.

Part VI

Conclusion

Chapter 21

Finding Common Ground: Emerging Principles for a Reconstructed Conservation

BEN A. MINTEER AND ROBERT E. MANNING

The preceding chapters have followed a wide-ranging but unbroken path through the fields of history, philosophy, political theory, sociology, anthropology, conservation biology, economics, and the applied professions engaged in conservation practice. Clearly, our authors have much to say about the shape and substance of a reformed conservationism, and they have provided an impressive pool of ideas to draw from in our efforts to move forward with this larger project. They have responded to the original challenge of providing a thoughtful assessment of the current theoretical and methodological trends in conservation thought and practice, and they have given us a clear-eyed appraisal of earlier conservation traditions and their bearing on present and future work. In this final chapter, we would like to bring together some of the major insights, arguments, and proposals contained in the individual contributions. We believe these ideas represent many of the key commitments required by a revivified conservationism in a new era of human action and reflection on the land.

Without question, the chapters in this volume offer a wealth of diverse perspectives on the conservation discussion. For example, on the preceding pages you have encountered projects focused on wilderness and protected areas (Trombulak; Callicott; Mitchell and Brown), cultural landscapes (Judd; Diamant, Eugster, and Mitchell), rural and agrarian landscapes (Vivanco, Thompson, Freyfogle), urban and built environments (McCullough, Minteer, Stokowski), and multiple points on the geographic map (Judd; Stokowski; Vivanco; Mitchell and Brown). You have come across chapters providing a fresh look at conservation icons (Lowenthal,

Flader) and those focused on the contributions of lesser-known figures and voices in the tradition (Judd, McCullough, Thompson, Minteer, Taylor). There have been discussions of the trends and challenges of domestic conservation planning and practice (Dizard; Trombulak; Diamant, Eugster, and Mitchell) and of international conservation agendas and efforts (Vivanco; Mitchell and Brown). You have seen enthusiastic endorsements of pluralism in conservation values and goals (Norton; Manning; Bengston and Iverson) and cautionary tales about the dangers of fragmentation and atomism in the conservation movement (Freyfogle, Trombulak). These examples—and there are many others—illustrate the multiple approaches and diverse applications pursued by the contributors to this book.

As we mentioned in the introduction, however, we are struck by the degree to which our authors' work converges in a number of significant ways in this book. This unity amid diversity, or common ground, can best be demonstrated through a cataloguing of what we see as a set of emerging "principles for reconstruction" that issue from the nineteen contributed chapters herein. Although we believe the following is a reasonably comprehensive list, there are no doubt additional principles, themes, and intersecting lines of argument to be uncovered in these chapters, and we encourage you to continue to explore and mine them for further insight in the course of your own reading. We hope, however, that the principles that follow provide a useful summary and synthesis of the work in this volume and that they set an agenda for further discussions and studies of the conservation tradition and its contemporary vitality in the literature and on the landscape.

Twelve Principles for Reconstructing Conservation

We have derived the following general principles for reconstructing conservation thought and practice from the nineteen contributed chapters in this book. As stated here, they are empirical observations about some of the major commitments and strategies of a new, revised conservation approach. Yet we believe these principles also possess an important normative force, especially for setting a thoughtful and innovative agenda for the scholarly fields that study conservation and the professions that carry out conservation projects on the ground.

1. A Reconstructed Conservation Will Adopt an Integrative Understanding of Nature and Culture

The authors in this volume endorse a model of conservation that recognizes the importance of the linkages between natural and cultural systems. Much of this view may be attributed to our improved understanding in recent years of the history (and prehistory) of human modifications of the environment. Indeed, as Callicott reminds us in his chapter, no landscape is really free of anthropogenic effects. This is ratified by Vivanco in his statement that "recent archaeological, ethnohistoric, and ethnographic research has adequately proven that in important instances Western projections of unpeopled wilderness are in fact artifactual landscapes manipulated by the hands of people."[1] This conclusion is clearly supported by Judd's discussion of the eastern conservation tradition of rural New Englanders: "The markers of eastern identity are more typically pastoral, distinctive not because of their natural *or* their cultural attributes but because these two are so inextricably combined."[2] Judd goes on to cite Henry David Thoreau in support of the linkages between nature and culture: "The eastern forest, with its legacy of disturbance and its explosive ecological succession, challenges the idea that nature and culture can be viewed as separate entities. Thoreau, for example, found the Maine woods authenticating in part because it invoked the lore of logging, hunting, guiding, exploring, and timber surveying: it was a cultural, as much as a natural, place."[3]

The fusion of systems of human meaning and activity with the cycles and processes of the natural world also has a number of implications for our understanding of the boundaries of the larger conservation discussion, one that challenges many of our previously held conceptual and professional categories. As McCullough points out in his chapter, if, as William Cronon and others have suggested, nature is a cultural construction, then our conservation emphasis should be on cultural resources as much as natural resources, or, alternatively, on their intersection. In fact, McCullough suggests that "the goals are so closely parallel and the task so enormous that one wonders why cultural and natural resource protection have remained separate for so long."[4] Yet, as Vivanco points out, the embrace of culture in conservation can be a very complicated move, especially when "culture" becomes inappropriately instrumentalized in the service of the conservationist agenda. "Thinking of culture as a mere tool to change behaviors," he writes, "may undermine the very reason we might want to bring it to bear in conservation, which is its ability to help focus attention on the highly specific and context-dependent processes and interactions that help determine why people relate with their natural surroundings in certain ways."[5]

2. A Reconstructed Conservation Will Be Concerned with Working and Cultural Landscapes as Well as More "Pristine" Environments

Many of the chapters in this volume warn us, directly or indirectly, of the dangers of embracing a "wilderness first" view of conservation, one that discredits or ignores cultural and working landscapes in favor of an idealized "pristine" nature. The majority of our authors would presumably agree with the sentiments of Diamant, Eugster, and Mitchell, who suggest that the concept of cultural landscapes "gives value and legitimacy to peopled places, a fundamentally different perspective from nature conservation's traditional focus on wild areas."[6] In this sense, Judd's account of the "long lived-in lands" of the Northeast offers a corrective to this wilderness bias in environmental history as it elevates "peopled" and transformed landscapes into the conservationist geography. As he puts it, "the oscillations of deforestation and reforestation, depletion and renewal, settlement and abandonment, and pollution and recovery suggest reciprocity rather than nature-as-victim. . . . One era's ecological disaster becomes the next era's textured landscape."[7] Dizard is even more direct: "'Undisturbed' nature is an oxymoron. . . . Put another way, to argue that the undisturbed (by humans) is to be preferred to the disturbed is to court a serious and disabling teleology."[8] The "altered lands" perspective is also on display in Thompson's portrait of the agrarian vision, one in which "human beings are hard at work within nature."[9] Thompson's account shows us how this agricultural modification of the land also transforms individual character and community values, in the process establishing close ties between rural producers and their supporting environments.

The contemporary notion of "sense of place" and its inherent blending of nature and culture is at the heart of working and cultural landscapes as suggested by Diamant, Eugster, and Mitchell; Freyfogle; Judd; Stokowski; and others. Quoting geographer E. C. Relph, Stokowski writes that "the relationship between community and place is a very powerful one in which each reinforces the identity of the other, and in which the landscape is very much an expression of communally held beliefs and values and of inter-personal involvements."[10] In the southern Appalachian context, Judd suggests that "mountain people saw the forest not simply as board feet but, historian Donald Davis asserts, also as a 'living matrix of plants, animals, and shared memories'" and that their "folk knowledge in turn cultured a sense of ownership,"[11] which ultimately developed into stewardship. In the agrarian tradition, Thompson notes that people's "actions shape and transform [nature] as surely as nature shapes and transforms them"[12] and that communities evolved in this way "will see no tension between conservation of wild nature and the duties of the steward."[13] Minteer suggests that the origins of regional planning, as espoused by Lewis Mumford, Benton MacKaye, and others, may offer an appropriately expansive model of a re-constructed conservation: "The task of regional planning, according to Mumford, was . . . more culturally and ecologically grounded than the approach taken by conservationists, which in his view merely attempted to protect wilderness areas from intrusion and sought to avoid the wasteful development of natural resources. Although he thought such a strategy was to be praised for protecting the rare and spectacular environments of the continent and for injecting efficiency measures into resource exploitation, he feared it was too limited in scope to serve as a guide for a true environmental ethic."[14] Building on their legacy, Minteer concludes that "a reconstructed conservation philosophy needs to address the complex whole of human experience in the environment, including the urban, the rural, and the wild."[15]

3. A Reconstructed Conservation Will Rely on a Wider and More Contextual Reading of the Conservation Tradition

Several of the chapters suggest that we already have many of the intellectual tools and resources of a new framework for conservation embedded in our history and culture; we need only adopt a more expansive and more nuanced approach to the conservation tradition for these ideas and commitments to come into sharper focus. In his case for an "eastern" conservation history, for example, Judd writes that we must adopt a regional and ethically textured understanding of the roots of the American conservation impulse, an interpretation that stands outside the conventional "western" environmental narrative. In his words, "plumbing the rhetoric of place in long-settled lands reveals a more nuanced set of motives behind the use of nature."[16] Similarly, in his attempt to recover the lost agrarian voice in conservationism, Thompson concludes that this tradition has been "so thoroughly neglected and forgotten that it is now possible to see it as something new, as an expansion of conservation thought that can play a significant role in its reconstruction."[17] Meine's plea for another look at the "radical center" of the conservation vision of the Progressive Era and Minteer's suggestion that we find a way to weave Lewis Mumford's "pragmatic conservationism" into the intellectual histories of conservation philosophy are further examples of this multi-vocal call for a contemporary rereading of conservation icons such as Henry David Thoreau, George Perkins Marsh, John Muir, Gifford Pinchot, and Aldo Leopold and for a revision and expansion of our received accounts of the tradition. "Any reconstructed conservation of today," concludes Minteer, "especially one in search of a philosophical 'usable past' to inform and guide future thought and practice, could not ask for a greater intellectual inheritance."[18]

4. A Reconstructed Conservation Will Require Long-Range Landscape Stewardship and Restoration Efforts

As David Lowenthal writes, one of George Perkins Marsh's most enduring lessons is that "stewardship, indispensable for the common good now and in the future, needs to be ceaselessly nurtured."[19] Although Lowenthal finds in Marsh the notion that we need to take greater control of nature, he suggests that this celebration of human agency is checked by the frank acknowledgment of our ignorance regarding the long-term effects of our actions on the land. Yet despite this "imperfect knowledge," Lowenthal concludes, following Marsh, that restorative actions designed to reverse severe human effects are urgently needed and well justified. In his chapter on large-scale restoration projects, however, Dizard points out that such restorative activities may actually present formidable obstacles to effective conservation stewardship, barriers due in part to some restoration advocates' absolutism about the "proper" methods and goals of environmentalism. Indeed, as we suggest later in this chapter, a necessarily active and reconstructed conservation requires a pluralistic and robustly democratic context.

Other chapters illustrate the importance of conservation stewardship not only for taking care of the land for future generations but also for building social capital and shoring up the realm of civil society. Stokowski writes that "conservation must also be about building community, so that people will be more likely to value others as well as value places."[20] Based on their wide-ranging program of international work, Mitchell and Brown enthusiastically observe that "one of the most exciting elements of stewardship work is that it often leads to advances in other social areas. Stewardship helps to build civil society by giving people opportunities to participate in shaping their environment and, therefore, their lives."[21]

5. A Reconstructed Conservation Will Have "Land Health" as One of Its Primary Socio-ecological Goals

The notion of health emerges from several of the chapters as an important overlapping normative goal of conservation, suggesting the need to understand and maintain the linkages between the reproduction of ecological and cultural processes over time. The chapters by Callicott and Freyfogle discuss how this unifying concept played a large part in Aldo Leopold's thinking about the aims of conservation—that is, a harmony between productive practices and ecological processes (or, as Dizard puts it, "land capable of sustaining a robust variety of living things, including humans"[22]). And in the agrarian context, as Thompson notes, "productive practices that cannot be passed down from parent to child fail to represent a heritable way of life, which (for an agrarian) is to say that they are no way of life at all."[23]

More strategically, Meine sees the goal of land health as uniting a broad coalition of interests, professions, and citizens. In his view, it is an area in which "people who care about land and communities and wild things and places, whatever their political stripe, may meet to make common cause."[24] We should also not be too concerned that we will continue to grope for empirical definitions of "land health" (definitions that might best be formulated at the community level). Bengston and Iverson note appropriate analogs between the case of conservation and normative notions of "human health" in medicine and "justice" in law. Perhaps, as Leopold anticipated in these matters of higher concern, it is as important to strive as to achieve.

6. A Reconstructed Conservation Will Be Adaptive and Open to Multiple Practices and Objectives

It is clear that our authors do not subscribe to a rigid "one size fits all" model of conservation. Instead, they describe in various ways a more flexible and adaptive approach to conserving the landscape. As Vivanco writes, "we need a conservationist culture based on dialogue—not domination—

that is not about simply facilitating an exchange of wisdom in order to convert people to some predetermined expectations of what conservation 'should be.' This dialogue should also involve a process of mutual enrichment in which the means and ends of conservation themselves are open to new contingencies and intercultural negotiations."[25] The specific practices of a reconstructed conservation will vary. Thompson's agrarian conservationist, for example, "would endorse parks and museums that memorialize farms and farming ways of particular note but would find it ultimately of greater importance to bring working farms into the conservation ideal. Activities such as farmer's markets and community-supported agriculture, which connect those who do not farm with those who do, could come to be understood as productive conservation activities."[26]

Many of the chapters also suggest that we must find ways to accommodate multiple social objectives (as well as ecological constraints) in framing significant conservation policies. As Manning writes in his chapter, variations in ecological conditions, cultural patterns, and institutional structure may lead to environmental policies and conservation models that vary across the natural and cultural landscape: "diverse environmental values and ethics offer empirical support for a correspondingly 'patchy' natural and cultural landscape."[27] As Manning notes, the U.S. public land system offers a model of such diversity in the conservation mission, with national forests displaying more utilitarian commitments and the national parks embodying more preservationist sentiments on the landscape. Likewise, Callicott's updating of the three paradigms of conservation philosophy in light of changes in ecological thought supports a multidimensional model of conservation action, as does Trombulak's discussion of dominant-use designations across a spectrum of land uses, from intensive human development to ecological lands managed to promote biodiversity and landscape-level processes. Diamant, Eugster, and Mitchell's example of the National Park Service's river conservation program provides a compelling illustration of how such broad-based, multi-objective, and multi-value conservation programs can meet with great success in practice. Further, it seems likely that conservation will continue to evolve, for, as Bengston and Iverson write, "the history of conservation in the United States is a history of responding to changing social, economic, political, technological, and environmental conditions."[28] In this respect, the *process* of conservation—its adaptive and open character—may be as important as the final product. The adaptive environmental and policy framework outlined by Norton, a process informed by science but considered within a multi-value, democratic context, may be a particularly appropriate model for this larger project.

7. A Reconstructed Conservation Will Embrace Value Pluralism

This endorsement of an integrated diversity of land-use types and objectives is reinforced by many of the authors' advocacy of pluralism in environmental values. Bengston and Iverson, in their defense of an evolving ecological economics against the traditional economic paradigm, argue that the latter is "inadequate to inform conservation thought and practice in the face of changed ecological and social contexts of the twenty-first century"[29] because it is unable to comprehend and incorporate all the diverse values people hold for the environment, especially noninstrumental moral and spiritual values and the value of life-supporting ecological services and functions. This value pluralism toward nature (including nonmaterial and noncommodity values) is supported in the empirical investigations Manning presents in his chapter and in the developing ecological science that, according to Callicott and Trombulak, recognizes "ecological services" (e.g., climate stabilization) as a natural resource as important as timber and other commodities, or more so. Such pluralism need not lead to political gridlock, however. Indeed, Norton's articulation of a multi-criteria approach to environmental valuation, one in which "good policies are marked by their robust performance over multiple criteria, which opens opportunities for win-win situations when one policy can support multiple values and goals,"[30] promises to offer a way out of the ideological logjams between intrinsic and instrumental values, conservation and preservation, and other rigid dualisms. In this way, according to Bengston and Iverson, "natural resource planners, managers, and policy makers need to grasp and incorporate the full range of environmental values and learn to manage for multiple values rather than multiple uses."[31]

8. A Reconstructed Conservation Will Promote Community-Based Conservation Strategies

One of the strongest points of consensus in this volume is that the centralized, command-and-control conservation approach is in many cases giving way to more grassroots and community-based conservation models. As Diamant, Eugster, and Mitchell note, "the emergence of community-based conservation has shifted the center of gravity from top-down management strategies toward more decentralized, localized, place-based approaches."[32]

An important consequence of this shift, one that Stokowski notes in her chapter, is that it affords a more expanded conservation vision: "The emphasis on community-based conservation focuses attention on people as well as on nature, assumes that natural landscapes will not be privileged over historical and cultural settings, and draws its power from collaboration by local leaders and citizens."[33]

This community-based conservationism is a theme picked up by many of our authors. Thompson, for example, notes that agrarian thought "holds great promise for the reconstruction of conservation and an empowering environmental philosophy emphasizing community-based practice."[34] Minteer's discussion of Lewis Mumford's approach to regional planning uncovers the latter's emphasis on the protection of human-scaled community values and institutions in the face of powerful metropolitan forces in the 1920s and 1930s. In her chapter, Flader suggests that Aldo Leopold would have approved of the new grassroots approaches: "As an inveterate organizer of local farmer-sportsman groups and other grassroots efforts at land restoration, [Leopold] would be heartened by the myriad watershed partnerships, community farms and forests, land trusts, urban wilderness projects, and other community-based efforts that have been thriving in recent years."[35] Leopold struggled professionally and personally with the tension between "scientist" and citizen and placed an increasing emphasis and importance on the latter as he matured. In a related manner, Freyfogle instructs conservationists to adopt a robust understanding and defense of community in the face of rampant moral individualism and the socially and ecologically corrosive effects of the market economy.

The international arena offers some of the most striking examples of successes and failures of conservation as it relates to community involvement. Vivanco writes that "as an applied concept, culture has become a key element in international development schemes, based on the recognition that local technologies and social institutions are often uniquely adaptive and that programs succeed by building upon, not sweeping aside, local situations, needs, and traditions."[36] Similarly, Mitchell and Brown caution us against "paper parks" and suggest that "managers of protected areas are turning instead to inclusive models, in which the interests of local communities are considered, resident populations are not displaced, and there is a high degree of local participation in planning and management of the protected area."[37]

Like most dualisms in conservation and in public policy more generally, there is a productive middle ground to be found between local control and the legitimate interests of scientific experts, regional and national contexts, and the financial aid and resources of centralized government. Conservation at any level should be informed by science, guided by larger-scale concerns about ecological health and integrity, and facilitated by government. As Stokowski observes, however, "newer participatory approaches reorient the work of conservation to local community settings and practices in which public resource protection and private development interests intersect."[38] And on the front lines of conservation practice, Diamant, Eugster, and Mitchell like what they see: "Local initiative . . . in partnership with government, has taken the form of land trusts, small watershed associations, greenway and trail groups, friends of parks, 'Main Street' organizations, and heritage area coalitions."[39] Likewise, speaking as conservation practitioners, Mitchell and Brown conclude that "public agencies still have a role; it is just different, concerned more with guiding than with dictating, and it is especially concerned with carefully constructing institutional frameworks that grant genuine authority to appropriate community groups while ensuring that conservation efforts succeed in their primary objectives."[40]

9. A Reconstructed Conservation Will Rely on an Engaged Citizenry

Directly linked with this turn to community-level conservation is the growing recognition of the relationship between conservation and citizen participation in conservation initiatives. Flader and Meine both find great inspiration for fostering individual initiative in conservation efforts in the thought and work of Aldo Leopold, who on both professional and personal fronts promoted various levels of citizen involvement in conservation. Minteer's account of Lewis Mumford's civic model of regional planning suggests additional foundations of citizen participation in the earlier conservation tradition. Writing from their experience with the contemporary management scene, Mitchell and Brown and Diamant, Eugster, and Mitchell also observe how the central role of citizens in environmental stewardship builds much-needed social capital and bolsters civil society, suggesting that conservation and citizenship are in many respects mutually reinforcing. Contemporary community-based conservation offers unlimited opportunities for all environmentally concerned citizens to become engaged: membership-based organizations, volunteer projects, informed consumerism, and the like.

10. A Reconstructed Conservation Will Engage Questions of Social Justice

It is clear that conservation in the twenty-first century will need to be more attentive to fundamental concerns of justice in environmental protective efforts. From the practitioner's perspective, Diamant, Eugster, and Mitchell note that such questions of social equity are indeed becoming more critical in discussions within the conservation professions. McCullough observes how the growing emphasis on community in conservation activities effectively opens the door for considerations of social issues related to community welfare, including housing, transportation, education, and social services. It is clear that issues of social justice are increasingly recognized as critical elements of the new landscape of conservation planning and goal setting. Vivanco's account of the struggles surrounding conservation efforts in Latin America illustrates just how central issues of justice are in these negotiations: "For many peoples of the South, nature conservation exists at a crossroads. Will it represent domination by a new set of elites, in this case scientifically trained natural resource administrators united with government or nongovernmental interests external to rural communities, or will conservation activists find ways to unite their struggles for nature with local struggles for equity, justice, and autonomy at the community level?"[41] Mitchell and Brown provide one indirect response to this question in their chapter, observing that the prospects for greater equity and accountability in international protected area management seem to be improving in many cases. As they write, a new paradigm for the world's protected areas is emerging, one "based on inclusive approaches, partnerships, and linkages, in which protected areas are no longer planned against local people but instead are planned with them."[42] Meine's impassioned call for a revived Progressivism in conservation—one built around a "radical center" that appeals to all peoples and interests—offers the hope that conservationists can construct a more tolerant and inclusive community focused on shared goals rather than partisan values and preferences.

11. A Reconstructed Conservation Will Be Politically Inclusive and Partnership Driven

In step with Meine's arguments, many of the chapters in this volume describe and defend a "big tent" approach to conservation, one characterized by multi-sector approaches, public–private partnerships, and new and creative relationships among organizations and institutions. Flader notes that Aldo Leopold anticipated (as he did many things) this collaborative model in the first half of the twentieth century. One of the driving forces behind these shifts toward partnerships appears to be an increased concern with producing measurable, tangible results on the landscape. "It is more important to be successful in conservation than it is to be in charge," write Diamant, Eugster, and Mitchell, suggesting that meaningful collaboration focused on real outcomes is part of strong conservation leadership.[43] As Mitchell and Brown point out, however (and as stated earlier), this shift toward cooperative models does not retreat from, nor does it preclude, the role of government in the conservation enterprise. There will always be conservation matters of scale or institutional complexity that require strong government leadership. The ecosystem-oriented and large-scale dimensions of many emerging conservation activities work to stimulate organized cooperation among different parties, including government, as Bengston and Iverson, Mitchell and Brown, and Trombulak discuss in their chapters. Furthermore, McCullough's chapter demonstrates how the conceptual revelations about the cultural dimensions of conservation also play a part in this redrawing (and erasing) of divisions between the academic and professional fields involved in conservation efforts, supporting his proposal to build "new green bridges of a collaborative nature" between the nature conservation and historic preservation communities.

12. A Reconstructed Conservation Will Embrace Its Democratic Traditions

Diamant, Eugster, and Mitchell write that "we will need a conservation community that is ethical, democratic, and humanistic in the broadest sense."[44] We believe that one of the most significant conclusions to be drawn from the chapters in this volume is that a reconstructed conservation needs to embody the democratic values and commitments found in the best parts of its intellectual inheritance. On this score, Flader and Minteer suggest (respectively) that Aldo Leopold and Lewis Mumford provide useful models for fashioning a democratic approach to conservation from the intellectual resources of the tradition. But this project is not as easy as it might seem. As Taylor points out, "a reconstructed oppositional conservationism, if such is to be found, must embrace the imperfections, even the modesty, of democratic political life."[45] This democratic humility does not seem to have been demonstrated by Scott Nearing's conservationism, the subject of Taylor's chapter. In fact, Taylor's conclusions about Nearing's stern moralizing and his failure to engage citizens in a broader, critical form of conservationism stand as a lesson to those conservationists tempted by either a moral purism or an overzealous scientism in their work. In a related vein, Dizard's post-mortem of the controversy surrounding the Chicago Wilderness Habitat Project suggests how the dogmatism of restorationists undercut their political objectives. "If the goal of environmentalists is to create as large a constituency as possible committed to environmental stewardship," Dizard writes, "the Chicago experience should be read more as a cautionary tale than as a model. The plain truth is that people resented being told that the nature they appreciated was bad and that they were ignorant and misguided. The Chicago restorationists came to sound suspiciously like evangelists who knew the one true path and who insisted that anyone rejecting that path was an enemy of the earth."[46]

To avoid these unproductive situations, we might subscribe to Norton's model of environmental valuation and policy argument, which focuses not on a defense of specific environmental commitments but rather on "democratic procedures designed to achieve a reasonable balance among multiple competing human values derived from, and attributed to, nature."[47] This embrace of a democratic politics in environmental valuation and goal setting finds support in Stokowski's discussion of deliberative approaches in community planning and development and also in Manning's chapter, which concludes that "it may not be productive to advocate any particular environmental value or ethic as a universal principle to be applied across a spectrum of people, places, or environmental problems." Instead, Manning writes, "environmental problem solving must be inclusive and democratic, not peremptory."[48]

Moving Forward

If the chapters in this volume are any indication, the conservation tradition is in very good hands during this moment of conceptual upheaval and skepticism in environmental thought. This does not mean, however, that our authors are at all complacent about the challenges presented by such criticisms. If the percussive force of the deconstructivist critique has not completely razed the foundations of conservation, it has certainly prompted many observers, including our writers, to reconsider the continuing appropriateness of the tradition for guiding our understandings of human–environment relationships and for shaping our practices on the landscape. But the message that emerges from these reconsiderations of conservation is, we believe, a hopeful one. For even if we agree that the deconstructivists have at times shown the environmentalist emperor to have no clothes (or at least to have a few holes in his socks), the emerging consensus in this book suggests that this by no means warrants a slippery "anything goes" relativism toward the natural world; it certainly does not imply a self-defeating nihilism about our conservation goals and commitments. Rather, we believe our contributors have demonstrated that a properly reconstructed conservation, one that is *pluralistic* in its value dimensions, *community oriented* in its goals and methods, *pragmatic* in its focus on conservation coalition building and its acceptance of sociophysical change and human fallibility, and *inclusive* in its policy agenda and intellectual temperament, possesses the moral and political resources—and the conceptual robustness—to lead citizens and professionals onto healthier and more sustainable development paths in the coming decades.

In many respects, then, the chapters in this volume may be read as attempts to cope with the increasing democratization of conservation thought and practice. From their rejection of privileged meanings, histories, and values regarding nature to their acceptance of multiple ways of knowing and prizing the landscape; from their elevation of citizens vis-à-vis experts in the responsibilities of conservation stewardship to the celebration of local community and grassroots action in environmental protection, our authors have provided many of the moral and empirical commitments of a more seriously democratic conservationism, one that draws its justification from the many converging arguments of a wide range of environmental fields, scholarly and professional. In this, they are advancing not only the main tenets of a new view of conservation but also some of the substantive content of a new generation's democratic values and commitments. It is our hope that this larger message—the faith in the capacity of citizens to respond intelligently and effectively to the evolving conservation challenge, and the accompanying judgment that this civic action is a critical part of a responsible conservationism in the twenty-first century—will continue to resonate long after you put down this book.

NOTES

Chapter 1. Minteer and Manning, *Conservation: From Deconstruction to Reconstruction*

1. W. Cronon, ed., *Uncommon Ground: Rethinking the Human Place in Nature* (New York: Norton, 1996).
2. W. Cronon, "The Trouble with Wilderness; or, Getting Back to the Wrong Nature," in Cronon, *Uncommon Ground*, pp. 69–90.
3. J. B. Callicott and M. P. Nelson, *The Great New Wilderness Debate* (Athens: University of Georgia Press, 1998).
4. D. Takacs, *The Idea of Biodiversity: Philosophies of Paradise* (Baltimore, Md.: Johns Hopkins University Press, 1996).
5. See L. S. Warren, *The Hunter's Game: Poachers and Conservationists in Twentieth-Century America* (New Haven, Conn.: Yale University Press, 1997); M. D. Spence, *Dispossessing the Wilderness: Indian Removal and the Making of the National Parks* (New York: Oxford University Press, 1999); and K. Jacoby, *Crimes against Nature: Squatters, Poachers, Thieves, and the Hidden History of American Conservation* (Berkeley and Los Angeles: University of California Press, 2001).
6. L. Mumford, *The Brown Decades* (1931; reprint, New York: Dover, 1971), p. 35.
7. See, e.g., D. Worster, *A River Running West: The Life of John Wesley Powell* (New York: Oxford University Press, 2001); D. Lowenthal, *George Perkins Marsh, Prophet of Conservation* (Seattle: University of Washington Press, 2000); and C. Miller, *Gifford Pinchot and the Making of Modern Environmentalism* (Washington, D.C.: Island Press, 2001).
8. See, e.g., R. McCullough, *The Landscape of Community: A History of Communal Forests in New England* (Hanover, N.H.: University Press of New England, 1995); Warren, *Hunter's Game*; R. W. Judd, *Common Lands, Common People: The Origins of Conservation in Northern New England* (Cambridge, Mass.: Harvard University Press, 1997); and Jacoby, *Crimes against Nature*.
9. J. Dewey, *Reconstruction in Philosophy* (1920; reprint, Boston: Beacon Press, 1957), p. viii.

Chapter 2. Judd, *Writing Environmental History from East to West*

1. On New England paradigms, see S. Nissenbaum, "New England as Region and Nation," in E. L. Ayers et al., eds., *All Over the Map: Rethinking American Regions* (Baltimore, Md.: Johns Hopkins University Press, 1996), p. 41.
2. F. A. Shannon, *The Farmer's Last Frontier: Agriculture, 1860–1897* (New York: Toronto, Farrar & Rinehart, 1945); W. P. Webb, *The Great Plains* (Boston: Ginn and Company, 1931); J. C. Malin, *The Grassland of North America: Prolegomena to Its History* (Lawrence, Kans.: James C. Malin, 1947); W. Stegner, *Beyond the Hundredth Meridian: John Wesley Powell and the Second Opening of the West* (Boston: Houghton Mifflin, 1954); R. A. Billington, *The Far Western Frontier, 1830–1860* (New York: Harper, 1956); P. W. Gates, *History of Public Land Law Development* (Washington, D.C.:

Government Printing Office, 1968); P. W. Gates, *The Farmer's Age: Agriculture, 1815–1860* (New York: Harper & Row, 1968).

3. K. Sivaramakrishnan, *Modern Forests: Statemaking and Environmental Change in Colonial Eastern India* (Stanford, Calif.: Stanford University Press, 1999), p. 24 n. 7.

4. B. Piasecki, ed., "A Sampler of Courses and Programs in Environmental Studies," *Environmental Review* 8 (winter 1984):312–26; W. Cronon, *Changes in the Land: Indians, Colonists, and the Ecology of New England* (New York: Hill and Wang, 1983); C. Merchant, *Ecological Revolutions: Nature, Gender, and Science in New England* (Chapel Hill: University of North Carolina Press, 1989); T. Silver, *A New Face on the Countryside: Indians, Colonists, and Slaves in South Atlantic Forests, 1500–1800* (New York: Cambridge University Press, 1990); E. Purchase, *Out of Nowhere: Disaster and Tourism in the White Mountains* (Baltimore, Md.: Johns Hopkins University Press, 1999), p. 4.

5. Some of these characteristics I have taken from W. Wyckoff, *Creating Colorado: The Making of a Western American Landscape, 1860–1940* (New Haven, Conn.: Yale University Press, 1999), p. 253; others, from P. N. Limerick, "Region and Reason," in Ayers et al., *All Over the Map*, pp. 89–91.

6. T. M. Bonnicksen, *America's Ancient Forests: From the Ice Age to the Age of Discovery* (New York: Wiley, 2000), p. 226; R. N. L. Andrews, *Managing the Environment, Managing Ourselves: A History of American Environmental Policy* (New Haven, Conn.: Yale University Press, 1999), p. 29; D. E. Davis, *Where There Are Mountains: An Environmental History of the Southern Appalachians* (Athens: University of Georgia Press, 2000), p. 125.

7. A. Daniel and T. Hanson, "'Remote, Rocky, Barren, Bushy Wild-Woody Wilderness': The Natural History of the Northeast," in *Wilderness Comes Home: Rewilding the Northeast,* edited by C. McGrory Klyza (Hanover, N.H.: Middlebury College Press, 2001), p. 41; L. C. Irland, *The Northeast's Changing Forest* (Petersham, Mass.: Harvard Forest, 1999), pp. 59, 115; D. Foster, preface to Irland, *Northeast's Changing Forest*, p. xix; K. Ryden (quoting J. Elder), *Landscape with Figures: Nature and Culture in New England* (Iowa City: University of Iowa Press, 2001), pp. 60, 220.

8. Davis, *Where There Are Mountains*, p. 207; G. P. Marsh, quoted in D. Lowenthal, *George Perkins Marsh, Prophet of Conservation* (Seattle: University of Washington Press, 2000), pp. 173, 287; J. W. Simpson, *Visions of Paradise: Glimpses of Our Landscape's Legacy* (Berkeley and Los Angeles: University of California Press, 1999), p. 24.

9. On Cronon's assumption of capitalist motives for colonialists, see Cronon, *Changes in the Land*. On Old World cultural transfers, see T. H. Breen, *Puritans and Adventures: Change and Persistence in Early America* (New York: Oxford University Press, 1980); D. G. Allen, *In English Ways: The Movement of Societies and the Transferal of English Local Law and Custom to Massachusetts Bay in the Seventeenth Century* (Chapel Hill: University of North Carolina Press, 1981); D. B. Hall, *Worlds of Wonder, Days of Judgment: Popular Religious Belief in Early New England* (New York: Knopf, 1989); M. J. Bowden, "Culture and Place: English Sub-Cultural Regions in New England in the Seventeenth Century," *Connecticut History* 35 (1994): 68–146. On the controversy over capitalist and precapitalist *mentalité*, see J. A. Henretta, "Families and Farms: *Mentalité* in Pre-industrial America," *William and Mary Quarterly*, 3rd ser., 35 (1978): 3–32; W. B. Rothenberg,

"The Market and Massachusetts Farmers, 1750–1855," *Journal of Economic History* 41 (1981): 283–314; R. E. Mutch, "The Cutting Edge: Colonial America and the Debate about the Transition to Capitalism," *Theory and Society* 9 (1980): 847–863; and S. Hahn and J. Prude, eds., *The Countryside in the Age of Capitalist Transformation: Essays in the Social History of Rural America* (Chapel Hill: University of North Carolina Press, 1985). See also G. G. Whitney, *From Coastal Wilderness to Fruited Plain: A History of Environmental Change in Temperate North America, 1500 to the Present* (New York: Cambridge University Press, 1994), p. 121.

10. R. W. Judd, *Common Lands, Common People: The Origins of Conservation in Northern New England* (Cambridge, Mass.: Harvard University Press, 1997); B. Donahue, *The Great Meadow* (New Haven, Conn.: Yale University Press, forthcoming); Andrews, *Managing the Environment, Managing Ourselves*, p. 16.

11. Judd, *Common Lands, Common People*, especially chap. 2; S. Hahn, "Hunting, Fishing, and Foraging: Common Rights and Class Relations in the Postbellum South," *Radical History Review* 26, no. 18 (1982): 38–39, 43; Andrews, *Managing the Environment, Managing Ourselves*, p. 49.

12. H. Baron, *Those Who Stayed Behind: Rural Society in Nineteenth-Century New England* (New York: Cambridge University Press, 1984), especially chap. 6. Baron did not discuss land use, but he demonstrated a growing cohesiveness in the community. For connections between sense of place and a land ethic, see L. Beam, *A Maine Hamlet* (New York: Wilfred Funk, 1957), and M. L. Brown, *The Wild East: A Biography of the Great Smoky Mountains* (Gainesville: University Press of Florida, 2000), p. 37.

13. Brown, *Wild East*, pp. 12, 15, 22, 24, 29, 30, 39, 41–42; Davis, *Where There Are Mountains*, pp. 41, 135, 179; G. Pinchot, in Davis, *Where There Are Mountains*, p. 179; V. Fowler, in T. Davis, *Sustaining the Forest, the People, and the Spirit* (Albany: State University of New York Press, 2000), p. 57. See D. S. Pierce, *The Great Smokies: From Natural Habitat to National Park* (Knoxville: University of Tennessee Press, 2000), pp. xiv, xviii; Wyckoff, *Creating Colorado*, p. 6.

14. T. Dwight, in Whitney, *From Coastal Wilderness to Fruited Plain*, p. 131.

15. T. Dwight, quoted in J. T. Cumbler, *Reasonable Use: The People, the Environment, and the State, New England, 1790–1930* (New York: Oxford University Press, 2001), p. 13; R. E. Walls, "Faith in a Seed: Northwest Timber Workers and the Tree Farm Ideal, 1940–1999" (paper presented at conference of the American Society for Environmental History and the Forest History Society, "Making Environmental History Relevant in the Twenty-First Century," Durham, N.C., March–April 2001). See also Lowenthal, *George Perkins Marsh*, p. 299; D. B. Botkin, *No Man's Garden: Thoreau and a New Vision for Civilization and Nature* (Washington, D.C.: Island Press, 2001), pp. 117–118; C. Tichi, *New World, New Earth: Environmental Reform in American Literature from the Puritans through Whitman* (New Haven, Conn.: Yale University Press, 1979).

16. J. Opie, *Nature's Nation: An Environmental History of the United States* (Fort Worth, Tex.: Harcourt Brace College Publishers, 1998), p. 2.

17. D. Worster, *Dust Bowl: The Southern Plains in the 1930s* (New York: Oxford University Press, 1979), pp. 6, 57.

18. Brown, *Wild East*, pp. 17, 32; Davis, *Where There Are Mountains*, pp. 175, 197; R. L. Lewis, quoted in Brown, *Wild East*, p. 73; K. Newfont, "No More Wilderness, No More Clearcuts: Commons Users and Forest Politics in Appalachian North Carolina, 1964–1994" (paper presented at conference of the American Society for Environmental History and the Forest History Society, "Making Environmental History Relevant in the Twenty-First Century," Durham, N.C., March–April 2001).

19. Brown, *Wild East*, p. 69; Judd, *Common Lands, Common People*, chap. 3.

20. A. McEvoy, *The Fisherman's Problem: Ecology and Law in the California Fisheries, 1850–1980* (New York: Cambridge University Press, 1986), p. 101, discussing the U.S. Fish Commission, created in 1871.

21. Cumbler, *Reasonable Use*, pp. 64, 175–177; G. Kulik, "Dams, Fish, and Farmers: Defense of Public Rights in Eighteenth-Century Rhode Island," in Hahn and Prude, *Countryside in the Age of Capitalist Transformation*, pp. 25–50; L. S. Warren, *The Hunter's Game: Poachers and Conservationists in Twentieth-Century America* (New Haven, Conn.: Yale University Press, 1997), especially the prologue (pp. 1–20) and chap. 2; E. D. Ives, *George Magoon and the Down-East Game Wars: History, Folklore, and the Law* (Urbana: University of Illinois Press, 1988); Judd, *Common Lands, Common People*, chap. 8.

22. T. Steinberg, *Nature Incorporated: Industrialization and the Waters of New England* (New York: Cambridge University Press, 1991), pp. xi, 11; Cumbler, *Reasonable Use*, p. 23; D. Muir, *Reflections in Bullough's Pond: Economy and Ecosystem in New England* (Hanover, N.H.: University Press of New England, 2000), p. 81.

23. Cumbler, *Reasonable Use*, pp. 6, 9, 10, 19, 52, 111, 116, 149, 155–157, 186; D. Muir, *Reflections in Bullough's Pond*.

24. S. P. Hays, *Beauty, Health, and Permanence: Environmental Politics in the United States, 1955–1985* (New York: Cambridge University Press, 1987), p. 52; S. P. Hays, "From Conservation to Environment: Environmental Politics in the United States since World War II," in *Out of the Woods: Essays in Environmental History*, edited by C. Miller and H. Rothman (Pittsburgh, Pa.: University of Pittsburgh Press, 1997), pp. 115–116.

25. On the balds, see Brown, *Wild East*, p. 281.

26. Irland, *Northeast's Changing Forest*, pp. 193, 199, 238, 329–332; C. McGrory Klyza, "An Eastern Turn for Wilderness," in Klyza, *Wilderness Comes Home*, pp. 3–26; J. W. Penfold, "Wilderness East—a Dilemma," *American Forests* 78 (April 1972): 24; F. C. Simmons, "Wilderness East?—No," *American Forests* 78 (July 1972): 3, 44–45; E. H. Ketchledge, "Born-Again Forest," *Natural History* (May 1992): pp. 34–39.

27. E. W. B. Russell, *People and the Land through Time: Linking Ecology and History* (New Haven, Conn.: Yale University Press, 1997), p. 16.

28. D. L. Donahue, *The Western Range Revisited: Removing Livestock from Public Lands to Conserve Native Biodiversity* (Norman: University of Oklahoma Press, 1999), p. 7.

29. Simpson, *Visions of Paradise*, p. 87.

30. Botkin, *No Man's Garden*, p. 156.

31. J. H. Mitchell, *Ceremonial Time: Fifteen Thousand Years on One Square Mile* (New York: Anchor Press, 1984); Muir, *Reflections in Bullough's Pond*, p. 31; K. Dann, *Lewis Creek Lost and Found* (Hanover, N.H.: Middlebury College Press, 2001).

32. G. B. Samuels, *Enduring Roots: Encounters with Trees, History, and the American Landscape* (New Brunswick, N.J.: Rutgers University Press, 1999), p. 9.

Chapter 3. McCullough, *The Nature of History Preserved; or The Trouble with Green Bridges*

1. W. Cronon, ed., *Uncommon Ground: Toward Reinventing Nature* (New York: Norton, 1995).
2. W. Cronon, "The Trouble with Wilderness; or, Getting Back to the Wrong Nature," *Environmental History* 1 (1996): 7–55.
3. Cronon, "Trouble with Wilderness"; M. Cohen, "Comment: Resistance to Wilderness," *Environmental History* 1 (1996): 42.
4. T. Dunlap, "Comment: But What Did You Go Out into the Wilderness to See?" *Environmental History* 1 (1996): 45.
5. B. MacKaye, "A New England Recreation Plan," *Journal of Forestry* 27 (1929): 927–930.
6. B. MacKaye, memorandum to Wilderness Society members, 9 November 1947, Dartmouth Archives, MacKaye Papers, box 187, folder 49.
7. K. Lynch, *What Time Is This Place?* (Cambridge, Mass.: MIT Press, 1972), pp. 29–64.
8. Ibid., p. 1.
9. D. Lowenthal, *The Past Is a Foreign Country* (New York: Cambridge University Press, 1985), pp. 326, 410–412.

Chapter 4. Dizard, *Going Native: Second Thoughts on Restoration*

1. D. Lowenthal, *George Perkins Marsh, Prophet of Conservation* (Seattle: University of Washington Press, 2000).
2. L. S. Warren, *The Hunter's Game: Poachers and Conservationists in Twentieth-Century America* (New Haven, Conn.: Yale University Press, 1997); D. J. Herman, *Hunting and the American Imagination* (Washington, D.C.: Smithsonian Institution Press, 2001).
3. J. F. Reiger, *American Sportsmen and the Origins of Conservation,* 3rd ed. (Corvallis: Oregon State University Press, 2001).
4. G. P. Marsh, *Man and Nature* (1864; reprint, Cambridge, Mass.: Belknap Press of Harvard University Press, 1965), p. 29.
5. Ibid., pp. 29–30.
6. P. Schullery, *Searching for Yellowstone* (Boston: Houghton Mifflin, 1997); A. Chase, *Playing God in Yellowstone* (New York: Harcourt Brace Jovanovich, 1987).
7. R. Lewontin, *The Triple Helix* (Cambridge, Mass.: Harvard University Press, 2000).
8. D. Botkin, *Discordant Harmonies* (New York: Oxford University Press, 1990).
9. J. H. Mitchell, *Ceremonial Time* (Reading, Mass.: Addison-Wesley, 1984), p. 7.
10. W. Cronon, "The Trouble with Wilderness; or, Getting Back to the Wrong Nature," in *Uncommon Ground: Toward Reinventing Nature,* edited by W. Cronon (New York: Norton, 1995).
11. My account of the Chicago initiative is based largely on two books: W. K. Stevens, *Miracle under the Oaks* (New York: Pocket Books, 1995), and P. H. Gobster and R. B. Hull, eds., *Restoring Nature: Perspectives from the Social Sciences and Humanities* (Washington, D.C.: Island Press, 2000). My account of the Buffalo Commons is based on A. Matthews, *Where the Buffalo Roam* (New York: Grove Weidenfeld, 1992); reports found

on the Great Plains Restoration Council's World Wide Web site, at http://www.gprc.org/; D. E. Popper and F. J. Popper, "The Buffalo Commons: Metaphor as Method," *Geographical Review* (October 1999): 491–510; and D. Leistra, "Buffalo Commons" (unpublished undergraduate research paper, Amherst College, 2001).

12. Popper and Popper, "Buffalo Commons," pp. 493–494.

13. D. Worster, *Rivers of Empire* (New York: Pantheon Books, 1985); D. Worster, *A River Running West: The Life of John Wesley Powell* (New York: Oxford University Press, 2001).

14. For one account, see D. O'Brian, *Buffalo for the Broken Heart* (New York: Random House, 2001).

15. P. F. Starrs, *Let the Cowboy Ride* (Baltimore, Md.: Johns Hopkins University Press, 1998).

16. S. Gatewood, "Update," *Wild Earth Journal* 8 (fall 1998): 17.

17. A. Light, "Ecological Restoration and the Culture of Nature: A Pragmatic Perspective," in *Restoring Nature: Perspectives from the Social Sciences and Humanities,* edited by P. H. Gobster and R. B. Hull (Washington, D.C.: Island Press, 2000).

Chapter 5. Vivanco, *Conservation and Culture, Genuine and Spurious*

1. G. Nabhan, *Cultures of Habitat: On Nature, Culture, and Story* (Washington, D.C: Counterpoint, 1997); W. Cronon, ed., *Uncommon Ground: Rethinking the Human Place in Nature* (New York: Norton, 1996).

2. J. Cohen, "Culture and Conservation," *BioScience* 38 (1988): 450–453.

3. D. Bates, *Human Adaptive Strategies: Ecology, Culture, and Politics* (Boston: Allyn and Bacon, 1998).

4. M. Cernea, ed., *Putting People First: Sociological Variables in Development* (London: Oxford University Press, 1991); R. Chambers, *Whose Reality Counts? Putting the First Last* (London: Intermediate Technology Publications, 1997); M. K. Nations and L. A. Rebhun, "Mystification of a Simple Solution: Oral Rehydration Therapy in Northeast Brazil," *Social Science and Medicine* 27, no. 1 (1988): 25–38.

5. N. Salafsky, "Community-Based Approaches for Combining Conservation and Development," in *The Biodiversity Crisis: Losing What Counts,* edited by M. J. Novacek (New York: New Press, 2001), p. 185.

6. J. Clifford, "On Ethnographic Authority," in *The Predicament of Culture: Twentieth-Century Ethnography, Literature, and Art* (Cambridge, Mass.: Harvard University Press, 1988); R. Rosaldo, *Culture and Truth: The Remaking of Social Analysis* (Boston: Beacon Press, 1993).

7. S. Alvarez, E. Dagnino, and A. Escobar, "Introduction: The Cultural and Political in Latin American Social Movements," in *Cultures of Politics/Politics of Cultures: Re-Visioning Latin American Social Movements*, edited by S. Alvarez, E. Dagnino, and A. Escobar (Boulder, Colo.: Westview Press, 1998), pp. 1–29; V. Toledo, *La Paz en Chiapas: Ecología, Luchas Indígenas, y Modernidad Alternativa* (Mexico City: Ediciones Quinto Sol, 2000).

8. H. Collinson, ed., *Green Guerillas: Environmental Conflicts and Initiatives in Latin America and the Caribbean* (London: Latin American Bureau, 1996).

9. W. Sachs, "The Need for the Home Perspective," *Interculture* 2 (winter 1996).

10. M. Dowie, *Losing Ground: American Environmentalism at the Close of the Twentieth Century* (Cambridge, Mass.: MIT Press, 1995); R. Guha, *Environmentalism: A Global History* (New York: Longman, 2000).

11. E. Sapir, "Cultures, Genuine and Spurious," in *Selected Writings of Edward Sapir in Language, Culture, and Personality*, edited by D. Mandelbaum (Berkeley and Los Angeles: University of California Press, 1949), p. 320.

12. Ibid., p. 323.

13. Cronon, *Uncommon Ground*; Nabhan, *Cultures of Habitat*.

14. M. Kearney, *Reconceptualizing the Peasantry: Anthropology in Global Perspective* (Boulder, Colo.: Westview Press, 1996).

15. Ibid., p. 8.

16. Ibid., p. 59.

17. K. Redford, "The Ecologically Noble Savage," *Cultural Survival Quarterly* 15, no. 1 (1991): 46–48.

18. J. Muir, Quoted in Nabhan, *Cultures of Habitat*, p. 156.

19. Redford, "Ecologically Noble Savage"; R. Reed, *Forest Dwellers, Forest Protectors: Indigenous Models for International Development* (Boston: Allyn and Bacon, 1997).

20. R. Ellen, "What Black Elk Left Unsaid: On the Illusory Images of Green Primitivism," *Anthropology Today* 2, no. 6 (1986): 8–12.

21. B. Street, *The Savage in Literature: Representations of "Primitive" Society in English Fiction, 1858–1920* (London: Routledge, 1975), quoted in Ellen, "What Black Elk Left Unsaid," p. 8.

22. For an overview of these arguments, see S. Krech, *The Ecological Indian: Myth and History* (New York: Norton, 1999); J. Petersen, E. Neves, and M. Heckenberger, "Gift from the Past: Terra Preta and Prehistoric Amerindian Occupation of Amazonia," in *Unknown Amazon*, edited by C. McEwan et al. (London: British Museum Press, 2001), pp. 86–105; C. Mann, "1491," *Atlantic Monthly*, March 2002, pp. 41–53. Regarding the Maya tropical forest, see J. D. Nations, "Indigenous Peoples and Conservation: Misguided Myths about the Maya Tropical Forest," in *On Biocultural Diversity: Linking Language, Knowledge, and the Environment*, edited by L. Maffi (Washington, D.C.: Smithsonian Institution Press, 2001), pp. 462–471.

23. Ellen, "What Black Elk Left Unsaid."

24. P. Erickson, "A-Whaling We Will Go: Encounters of Knowledge and Memory at the Makah Cultural and Research Center," *Cultural Anthropology* 14, no. 4 (1999): 556–583.

25. Ibid., p. 563.

26. M. Colchester, comment on "Defining Oneself, and Being Defined, as Indigenous," *Anthropology Today* 18, no. 3 (June 2002): 24.

27. B. Conklin, "Body Paint, Feathers, and VCRs: Aesthetics and Authenticity in Amazonian Activism," *American Ethnologist* 24, no. 4 (1997): 711–737.

28. Ibid.

29. Kearney, *Reconceptualizing the Peasantry*.

30. N. Myers, *The Primary Source: Tropical Forests and Our Future* (New York: Norton, 1992), p. 143.

31. Ibid., p. xx.

32. Nations, "Indigenous Peoples and Conservation"; J. Fairhead and M. Leach, *Misreading the African Landscape: Society and Ecology in a Forest-Savanna Mosaic* (Cambridge, England: Cambridge University Press, 1996).

33. W. H. Allen, "Biocultural Restoration of a Tropical Forest," *BioScience* 38, no. 3 (1988): 156.

34. L. Thrupp, "Environmental Initiatives in Costa Rica: A Political Ecology Perspective," *Society and Natural Resources* 3 (1990): 243–256.

35. Ibid., p. 244. See also J. Vandermeer and I. Perfecto, *Breakfast of Biodiversity: The Truth about Rain Forest Destruction* (Oakland, Calif.: Food First, 1995).

36. Monteverde Conservation League, "Saving the Monteverde Cloud Forest," proposal to the World Wildlife Fund (Washington, D.C.: World Wildlife Fund Files, 1986), p. 3.

37. A. Forsyth, "The Lessons of Monteverde," *Equinox* (March–April 1988): 56–61.

38. See L. Vivanco, "Environmentalism, Democracy, and the Cultural Politics of Nature in Monte Verde, Costa Rica," in *Democracy and the Claims of Nature: Critical Perspectives for a New Century,* edited by B. A. Minteer and B. P. Taylor (Lanham, Md.: Rowman and Littlefield, 2002), pp. 215–236.

39. Ibid., pp. 230–231.

40. J. Simon, *Endangered Mexico: An Environment on the Edge* (San Francisco: Sierra Club Books, 1997), p. 35; J. J. Consejo, "La Protección de Espacios Naturales en Oaxaca: Estado Actual y Perspectivas," in *Etnias, Desarrollo, Recursos, y Tecnologias en Oaxaca,* edited by A. Gonzalez and M. A. Vasquez (Mexico City: Centro de Investigaciones y Estudios Superiores en Antropologia Social, 1996), pp. 23–39.

41. Simon, *Endangered Mexico*; D. Barkin et al., "Globalization and Resistance: The Remaking of Mexico," *NACLA Report on the Americas* 30, no. 4 (1997): 13–27.

42. Centro de Encuentros y Dialogos Interculturales (CEDI) and the John Dewey Project, "New Approaches to Governance in the Context of Rapid Globalization: Constructing Environmental Security and Political Pluralism in Oaxaca, Mexico," proposal to The John D. and Catherine T. MacArthur Foundation (Burlington, Vt.: John Dewey Project on Progressive Education, 2000).

43. V. Rodriguez, *Decentralization in Mexico: From Municipal Reform to Solidaridad to Nuevo Federalismo* (Boulder, Colo.: Westview Press, 1997).

44. G. Esteva, "Basta! Mexican Indians Say Enough!" *Ecologist* 24, no. 3 (1994): 84. See also G. Esteva and M. Prakash, *Grassroots Postmodernism: Remaking the Soil of Cultures* (London: Zed Books, 1998).

45. Toledo, *La Paz en Chiapas.*

46. CEDI and John Dewey Project, "New Approaches to Governance."

47. J. J. Consejo, "The Twilight of the Environmentalist Era," *NGONet in Rio* (ngonet@chasque.org.uy), n.d., p. 1.

48. Ibid., p. 1.

49. Ibid., p. 2.

50. Esteva and Prakash, *Grassroots Postmodernism.*

51. Ellen, "What Black Elk Left Unsaid," p. 10.

52. P. Raine, "The Shaman and the Ecologist: Beyond Universalism, an Ever Open Horizon," *Interculture* 140 (April 2001): 3.

53. Ibid., p. 5.

Chapter 6. Thompson, *Expanding the Conservation Tradition:*
The Agrarian Vision

1. V. D. Hanson, *The Other Greeks: The Family Farm and the Agrarian Roots of Western Civilization* (New York: Free Press, 1995).

2. P. B. Thompson, "Agrarianism as Philosophy," in *The Agrarian Roots of Pragmatism,* edited by P. B. Thompson and T. C. Hilde (Nashville, Tenn.: Vanderbilt University Press, 2000), pp. 25–50.

3. For the links to Nazism, see T. Rockmore, *On Heidegger's Nazism and Philosophy* (Berkeley and Los Angeles: University of California Press, 1992). For the connection to bin Laden, see I. Buruma and A. Margalit, "Occidentalism," *New York Review of Books* 49, no. 1 (17 January 2002): 4–7.

4. M. Weber, *The Protestant Ethic and the Spirit of Capitalism* (London: Butler and Tanner, 1930, 1948).

5. T. M. Power, "Trapped in Consumption: Modern Social Structure and the Entrenchment of the Device," *Technology and the Good Life?* edited by E. Higgs, A. Light, and D. Strong (Chicago: University of Chicago Press, 2000), pp. 271–293.

6. D. A. Crocker and T. Linden, eds., *The Ethics of Consumption: The Good Life, Justice, and Global Stewardship* (Lanham, Md.: Rowman and Littlefield, 1998).

7. A. Leopold, *A Sand County Almanac, and Sketches Here and There* (New York: Oxford University Press, 1949), p. 6.

8. W. Berry, *The Unsettling of America: Culture and Agriculture* (San Francisco: Sierra Club Books, 1977); see especially chap. 7, "The Body and the Earth." See also W. Berry, *Home Economics* (San Francisco: North Point Press, 1987).

9. For a perceptive discussion of landscape mythology and its connections to fascism, see S. Schama, *Landscape and Memory* (New York: Knopf, 1996).

10. P. B. Thompson, "Thomas Jefferson and Agrarian Philosophy," in *The Agrarian Roots of Pragmatism,* edited by P. B. Thompson and T. C. Hilde (Nashville, Tenn.: Vanderbilt University Press, 2000), pp. 118–139.

11. R. S. Corrington, "Emerson and the Agricultural Midworld," *Agriculture and Human Values* 7 (1990): 20–26.

12. For a discussion of the 1972 corn blight, see J. Doyle, *Altered Harvest: Agriculture, Genetics, and the Fate of the World's Food Supply* (New York: Viking Penguin, 1985). For peasant farming practices and the limitation of risk, see J. C. Scott, *The Moral Economy of the Peasant* (New Haven, Conn.: Yale University Press, 1976).

13. See B. Norton, *Why Preserve Natural Variety?* (Princeton, N.J.: Princeton University Press, 1987).

14. In mentioning Edmund Burke, I link conservation to conservative political thought, yet the view being developed here owes more to John Dewey. Dewey's 1897 writings on the reflex arc note that interactions between organism and environment are seldom as simple as the physician tapping on the knee. Instead, response is possible because

attention has already been framed by the accretion of past experiences, which take the form of habits in individuals, and of institutions for social groups. See J. Dewey, "The Reflex-Arc Concept in Psychology," in *The Early Works of John Dewey*, vol. 5 (Carbondale: Southern Illinois University Press, 1967), pp. 96–109. Rejecting simple means–ends notions of rationality, Dewey believed that reconstruction must always focus on the habits and institutions that filter and frame capacities for future interaction. Yet as Ben A. Minteer notes in his chapter in this volume, a Deweyan is unlike Burke in believing that planned experimentation can improve these capacities over time.

15. See P. B. Thompson, *Agricultural Ethics: Research, Teaching, and Public Policy* (Ames: Iowa State University Press, 1998), especially the concluding chapter, "Markets, Moral Economy, and the Ethics of Sustainable Agriculture."

16. So, one might link feminist thought that stresses embodiment, such as S. Bordo, *Unbearable Weight* (Berkeley and Los Angeles: University of California Press, 1997), with Wendell Berry's keystone chapter "The Body and the Earth" in *The Unsettling of America*.

17. See especially "The Farmer as Conservationist," in A. Leopold, *For the Health of the Land: Previously Unpublished Essays and Other Writings*, edited by J. B. Callicott and E. T. Freyfogle (Washington, D.C.: Island Press, 1999).

Chapter 7. Minteer, *Regional Planning as Pragmatic Conservationism*

1. This almost teleological account of the rise of nonanthropocentrism appears in the work of many environmental philosophers. See, e.g., E. Katz, "The Traditional Ethics of Nature Resource Management," in *A New Century for Natural Resources Management*, edited by R. L. Knight and S. F. Bates (Washington, D.C.: Island Press, 1995), pp. 101–116; and J. B. Callicott, *Beyond the Land Ethic: More Essays in Environmental Philosophy* (Albany: State University of New York Press), especially pp. 321–331.

2. S. P. Hays, *Conservation and the Gospel of Efficiency: The Progressive Conservation Movement, 1890–1920* (Cambridge, Mass.: Harvard University Press, 1959); R. Nash, *Wilderness and the American Mind*, 3rd ed. (New Haven, Conn.: Yale University Press, 1983); and S. Fox, *John Muir and His Legacy: The American Conservation Movement* (Boston: Little, Brown, 1981).

3. See, e.g., R. Judd, *Common Lands, Common People: The Origins of Conservation in Northern New England* (Cambridge, Mass.: Harvard University Press, 1997); R. McCullough, *The Landscape of Community: A History of Communal Forests in New England* (Hanover, N.H.: University Press of New England, 1995); K. Jacoby, *Crimes against Nature: Squatters, Poachers, Thieves, and the Hidden History of American Conservation* (Berkeley and Los Angeles: University of California Press, 2001); and L. S. Warren, *The Hunter's Game: Poachers and Conservationists in Twentieth-Century America* (New Haven, Conn.: Yale University Press, 1997).

4. Such alternative interpretations of the environmental thought of Pinchot and Muir may be found in B. Norton, *Toward Unity among Environmentalists* (New York: Oxford University Press, 1991), and B. P. Taylor, *Our Limits Transgressed: Environmental Political Thought in America* (Lawrence: University Press of Kansas, 1992).

5. The arguments of the present chapter join my earlier claim that Mumford's regionalist ally and friend Benton MacKaye was also influenced by the American philosophical tradition (specifically the social philosophy of Josiah Royce); see B. A. Minteer, "Wilderness and the Wise Province: Benton MacKaye's Pragmatic Vision," *Philosophy and Geography* 4 (2001): 187–204. I should note that Curt Meine (personal communication; see also his chapter in this volume) has made me more sensitive to the potential historiographic and normative distinctions between conservation philosophy and environmental philosophy. Although a sufficiently developed treatment of the differences between the two traditions is beyond the scope of this chapter, I will point out here that I believe Mumford's pragmatic conservationism was forged in a very different fire from most contemporary environmental philosophy, an intellectual development marked by its traffic with the ideas of the conservation movement *and* American philosophy (not to mention those of early planning thinkers such as Ebenezer Howard and Patrick Geddes). As I suggest, this account would seem to challenge many presuppositions of environmental philosophers about the progressive evolution of classic conservation period philosophy into full-blown "environmental philosophy" later in the twentieth century.

6. R. Fishman, *Urban Utopias in the Twentieth Century: Ebenezer Howard, Frank Lloyd Wright, and Le Corbusier* (Cambridge, Mass.: MIT Press, 1982), pp. 29–39.

7. E. Howard, *Garden Cities of Tomorrow* (1902; reprint, Cambridge, Mass.: MIT Press, 1965), pp. 50–57; P. Hall, *Cities of Tomorrow*, updated ed. (Oxford, England: Blackwell, 1996), pp. 87–94.

8. Howard, *Garden Cities*, p. 146.

9. L. Mumford, introduction to Howard, *Garden Cities*, p. 33.

10. H. Meller, *Patrick Geddes: Social Evolutionist and City Planner* (London: Routledge, 1990); W. M. Welter, *Biopolis: Patrick Geddes and the City of Life* (Cambridge, Mass.: MIT Press, 2002).

11. Welter, *Biopolis*, pp. 109–112.

12. Geddes, quoted in Meller, *Patrick Geddes*, p. 179.

13. Welter, *Biopolis*.

14. Meller, *Patrick Geddes*, p. 134.

15. See the discussions of the RPAA's regionalist agenda and design principles in M. Luccarelli, *Lewis Mumford and the Ecological Region* (New York: Guilford Press, 1995), pp. 76–83, and E. K. Spann, *Designing Modern America: The Regional Planning Association of America and Its Members* (Columbus: Ohio State University Press, 1996).

16. L. Mumford, "The Fourth Migration," reprinted in *Planning the Fourth Migration: The Neglected Vision of the Regional Planning Association of America*, edited by C. Sussman (Cambridge, Mass.: MIT Press, 1976), pp. 55–64.

17. B. MacKaye, *The New Exploration: A Philosophy of Regional Planning*, 2nd ed. (Urbana: University of Illinois Press, 1962).

18. B. MacKaye, "An Appalachian Trail: A Project in Regional Planning," *Journal of the American Institute of Architects* 9 (1921): 3–8.

19. Several excellent treatments of MacKaye's environmental thought have appeared in recent years. See P. S. Sutter, *Driven Wild: How the Fight against Automobiles Launched the*

Modern Wilderness Movement (Seattle: University of Washington Press, 2002); K. Easterling, *Organization Space: Landscapes, Highways, and Houses in America* (Cambridge, Mass.: MIT Press, 1999); T. Hiss, *The Experience of Place* (New York: Random House, 1990); and the work of Luccarelli, Spann, McCullough, and Minteer, cited earlier. MacKaye has finally received a full biographical treatment in Larry Anderson's fine book *Benton MacKaye: Conservationist, Planner, and Creator of the Appalachian Trail* (Baltimore, Md.: Johns Hopkins University Press, 2002).

20. L. Marx, "Lewis Mumford: Prophet of Organicism," in *Lewis Mumford: Public Intellectual,* edited by T. P. Hughes and A. C. Hughes (New York: Oxford University Press, 1990), p. 164.

21. D. L. Miller, *Lewis Mumford: A Life* (New York: Weidenfeld & Nicolson, 1989), pp. 57–60.

22. Spann, *Designing Modern America*, p. 46.

23. R. Fishman, "The Metropolitan Tradition in American Planning," in *The American Planning Tradition: Culture and Policy,* edited by R. Fishman (Washington, D.C.: Woodrow Wilson Center Press, 2000), pp. 65–85.

24. L. Mumford, "Regions—to Live In," in Sussman, *Planning the Fourth Migration*, p. 92 (emphasis added).

25. Mumford, "Regions—to Live In," p. 90 (emphasis added).

26. L. Mumford, *The Culture of Cities* (New York: Harcourt, Brace, 1938), p. 332.

27. W. Cronon, "The Trouble with Wilderness; or, Getting Back to the Wrong Nature," in *Uncommon Ground: Rethinking the Human Place in Nature,* edited by W. Cronon (New York: Norton, 1996), pp. 69–90.

28. Mumford, *Culture*, p. 327.

29. L. Mumford, quoted in J. Friedmann and C. Weaver, *Territory and Function: The Evolution of Regional Planning* (Berkeley and Los Angeles: University of California Press, 1979), p. 29.

30. L. Mumford, *Sketches from Life* (Boston: Beacon Press, 1982), pp. 135–136.

31. Dewey himself, though, would devote a good deal of attention to aesthetic concerns in the 1930s. See, e.g., his *Art as Experience* (New York: Minton, Balch & Company, 1934).

32. Mumford's criticisms of pragmatic instrumentalism in his 1926 book *The Golden Day* (New York: Harcourt, Brace) and his subsequent exchange with Dewey in the pages of the *New Republic* indicate that there were significant differences between their two projects when it came to questions of aesthetic theory and value. More recent accounts of this debate, however, such as those offered by Robert Westbrook and Casey Blake, suggest that the tenor of the Mumford–Dewey exchange tended to mask several important similarities between their projects. See the discussion of this exchange in R. Westbrook, *John Dewey and American Democracy* (Ithaca, N.Y.: Cornell University Press, 1991), and C. Blake, *Beloved Community: The Cultural Criticism of Randolph Bourne, Van Wyck Brooks, Waldo Frank, and Lewis Mumford* (Chapel Hill: University of North Carolina Press, 1990).

33. Mumford, *Culture*, p. 384.

34. See J. Dewey, "Logic: The Theory of Inquiry," in *The Later Works, 1925–1953,* edited by J. A. Boydston, vol. 12, and J. Dewey, *Reconstruction in Philosophy* (New York: Henry Holt, 1920).

35. Dewey, "Logic."

36. Mumford, *Culture,* pp. 376–380.

37. J. Dewey, *Liberalism and Social Action* (1935; reprint, Amherst, N.Y.: Prometheus Books, 2000), p. 55.

38. Mumford, *Culture,* p. 379.

39. See C. S. Holling, *Adaptive Environmental Assessment and Management* (London: Wiley, 1978); C. J. Walters, *Adaptive Management of Renewable Resources* (New York: Macmillan, 1986); K. N. Lee, *Compass and Gyroscope: Integrating Science and Politics for the Environment* (Washington, D.C.: Island Press, 1993); and L. H. Gunderson, C. S. Holling, and S. S. Light, eds., *Barriers and Bridges to the Renewal of Ecosystems and Institutions* (New York: Columbia University Press, 1995).

40. Mumford, *Culture,* pp. 380–381 (emphasis added). Bryan Norton and his colleagues have written about the connections between the classical American pragmatists and the goals and methods of contemporary adaptive management. See B. Norton, "Integration or Reduction: Two Approaches to Environmental Values," in *Environmental Pragmatism,* edited by A. Light and E. Katz (London: Routledge, 1996), pp. 105–138; B. Norton and A. Steinemann, "Environmental Values and Adaptive Management," *Environmental Values* 10 (2001): 473–506; and B. Norton and B. A. Minteer, "From Environmental Ethics to Environmental Public Philosophy: Ethicists and Economists, 1973–Future," in *The International Yearbook of Environmental and Resource Economics, 2002/2003,* edited by T. Tietenberg and H. Folmer (Cheltenham, UK and Northampton, Mass.: Edward Elgar, 2002), pp. 373–407.

41. Mumford, *Culture,* p. 377.

42. J. Dewey, *The Public and Its Problems* (1927; reprint, Athens: Ohio University Press, 1954), p. 207.

43. Dewey develops this line of argument in numerous works, including *The Public and Its Problems* and *Liberalism and Social Action.* For a discussion of this project and its implications for environmental ethics, see B. A. Minteer, "Deweyan Democracy and Environmental Ethics," in *Democracy and the Claims of Nature: Critical Perspectives for a New Century,* edited by B. A. Minteer and B. P. Taylor (Lanham, Md.: Rowman and Littlefield, 2002), pp. 33–48.

44. For a revealing comparison of Dewey's and Mill's approaches to liberalism and public deliberation, see J. Gouinlock, *Excellence in Public Discourse: John Stuart Mill, John Dewey, and Social Intelligence* (New York: Teachers College Press, 1986).

45. Dewey, *Liberalism and Social Action,* p. 81.

46. Dewey, *Public and Its Problems,* p. 148.

47. Ibid., p. 154.

48. Mumford, *Culture,* p. 380.

49. Ibid., p. 384.

50. Mumford, *Culture,* p. 387.

51. Ibid., p. 386.

52. Dewey, *Public and Its Problems*, p. 216.

53. On this, I clearly disagree with John Friedmann's conclusion that Mumford's intellectual foundations were not pragmatic, even if Friedmann does recognize that Mumford expressed a Deweyan approach to social learning in the 1930s. See J. Friedmann, *Planning in the Public Domain: From Knowledge to Action* (Princeton, N.J.: Princeton University Press, 1987), pp. 198–200. I think Friedmann misses the pragmatic logic of Mumford's planning method and the degree to which Mumford's social democratic commitments mirrored Dewey's own. Friedmann's characterization of Dewey as a technocrat who favored the opinion of experts in planning and policy argument is, I think, the primary culprit in this misreading. In fact, Dewey was much more of a radical democrat than Friedmann suggests. See Westbrook, *John Dewey and American Democracy*, for one of the more compelling discussions of Dewey's strong democratic credentials.

54. Minteer, "Wilderness and the Wise Province."

55. B. Norton, "The Constancy of Leopold's Land Ethic," *Conservation Biology* 2 (1988): 93–102. See also Norton's discussion of Leopold in his *Toward Unity among Environmentalists* (New York: Oxford University Press, 1991).

56. D. Worster, *A River Running West: The Life of John Wesley Powell* (New York: Oxford University Press, 2001), p. 552.

Chapter 8. Flader, *Building Conservation on the Land: Aldo Leopold and the Tensions of Professionalism and Citizenship*

1. A. Leopold, *A Sand County Almanac, and Sketches Here and There* (New York: Oxford University Press, 1949); S. L. Flader, *Thinking Like a Mountain: Aldo Leopold and the Evolution of an Ecological Attitude toward Deer, Wolves, and Forests* (Columbia: University of Missouri Press, 1974). See also the preface to the University of Wisconsin Press edition, 1994. Some portions of this essay are substantially recast from S. Flader, "Aldo Leopold and Environmental Citizenship," *Transactions of the Wisconsin Academy of Sciences, Arts, and Letters* 87 (1999): 23–35.

2. F. D. Robertson, "Ecosystem Management of the National Forests and Grasslands," memorandum to regional foresters and station directors, 4 June 1992.

3. See National Commission on Civic Renewal, *A Nation of Spectators: How Civic Disengagement Weakens America and What We Can Do about It* (College Park: University of Maryland, 1998), available on-line at http://www.puaf.umd.edu/Affiliates/CivicRenewal/finalreport/table_of_contentsfinal_report.htm, and R. D. Putnam, "Bowling Alone: America's Declining Social Capital," *Journal of Democracy* 6 (January 1995): 65–78. Much of the recent attention to citizenship has been stimulated by scholarly writing concerning the forging of civil society in new democracies around the world, especially since the fall of the Iron Curtain. See, e.g., A. Arato, "Interpreting 1989," *Social Research* 60 (fall 1993): 609–646; M. Bernhard, "Civil Society after the First Transition: Dilemmas of Post-Communist Democratization in Poland and Beyond," *Communist and Post-Communist Studies* 29 (1996): 309–330; and N. Fraser, "Rethinking the Public Sphere: A Contribution to the Critique of Actually Existing Democracy," in *Justice Interruptus: Critical Reflections on the "Postsocialist" Condition* (New York: Routledge, 1997), pp. 69–98. For a probing historical analysis of American political culture

that comes to more sanguine conclusions, see M. Schudson, *The Good Citizen: A History of American Civic Life* (New York: Free Press, 1998).

4. See, e.g., B. Donahue, *Reclaiming the Commons: Community Farms and Forests in a New England Town* (New Haven, Conn.: Yale University Press, 1999), and J. Richardson, *Partnerships in Communities: Reweaving the Fabric of Rural America* (Washington, D.C.: Island Press, 2000).

5. S. L. Flader, "Citizenry and the State in the Shaping of Environmental Policy," *Environmental Review* 3 (January 1998): 8–24.

6. See S. Skowronek, *Building a New American State: The Expansion of National Administrative Capacities, 1877–1920* (New York: Cambridge University Press, 1982); S. P. Hays, *Conservation and the Gospel of Efficiency: The Progressive Conservation Movement, 1890–1920* (Cambridge, Mass.: Harvard University Press, 1959); H. Kaufman, *The Forest Ranger: A Study in Administrative Behavior* (Baltimore, Md.: Johns Hopkins University Press, 1960); and Schudson, *Good Citizen*.

7. G. Pinchot, *The Fight for Conservation,* (Garden City, N.Y.: Doubleday, 1910), IV:6. Cf. A. Leopold, "It is no prediction, but merely an assertion that the idea of controlled environment contains colors and brushes wherewith society may some day paint a new and possibly a better picture of itself," in "The Conservation Ethic," *Journal of Forestry* 31 (October 1933): 634–643.

8. For details of Leopold's biography, see C. Meine, *Aldo Leopold: His Life and Work* (Madison: University of Wisconsin Press, 1988), and Flader, *Thinking Like a Mountain*.

9. A. Leopold, "To the Forest Officers of the Carson," *Carson Pine Cone* (July 1913), reprinted in *The River of the Mother of God and Other Essays by Aldo Leopold*, edited by S. L. Flader and J. B. Callicott (Madison: University of Wisconsin Press, 1991), pp. 41–46; quote, p. 44.

10. A. Leopold, "Forest Inspection as Developed in the Southwest" (address to New York Forest Club, 25 November 1924), General Files—Aldo Leopold, Series 9/25/10-6, box 16, University of Wisconsin Division of Archives, hereafter cited as LP 6B16 (Leopold Papers, Series 6, box 16); S. Flader, "Aldo Leopold and the Evolution of Ecosystem Management," in *Sustainable Ecological Systems: Implementing an Ecological Approach to Land Management*, edited by W. W. Covington and L. F. DeBano, USDA Forest Service General Technical Report RM-247 (Ft. Collins, CO: USDA Forest Service, 1994), pp. 15–19.

11. A. Leopold, "Standards of Conservation" (6p. hdw., ca. 1922), LP 6B16; published in Flader and Callicott, *River*, pp. 82–85; A. Leopold, "Skill in Forestry" (10p. tps., ca. 1922), LP 6B16. See also A. Leopold, "Conservation Economics," *Journal of Forestry* 32, no. 5 (May 1934): pp. 537–544, reprinted in Flader and Callicott, *River*, 201. For a discussion of the problem of authority as related to the relationship between professionals and citizens, see T. L. Cooper, "Citizenship and Professionalism in Public Administration," *Public Administration Review* 44 (1984): 143–149, and J. D. Wellman and T. J. Tipple, "Public Forestry and Direct Democracy," *Environmental Professional* 12 (1990): 77–86.

12. A. Leopold, "Home Gardens and Citizenship" (7pp. tps., 23 April 1917), LP 8B8.

13. A. Leopold, "The Civic Life of Albuquerque" (9pp. tps., 27 September 1918), LP 8B8.

14. G. S. Wood, *The Creation of the American Republic, 1776–1787* (New York: Norton, 1972); R. E. Shalhope, "Republicanism and Early American Historiography," *William and Mary Quarterly* 39 (1982): 334–356; J. Appleby, ed., "Special Issue: Republicanism in the History and Historiography of the United States," *American Quarterly* 37 (1985); G. S. Wood, *The Radicalism of the American Revolution* (New York: Knopf, 1992).

15. See J. N. Rakove, "Parchment Barriers and the Politics of Rights," in *A Culture of Rights: The Bill of Rights in Philosophy, Politics, and Law—1791 and 1991*, edited by M. J. Lacey and K. Haakonssen (Cambridge, England: Cambridge University Press, 1992), p. 103, and W. A. Galston, "Practical Philosophy and the Bill of Rights: Perspectives on Some Contemporary Issues," in Lacey and Haakonssen, *Culture of Rights*, p. 234.

16. Wood, *Creation of the American Republic*, pp. 319–328. See, e.g., G. Kulik, "Dams, Fish, and Farmers: Defense of Public Rights in Eighteenth-Century Rhode Island," in *The Countryside in the Age of Capitalist Transformation*, edited by S. Hahn and J. Prude (Chapel Hill: University of North Carolina Press, 1985), pp. 25–50.

17. A. de Tocqueville, *Democracy in America*, edited by P. Bradley (New York: Vintage, 1945), vol. 1, chap. 12; vol. 2, chap. 5.

18. A. Leopold, "A Criticism of the Booster Spirit" (10pp. tps. speech to Ten Dons, 6 November 1923), LP 6B16, published in *River*, pp. 98–105. The national park reference may have been to a proposal by Secretary of the Interior Albert Fall for establishment of a park from a series of discontinuous segments of land near his home in south-central New Mexico, part of which is now White Sands National Monument.

19. A. Leopold, "Pioneers and Gullies," *Sunset* 52, no. 5 (May 1924): 15–16, 91–95, reprinted in Flader and Callicott, *River*, pp. 106–113. Leopold's language regarding the obligation of landowners was similar to that in a speech he had written in December 1922 for the New Mexico Association for Science, "Erosion as a Menace to the Social and Economic Future of the Southwest." The speech was published many years later in *Journal of Forestry* 44, no. 9 (September 1946): 627–633.

20. A. Leopold, "The Homebuilder Conserves," *American Forests and Forest Life* 34, no. 413 (May 1928): 276–278, 297, reprinted in Flader and Callicott, *River*, pp. 143–147; A. Leopold, "Land-Use and Democracy," *Audubon Magazine* 44, no. 5 (September–October 1942): 259–265, reprinted in Flader and Callicott, *River*, pp. 295–300.

21. A. Leopold, "Izaac Walton League and Its Relation to Forestry in Wisconsin" (10pp. tps., ca. 1925), LP 6B16.

22. A. Leopold to C. V. Campbell, 15 October 1932, LP 3B5, and associated correspondence. See also J. L. Crane Jr. and G. W. Olcott, *Report on the Iowa Twenty-Five-Year Conservation Plan* (Des Moines, Iowa: Meredith, 1933).

23. A. Leopold, "A Conservation Plan for Wisconsin Farms" (6pp. tps., 23 October 1933), LP 6B16.

24. A. Leopold to W. Schuenke, 10 July 1935; I. T. Bode to A. Leopold, ca. July 1935; A. Leopold to I. T. Bode, 19 July 1935; all in LP 3B5. See also R. Conard, *Places of Quiet Beauty: Parks, Preserves, and Environmentalism* (Iowa City: University of Iowa Press, 1997), pp. 120–136.

25. A. Leopold to P. S. Lovejoy, 18 July 1935, P. S. Lovejoy Papers, Michigan Historical Commission Archives, Lansing, RG63-12 B12F6.

26. A. Leopold, "A House Divided," *Wisconsin Sportsman* (October 1940): 5. See also A. Leopold, "Game and Wild Life Conservation," *Condor* 34, no. 2 (March–April 1932): 103–106, reprinted in Flader and Callicott, *River*, pp. 164–168.

27. A. Leopold, "Notes on Game Administration in Germany," *American Wildlife* 25, no. 6 (November–December 1936): 85, 92–93.

28. Leopold, "Conservation Economics," *Journal of Forestry* 32, no. 5 (1934): 537–544, reprinted in Flader and Callicott, *River*, pp. 193–202. See also A. Leopold, "The Conservation Ethic," *Journal of Forestry* 31, no. 6 (October 1933): 634–643, reprinted in Flader and Callicott, *River*, pp. 181–192; A. Leopold, "Conservation in the World of Tomorrow," lecture notes (5pp. tps., 29 March 1937), LP 6B14; and A. Leopold, "The Farmer as a Conservationist," *American Forests* 45, no. 6 (June 1939): 294–299, 316, 323, reprinted in Flader and Callicott, *River*, pp. 255–265.

29. A. Leopold, "Land Pathology" (8pp. tps., 15 April 1935), LP 6B16, published in Flader and Callicott, *River*, pp. 212–217. Leopold observed that mechanisms, economic and moral, to encourage conservation of landscape beauty on private lands might also help prevent the otherwise inevitable degradation of public parks: "Parks are over-crowded hospitals trying to cope with an epidemic of esthetic rickets; the remedy lies not in hospitals, but in daily dietaries."

30. J. N. Darling to A. Leopold, 20 November 1935, LP 6B16.

31. A. Leopold, "Coon Valley: An Adventure in Cooperative Conservation," *American Forests* 41, no. 5 (May 1935): 205–208, reprinted in Flader and Callicott, *River*, pp. 218–223.

32. A. Leopold, "Farmer-Sportsman Set-ups in the North Central Region," *Proceedings, North American Wildlife Conference*, 3–7 February 1936 (Senate Committee Print, 74th Cong., 2d sess., 1936), pp. 279–285; A. Leopold, "Helping Ourselves" (with R. Paulson), *Field and Stream* 39, no. 4 (August 1934): 32–33, 56, reprinted in Flader and Callicott, *River*, pp. 203–208; and A. Leopold, "History of the Riley Game Cooperative, 1931–1939," *Journal of Wildlife Management* 4, no. 3 (July 1940): 291–302. See also R. E. McCabe, ed., *Aldo Leopold: Mentor, by His Graduate Students*, proceedings of an Aldo Leopold centennial symposium held in Madison, Wisconsin, 23–24 April 1987 (Madison: University of Wisconsin, Department of Wildlife Ecology, 1988).

33. A. Leopold, "Threatened Species: A Proposal to the Wildlife Conference for an Inventory of the Needs of Near-Extinct Birds and Animals," *American Forests* 42, no. 3 (March 1936): 116–119, reprinted in Flader and Callicott, *River*, pp. 230–234.

34. Leopold, *Sand County Almanac*, pp. viii, 204. See also S. Flader, "The Person and the Place," in C. Steinhacker and S. Flader, *The Sand Country of Aldo Leopold* (San Francisco: Sierra Club Books, 1973), pp. 7–49.

35. Leopold, *Sand County Almanac*, pp. 4, 87.

36. Ibid., pp. 138, 161. For a discussion of definitions or dimensions of citizenship, see, e.g., Cooper, "Citizenship and Professionalism," n. 11.

37. Leopold, *Sand County Almanac*, pp. 166–167, 175.

38. Ibid., pp. 207–208.

39. A. Leopold, "Memo for Dean Christensen," 29 July 1935, Department of Wildlife Ecology Papers, Series 9/25/3, box 1, University of Wisconsin Division of Archives; A.

Leopold, "A Biotic View of Land," *Journal of Forestry* 37, no. 9 (September 1939): 727–730, reprinted in Flader and Callicott, *River*, pp. 266–273; A. Leopold, "The Role of Wildlife in a Liberal Education," *Transactions, Seventh North American Wildlife Conference* (8–10 April 1942), pp. 485–489, reprinted in Flader and Callicott, *River*, pp. 301–305. See also S. Flader, "Aldo Leopold's Challenge to Educators," *Transactions, Forty-Eighth North American Wildlife and Natural Resources Conference* (1983), pp. 33–41, and C. Meine, "Reading the Landscape: Aldo Leopold and Wildlife Ecology 118," *Forest History Today* (fall 1999): 35–42.

40. A. Leopold, "Ecology and Politics," WLE 118 Introductory Lecture (7pp. tps., ca. 1941), LP 6B16, reprinted in Flader and Callicott, *River*, pp. 281–289.

41. A. Leopold, "Land-Use and Democracy," *Audubon Magazine* 44, no. 5 (September–October 1942): 259–265, reprinted in Flader and Callicott, *River*, pp. 295–300.

42. See Flader, *Thinking Like a Mountain*, pp. 168–260.

43. A. Leopold, "Deer Irruptions," *Wisconsin Conservation Bulletin* 8 (August 1943): 1–11; J. M. Larkin, "A Report on the Deer Situation in Vilas County, 23 January 1943," Wisconsin Conservation Department Files, State Historical Society of Wisconsin Archives; J. M. Larkin, "Comments on the Deer Situation in General and in Vilas County in Particular" (15pp. tps., ca. spring 1943), ibid. For a news report on the deer yard tour, see G. MacQuarrie, "Death Stalks Deer Country," *Milwaukee Journal* (4 April 1943).

44. Personal conversations with W. Noble Clark and A. Starker Leopold, ca. 1970.

45. Flader, *Thinking Like a Mountain*, pp. 217–256.

46. Leopold, *Sand County Almanac*, p. 68.

47. M. Sagoff, "The View from Quincy Library: Civic Engagement in Environmental Problem-Solving," Working Paper no. 16, National Commission on Civic Renewal; M. Mossman, "Of People and Prairie," *Wisconsin Academy Review* (fall 2000): 24–26, 33–34. For other examples of local democratic participation in decision making, see D. Kemmis, *Community and the Politics of Place* (Norman: University of Oklahoma Press, 1991). For a discussion of the Quincy group's trajectory from collaboration to confrontation, see J. B. Little, "Coming of Age for Quincy Experiment," *Forest* (spring 2002): 38–43.

48. For recent examples of the burgeoning movement in community-based conservation, see the *Journal of Forestry* 96, no. 3 (March 1998), a special issue on community forestry; and the references in note 3. For a discussion of the interaction of professionals and ordinary citizens in Chicago Wilderness and other restoration projects, see P. H. Gobster and R. B. Hull, *Restoring Nature: Perspectives from the Social Sciences and Humanities* (Washington, D.C.: Island Press, 2000).

49. Farming and Conservation Together Committee (FACT), "Proposal to the U.S. Fish and Wildlife Service, Alternative to the Aldo Leopold National Wildlife Refuge," submitted 28 September 2000, in U.S. Fish and Wildlife Service, *The Fairfield Marsh: A Conservation Partnership*, Revised Draft Environmental Assessment (7 February 2001). The FACT alternative was accepted as the preferred alternative by the U.S. Fish and Wildlife Service, and the first $2 million was appropriated in 2001 to fund the local initiative; see "Federal Dollars Spur FACT Programs," *Leopold Outlook* 4, no. 1 (winter 2002): 1, 6.

50. See, e.g., "Certified Woods: Ingraining Sustainable Forestry," *Wisconsin Natural Resources* 26 (February 2002): 1–16.

51. See, e.g., T. L. Cooper, "Citizenship and Professionalism in Public Administration," *Public Administration Review* 44 (March 1984): 143–149; J. D. Wellman and T. J. Tipple, "Public Forestry and Direct Democracy," *Environmental Professional* 12 (1990): 77–86; L. H. Gunderson, C. S. Holling, and S. S. Light, eds., *Barriers and Bridges to the Renewal of Ecosystems and Institutions* (New York: Columbia University Press, 1995); and S. S. Light, "Adaptive Ecosystem Assessment and Management: The Path of Last Resort?" (unpublished manuscript ca. 1999f).

Chapter 9. Taylor, *Scott Nearing and the American Conservation Tradition*

1. R. Gottlieb, *Forcing the Spring: The Transformation of the American Environmental Movement* (Washington, D.C.: Island Press, 1993), p. 7.
2. Ibid., p. 8.
3. H. Nearing and S. Nearing, *Continuing the Good Life: Half a Century of Homesteading* (New York: Schocken Books, 1979), p. 153.
4. H. Nearing and S. Nearing, *Living the Good Life: How to Live Sanely and Simply in a Troubled World* (1954; reprint, New York: Schocken Books, 1970), p. xv.
5. See also S. Nearing, *Man's Search for the Good Life* (Harborside, Maine: Social Science Institute, 1974), and Nearing and Nearing, *Continuing the Good Life*.
6. J. A. Saltmarsh, *Scott Nearing: An Intellectual Biography* (Philadelphia: Temple University Press, 1991), p. 254.
7. Thoreau's famous command "Simplify, simplify, simplify!" was taken very seriously by the Nearings. Their diets alone were models of simplicity; they ate almost entirely unprocessed raw fruits and vegetables, with only a little soup and cooked grain at lunch. See H. D. Thoreau, *Walden,* in *A Week on the Concord and Merrimack Rivers; Walden, or Life in the Woods; The Maine Woods; Cape Cod* (New York: Library of America, 1985), p. 395; Nearing and Nearing, *Living the Good Life,* pp. 109–141.
8. The Nearings tried valiantly to organize political discussion groups among their neighbors, but never with much success. They were distressed that only (what were in their view) frivolous activities, such as dances, really brought people together socially. "In other words," they wrote contemptuously, "activities were to be leveled down to the lowest common denominator." Nearing and Nearing, *Living the Good Life*, p. 170. Stephen Whitfield dryly observes that Nearing's "excoriation of the hedonism of Vermonters must be virtually unique in the history of moralist literature." S. Whitfield, *Scott Nearing: Apostle of American Radicalism* (New York: Columbia University Press, 1974), p. 178.
9. The Nearings admitted, for example, that their lifestyle would have prevented them from being able to afford to send a child to college. Whitfield, *Scott Nearing*, p. 191.
10. Consider this, from Nearing and Nearing, *Living the Good Life:* "There is something extravagant and irresponsible about eating strawberries and green peas in a cold climate, every month in the year. Such practices ignore the meaningful cycle of the seasons. Those who dodge it or slight it are like children who skip a grade in school, pass over its drill and discipline, and ever after have the feeling that they have missed something" (p. 97).

11. "As I have said, I do not propose to write an ode to dejection, but to brag as lustily as chanticleer in the morning, standing on his roost, if only to wake my neighbors up." Thoreau, *Walden*, p. 389.

12. "If I seem to boast more than is becoming, my excuse is that I brag for humanity rather than for myself; and my shortcomings and inconsistencies do not affect the truth of my statement." Ibid., p. 361. I have discussed this quality of Thoreau's criticism of American society in my *America's Bachelor Uncle: Henry Thoreau and the American Polity* (Lawrence: University Press of Kansas, 1996). See chap. 5, "Independence," and p. 81 in particular.

13. See Nearing and Nearing, *Living the Good Life,* pp. 173, 196.

14. The Nearings generated a ten-year economic development plan, a constitution, and by-laws for their household, and they kept records of almost every imaginable activity. "Some of our readers will feel that such a life pattern is overorganized," the Nearings commented. "They would not wish to plan their activities so completely. After having tried it out, day after day, and year after year, we know it is the way to get things done." Nearing and Nearing, *Living the Good Life*, p. 36.

15. H. D. Thoreau, "The Pond in Winter," in *Walden*, pp. 547–560.

16. Whitfield, *Scott Nearing*, p. 51.

17. Ibid., p. 95.

18. The standard biographies are Whitfield's and Saltmarsh's, both referred to earlier. Whitfield's is the first and the more critical (and critically adept) of the two.

19. J. Field and S. Nearing, *Community Civics* (New York: Macmillan, 1916); S. Nearing, *The New Education* (1915; reprint, New York: Arno Press and New York Times, 1969); and articles on women in political life, social science, religious ideals, and socialism can all be found in S. Sherman, ed., *A Scott Nearing Reader: The Good Life in Bad Times* (Metuchen, N.J.: Scarecrow Press, 1989). See especially p. 39 ("It is the women who realize the needs of a social housecleaning,—who are demanding an opportunity for real service in the state"); p. 42 ("Social Sanity can be based on nothing less than a scientific attitude toward the facts of social life"); p. 57 ("We want heaven on earth, and we can have it if we will"); and p. 65 ("In so far as the community fails to give first place to the welfare of the wage-earners, who make up the greatest number in an industrial society, it fails in its efforts to establish democracy"). All these passages are from articles written between 1912 and 1916.

20. Consider, for example, his comment in *Man's Search for the Good Life* that "man is a child of nature" (p. 52). At the very least, this seems to express a rather different sensibility from that found in the comments building to the conclusion of the book, such as "Waste and pollution of nature, like inadequacies and defects in the social environment require the attention of trained, experienced social engineers" (p. 126). For another example, consider what Nearing identified as the most crucial environmental contribution he could make: "At the top of our priority list for the well-being of the earth stands the injunction: conserve and build good topsoil." See S. Nearing, *Civilization and Beyond: Learning from History* (Harborside, Maine: Social Sciences Institute, 1975), p. 224.

21. For a classic theoretical text that grew from this strain of the Progressive movement, see W. Lippmann, *Public Opinion* (1922; reprint, New York: Macmillan, 1930).

22. S. Nearing, *The Conscience of a Radical* (Harborside, Maine: Social Science Institute, 1965), pp. 168–169.

23. Nearing, *Man's Search for the Good Life*, p. 103.

24. It was also, incidentally, what informed his version of socialism. Whitfield observes that Nearing's focus was always on "the ideals of control and efficiency, in the harnessing of social forces, and in the development of political and technical mastery." Whitfield, *Scott Nearing*, p. 210.

25. For a discussion of the politics of Pinchot's conservationism, see B. P. Taylor, *Our Limits Transgressed: Environmental Political Thought in America* (Lawrence: University Press of Kansas, 1992), pp. 18–22.

26. Nearing and Nearing, *Living the Good Life*, p. 33.

27. Nearing and Nearing, *Continuing the Good Life*, p. 183.

28. Nearing and Nearing, *Living the Good Life*, p. 22.

29. "The word 'discipline' was in such disrepute among the families in the valley, that its mention aroused sharp opposition." Nearing and Nearing, *Living the Good Life*, p. 195.

30. Ibid., p. xv.

31. Whitfield notes the irony that this humane sensibility was found in the same man who supported the Soviet Union's brutality in Hungary. Whitfield, *Scott Nearing*, p. 199.

32. Nearing and Nearing, *Continuing the Good Life*, p. 184.

33. Nearing, *Civilization and Beyond*, p. 227.

34. In one of the most remarkable passages in his writings, Nearing referred to modern cities as "squalid and corrupt; ruthless, policemanized concentration camps in which men and women were persuaded or compelled to spend their lives and in which children were forced to grow up unaware of any alternative to the wealth-poverty pattern." S. Nearing and H. Nearing, *The Maple Sugar Book* (New York: J. Day, 1950).

35. Nearing and Nearing, *Living the Good Life*, p. 173.

36. Ibid., p. 196.

37. Saltmarsh, *Scott Nearing*, p. 264.

38. Whitfield, *Scott Nearing*, p. 219.

39. And, as Saltmarsh points out, the young never really understood Nearing either. Saltmarsh, *Scott Nearing*, p. 263.

40. Note the new use of the word "Establishment" in the passage quoted earlier from *Continuing the Good Life* (p. 183): "Our general aim was to set up a use economy for ourselves independent of the established market economy and for the most part under our own control, thereby freeing ourselves from undue dependence on the Establishment." Prior to this time in his life, Nearing would attack capitalism, not anything so vague as "the Establishment."

41. One way of looking at this distance between Nearing and the counterculture of the 1960s and 1970s is to consider the harsh but not entirely unfair assessment by Whitfield that Nearing despised "the pleasures of others." This, of course, is a far cry from the playful hedonism of the youth movement. Whitfield, *Scott Nearing*, p. 212.

42. Nearing and Nearing, *Continuing the Good Life*, p. 152.

43. This is a man, for example, who resigned from the War Resisters League in protest over the use of the word "shit" in one of their publications. Whitfield, *Scott Nearing*, p. 221.

Paul Goodman observed, in his 1970 introduction to *Living the Good Life*, "Certainly our communal hippies will be appalled by the Puritan rectitude of the Nearings, their extraordinary prudence in gathering stones for a ten-year building plan, their almost cash-accounting of labor time, and their rigorously hygienic pleasures" (p. x).

44. See W. C. McWilliams, "Standing at Armageddon: Morality and Religion in Progressive Thought," in S. M. Milkis and J. M. Mileur, eds., *Progressivism and the New Democracy* (Amherst: University of Massachusetts Press, 1999), p. 112.

45. Whitfield, *Scott Nearing*, p. 211.

46. His own publishing project was called the Social Science Institute. For his view of himself as a social scientist, see S. Nearing, *The Making of a Radical: A Political Autobiography* (New York: Harper & Row, 1972), p. 136.

47. In this sense, his democratic theory paralleled his theory about the promotion of personal health (always a major preoccupation for him): his assumption was always that it was the corrupting influence of capitalism that was responsible for creating poor human health, and this assumption was so strong that he never needed a serious biological science to support, in his own mind, his claims about the healthful consequences of organic food. If all bad human works disappeared, all good things, he thought, could be expected to come to us in the natural order of things.

48. S. Nearing, *Democracy Is Not Enough* (New York: Island Workshop Press, 1945), p. 106.

49. See note 31 earlier. For a particularly distressing example of the brutality of Nearing's political views, see Nearing, *Making of a Radical*, pp. 282–284. Here he tells the story of two letters he wrote to the mother of a son killed in World War II, and the telling makes for chilling reading. The following is a passage from the first of these: "So long . . . as fine, capable young men respond thus to the call of the big shots, destroying and murdering at the word of command, fine young men will be snuffed out in their early years, leaving mothers and wives to lament their loss. This holds true whether they respond to the orders of Roosevelt, Hitler, or any other commander-in-chief" (p. 282). This is a classic Nearing performance on two grounds: in his equation of Franklin D. Roosevelt with Adolf Hitler, combined with his unwillingness to mention Joseph Stalin by name; and in his willingness to be cruel in the name of principle and to pass harsh judgment even on those least morally culpable. ("This was not a kind letter under the circumstances, but it was true. I wrote it because I thought the time had come for John [the young soldier's father] and Mary to face the music of a comfortable, secure life built on a foundation of exploitation and war." Nearing, *Making of a Radical,* p. 282.)

50. Consider this: "Providing sufficient relief to end physical hardship and formulating a program aimed to achieve social justice is outside the scope of western civilization." Nearing, *Conscience of a Radical*, 145.

51. A telling expression of this failure can be found in Nearing's pedagogy. For his entire life, he thought of himself as a teacher above all else, but as a teacher he never took his students seriously as independent thinkers and moral agents. As a result, he never learned to listen to his students, any more than to his fellow citizens; either they listened to him and accepted what he had to say or they were simply viewed as intractable or stubborn or corrupt. "Teaching is my job. Teaching, in its largest sense,

means searching out the truth, telling it to those who are willing to learn, and building it into the life of the community." Nearing, *Making of a Radical*, p. 299.

52. Saltmarsh, *Scott Nearing*, p. 1.

53. "The insistence on categorical [environmental] principles that are nonnegotiable or amenable to majoritarian choices, is revolutionary in itself in today's moral climate." L. Westra, *An Environmental Proposal for Ethics* (Lanham, Md.: Rowman and Littlefield, 1994), p. 189.

54. J. B. Elshtain, *Jane Addams and the Dream of American Democracy* (New York: Basic Books, 2002), p. 19.

Chapter 10. Freyfogle, *Conservation and the Four Faces of Resistance*

1. W. Berry, "Conserving Communities," in *Another Turn of the Crank* (Washington, D.C.: Counterpoint, 1995), p. 16.

2. His other commentaries on the global economy include W. Berry, "A Bad Big Idea," in *Sex, Economy, Freedom, and Community* (New York: Pantheon Books, 1993), p. 45; W. Berry, "Farming and the Global Economy," in *Another Turn of the Crank*, p. 1; and W. Berry, "The Whole Horse," in *The New Agrarianism: Land, Culture, and the Community of Life*, edited by E. T. Freyfogle (Washington, D.C.: Island Press, 2001), p. 63.

3. See, e.g., D. Worster, *The Wealth of Nature: Environmental History and the Ecological Imagination* (New York: Oxford University Press, 1993).

4. A. Leopold, *A Sand County Almanac, and Sketches Here and There* (New York: Oxford University Press, 1949), p. vii.

5. Ibid., pp. 224–225.

6. See S. L. Flader, *Thinking Like a Mountain: Aldo Leopold and the Evolution of an Ecological Attitude toward Deer, Wolves, and Forests* (Columbia: University of Missouri Press, 1974).

7. A key essay, recording Leopold's progress in providing an ecological grounding for his holistic thinking, was A. Leopold, "A Biotic View of Land" (1939), reprinted in *The River of the Mother of God and Other Essays by Aldo Leopold*, edited by S. L. Flader and J. B. Callicott (1936; reprint, Madison: University of Wisconsin Press, 1991), p. 266.

8. A. Leopold, "The Conservation League," unpublished manuscript (1940), Leopold Papers (LP), University of Wisconsin Archives, Series 10-6, box 16.

9. A. Leopold, "Ecology, Philosophy, and Conservation," unpublished, undated manuscript, LP 10-6, box 16.

10. A. Leopold, "Threatened Species" (1936), in Flader and Callicott, *River*, pp. 230–231.

11. A. Leopold, "The Conservation Ethic" (1933), reprinted in Flader and Callicott, *River*, pp. 181, 187.

12. A. Leopold, "Land Pathology" (1935), in Flader and Callicott, *River*, pp. 212–213.

13. Leopold, "Land Pathology," pp. 212–213.

14. One of Leopold's clearest calls for conservationists to rally around the goal, and for ecologists to use their best guesses about what it meant for land to possess health, was left unpublished at his death. "The Land-Health Concept and Conservation," in A. Leopold, *For the Health of the Land: Previously Unpublished Essays and Other Writings*, edited by J. B. Callicott and E. T. Freyfogle (Washington, D.C.: Island Press, 1999), p. 218 (originally written in 1946).

15. A. Leopold, "Conservation: In Whole or in Part" (1944); first published in 1991 in Flader and Callicott, *River*, pp. 311, 318. Leopold's concept of land health is considered in part 6 of J. B. Callicott, *Beyond the Land Ethic: More Essays in Environmental Philosophy* (Albany: State University of New York Press, 1999), and E. T. Freyfogle, "*A Sand County Almanac* at 50: Leopold in the New Century," *Environmental Law Reporter* 30:10058 (2000).

16. A. Leopold, "Land-Use and Democracy" (1942), in Flader and Callicott, *River*, pp. 295, 300.

17. A. Leopold, "Biotic Land-Use," in Leopold, *For the Health of the Land*, pp. 198, 201.

18. Ibid., p. 205.

19. Leopold explored the economics of private lands conservation, beginning with his important trio of essays, "The Conservation Ethic" (1933), "Conservation Economics" (1934), and "Land Pathology" (1935), published in Flader and Callicott, *River*, pp. 181, 193, 212. His many unpublished manuscripts touching on the subject include (from LP 10-6, boxes 16–18) "Armaments for Conservation," "Conservation and Politics," "Motives for Conservation," "Economics of the Wild," "Ecology and Economics in Land Use," and "Economics, Philosophy, and Land."

20. Leopold, "Land Pathology," p. 215.

21. Ibid., p. 214.

22. A. Leopold, "Conservation and Politics," unpublished, undated manuscript, LP 10-6, box 16.

23. A. Leopold, "Pioneers and Gullies" (1924), in Flader and Callicott, *River*, pp. 106, 111.

24. Leopold, *Sand County Almanac*, p. 225.

25. Ibid., p. 210.

26. A. Leopold, "The State of the Profession" (1940), in Flader and Callicott, *River*, pp. 276, 280.

27. No biography of Berry has yet been undertaken. Information about his life is included in A. Angyal, *Wendell Berry* (New York: Twayne, 1995).

28. Berry, "Whole Horse," pp. 63, 67.

29. W. Berry, "Discipline and Hope," in *A Continuous Harmony: Essays Cultural and Agricultural* (New York: Harcourt Brace Jovanovich, 1972), pp. 86, 164; W. Berry, *Sex, Economy, Freedom, and Community* (New York: Pantheon Books, 1993), pp. 14–15, 40; W. Berry, *What Are People For?* (San Francisco: North Point Press, 1990), pp. 149, 206–207.

30. A. Howard, *The Soil and Health: A Study of Organic Agriculture* (New York: Devin-Adair, 1947), p. 11. Berry's usages include *What Are People For?* p. 149, and *Another Turn of the Crank*, pp. 89–90.

31. W. Berry, "Health Is Membership," in *Another Turn of the Crank*, pp. 86, 90.

32. See, e.g., W. Berry, "Conservation and Local Economy," in *Sex, Economy, Freedom, and Community*, p. 3.

33. See, e.g., W. Berry, "Private Property and the Common Wealth," in *Another Turn of the Crank*, pp. 46, 48.

34. B. Field, *Environmental Economics: An Introduction*, 2nd ed. (New York: McGraw-Hill, 1997), pp. 69–73.

35. E. Freyfogle, "The Tragedy of Fragmentation," *Environmental Law Reporter* 32(2002): 11321–11335.

36. An important work addressing common-property management possibilities is E. Ostrom, *Governing the Commons: The Evolution of Institutions for Collective Action* (Cambridge, England: Cambridge University Press, 1990).

37. See W. Kempton, J. Boster, and J. Hartley, *Environmental Values in American Culture* (Cambridge, Mass.: MIT Press, 1995).

38. See, e.g., A. Arblaster, *Democracy,* 2nd ed. (Minneapolis: University of Minnesota Press, 1994).

39. Useful surveys of ideas about property in the United States are W. Scott, *In Pursuit of Happiness: American Conceptions of Property from the Seventeenth to the Twentieth Century* (Bloomington: Indiana University Press, 1977), and G. Alexander, *Commodity and Propriety: Competing Visions of Property in American Legal Theory, 1776–1970* (Chicago: University of Chicago Press, 1997).

40. See J. Echeverria, "The Politics of Property Rights," *Oklahoma Law Review* 50, no. 351 (1997).

41. Differing visions of private landownership are considered in E. T. Freyfogle, *Bounded People, Boundless Lands: Envisioning a New Land Ethic* (Washington, D.C.: Island Press, 1998), chap. 6.

42. See P. Westen, *Speaking of Equality* (Princeton, N.J.: Princeton University Press, 1990).

43. A sensitive, probing critique of environmentalism, highlighting the failings of conservationists to respond to cultural critiques, is offered in S. Hays, *A History of Environmental Politics, 1945–1995* (Pittsburgh: University of Pittsburgh Press, 2000).

44. A. Leopold, "The Conservation Ethic," in Flader and Callicott, *River,* pp. 181, 187.

45. See, e.g., J. Gray, *Liberalism* (Minneapolis: University of Minnesota Press, 1986).

46. A perceptive exploration that reconciles environmentalism with liberalism—although only after refining the latter—is M. Sagoff, *The Economy of the Earth: Philosophy, Law, and the Environment* (Cambridge, England: Cambridge University Press, 1988), pp. 146–170.

47. A. Leopold, "The Farm Wildlife Program: A Self-Scrutiny" (undated, ca. 1937), LP 10-6, box 16.

48. Good sources include H. Daly and J. Cobb Jr., *For the Common Good: Redirecting the Economy toward Community, the Environment, and a Sustainable Future* (Boston: Beacon Press, 1989); L. Brown, *Eco-Economy: Building an Economy for the Earth* (New York: Norton, 2001); E. Davidson, *You Can't Eat GNP: Economics as if Ecology Mattered* (Cambridge, Mass.: Perseus, 2000).

49. A standard libertarian work is R. Epstein, *Takings: Private Property and the Power of Eminent Domain* (Cambridge, Mass.: Harvard University Press, 1985).

Chapter 11. Meine, *Conservation and the Progressive Movement:*
Growing from the Radical Center

1. S. Stromquist, "Prairie Politics and the Landscape of Reform," in *Recovering the Prairie,* edited by R. Sayre (Madison: University of Wisconsin Press, 1999), pp. 107–123. We have recently received a windfall of biographical and topical coverage of these times.

See D. Lowenthal, *George Perkins Marsh, Prophet of Conservation* (Seattle: University of Washington Press, 2000), C. Miller, *Gifford Pinchot and the Making of Modern Environmentalism* (Washington, D.C.: Island Press, 2001), E. Morris, *Theodore Rex* (New York: Random House, 2001), J. Reiger, *American Sportsmen and the Origins of Conservation*, 3rd ed. (Corvallis: Oregon State University Press, 2001), and D. Worster, *A River Running West: The Life of John Wesley Powell* (New York: Oxford University Press, 2001).

2. T. Roosevelt, *Theodore Roosevelt: An Autobiography* (New York: Da Capo Press, 1985), pp. 408–436. See C. Meine, "Roosevelt, Conservation, and the Revival of Democracy," *Conservation Biology* 15 (2001): 829–831.

3. The most recent biography is N. C. Unger, *Fighting Bob La Follette: The Righteous Reformer* (Chapel Hill: University of North Carolina Press, 2000). For an account of the shift in the lumber industry away from the Lake States, see M. Williams, *Americans and Their Forests: A Historical Geography* (Cambridge, England: Cambridge University Press, 1989), pp. 193–330.

4. T. Roosevelt, introduction to C. McCarthy, *The Wisconsin Idea* (New York: Macmillan, 1912), p. vii.

5. Quoted in Roosevelt, *Theodore Roosevelt: An Autobiography*, pp. 406–407.

6. W. Berry, "A Few Words in Praise of Edward Abbey," in *Resist Much, Obey Little: Remembering Ed Abbey*, edited by J. R. Hepworth and G. McNamee (San Francisco: Sierra Club Books, 1996), p. 3.

7. Roosevelt, *Theodore Roosevelt: An Autobiography*, p. 437.

8. T. Roosevelt, introduction to *Wisconsin Idea*, p. ix.

9. G. Pinchot, *The Fight for Conservation* (1910; reprint, Seattle: University of Washington Press, 1967), p. 88.

10. C. Van Hise, *The Conservation of Natural Resources in the United States* (New York: Macmillan, 1910), p. 397.

11. See J. Nichols, "Questioning Leaders a Progressive Tradition," *Capital Times* (Madison, Wisconsin), 25 September 2002.

12. P. Sauer, "Reinhabiting Environmentalism: Picking Up Where Leopold and Carson Left Off," *Orion* 18, no. 3 (summer 1999): 31.

13. J. B. Callicott and M. P. Nelson, eds., *The Great New Wilderness Debate* (Athens: University of Georgia Press, 1998). See also W. Cronon, ed., *Uncommon Ground: Toward Reinventing Nature* (New York: Norton, 1995), and M. E. Soulé and G. Lease, eds., *Reinventing Nature? Responses to Postmodern Deconstruction* (Washington, D.C.: Island Press, 1995).

14. K. DeLuca, "Environmental Justice," *New York Times*, 18 July 2002, p. A22.

15. O. Murie, "Ethics in Wildlife Management," *Journal of Wildlife Management* 18, no. 3 (1954): 292, 293. See C. Meine, "Murie's Choice: An Introduction to the Essay 'Ethics in Wildlife Management,'" in *The Muries: Voices for Wilderness and Wildlife*, edited by N. Shea et al. (Shepardstown, W.V.: U.S. Fish and Wildlife Service, National Conservation Training Center, 2001), pp. 51–52. Two useful explorations of the relationship between social justice and conservation are W. Berry, *The Hidden Wound* (San Francisco: North Point Press, 1989), and A. L. Herman, *Community, Violence, and Peace: Aldo Leopold, Mohandas K. Gandhi, Martin Luther King Jr., and Gautama the Buddha in the Twenty-First*

Century (Albany: State University of New York Press, 1999). For a helpful discussion of the need to clarify the "linguistic muddle" in environmental history, see J. M. Turner, "Charting American Environmentalism's Early (Intellectual) Geography, 1890–1920," *Wild Earth Journal* 10, no. 2 (summer 2000): 18–26.

16. C. Meine, "Conservation Movement, Historical," in *Encyclopedia of Biodiversity,* vol. 1, edited by S. Levin (San Diego: Academic Press, 2001), pp. 883–896.

17. Pinchot, *Fight for Conservation*, p. 43.

18. Ibid., p. 46.

19. Miller, *Pinchot and the Making of Modern Environmentalism*, p. 11. The classic commentary is S. P. Hays, *Conservation and the Gospel of Efficiency* (Cambridge, Mass.: Harvard University Press, 1959).

20. J. M. Turner writes in "Charting Environmentalism's Early Geography": "Little evidence exists that in the 1890s [the] 'preservationists' considered themselves the foes of any emerging group of 'conservationists.' Ambiguities in the 1890s language have made it easy for historians and environmentalists alike to overemphasize [these] early divisions underlying the nation's environmental movement." See C. Meine, "The Utility of Preservation and the Preservation of Utility: Leopold's Fine Line," in *The Wilderness Condition: Essays on Environment and Civilization,* edited by M. Oelschlaeger (San Francisco: Sierra Club Books, 1992), pp. 131–172. See also Miller, *Pinchot and the Making of Modern Environmentalism*, pp. 1–12.

21. T. Roosevelt, annual address to the United States Senate and House of Representatives, 8 December 1908.

22. A. Schlesinger Jr., "A Question of Power," *American Prospect* 12, no. 7 (23 April 2001), pp. 26–29.

23. D. Kemmis, *This Sovereign Land: A New Vision for Governing the West* (Washington, D.C.: Island Press, 2001), p. 38.

24. Ibid., p. 25.

25. Pinchot, *Fight for Conservation*, p. 60.

26. Miller, *Pinchot and the Making of Modern Environmentalism*, p. 155.

27. H. Clepper, ed., *Origins of American Conservation* (New York: Ronald Press, 1966).

28. R. S. Beeman and J. A. Pritchard, *A Green and Permanent Land: Ecology and Agriculture in the Twentieth Century* (Lawrence: University Press of Kansas, 2001), p. 82.

29. C. Meine and R. L. Knight, *The Essential Aldo Leopold: Quotations and Commentaries* (Madison: University of Wisconsin Press, 1999), p. 162. For a compilation of Leopold's writing on the theme of private land stewardship, see A. Leopold, *For the Health of the Land: Previously Unpublished Essays and Other Writings,* edited by J. B. Callicott and E. T. Freyfogle (Washington, D.C.: Island Press, 1999).

30. See S. Flader, "Building Conservation on the Land: Aldo Leopold and the Tensions of Professionalism and Citizenship," this volume.

31. A. Leopold, *A Sand County Almanac, and Sketches Here and There* (New York: Oxford University Press, 1949), p. 210.

32. See Kemmis, *This Sovereign Land,* pp. 45–69; J. L. Thomas, *A Country in the Mind: Wallace Stegner, Bernard De Voto, History, and the American Land* (New York: Routledge, 2001), pp. 129–138.

33. R. H. Nelson, "The Public Land Management Agencies," in *A New Century for Natural Resources Management,* edited by R. L. Knight and S. F. Bates (Washington, D.C: Island Press, 1995), p. 54.

34. A. Leopold, *A Sand County Almanac, and Sketches Here and There* p. 210.

35. Meine, "Roosevelt, Conservation, and the Revival of Democracy," p. 830.

36. K. Brower, introduction to A. Leopold, *A Sand County Almanac: With Essays on Conservation* (New York: Oxford University Press, 2001), p. 9.

37. See E. T. Freyfogle, *Bounded People, Boundless Lands: Envisioning a New Land Ethic* (Washington, D.C.: Island Press, 1998); E. T. Freyfogle and J. L. Newton, "Putting Science in Its Place," *Conservation Biology* 16, no. 4 (2002): 863–873.

38. R. L. Knight, "The Ecology of Ranching," in *Ranching West of the Hundredth Meridian: Culture, Ecology, and Economics,* edited by R. L. Knight, W. C. Gilgert, and E. Marston (Washington, D.C.: Island Press, 2002), pp. 123–144; C. Meine, "Homegrown Conservation: The Revolution Is Here," *Wisconsin Academy Review* 48 (2002): 49–50.

39. Meine and Knight, *Essential Aldo Leopold,* p. 239.

Chapter 12. Norton, *Conservation: Moral Crusade or Environmental Public Policy?*

1. J. Muir, in *Century Magazine,* 1895, quoted in R. Nash, *Wilderness and the American Mind* (New Haven, Conn.: Yale University Press, 1967): pp. 158; 264; 167–8.

2. G. Pinchot, *Breaking New Ground* (New York: Harcourt Brace, 1947), p. 325.

3. L. White, "The Historical Roots of Our Ecologic Crisis," reprinted in *Environmental Ethics: Readings in Theory and Application,* edited by L. Pojman (Belmont, CA: Wadsworth), pp. 13–19.

4. Ibid., p. 16.

5. See, e.g., R. Routley, "Is There a Need for a New Environmental Ethic?" *Proceedings of the Fifteenth World Congress of Philosophy* 1 (1973): 205–210; H. Rolston III, "Is There an Ecological Ethic?" *Ethics* 85, no. 2 (1975): 93–109; T. Regan, *The Case for Animal Rights* (Berkeley and Los Angeles: University of California Press, 1985); J. B. Callicott, *In Defense of the Land Ethic* (Albany: State University of New York Press, 1989).

6. J. Passmore, *Man's Responsibility for Nature* (New York: Scribner, 1974).

7. Regan, *Case for Animal Rights*; Callicott, *In Defense of the Land Ethic.*

8. See, e.g., Routley, "Is There a Need?"; Rolston, "Is There an Ecological Ethic?"; R. Routley and V. Routley, "Against the Inevitability of Human Chauvinism," in *Ethics and Problems of the Twenty-First Century,* edited by K. E. Goodpaster and K. M. Sayre (Notre Dame, Ind.: Notre Dame University Press, 1989); C. D. Stone, *Should Trees Have Standing? Toward Legal Rights for Natural Objects* (Los Altos, Calif.: William Kaufmann, 1974); C. D. Stone, *Earth and Other Ethics: A Case for Moral Pluralism* (New York: Harper & Row, 1987). Passmore, in *Man's Responsibility,* states the case against intrinsic value theory.

9. See Rolston, "Is There an Ecological Ethic?"; H. Rolston III, *Conserving Natural Value* (New York: Columbia University Press, 1994), p. 173; Regan, *Case for Animal Rights;* P. Taylor, *Respect for Nature* (Princeton, N.J.: Princeton University Press, 1986).

10. J. B. Callicott, "On the Inherent Value of Non-human Species," in *The Preservation of Species,* edited by B. G. Norton (Princeton, N.J.: Princeton University Press, 1986), p. 157.

11. B. G. Norton, "Epistemology and Environmental Values," *Monist* 75 (1992): 208–226.

12. B. G. Norton, "Democracy and Environmentalism: Foundations and Justifications in Environmental Policy," in *Democracy and the Claims of Nature: Critical Perspectives for a New Century,* edited by B. A. Minteer and B. P. Taylor (Lanham, Md.: Rowman and Littlefield, 2002).

13. See, e.g., Regan, *Case for Animal Rights;* P. Singer, *Animal Liberation: A New Ethics for Our Treatment of Animals* (New York: New York Review, 1975).

14. J. B. Callicott, "Animal Liberation: A Triangular Affair," reprinted in Callicott, *In Defense of the Land Ethic,* p. 29.

15. Regan, *Case for Animal Rights,* p. 362.

16. B. G. Norton, *Toward Unity among Environmentalists* (New York: Oxford University Press, 1991).

17. See B. G. Norton, "Pragmatism, Adaptive Management, and Sustainability," *Environmental Values* 8 (1999): 451–466, for a brief review. A. Light and E. Katz, *Environmental Pragmatism* (London: Routledge, 1996), provides a selection of pragmatist writings on environmental values and policy.

18. See, e.g., J. B. Callicott, "Environmental Philosophy *Is* Environmental Activism: The Most Effective and Radical Kind," in *Environmental Philosophy and Environmental Activism,* edited by D. E. Marietta Jr. and L. Embree (Lanham, Md.: Rowman and Littlefield, 1995), and J. B. Callicott, "Silencing Philosophers: Minteer and the Foundations of Anti-foundationalism," *Environmental Values* 8 (1999): 499–516.

19. Muir, in *Century Magazine,* 1895, quoted in Nash, *Wilderness and the American Mind,* p. 134.

20. H. Rittel and M. Webber, "Dilemmas in a General Theory of Planning," *Policy Sciences* 4 (1973): 155–169.

21. E. N. Novakowski and B. G. Norton, "Revisiting Wicked Problems," in preparation.

22. L. W. Milbrath, *Environmentalists: Vanguard for a New Society* (Albany: State University of New York Press, 1984); S. Kellert and T. Clark, "The Theory and Application of a Wildlife Policy Framework," in *Public Policy and Wildlife Conservation,* edited by W. R. Magnum and S. S. Nagel (New York: Greenwood, 1991); W. Kempton, J. S. Boster, and J. A. Hartley, *Environmental Values in American Culture* (Cambridge, Mass.: MIT Press, 1995); B. A. Minteer and R. E. Manning, "Pragmatism in Environmental Ethics: Democracy, Pluralism, and the Management of Nature," *Environmental Ethics* 21 (1999): 191–207.

23. Norton, *Toward Unity.*

24. Stone, *Earth and Other Ethics.*

25. A. M. Freeman III, *The Measurement of Environmental and Resource Values: Theory and Methods* (Washington, D.C.: Resources for the Future, 1994), p. 485. For a detailed explanation of the parameters of the crisis in conceptualization of environmental values, see B. G. Norton, "Evaluation and Ecosystem Management: New Directions Needed?" *Landscape and Urban Planning* 40 (1998): 185–194.

26. W. Leach and N. Pelkey, "Making Watershed Partnerships Work: A Review of the Empirical Literature," *Journal of Water Resources Planning and Management* 127, no. 6 (2001): 353–418.

27. See, e.g., J. Robinson and D. Rothman, "Growing Pains: A Conceptual Framework for Considering Integrated Assessments," *Environmental Monitoring and Assessment* 46 (1997): 23–43.

28. See T. Page, *Conservation and Economic Efficiency: An Approach to Materials Policy* (Washington D.C.: Resources for the Future, 1977); B. G. Norton, "Reduction or Integration: Two Approaches to Environmental Values," in *Environmental Pragmatism,* edited by A. Light and E. Katz (London: Routledge, 1995); B. G. Norton and M. Toman, "Sustainability: Ecological and Economic Perspectives," *Land Economics* 73, no. 4 (1997): 553–568; B. G. Norton and A. C. Steinemann, "Environmental Values and Adaptive Management," *Environmental Values* 10, no. 4 (2001): 473–506; M. A. Toman, "Economics and Sustainability: Balancing Tradeoffs and Imperatives," *Land Economics* 70 (1994): 399–413.

29. See, e.g., J. Rotmans and H. Dowlatabadi, "Integrated Assessment Modeling," in *Human Choices and Climate Change: Tools for Policy Analysis,* edited by S. Rayner and E. L. Malone (Columbus, Ohio: Batelle Press, 1998); J. Rotmans and M. Van Asselt, "Uncertainty Management in Integrated Assessment Modeling: Towards a Pluralistic Approach," *Environmental Monitoring and Assessment* 69 (2001): 101–130; J. B. Robinson et al., *Life in 2030: Exploring a Sustainable Future for Canada* (Vancouver, B.C., Canada: University of British Columbia Press, 1996); Robinson and Rothman, "Growing Pains."

Chapter 13. Manning, *Social Climate Change: A Sociology of Environmental Philosophy*

1. See, e.g., R. Dunlap and K. Van Liere, "The New Environmental Paradigm," *Journal of Environmental Education* 9 (1978): 10–17; R. Dunlap, *Trends in Public Opinion toward the Environment* (Washington, D.C.: Taylor and Francis, 1992).

2. See, e.g., Y. Tuan, *Topophilia: A Study of Environmental Perception, Attitudes, and Values* (Englewood Cliffs, N.J.: Prentice-Hall, 1974); E. Relph, *Place and Placelessness* (London: Pion, 1976); R. Steele, *The Sense of Place* (Boston: CBI, 1981); J. Entrikin, *The Betweenness of Place* (Baltimore, Md.: Johns Hopkins University Press, 1991); and A. Brandenburg and M. Carroll, "Your Place or Mine? The Effect of Place Creation on Environmental Values and Landscape Meaning," *Society and Natural Resources* 8 (1995): 381–398.

3. B. A. Minteer and R. E. Manning, "Pragmatism in Environmental Ethics: Democracy, Pluralism, and the Management of Nature," *Environmental Ethics* 21 (1999): 191–207; R. Manning, W. Valliere, and B. Minteer, "Values, Ethics, and Attitudes toward National Forest Management," *Society and Natural Resources* 12 (1999): 421–436; B. A. Minteer and R. E. Manning, "Convergence in Environmental Values: An Empirical and Conceptual Defense," *Ethics, Place and Environment* 3 (2000): 47–60; J. Morrissey and R. Manning, "Race, Residence, and Environmental Concern: New Englanders and the White Mountain National Forest," *Human Ecology Review* 7 (2000): 12–24; B. A. Minteer, E. A.

Corley, and R. E. Manning, "Environmental Ethics Beyond Principle? The Case for a Pragmatic Contextualism," *Journal of Agricultural and Environmental Ethics* (in press).

4. D. A. Dillman, *Mail and Telephone Surveys: The Total Design Method* (New York: Wiley, 1978).

5. See M. Rokeach, *The Nature of Human Values* (New York: Free Press, 1973); R. Andrews and M. Waits, "Theory and Methods of Environmental Values Research," *Interdisciplinary Science Review* 5 (1980): 71–78; D. Bengston, "Changing Forest Values and Ecosystem Management," *Society and Natural Resources* 7 (1994): 515–533; and W. Kempton, J. Boster, and J. Hartley, *Environmental Values in American Culture* (Cambridge, Mass.: MIT Press, 1995).

6. T. Brown, "The Concept of Value in Resource Allocation," *Land Economics* 60 (1984): 232.

7. Bengston, "Changing Forest Values and Ecosystem Management," p. 520.

8. Bengston, "Changing Forest Values and Ecosystem Management"; J. Heatherington, T. Daniel, and T. Brown, "Anything Goes Means Everything Stays: The Perils of Uncritical Pluralism in the Study of Ecosystem Values," *Society and Natural Resources* 7 (1994): 535–546.

9. H. Rolston III, *Environmental Ethics* (Philadelphia: Temple University Press, 1988); H. Rolston and J. Coufal, "A Forest Ethic and Multivalue Forest Management," *Journal of Forestry* 89 (1991): 35–40; R. Manning, "The Nature of America: Visions and Revisions of America," *Natural Resources Journal* 29 (1989): 25–40; S. Kellert, "Historical Trends in Perceptions and Uses of Animals in Twentieth Century America," *Environmental Review* 9 (1985): 19–33.

10. D. Runes, *Dictionary of Philosophy* (New York: Philosophical Library, 1983), p. 113.

11. K. Bailes, *Environmental History: Critical Issues in Comparative Perspective* (Lanham, Mass.: University Press of America, 1985); J. B. Callicott, *Earth's Insights: A Survey of Ecological Ethics from the Mediterranean Basin to the Australian Outback* (Berkeley and Los Angeles: University of California Press, 1995); J. Des Jardins, *Environmental Ethics: An Introduction to Environmental Philosophy* (Belmont, Calif.: Wadsworth, 1993); R. Elliot and A. Gare, eds., *Environmental Philosophy: A Collection of Readings* (University Park: Pennsylvania State University Press, 1983); E. Hargrove, *Foundations of Environmental Ethics* (Englewood Cliffs, N.J.: Prentice-Hall, 1989); C. Merchant, *Major Problems in American Environmental History* (Lexington, Mass.: D.C. Heath, 1993); R. Nash, *The Rights of Nature* (Madison: University of Wisconsin Press, 1989); P. Taylor, *Respect for Nature: A Theory of Environmental Ethics* (Princeton, N.J.: Princeton University Press, 1986); Rolston, *Environmental Ethics;* D. VanDeVeer and C. Pierce, *The Environmental Ethics and Policy Book* (Belmont, Calif.: Wadsworth, 1994); D. Worster, *Nature's Economy: A History of Ecological Ideas* (Cambridge, Mass.: Cambridge University Press, 1977); D. Worster, *The Wealth of Nature: Environmental History and the Ecological Imagination* (New York: Oxford University Press, 1993); and M. Zimmerman, *Environmental Philosophy: From Animal Rights to Radical Ecology* (Englewood Cliffs, N.J.: Prentice-Hall, 1993).

12. G. Theodorson and A. Theodorson, *A Modern Dictionary of Sociology* (New York: Crowell, 1969), p. 19.

13. R. Dunlap, *Trends in Public Opinion toward the Environment* (Washington, D.C.: Taylor and Francis, 1992).

14. B. Shindler, P. List, and B. Steel, "Managing Federal Forests: Public Attitudes in Oregon and Nationwide," *Journal of Forestry* 91 (1993): 36–42; B. Steel, P. List, and B. Shindler, "Conflicting Values about Federal Forests: A Comparison of National and Oregon Publics," *Society and Natural Resources* 7 (1994): 137–153; D. Bengston, "Changing Forest Values and Ecosystem Management," *Society and Natural Resources* 7 (1994): 515–533; D. Bengston and Z. Xu, *Changing National Forest Values: A Content Analysis,* Research Paper NC-323 (St. Paul, Minn.: USDA Forest Service, North Central Research Station, 1995); D. Bengston and D. Z. Xu, "Shifting and Expanding Forest Values: The Case of the U.S. National Forests," *George Wright Forum* 13 (1996): 10–19.

15. B. Shindler, P. List, and B. Steel, "Managing Federal Forests: Public Attitudes in Oregon and Nationwide," *Journal of Forestry* 91 (1993): 36–42.

16. R. Grumbine, "What Is Ecosystem Management?" *Conservation Biology* 8 (1994): 24–38.

17. J. Morrissey and R. Manning, "Race, Residence, and Environmental Concern: New Englanders and the White Mountain National Forest," *Human Ecology Review* 7 (2000): 12–24.

18. This notion of policy convergence is discussed in a number of Norton's writings, including "Conservation and Preservation: A Conceptual Rehabilitation," *Environmental Ethics* 8 (1986): 195–220; *Toward Unity among Environmentalists* (New York: Oxford University Press, 1991); "Applied Philosophy versus Practical Philosophy: Toward an Environmental Philosophy According to Scale," in *Environmental Philosophy and Environmental Activism,* edited by D. E. Marietta Jr. and L. Embree (Lanham, Md.: Rowman and Littlefield, 1995), pp. 125–148; "Why I Am Not a Nonanthropocentrist: Callicott and the Failure of Monistic Inherentism," *Environmental Ethics* 17 (1995): 341–358; "Integration or Reduction: Two Approaches to Environmental Values," in *Environmental Pragmatism,* edited by A. Light and E. Katz (London: Routledge, 1996), pp. 105–138; and "Convergence and Contextualism: Some Clarifications and a Reply to Steverson," *Environmental Ethics* 19 (1997): 87–100.

19. Bengston and Xu, *Changing National Forest Values;* Bengston and Xu, "Shifting and Expanding Forest Values."

Chapter 14. Bengston and Iverson, *Reconstructing Conservation in an Age of Limits: An Ecological Economics Perspective*

1. S. P. Hays, *Conservation and the Gospel of Efficiency: The Progressive Conservation Movement, 1890–1920* (Cambridge, Mass.: Harvard University Press, 1959).

2. R. Bellah et al., *The Good Society* (New York: Knopf, 1991); J. Turner, *The Abstract Wild* (Tucson: University of Arizona Press, 1996).

3. J. J. Kennedy, "Conceiving Forest Management as Providing for Current and Future Social Value," *Forest Ecology and Management* 13 (1985): 121–132; A. G. McQuillan, "New Perspectives: Forestry for a Post-Modern Age," *Western Wildlands* 17 (1992): 13–20.

4. R. B. Norgaard, "Economics as Mechanics and the Demise of Biological Diversity," *Ecological Modelling* 38 (1987): 107–121; R. B. Norgaard, *Development Betrayed: The End of Progress and a Coevolutionary Revisioning of the Future* (New York: Routledge, 1994).

5. This section draws on C. Hamilton, "Foundations of Ecological Economics," in *Human Ecology, Human Economy: Ideas for an Ecologically Sustainable Future,* edited by M. Diesendorf and C. Hamilton (St. Leonards, N.S.W., Australia: Allen & Unwin, 1997), pp. 35–63, and C. L. Spash, "The Development of Environmental Thinking in Economics," *Environmental Values* 8 (1999): 413–435.

6. H. R. Sewall, *The Theory of Value before Adam Smith* (1901; reprint, New York: Augustus M. Kelley, 1971), p. 80. See also P. Christensen, "Historical Roots for Ecological Economics," *Ecological Economics* 1 (1989): 17–36.

7. H. E. Daly, *Economics, Ecology, Ethics: Essays toward a Steady-State Economy* (San Francisco: Freeman, 1980), p. 3.

8. A. W. Coats, *The Sociology and Professionalization of Economics* (New York: Routledge, 1983).

9. L. C. Gray, "Rent under the Assumption of Exhaustibility," *Quarterly Journal of Economics* 28 (1914): 466–498; P. J. Crabbe, "The Contribution of L. C. Gray to the Economic Theory of Exhaustible Resources," *Journal of Environmental Economics and Management* 10 (1983): 195–220.

10. S. V. Ciriacy-Wantrup, *Resource Conservation: Economics and Policies* (Berkeley and Los Angeles: University of California Press, 1952).

11. M. Sagoff, "Ancient Astronomers and Modern Economists," *Nature Conservancy* 41 (1991): 38.

12. A. C. Fisher and F. M. Peterson, "The Environment in Economics: A Survey," *Journal of Economic Literature* 14 (1976): 1–33; quote, p. 1.

13. P. Portney, ed., *Public Policies for Environmental Protection* (Washington, D.C.: Resources for the Future, 1990), p. 282. See also J. F. Shogren, "A Political Economy in an Ecological Web," *Environmental and Resource Economics* 11 (1998): 557–570.

14. USDA Forest Service, *Southern Forest Resource Assessment,* Draft Report (Asheville, N.C.: USDA Forest Service, Southern Research Station, 2001), available on-line at http://www.srs.fs.fed.us/sustain/index.htm; B. Czech, P. R. Krausman, and P. K. Devers, "Economic Associations among Causes of Species Endangerment in the United States," *BioScience* 50 (2000): 593–601.

15. U.S. Bureau of the Census, *Statistical Abstract of the United States: 2000* (Washington, D.C.: Government Printing Office, 2000).

16. W. Kempton, J. S. Boster, and J. A. Hartley, *Environmental Values in American Culture* (Cambridge, Mass.: MIT Press, 1995); D. N. Bengston, D. P. Fan, and D. N. Celarier, "A New Approach to Monitoring the Social Environment for Natural Resource Management and Policy: The Case of U.S. National Forest Benefits and Values," *Journal of Environmental Management* 56 (1999): 181–193; R. Manning, W. Valliere, and B. Minteer, "Values, Ethics, and Attitudes toward National Forest Management: An Empirical Study," *Society and Natural Resources* 12 (1999): 421–436.

17. E. c. Ladd and K. Bowman, "Public Opinion and the Environment," *Resources* 124 (summer 1996): 5–7; quote, p. 5.

18. S. Boyden, *Biohistory: The Interplay between Human Society and the Biosphere, Past and Present* (Park Ridge, N.J.: Parthenon, 1992); J. D. Hughes and J. Donald, *Pan's Travail: Environmental Problems of the Ancient Greeks and Romans* (Baltimore, Md.: Johns Hopkins University Press, 1994).

19. Citations for these global environmental trends include D. Bryant, D. Nielsen, and L. Tangley, *The Last Frontier Forests* (Washington, D.C.: World Resources Institute, 1997); E. O. Wilson, *The Diversity of Life* (Cambridge, Mass.: Belknap Press of Harvard University Press, 1992); S. M. Garcia and I. De Leiva Moreno, "Trends in World Fisheries and Their Resources: 1974–1999," in *The State of World Fisheries and Aquaculture, 2000* (Rome: Food and Agriculture Organization of the United Nations, 2000); S. L. Postel, G. C. Daily, and P. R. Ehrlich, "Human Appropriation of Renewable Fresh Water," *Science* 271 (1996): 785–788; S. Postel, *Pillar of Sand* (New York: Norton, 1999); S. Wood, K. Sebastian, and S. Scherr, *Pilot Analysis of Global Ecosystems: Agroecosystems Technical Report* (Washington, D.C.: World Resources Institute and International Food Policy Research Institute, 2000); G. C. Daily, "Restoring Value to the World's Degraded Lands," *Science* 269 (1995): 350–354; P. M. Vitousek et al., "Human Appropriation of the Products of Photosynthesis," *BioScience* 36 (1986): 368–373; J. Houghton, *Global Warming: The Complete Briefing,* 2nd ed. (Cambridge, England: Cambridge University Press, 1997); R. L. Hooke, "On the History of Humans as Geomorphic Agents," *Geology* 28 (2000): 843–846; and T. E. Dahl, *Wetlands Losses in the United States 1780's to 1980's* (Jamestown, N.D.: U.S. Department of the Interior, U.S. Fish and Wildlife Service, Northern Prairie Wildlife Research Center, 1990), version 16JUL97, available on-line at http://www.npwrc.usgs.gov/resource/othrdata/wetloss/wetloss.htm.

20. H. E. Daly, "From Empty-World Economics to Full-World Economics: A Historical Turning Point in Economic Development," in *World Forests for the Future: Their Use and Conservation,* edited by K. Ramakrishna and G. M. Woodwell (New Haven, Conn.: Yale University Press, 1993), pp. 79–91.

21. H. E. Daly and J. B. Cobb Jr., *For the Common Good* (Boston: Beacon Press, 1994); C. Cobb, M. Glickman, and C. Cheslog, *Genuine Progress Indicator: Gross Production versus Genuine Progress, 1950 to 1999*, Redefining Progress Issue Brief (Oakland, Calif.: Redefining Progress, 2001), available on-line at http://www.rprogress.org/projects/gpi/.

22. Union of Concerned Scientists, *World Scientists' Warning to Humanity* (Cambridge, Mass.: Union of Concerned Scientists, 1992), available on-line at http://www.ucsusa.org/ucs/about/page.cfm?pageID=1009.

23. For an example of the catastrophic collapse view, see D. H. Meadows, D. L. Meadows, and J. Randers, *Beyond the Limits: Confronting Global Collapse, Envisioning a Sustainable Future* (Post Mills, Vt.: Chelsea Green, 1992). For an example of the view that limits will be gradual, see C. Davidson, "Economic Growth and the Environment: Alternatives to the Limits Paradigm," *BioScience* 50 (2000): 433–440.

24. R. P. Gale and S. Cordray, "Making Sense of Sustainability: Nine Answers to 'What Should Be Sustained?'" *Rural Sociology* 59 (1994): 311–332.

25. M. A. Toman, *Sustainable Decisionmaking: The State of the Art from an Economics Perspective,* Discussion Paper 98-39 (Washington, D.C.: Resources for the Future, 1998).

26. T. Prugh, *Natural Capital and Human Economic Survival* (Solomons, Md.: ISEE Press, 1995).

27. W. A. Morrissey, J. A. Zinn, and M. L. Corn, comps., *Ecosystem Management: Federal Agency Activities*, CRS Report for Congress 94-339 ENR (Washington, D.C.: Congressional Research Service, 1994); R. S. Brown and K. Marshall, "Ecosystem Management in State Governments," *Ecological Applications* 6 (1996): 721–723.

28. P. W. Hirt, *A Conspiracy of Optimism: Management of the National Forests since World War Two* (Lincoln: University of Nebraska Press, 1994).

29. T. A. More, "Forestry's Fuzzy Concepts: An Examination of Ecosystem Management," *Journal of Forestry* 94 (August 1996): 19–23; quote, p. 21.

30. See, e.g., H. J. Cortner and M. A. Moote, *The Politics of Ecosystem Management* (Washington, D.C.: Island Press, 1999); L. P. Gerlach and D. N. Bengston, "If Ecosystem Management Is the Solution, What's the Problem?" *Journal of Forestry* 92 (August 1994): 18–21; R. E. Grumbine, "What Is Ecosystem Management?" *Conservation Biology* 8 (1994): 27–38; More, "Forestry's Fuzzy Concepts."

31. Some have argued that value pluralism is essential to fully incorporating the human dimensions in ecosystem management. See, e.g., A. G. McQuillan, "Cabbages and Kings: The Ethics and Aesthetics of New Forestry," *Environmental Values* 2 (1993): 191–222; D. N. Bengston, "Changing Forest Values and Ecosystem Management," *Society and Natural Resources* 7 (1994): 515–533.

32. Grumbine, "What Is Ecosystem Management?" p. 31.

33. C. Folke et al., "Investing in Natural Capital: Why, What, and How?" in *Investing in Natural Capital: The Ecological Economics Approach to Sustainability,* edited by A. Jansson et al. (Washington, D.C.: Island Press, 1994), pp. 1–20; quote, p. 2.

34. K. E. Boulding, "The Economics of the Coming Spaceship Earth," in *Environmental Quality in a Growing Economy,* edited by H. Jarrett (Baltimore, Md.: Johns Hopkins University Press, 1966), pp. 3–14; H. E. Daly, "On Economics as a Life Science," *Journal of Political Economy* 76 (1968): 392–406; N. Georgescu-Roegen, *The Entropy Law and the Economic Process* (Cambridge, Mass.: Harvard University Press, 1971).

35. See, e.g., Daly and Cobb, *For the Common Good*; Prugh, *Natural Capital*; Hamilton, "Foundations of Ecological Economics."

36. Space also does not allow us to explore some newly discovered paths in economics. In particular, we do not address recent advances in game theory that allow us to better examine behavior in political economic games on the part of powerful players capable of manipulating tastes and preferences and moving economics far away from the Arcadian settings that form the backdrop for much classical and neoclassical economic theory. Similarly, we do not address recent advances in complexity theory that allow us to better examine problems associated with "increasing returns to scale," "path dependency," and vagaries of history and "place" that influence development and exploitation patterns. Since ecological economics is based on interrelated systems concepts and recognizes the importance of both actors and emergent characteristics of open adaptive systems, extensions of ecological economics to both game theory and complexity theory are ongoing.

37. J. A. Schumpeter, *History of Economic Analysis* (New York: Oxford University Press, 1954), p. 588.

38. E. Anderson, *Value in Ethics and Economics* (Cambridge, Mass.: Harvard University Press, 1993).

39. R. C. Bishop, "Economic Values Defined," in *Valuing Wildlife: Economic and Social Perspectives,* edited by D. G. Decker and G. R. Goff (Boulder, Colo.: Westview Press, 1987), pp. 24–33; quote, p. 31.

40. For a discussion of energy theories of value, see D. H. Judson, "The Convergence of Neo-Ricardian and Embodied Energy Theories of Value and Price," *Ecological Economics* 1 (1989): 261–281.

41. M. Sagoff, "Zuckerman's Dilemma: A Plea for Environmental Ethics," *Hastings Center Report* 21, no. 5 (1991): 32–40; quote, p. 32.

42. Kempton, Boster, and Hartley, *Environmental Values.*

43. M. Sagoff, *The Economy of the Earth* (New York: Cambridge University Press, 1988), pp. 68–69 (emphasis in original).

44. A. K. Sen, "Rational Fools: A Critique of the Behavioural Foundations of Economic Theory," *Philosophy and Public Affairs* 6 (1977): 317–344; quote, p. 336.

45. Hays, *Conservation and the Gospel of Efficiency.*

46. See D. C. Iverson and R. M. Alston, "A New Role for Economics in Integrated Environmental Management," in *Implementing Integrated Environmental Management,* edited by J. Cairns Jr., T. Crawford, and H. Salwasser (Blacksburg: Virginia Polytechnic Institute and State University, University Center for Environmental and Hazardous Materials Studies, 1994), pp. 27–40, for a discussion of appropriate roles for traditional economic analysis in environmental management and decision making, including least-cost analysis, identification of nonmonetary costs of output or input substitution, and analysis of cost shifting, employment, and income distribution effects of alternative policies. Citing specific cases of widespread abuse of so-called efficiency analysis, they advise that such analysis not be pushed beyond its appropriate domain of improving means to socially desired and previously defined ends.

Chapter 15. Callicott, *The Implication of Shifting Paradigm in Ecology for Paradigm Shifts in the Philosophy of Conservation*

1. R. P. McIntosh, "The Myth of Community as Organism," *Perspectives in Biology and Medicine* 41 (1998): 426–438; S. T. A. Pickett and R. S. Ostfeld, "The Shifting Paradigm in Ecology," in *A New Century for Natural Resources Management,* edited by R. L. Knight and S. F. Bates (Washington, D.C.: Island Press, 1995), pp. 261–277.

2. D. B. Botkin, *Discordant Harmonies: A New Ecology for the Twenty-First Century* (New York: Oxford University Press, 1990); D. Worster, "The Ecology of Order and Chaos," *Environmental History Review* 14 (1990): 1–18.

3. A. W. Crosby, "Virgin Soil Epidemics as a Factor in the Aboriginal Depopulation of America," *William and Mary Quarterly* 33 (1976): 289–299; W. M. Denevan, "Native American Populations in 1492: Recent Research and a Revised Hemispheric Estimate," in *Native Populations of the Americas in 1492,* 2nd ed., edited by W. M. Denevan (Madison: University of Wisconsin Press, 1992), pp. xvii–xxix.

4. W. M. Denevan, "Pristine Myth," in *Encyclopedia of Cultural Anthropology*, vol. 3, edited by D. Levinson and M. Ember (New York: Henry Holt and Company, 1996), pp. 1034–1036.

5. F. J. Turner, *The Frontier in American History* (New York: Henry Holt and Company, 1920).

6. R. W. Emerson, *Nature* (Boston: James Monroe and Company, 1836).

7. Ibid., pp. 9; 12–13.

8. J. Edwards, "The Shadows and Images of Divine Things," in *The Great New Wilderness Debate* (New York: New American Library, 1978), pp. 23–25; quote p. 23.

9. P. Miller, *Errand into the Wilderness* (New York: Harper and Row, 1964).

10. R. Nash, *Wilderness and the American Mind* (New Haven, Conn.: Yale University Press, 1967).

11. H. D. Thoreau, *Walden, or Life in the Woods* (Boston: Ticknor and Fields, 1854).

12. H. D. Thoreau, "Walking," in H. D. Thoreau, *Excursions* (Boston: Tichnor and Fields, 1863), pp. 161–214; quote, p. 185.

13. H. D. Thoreau, "Huckleberries" in *The Great New Wilderness Debate*, (Iowa City: University of Iowa Press, 1970) pp. 41–47; quote, p. 45.

14. S. Fox, *John Muir and His Legacy: The American Conservation Movement* (Boston: Little, Brown, 1981).

15. D. Worster, review of M. P. Cohen, *The Pathless Way: John Muir and American Wilderness*, in *Environmental Ethics* 10 (1988): 277–281; quote, p. 268.

16. Emerson, *Nature*, p. 13.

17. V. Plumwood, "Wilderness Skepticism and Wilderness Dualism," in *The Great New Wilderness Debate*, edited by J. B. Callicott and M. P. Nelson (Athens: University of Georgia Press, 1998), pp. 652–690; quote, p. 684–685.

18. D. Lowenthal, *George Perkins Marsh: Versatile Vermonter* (New York: Columbia University Press, 1958); D. Lowenthal, *George Perkins Marsh, Prophet of Conservation* (Seattle: University of Washington Press, 2000).

19. G. P. Marsh, *Man and Nature; or, Physical Geography as Modified by Human Action* (New York: Charles Scribner, 1864), p. 35.

20. C. Miller, *Gifford Pinchot and the Making of Modern Environmentalism* (Washington, D.C.: Island Press, 2001).

21. G. Pinchot, *Breaking New Ground* (New York: Harcourt, Brace, 1947), p. 326.

22. Plumwood, "Wilderness Skepticism and Wilderness Dualism."

23. Pinchot, *Breaking New Ground*, p. 325–326.

24. Fox, *Muir and His Legacy*.

25. A. Leopold, "Forestry and Game Conservation," *Journal of Forestry* 16 (1918): 404–411.

26. C. Meine, *Aldo Leopold: His Life and Work* (Madison: University of Wisconsin Press, 1988).

27. Ibid.

28. A. Leopold, "Wilderness as a Form of Land Use," *Journal of Land and Public Utility Economics* 1 (1925): 348–350.

29. Ibid.

30. S. L. Flader, *Thinking Like a Mountain: Aldo Leopold and the Evolution of an Ecological Attitude toward Deer, Wolves, and Forests* (Columbia: University of Missouri Press, 1974); Meine, *Aldo Leopold.*

31. A. Leopold, "A Biotic View of Land," *Journal of American Forestry* 37 (1939): 727–730, 316, 323; quote, p. 727.

32. Meine, *Aldo Leopold.*

33. A. Leopold, *For the Health of the Land: Previously Unpublished Essays and Other Writings,* edited by J. B. Callicott and E. T. Freyfogle (Washington, D.C.: Island Press, 1999).

34. B. Balogh, "Scientific Forestry and the Roots of the Modern American State: Gifford Pinchot's Path to Progressive Reform," *Environmental History* 7 (2002): 198–225; quote, p. 202.

35. Fox, *Muir and His Legacy.*

36. Leopold, *For the Health of the Land.*

37. A. Leopold, "Threatened Species: A Proposal to the Wildlife Conference for an Inventory of the Needs of Near-Extinct Birds and Animals," *American Forests* 42 (1936): 116–119.

38. A. Leopold, "Wilderness as a Land Laboratory," *Living Wilderness* 6 (1941): 3.

39. Leopold, "Wilderness as a Form of Land Use."

40. Leopold, "Wilderness as a Land Laboratory."

41. W. Forbes and T. Haas, "Leopold's Legacy in the Rio Gavilan: Revisiting an Altered Mexican Wilderness," *Wild Earth* 10 (2000): 61–67.

42. F. E. Clements, *Research Methods in Ecology* (Lincoln, Nebr.: University Publishing Company, 1905), and F. E. Clements, *Plant Succession: An Analysis of the Development of Vegetation,* Publication no. 242 (Washington, D.C.: Carnegie Institution, 1916).

43. E. Cittadino, "Ecology and the Professionalization of Botany in America, 1890–1905," *Studies in the History of Biology* 4 (1980): 171–198; R. P. McIntosh, "Pioneer Support for Ecology," *BioScience* 33 (1983): 107–112.

44. C. Elton, *Animal Ecology* (London: Sidgwick and Jackson, 1927).

45. A. G. Tansley, "The Use and Abuse of Vegetational Concepts and Terms," *Ecology* 16 (1935): 284–307.

46. Ibid.,; J. Philips, "Succession, Development, the Climax and the Complete Organism: An Analysis of Concepts I," *Journal of Ecology* 22 (1934): 554–571; Idem II, III, *Journal of Ecology* 23 (1935): 216–264, 488–508.

47. Tansley, "Use and Abuse of Vegetational Concepts," quote, pp. 290–291.

48. Ibid.; also quote, p. 291.

49. R. L. Lindeman, "The Trophic-Dynamic Aspect of Ecology," *Ecology* 23 (1942): 399–418.

50. G. E. Hutchinson, "Review of Bio-Ecology," *Ecology* 21 (1940): 267–268.

51. E. P. Odum, "The Strategy of Ecosystem Development," *Science* 164 (1969): 262–270.

52. Ibid., p. 262.

53. D. Simberloff, "A Succession of Paradigms in Ecology: Essentialism to Materialism and Probabilism," in *Conceptual Issues in Ecology,* edited by E. Saarinen (Boston: Reidel, 1982), pp. 63–99.

54. Odum, "Strategy of Ecosystem Development," p. 266.

55. G. E. Hutchinson, "Homage to Santa Rosalie; or, Why There Are So Many Kinds of Animals," *American Naturalist* 93 (1959): 145–159.

56. H. A. Gleason, "The Individualistic Concept of the Plant Association," *Bulletin of the Tory Botanical Club* 53 (1926): 7–26.

57. Ibid., p. 16.

58. J. T. Curtis and R. P. McIntosh, "An Upland Forest Continuum in the Prairie-Forest Border Region of Wisconsin," *Ecology* 32 (1951): 476–496; R. H. Whittaker, "A Criticism of the Plant Association and Climatic Climax Concepts," *Northwest Science* 25 (1951): 18–31.

59. G. C. Williams, *Adaptation and Natural Selection* (Princeton, N.J.: Princeton University Press, 1966).

60. Simberloff, "A Succession of Paradigms in Ecology," pp. 63–99.

61. Tansley, "Use and Abuse of Vegetational Concepts," p. 302.

62. M. B. Davis, "Climatic Instability, Time Lags, and Community Disequilibrium," in *Community Ecology,* edited by J. Diamond and T. J. Case (New York: Harper & Row, 1984), pp. 264–284.

63. S. T. A. Pickett and P. S. White, eds., *The Ecology of Natural Disturbance and Patch Dynamics* (Orlando, Fla.: Academic Press, 1995).

64. D. Goodman, "The Theory of Diversity–Stability Relationships in Ecology," *Quarterly Review of Biology* 50 (1975): 237–266.

65. B. H. Walker, "Biological Diversity and Ecological Redundancy," *Conservation Biology* 6 (1992): 18–23.

66. Botkin, *Discordant Harmonies.*

67. R. M. May, "Biological Populations and Nonoverlapping Generations: Stable Points, Stable Cycles, and Chaos," *Science* 186 (1974): 645–647; D. Worster, "The Ecology of Order and Chaos," *Environmental History Review* 14 (1990): 1–18.

68. C. S. Holling, "Resilience and Stability of Ecology Systems," *Annual Review of Ecology and Systematics* 4 (1973): 1–23.

69. A. Leopold, "Grass, Brush, Timber, and Fire in Southern Arizona," *Journal of Forestry* 22 (1924): 1–10.

70. W. Ashworth, *The Late, Great Lakes: An Environmental History* (New York: Knopf, 1986).

71. J. B. Callicott and M. P. Nelson, *The Great New Wilderness Debate* (Athens: University of Georgia Press, 1998).

72. S. J. Pyne, *Fire in America: A Cultural History of Wildland and Rural Fire* (Seattle: University of Washington Press, 1982).

73. C. Kay, "Aboriginal Overkill: The Role of Native Americans in Structuring Western Ecosystems," *Human Nature* 5 (1994): 359–398; C. Kay, "Aboriginal Overkill and Native Burning: Implications for Modern Ecosystem Management," *Western Journal of Applied Forestry* 10 (1995): 121–126.

74. Pickett and Ostfeld, "Shifting Paradigm in Ecology," p. 267.

75. T. F. H. Allen and T. Hoekstra, *Toward a Unified Ecology* (New York: Columbia University Press, 1992).

76. D. Worster, *Nature's Economy: The Roots of Ecology,* 2nd ed. (New York: Anchor Books, 1994), p. 429.

77. Botkin, *Discordant Harmonies.*
78. May, "Biological Populations and Nonoverlapping Generations."
79. R. P. McIntosh, "The Myth of Community as Organism," *Perspectives in Biology and Medicine* 41 (1998): 426–438; quote, p. 431.
80. Pickett and Ostfeld, "Shifting Paradigm in Ecology," p. 266.
81. J. B. Callicott, "Aldo Leopold's Metaphor," in *Ecosystem Health: New Goals for Environmental Management,* edited by R. Costanza, B. G. Norton, and B. D. Haskell (Washington, D.C.: Island Press, 1992), pp. 42–56; J. B. Callicott, "The Value of Ecosystem Health," *Environmental Values* 4 (1995): 345–361.
82. E. O. Wilson, *Biodiversity* (Washington, D.C.: National Academy Press, 1988).
83. E. O. Wilson, *The Diversity of Life* (Cambridge, Mass.: Belknap Press of Harvard University Press, 1992).
84. R. L. Knight and S. F. Bates, eds., *A New Century for Natural Resources Management* (Washington, D.C.: Island Press, 1995).
85. S. T. A. Pickett and P. S. White, eds., *The Ecology of Natural Disturbance and Patch Dynamics* (Orlando, Fla.: Academic Press, 1995).
86. D. B. Osmundson, *Flow Regimes for Restoration and Maintenance of Sufficient Habitat to Recover Endangered Razorback Sucker and Colorado Pikeminnow in the Upper Colorado River: Interim Recommendations for the Palisade-to-Rifle Reach: Final Report* (Grand Junction, Colo.: U.S. Fish and Wildlife Service, Colorado River Fishery Project, 2001).
87. Kirtland's Warbler Recovery Team, *Kirtland's Warbler Recovery Plan* (Twin Cities, Minn.: U.S. Fish and Wildlife Service, 1985).
88. R. Costanza et al., "The Value of the World's Ecosystem Services and Natural Capital," *Nature* 387 (1997): 253–260.
89. R. F. Noss and A. Y. Cooperrider, *Saving Nature's Legacy: Protecting and Restoring Biodiversity* (Washington, D.C.: Island Press, 1994).
90. Leopold, *For the Health of the Land.*
91. A. Leopold, "The Farmer as a Conservationist," *American Forests* 45 (1939): 294–299, 316, 323.
92. W. Jackson, *Altars of Unhewn Stone: Science and the Earth* (San Francisco: North Point Press, 1987).

Chapter 16. Trombulak, *An Integrative Model for Landscape-Scale Conservation in the Twenty-First Century*

1. Detailed histories of the conservation movement in the twentieth century are offered in numerous sources, including D. Worster, *The Ends of the Earth: Perspectives on Modern Environmental History* (New York: Cambridge University Press, 1988), and R. Nash, *Wilderness and the American Mind* (New Haven, Conn.: Yale University Press, 1982).
2. C. Krauthammer, "Saving Nature, but Only for Man," *Time* 137 (17 June 1991): 82.
3. Nash, *Wilderness and the American Mind.*
4. A. Leopold, *A Sand County Almanac: With Other Essays on Conservation from Round River* (New York: Oxford University Press, 1966), p. 240.
5. P. L. Angermeier and J. R. Karr, "Biological Integrity versus Biological Diversity as Policy Directives—Protecting Biotic Resources," *BioScience* 44 (1994): 690–697; C. Folke,

C. S. Holling, and C. Perrings, "Biological Diversity, Ecosystems, and the Human Scale," *Ecological Applications* 64 (1996): 1018–1024; G. K. Meffe and C. R. Carroll, *Principles of Conservation Biology* (Sunderland, Mass.: Sinauer Associates, 1996); J. B. Callicott, L. B. Crowder, and K. Mumford, "Current Normative Concepts in Conservation," *Conservation Biology* 13 (1999): 22–35.

6. J. E. Anderson, "A Conceptual Framework for Evaluating and Quantifying Naturalness," *Conservation Biology* 5 (1991): 347–352; P. L. Angermeier, "The Natural Imperative for Biological Conservation," *Conservation Biology* 14 (2000): 373–381.

7. J. R. Karr and D. R. Dudley, "Ecological Perspective on Water Quality Goals," *Environmental Management* 5 (1981): 55–68.

8. R. F. Noss, "The Wildlands Project: Land Conservation Strategy," *Wild Earth Journal,* Special Issue 1 (1992): 10–25.

9. B. Rogers, "The Nature of Value and the Value of Nature: A Philosophical Overview," *International Affairs* 76 (2000): 315–323; R. Attfield, "Postmodernism, Value, and Objectivity," *Environmental Values* 10 (2001): 145–162; B. A. Minteer, "Intrinsic Value for Pragmatists?" *Environmental Ethics* 23 (2001): 57–75; H. P. McDonald, "Toward a Deontological Environmental Ethic," *Environmental Ethics* 23 (2001): 411–430.

10. G. P. Marsh, *Man and Nature,* edited by D. Lowenthal (1864; reprint, Cambridge, Mass.: Belknap Press of Harvard University Press, 1965), quotes, pp. 111, 112.

11. Angermeier and Karr, "Biological Integrity versus Biological Diversity"; R. E. Grumbine, "What Is Ecosystem Management?" *Conservation Biology* 8 (1994): 27–38.

12. U.S. Department of Transportation, *Highway Statistics, 1996,* FHWA-PL-98-003 (Lanham, Md.: U.S. Department of Transportation, Office of Highway Policy Information, 1996).

13. R. T. T. Forman, "Estimate of the Area Affected Ecologically by the Road System in the United States," *Conservation Biology* 14 (2000): 31–35.

14. U.S. Department of Energy, *Electricity End Use, 1949–2001,* 7 April 2003. available online at http://www.eia.doe.gov/emeu/aer/txt/ptb0805.html.

15. H. Haberl et al., "Human Appropriation of Net Primary Production," *Science* 296 (2002): 1968–1969.

16. R. F. Noss and A. Y. Cooperrider, *Saving Nature's Legacy: Protecting and Restoring Biodiversity* (Washington, D.C.: Island Press, 1994); R. F. Noss and R. L. Peters, *Endangered Ecosystems: A Status Report on America's Vanishing Habitat and Wildlife* (Washington, D.C.: Defenders of Wildlife, 1995); B. A. Stein, L. S. Kutner, and J. S. Adams, *Precious Heritage: The Status of Biodiversity in the United States* (New York: Oxford University Press, 2000).

17. W. S. Alverson, W. Kuhlmann, and D. M. Waller, *Wild Forests: Conservation Biology and Public Policy* (Washington, D.C.: Island Press, 1994).

18. *Burlington (Vermont) Free Press,* "Seniors Village Denied Act 250 Permit," *Burlington (Vermont) Free Press,* 24 February 2001, p. 48.

19. W. Cronon, "The Trouble with Wilderness; or, Getting Back to the Wrong Nature," in *Uncommon Ground: Toward Reinventing Nature,* edited by W. Cronon (New York: Norton, 1995); J. B. Callicott, "The Wilderness Idea Revisited: The Sustainable Development Alternative," in *Earth Summit Ethics: Toward a Reconstructive Postmodern Philosophy*

of Environmental Education, edited by J. B. Callicott and F. J. R. daRocha (Albany: State University of New York Press, 1998).

20. Cronon, "Trouble with Wilderness," p. 81.

21. S. Rampton and J. Stauber, *Trust Us, We're Experts! How Industry Manipulates Science and Gambles with Your Future* (New York: Jeremy P. Tarcher/Putnam, 2001).

22. R. L. Pressey et al., "Beyond Opportunism: Key Principles for Systematic Reserve Selection," *Trends in Ecology and Evolution* 8 (1993): 124–128; L. G. Underhill, "Optimal and Suboptimal Reserve Selection Algorithms," *Biological Conservation* 70 (1994): 85–87; C. H. Flather et al., "Identifying Gaps in Conservation Networks: Of Indicators and Uncertainty in Geographic-Based Analyses," *Ecological Applications* 7 (1997): 531–542; H. Possingham, I. Ball, and S. Andelman, "Mathematical Methods for Identifying Representative Reserve Networks," in *Quantitative Methods for Conservation Biology,* edited by S. Ferson and M. Burgman (New York: Springer, 2000).

23. *Sites: An Analytical Toolbox for Ecoregional Conservation Planning,* University of California, Santa Barbara, 1 November 2000, available on-line at http://www.biogeog.ucsb.edu/projects/tnc/toolbox.html.

24. I. R. Ball and H. P. Possingham, *MARXAN—a Reserve System Selection Tool,* University of Queensland, 1 November 2001, available on-line at http://www.ecology.uq.edu.au/marxan.htm.

25. United Nations Educational, Scientific and Cultural Organization (UNESCO), *Task Force on Criteria and Guidelines for the Choice and Establishment of Biosphere Reserves,* Man and the Biosphere Report 22 (Paris: UNESCO, 1974).

26. Noss, "Wildlands Project."

27. R. G. Bailey, *Description of the Ecoregions of the United States,* Miscellaneous Publication 1391 (Washington, D.C.: U.S. Department of Agriculture, Forest Service, 1995).

28. C. M. Rigg, "Orchestrating Ecosystem Management: Challenges and Lessons from Sequoia National Forest," *Conservation Biology* 15 (2001): 78–90.

29. R. F. Noss, *Conserving Oregon's Coast Range Biodiversity: A Conservation and Restoration Plan* (Newport, Oreg.: Coast Range Association, 1992).

30. R. F. Noss et al., "A Conservation Plan for the Klamath-Siskiyou Ecoregion," *Natural Areas Journal* 19 (1999): 392–411.

31. D. Forman et al., "The Elements of a Wildlands Network Conservation Plan: An Example from the Sky Islands," *Wild Earth Journal* 10 (2000): 17–30.

32. R. S. Kautz and J. A. Cox, "Strategic Habitats for Biodiversity Conservation in Florida," *Conservation Biology* 15 (2001): 55–77.

33. D. R. Field, "Symbiotic Relationships between National Parks and Neighboring Social-Biological Regions," in *National Parks and Rural Development: Practice and Policy in the United States,* edited by G. E. Machlis and D. R. Field (Washington, D.C.: Island Press, 2000).

Chapter 17. Stokowski, *Community Values in Conservation*

1. R. J. Brulle, *Agency, Democracy, and Nature: The U.S. Environmental Movement from a Critical Theory Perspective* (Cambridge, Mass.: MIT Press, 2000).

2. W. R. Burch Jr., *Daydreams and Nightmares: A Sociological Essay on the American Environment* (Middleton, Wis.: Social Ecology Press, 1997), pp. vii–viii.

3. Ibid.

4. D. A. Mazmanian and M. E. Kraft, eds., *Toward Sustainable Communities: Transition and Transformations in Environmental Policy* (Cambridge, Mass.: MIT Press, 1999).

5. K. Hess Jr., *Visions Upon the Land: Man and Nature on the Western Range* (Washington, D.C.: Island Press, 1992), pp. 219–220.

6. J. Friedmann, "Two Centuries of Planning Theory," in *Planning in the Public Domain* (Princeton, N.J.: Princeton University Press, 1987), pp. 51–85.

7. George A. Hillery Jr. identified more than ninety separate definitions of the term; see G. A. Hillery Jr., "Definitions of Community: Areas of Agreement," *Rural Sociology* 20 (1955): 779–791.

8. L. Lyon, *The Community in Urban Society* (Chicago: Dorsey Press, 1987), p. 5.

9. T. Bender, *Community and Social Change in America* (Baltimore, Md.: Johns Hopkins University Press, 1978), p. 7.

10. A. P. Cohen, *The Symbolic Construction of Community* (Chichester, England: Ellis Horwood, 1985), p. 118.

11. C. B. Flora et al., *Rural Communities: Legacy and Change* (Boulder, Colo.: Westview Press, 1992), p. 66.

12. S. Schama, *Landscape and Memory* (New York: Knopf, 1995), pp. 6–7.

13. T. Greider and L. Garkovich, "Landscapes: The Social Construction of Nature and the Environment," *Rural Sociology* 59 (1994): 1–24; quote, p. 2.

14. R. D. Putnam, *Making Democracy Work: Civic Traditions in Modern Italy* (Princeton, N.J.: Princeton University Press, 1993).

15. J. C. Bridger and A. E. Luloff, "Building the Sustainable Community: Is Social Capital the Answer?" *Sociological Inquiry* 71 (2001): 458–472; quote, p. 464.

16. D. Kemmis, *Community and the Politics of Place* (Norman: University of Oklahoma Press, 1990), p. 117.

17. D. Snow, "Coming Home: An Introduction to Collaborative Conservation," in *Across the Great Divide: Explorations in Collaborative Conservation and the American West*, edited by P. Brick, D. Snow, and S. Van de Wetering (Washington, D.C.: Island Press, 2000), pp. 1–11; quote, p. 6.

18. C. B. Flora and J. L. Flora, "Creating Social Capital," in *Rooted in the Land: Essays on Community and Place*, edited by W. Vitek and W. Jackson (New Haven, Conn.: Yale University Press, 1996), pp. 217–225; quote, p. 223.

19. D. R. Williams et al., "Beyond the Commodity Metaphor: Examining Emotional and Symbolic Attachment to Place," *Leisure Sciences* 14 (1992): 29–46; R. L. Moore and A. R. Graefe, "Attachments to Recreation Settings: The Case of Rail-Trail Users," *Leisure Sciences* 16 (1994): 17–31.

20. P. Berger and H. Kellner, "Marriage and the Construction of Reality," *Diogenes* 46 (1964): 1–24.

21. E. C. Relph, *Place and Placelessness* (London: Pion, 1976), p. 34.

22. Greider and Garkovich, "Landscapes," p. 2.

23. W. Stegner, *Where the Bluebird Sings to the Lemonade Springs: Living and Writing in the West* (New York: Random House, 1992), p. 202.

24. B. Johnstone, *Stories, Community, and Place: Narratives from Middle America* (Bloomington: Indiana University Press, 1990), p. 5.

25. K. C. Ryden, *Mapping the Invisible Landscape: Folklore, Writing, and the Sense of Place* (Iowa City: University of Iowa Press, 1993), p. 241.

26. Brulle, *Agency, Democracy, and Nature.*

27. M. A. Hajer, *The Politics of Environmental Discourse: Ecological Modernization and the Policy Process* (Oxford: Clarendon Press, 1995); J. Forester, *The Deliberative Practitioner: Encouraging Participatory Planning Processes* (Cambridge, Mass.: MIT Press, 1999).

28. Colorado Division of Gaming, *Gaming in Colorado: Fact Book and 2001 Abstract,* June 2002, available on-line at http://www.gaming.state.co.us.

29. *Weekly Register-Call,* "Shady Ladies Promote Central City by Celebrating Role of Women in the Old West," *Weekly Register-Call,* 25 November 1994, p. 1.

30. P. A. Stokowski, *Riches and Regrets: Betting on Gambling in Two Colorado Mountain Towns* (Niwot: University Press of Colorado, 1996).

31. William R. Freudenburg and Robert Gramling termed this "bureaucratic slippage"; see W. R. Freudenburg and R. Gramling, "Bureaucratic Slippage and Failures of Agency Vigilance: The Case of the Environmental Studies Program," *Social Problems* 41 (1994): 214–239.

32. See the work of Charles F. Cortese and Bernie Jones—for example, C. F. Cortese and B. Jones, "The Sociological Analysis of Boom Towns," *Western Sociological Review* 8 (1977): 76–90.

33. Stokowski, *Riches and Regrets,* p. 302.

34. Snow, "Coming Home," p. 4.

35. Cited in Snow, "Coming Home," p. 2.

36. G. C. Coggins, "Of Californicators, Quislings, and Crazies: Some Perils of Devolved Collaboration," in Brick, Snow, and Van de Wetering, *Across the Great Divide,* pp. 163–171.

37. B. Cooke and U. Kothari, *Participation: The New Tyranny?* (London: Zed Books, 2001), p. 235.

38. N. L. Peluso, "'Reserving' Value: Conservation Ideology and State Protection of Resources," in *Creating the Countryside: The Politics of Rural and Environmental Discourse,* edited by E. M. DuPuis and P. Vandergeest (Philadelphia: Temple University Press, 1996), pp. 135–165.

39. R. T. Hester Jr., "The Sacred Structure in Small Towns: A Return to Manteo, North Carolina," *Small Town* 20 (1990): 5–21.

40. W. Berry, "Conserving Communities," in *Rooted in the Land: Essays on Community and Place,* edited by W. Vitek and W. Jackson (New Haven, Conn.: Yale University Press, 1996), pp. 76–84.

41. D. R. Maines and J. C. Bridger, "Narratives, Community, and Land Use Decisions," *Social Science Journal* 29 (1992): 363–380.

42. G. Snyder, *A Place in Space: Ethics, Aesthetics, and Watersheds* (Washington, D.C.: Counterpoint, 1995).

43. Mazmanian and Kraft, *Toward Sustainable Communities,* p. 286.

44. T. Shibutani, *Social Processes: An Introduction to Sociology* (Berkeley and Los Angeles: University of California Press, 1986).

45. Hess, *Visions Upon the Land*, p. 247.

46. C. Merchant, *Radical Ecology: The Search for a Livable World* (New York: Routledge, 1992), p. 129.

Chapter 18. Mitchell and Brown, *Stewardship and Protected Areas in a Global Context: Coping with Change and Fostering Civil Society*

1. D. Lowenthal, *George Perkins Marsh, Prophet of Conservation* (Seattle: University of Washington Press, 2000), p. 405.

2. International Union for the Conservation of Nature and Natural Resources, statement adopted by the IUCN World Commission on Protected Areas (WCPA) Symposium, "Protected Areas in the 21st Century: From Islands to Networks," Albany, W.A., Australia, November 1997.

3. K. H. Redford, "Getting to Conservation," in *Traditional Peoples and Biodiversity Conservation in Large Tropical Landscapes,* edited by K. H. Redford and J. A. Mansour (Arlington, Va.: Nature Conservancy, 1994), p. 251.

4. G. Borrini-Feyerabend, "Collaborative Management of Protected Areas: Tailoring the Approach to the Context" (Gland, Switzerland: IUCN, 1996), p. 5.

5. J. Brown and A. Kothari, editorial, *PARKS* 12 no. 2 (2002), p. 1.

6. M. Beresford and A. Phillips, "Protected Landscapes: A Conservation Model for the Twenty-first Century," *George Wright Forum* 17 (2000), p. 19.

7. B. A. Mitchell and J. L. Brown, "Stewardship: A Working Definition," *Environments* 26 no. 1 (1998): p. 8.

8. D. Western and R. M. Wright, *Natural Connections: Perspectives in Community-Based Conservation* (Washington, D.C.: Island Press, 1994), p. 1–12.

9. These figures, and several other cases included here, have been reported to the authors by past participants in QLF/Atlantic Center for the Environment's international fellowship program. They have been instrumental in establishing trusts and other conservation vehicles and creating the legal and institutional environment to support conservation.

10. L. Ptacek, "Czech Land Trusts" (presentation to Land Trust Rally, Baltimore, Md., 2001).

11. Past participants in the international fellowship programs have been instrumental in piloting the first conservation easements in Mexico, Guatemala, Belize, and Paraguay as well as private reserve networks in many other countries of Latin America and the Caribbean region.

12. J. Brown and B. Mitchell, "Private Initiatives for Protected Areas in South America," in *Partnerships for Protection: New Strategies for Planning and Management of Protected Areas,* edited by S. Stolton and N. Dudley (London: Earthscan, 1999), p. 173–183.

13. W. Maheia, personal communication, and site visits by Brent Mitchell.

14. T. Geoghegan and Y. Renard, "Beyond Community Involvement: Lessons from the Insular Caribbean," *PARKS* 12, no. 2 (2002), pp. 16–27.

15. Ibid. See also L. Hudson, Y. Renard, and G. Romulus, *A System of Protected Areas for St. Lucia* (Castries, St. Lucia: St. Lucia National Trust, 1992).

16. The Zanzibar Commission for Natural Resources is now absorbed into the Department of Commercial Crops, Fruits, and Forestry (DCCFF).

17. J. M. Chernela et al., "Innovative Governance of Fisheries and Ecotourism in Community-Based Protected Areas," *Parks* 12, no. 2 (2002): 28–41.

18. See the profile of the South Pacific Biodiversity Conservation Programme in *The Landscape of Conservation Stewardship,* edited by J. Tuxill (Woodstock, Vt.: Marsh-Billings-Rockefeller National Historical Park, Woodstock Foundation, and Conservation Study Institute, 2000), pp. 52–53.

19. A. Argumedo, "Agriculture and Working Landscapes in the Andes," in *Landscape Conservation: An International Working Session on the Stewardship of Protected Landscapes,* Conservation and Stewardship Publication no. 1 (Woodstock, Vt.: Conservation Study Institute, IUCN—the World Conservation Union, and QLF/Atlantic Center for the Environment, 2001).

20. A. Beckmann et al., *Caring for the Land: A Decade of Promoting Landscape Stewardship in Central Europe* (Ipswich, Mass., and Brno, Czech Republic: QLF/Atlantic Center for the Environment and Environmental Partnership for Central Europe, 2000).

21. J. Brown and B. Mitchell, *Landscape Conservation and Stewardship in Central Europe,* Nexus Occasional Paper no. 10 (Ipswich, Mass.: QLF/Atlantic Center for the Environment, 1994); J. Brown and B. Mitchell, "Extending the Reach of National Parks and Protected Areas: Local Stewardship Initiatives," in *National Parks and Protected Areas: Keystones to Conservation and Sustainable Development,* NATO ASI Series, Vol. G 40, edited by J. G. Nelson and R. Serafin (Berlin, Heidelberg: Springer-Verlag, 1997).

22. B. Mitchell, "CAMPFIRE and Conservancies Policy Seminar," in *Wildlife Resource Management Outside Parks Estate Seminar Report* (Harare, Zimbabwe: Department of National Parks and Wildlife Management, 1997).

23. H. Joseph, "Friend to Farmers: John Ogonowski, American Airlines Flight 11 Pilot," *Tufts Nutrition News,* 24 September 2001, available on-line at http://nutrition.tufts.edu/feature/ogonowski.shtml.

24. Geoghegan and Renard, "Beyond Community Involvement," pp. 16–27.

25. G. Borrini-Feyerabend, "Indigenous and Local Communities and Protected Areas: Rethinking the Relationship," *PARKS,* 12, no. 2 (2002): 5–15."

26. D. Western, "Vision of the Future: The New Focus of Conservation," in Western and Wright, *Natural Connections,* p. 554.

27. Lowenthal, *George Perkins Marsh,* p. 423.

Chapter 19. Diamant, Eugster, and Mitchell, *Reinventing Conservation: A Practitioner's View*

1. R. Bass, interview for Marsh-Billings-Rockefeller National Historical Park exhibit "Celebrating Stewardship," August 2000.

2. S. Van der Ryn and S. Cowan, *Ecological Design* (Washington, D.C.: Island Press, 1996), p. 146.

3. J. Elder, "Rediscovering Mt. Tom," *Orion* (spring 1997): 31.

4. D. Hayden, *The Power of Place: Urban Landscapes as Public History* (Cambridge, Mass.: MIT Press, 1995), p. 19.

5. D. T. Pitcaithley, "The Future of the NPS History Program," *George Wright Society Forum* 13, no. 5 (1996): 51–56.

6. See, e.g., National Park Service Advisory Board, *National Parks for the 21st Century* (Washington, D.C.: National Geographic Society, 2001); M. Rossler, "World Heritage Cultural Landscapes," *George Wright Forum* 17, no. 1 (2000): 27–34; B. von Droste, H. Plachter, and M. Rossler, eds., *Cultural Landscapes of Universal Value: Components of a Global Strategy* (Jena, Germany: Gustav Fischer Verlag, 1995).

7. A. Phillips, "The Nature of Cultural Landscapes: A Nature Conservation Perspective," *Landscape Research* 23, no. 1 (2001): 37.

8. See, e.g., C. O. Sauer, "The Morphology of Landscape," in *Land and Life: A Selection from the Writings of Carl Otwin Saue,* edited by J. Leighly (Berkeley and Los Angeles: University of California Press, 1963); R. Z. Melnick, with D. Sponn and E. J. Saxe, *Cultural Landscapes: Rural Historic Districts in the National Park System* (Washington, D.C.: U.S. Department of the Interior, National Park Service, 1984); and W. Cronon, ed., *Uncommon Ground: Rethinking the Human Place in Nature* (New York: Norton, 1995).

9. von Droste, Plachter, and Rossler, *Cultural Landscapes of Universal Value.*

10. R. D. Putnam, *Bowling Alone: The Collapse and Revival of American Community* (New York: Simon & Schuster, 2000), p. 19.

11. G. Speth, "A New Paradigm: Bring It On!" (speech given at the Environmental Law Institute's thirtieth annual award dinner, Washington, D.C., 1999).

12. P. Forbes, "A Conservation Eulogy," speech to the Land Trust Rally, Baltimore, 2001. Available on-line at http://www.tpl.org/tier3_cd.cfm?content_item_id=5482&folder_id=831.

13. Ibid.

14. Northern Forest Center, *Northern Forest Wealth Index: Exploring a Deeper Meaning of Wealth* (Concord, N.H.: Northern Forest Center, 2000), available on-line at http://www.northernforest.org/techwindex.htm.

15. J. Chin, "Connecting Schools and Communities through Place-Based Education" (paper presented at Essex Conference Center, Essex, Mass., April 2001).

16. D. Lacy, presentation to "Forest for Every Classroom: Learning to Make Choices for the Future of Vermont Forests" workshop at Blueberry Hill Inn, Goshen, VT, 2002.

17. See, e.g., D. Western and R. M. Wright, eds., *Natural Connections: Perspectives in Community-Based Conservation* (Washington, D.C.: Island Press, 1994); T. Bernard and J. Young, *The Ecology of Hope: Communities Collaborate for Sustainability* (Gabriola Island, B.C., Canada: New Society Publishers, 1997); J. Howe, E. McMahon, and L. Propst, *Balancing Nature and Commerce in Gateway Communities* (Washington, D.C.: Island Press, 1997); R. L. Knight and P. B. Landres, eds., *Stewardship across Boundaries* (Washington, D.C.: Island Press, 1998); S. Stolton and N. Dudley, eds., *Partnerships for Protection: New Strategies for Planning and Management for Protected Areas* (London: Earthscan, 1999); J. Brown, N. Mitchell, and F. Sarmiento, "Landscape Stewardship: New Directions in Conservation of Nature and Culture," *George Wright Forum* 17, no. 1 (2000); J. L. Tuxill, ed., *The Landscape of Conservation Stewardship: The Report of the Stewardship Initiative Feasibility Study* (Woodstock, Vt.: Marsh-Billings-Rockefeller National Historical Park, Woodstock Foundation, and Conservation Study Institute,

2000); J. M. Wondolleck and S. L. Yaffee, *Making Collaboration Work: Lessons from Innovation in Natural Resource Management* (Washington, D.C.: Island Press, 2000); and J. L. Tuxill and N. J. Mitchell, eds., *Collaboration and Conservation: Lessons Learned in Areas Managed through National Park Service Partnership* (Woodstock, Vt.: Conservation Study Institute, 2001).

18. A. P. Swanson, M. S. Haire, and P. O. Schwartz, "Chesapeake Bay: Managing an Ecosystem: The Federal Role in Ecosystem Management," report on seminar sponsored by the Library of Congress (Annapolis, Md.: Chesapeake Bay Commission, n.d.), p. 6.

19. I. L. McHarg, *Design with Nature* (Philadelphia: Natural History Press, Falcon Press, 1969).

20. F. J. Seymour, "Are Successful Community-Based Conservation Projects Designed or Discovered?" in Western and Wright, *Natural Connections,* p. 473.

21. W. Berry, "In Distrust of Movements," *Orion* (summer 1999): 16.

Chapter 20. Lowenthal, *Conservation Stewardship: Legacies from Vermont's Marsh*

1. G. P. Marsh, *Man and Nature; or, Physical Geography as Modified by Human Action* (1864; reprint, Cambridge, Mass.: Belknap Press of Harvard University Press, 1965), pp. 42–43.

2. This history is discussed in detail in D. Lowenthal, *George Perkins Marsh, Prophet of Conservation* (Seattle: University of Washington Press, 2000), especially chaps. 13, 14, and 18.

3. Ibid., p. 41.

4. Ibid.

5. K. Erikson, *A New Species of Trouble: Explorations in Disaster, Trauma, and Community* (New York: Norton, 1994), pp. 203–225.

6. Marsh, *Man and Nature,* p. 52.

7. G. P. Marsh to Charles Sprague Sargent, 12 June 1879, Marsh Collection, University of Vermont.

8. For an extended discussion of stewardship concerns, see D. Lowenthal, *Forest Stewardship: Marsh, Pinchot, and America Today,* Pinchot Lecture Series (Milford, Pa.: Grey Towers Press, 2001), pp. 14–17.

9. Marsh, *Man and Nature,* pp. 277–280.

10. George P. Marsh, *Address Delivered before the Agricultural Society of Rutland County, Sept. 30, 1847* (Rutland, Vt., 1848), pp. 17–19; *Man and Nature,* pp. 51–51 n. 53, 202–2.

11. G. P. Marsh, *Lectures on the English Language* (New York: C. Scribner, 1861), pp. 637, 678.

12. Marsh, *Man and Nature,* p. 286 n. 4.

13. Giuseppe Garibaldi to G. P. Marsh, 20 January 1865, Marsh Collection, University of Vermont.

Chapter 21. Minteer and Manning, *Finding Common Ground: Emerging Principles for a Reconstructed Conservation*

1. L. A. Vivanco, "Conservation and Culture, Genuine and Spurious," this volume, p. 61.

2. R. W. Judd, "Writing Environmental History from East to West," this volume, p. 29.

3. Ibid., p. 29.

4. R. McCullough, "The Nature of History Preserved, or The Trouble with Green Bridges," this volume, p. 35.

5. Vivanco, "Conservation and Culture," p. 58.

6. R. Diamant, J. G. Eugster, and N. J. Mitchell, "Reinventing Conservation: A Practitioner's View," this volume, p. 316.

7. Judd, "Writing Environmental History," p. 22.

8. J. E. Dizard, "Going Native: Second Thoughts on Restoration," this volume, p. 46.

9. P. B. Thompson, "Expanding the Conservation Tradition: The Agrarian Vision," this volume, p. 78.

10. P. A. Stokowski, "Community Values in Conservation," this volume, pp. 284–285.

11. Judd, "Writing Environmental History," p. 24.

12. Thompson, "Expanding the Conservation Tradition," p. 78.

13. Ibid., p. 83.

14. B. A. Minteer, "Regional Planning as Pragmatic Conservationism," this volume, p. 103.

15. Ibid., p. 145.

16. Judd, "Writing Environmental History," p. 24.

17. Thompson, "Expanding the Conservation Tradition," p. 78.

18. Minteer, "Regional Planning as Pragmatic Conservationism," p. 113.

19. D. Lowenthal, "Conservation Stewardship: Legacies from Vermont's Marsh," this volume, p. 329.

20. Stokowski, "Community Values in Conservation," p. 283.

21. B. Mitchell and J. Brown, "Stewardship and Protected Areas in a Global Context: Coping with Change and Fostering Civil Society," this volume, p. 305.

22. Dizard, "Going Native," p. 48.

23. Thompson, "Expanding the Conservation Tradition," pp. 82–83.

24. Meine, p. 183.

25. Vivanco, "Conservation and Culture," p. 72.

26. Thompson, "Expanding the Conservation Tradition," p. 92.

27. Manning, p. 221.

28. Bengston and Iverson, p. 237.

29. Ibid., pp. 223–224.

30. Norton, p. 204.

31. Bengston and Iverson, p. 138.

32. Diamant, Eugster, and Mitchell, "Reinventing Conservation," p. 322.

33. Stokowski, "Community Values in Conservation," p. 281.

34. Thompson, "Expanding the Conservation Tradition," p. 91.

35. Flader, p. 132.

36. Vivanco, "Conservation and Culture," p. 58.

37. Mitchell and Brown, "Stewardship and Protected Areas in a Global Context," p. 299.

38. Stokowski, "Community Values in Conservation," p. 281.

39. Diamant, Eugster, and Mitchell, "Reinventing Conservation," p. 315.

40. Mitchell and Brown, "Stewardship and Protected Areas in a Global Context," p. 308.

41. Vivanco, "Conservation and Culture," p. 71.

42. Mitchell and Brown, "Stewardship and Protected Areas in a Global Context," p. 299.

43. Diamant, Eugster, and Mitchell, "Reinventing Conservation," p. 324.

44. Ibid., p. 326.

45. B. P. Taylor, "Scott Nearing and the American Conservation Tradition," this volume, pp. 143–144.

46. Dizard, "Going Native," p. 54.

47. B. Norton, "Conservation: Moral Crusade or Environmental Public Policy?" this volume, p. 188.

48. R. E. Manning, "Social Climate Change: A Sociology of Environmental Philosophy," this volume, p. 221.

ABOUT THE CONTRIBUTORS

David N. Bengston is an ecological economist and social scientist with the USDA Forest Service, North Central Research Station, in St. Paul, Minnesota, and an adjunct professor in the College of Natural Resources at the University of Minnesota. His research focuses on environmental values and attitudes and on public policies for managing landscape change.

Jessica Brown is vice president for international programs at the QLF/Atlantic Center for the Environment (QLF), a nongovernmental organization working in rural areas of New England and eastern Canada. Her work focuses on stewardship and the changing role of protected areas in society. Since the 1980s, she has worked in countries of the Caribbean region, Latin America, and central Europe. She is a member of the World Conservation Union's (IUCN's) World Commission on Protected Areas and its Task Force on Protected Landscapes, and she serves on the governing and advisory boards of several nonprofit organizations. In the United States, she works closely with the National Park Service through the Conservation Study Institute.

J. Baird Callicott is professor of philosophy and religion studies in the Institute of Applied Sciences at the University of North Texas. His research proceeds on four major fronts: theoretical environmental ethics, land ethics, the philosophy of ecology and conservation, and comparative environmental philosophy. He is the author or editor of many books, including *Earth's Insights: A Multicultural Survey of Ecological Ethics from the Mediterranean Basin to the Australian Outback; In Defense of the Land Ethic: Essays in Environmental Philosophy; Beyond the Land Ethic: More Essays in Environmental Philosophy;* and *The Great New Wilderness Debate.*

Rolf Diamant is superintendent of Marsh-Billings-Rockefeller National Historical Park, a national park telling the story of conservation history, the evolution of land stewardship, and the emergence of a conservation ethic. In his career with the National Park Service, he has been a resource manager, planner, and superintendent and has worked on new conservation strategies for wild and scenic rivers, national heritage areas, landscape corridors, and urban parks. He is a contributing author to *Wilderness Comes Home: Rewilding the Northeast* and is a coauthor of *A Citizen's Guide to River Conservation.*

Jan E. Dizard teaches sociology and environmental studies at Amherst College, where he is Charles Hamilton Houston Professor of American Culture and Pick Professor of Environmental Studies. His recent books include *Going Wild: Hunting, Animal Rights and the Contested Meaning of Nature* and *Mortal Stakes: Hunters and Hunting in Contemporary America.*

J. Glenn Eugster is assistant regional director for partnerships at the National Park Service, National Capital Region, in Washington, D.C. He has worked for twenty-six years locally, regionally, nationally, and internationally helping communities and park managers regenerate economies and ecosystems. His experience includes an emphasis on watershed stewardship, wetlands protection, heritage conservation, sustainable development, and fundraising.

Susan Flader is professor of history at the University of Missouri–Columbia, where she teaches American and world environmental history and the history of Missouri and the

American West. She has served as president of the American Society for Environmental History and the Missouri Parks Association and served on the boards of numerous other national and state organizations, including the National Audubon Society, the American Forestry Association, the Aldo Leopold Foundation, and the Citizens Committee for Soil, Water, and State Parks. She has published several books and numerous articles on the career and thought of Aldo Leopold, including *Thinking Like a Mountain* and *The River of the Mother of God and Other Essays*, and she has edited works such as *The Great Lakes Forest: An Environmental and Social History; Exploring Missouri's Legacy: State Parks and Historic Sites*, and the forthcoming *Toward Sustainability for Missouri Forests*.

Eric T. Freyfogle is Max L. Rowe Professor of Law at the University of Illinois, where he teaches courses on environmental law, natural resources law, and modern environmental thought. A native of central Illinois, he has long been active in state and local conservation causes. He currently serves as president of Prairie Rivers Network, the Illinois affiliate of the National Wildlife Federation. His books include *Bounded People, Boundless Lands; Justice and the Earth*; and an edited volume, *The New Agrarianism*.

David C. Iverson is an economist for the Intermountain Region of the USDA Forest Service. He also serves as social science coordinator for the Intermountain Region. As a practicing social scientist, he divides his time between government work and nonprofit work. He is a founding board member of Forest Service Employees for Environmental Ethics, a nonprofit organization that works with (and sometimes against) the Forest Service in identifying and establishing policy, programs, and practices in harmony with the environment.

Richard W. Judd is Adelaide C. and Alan L. Bird Professor of History at the University of Maine. He is the author of many works of environmental history, including *Common Lands, Common People: The Origins of Conservation in Northern New England; Maine: The Pine Tree State from Prehistory to the Present*, and the forthcoming *Natural States: The Environmental Imagination in Maine, Oregon, and the Nation*. His current research involves early scientific exploration and inquiry into the process of settlement along the trans-Appalachian frontier, 1790–1860.

David Lowenthal, emeritus professor of geography and honorary research fellow at University College London, is a gold medalist of the Royal and the American Geographical Societies and a senior fellow of the British Academy. Among his books are *The Past Is a Foreign Country; Landscape Meanings and Values; The Politics of the Past; The Heritage Crusade and the Spoils of History; George Perkins Marsh, Prophet of Conservation*; and *Our Past before Us: Why Do We Save It?*

Robert McCullough teaches in the Graduate Program in Historic Preservation at the University of Vermont. He is also co-manager of the Vermont Historic Bridge Program, which he helped to establish at the Vermont Agency of Transportation in 1998. McCullough is the author of *The Landscape of Community: A History of Communal Forests in New England* and a contributing author to *Stepping Back to Look Forward: A History of the Massachusetts Forest*.

Robert E. Manning is professor of natural resources at the University of Vermont, where he chairs the Recreation Management Program. He teaches and conducts research on the history, philosophy, and management of parks and protected areas. He is the author of *Studies* in *Outdoor Recreation* (2nd edition), published by Oregon State University Press, and editor of *Mountain Passages,* published by The Appalachian Mountain Club.

Curt Meine is director of conservation programs at the Wisconsin Academy of Sciences, Arts and Letters in Madison, Wisconsin. Meine is a member of the Crane Specialist Group of the World Conservation Union (IUCN) and is a research associate with the International Crane Foundation in Baraboo, Wisconsin. He is author of the biography *Aldo Leopold: His Life and Work*, among other works, and serves on the board of governors of the Society for Conservation Biology.

Ben A. Minteer is assistant research professor in the Human Dimensions of Biology Faculty, School of Life Sciences, Arizona State University. His work focuses on the moral and political dimensions of American environmental policy and the intellectual and cultural history of the conservation and environmental movements. He is co-editor (with Bob Pepperman Taylor) of *Democracy and the Claims of Nature* and is currently at work on a book exploring the role of democratic ideals in the American environmental tradition.

Brent Mitchell is director of stewardship at QLF/Atlantic Center for the Environment. His current focus is on exchange among professional peers working to protect conservation values of working landscapes in central Europe, Latin America and the Caribbean region, and the Middle East. He is a member of IUCN's World Commission on Protected Areas and works closely with the National Park Service through the Conservation Study Institute.

Nora J. Mitchell is director of the National Park Service's Conservation Study Institute, a national program based at Marsh-Billings-Rockefeller National Historical Park in Woodstock, Vermont. In her career with the National Park Service, she has worked on the management of natural and cultural resources of many national parks, most recently on leadership development for new collaborative models of landscape conservation.

Bryan Norton is professor of philosophy, science, and technology in the School of Public Policy of the Georgia Institute of Technology. His research explores biodiversity policy, adaptive management theory, and sustainability theory. He is the author or editor of a number of books, including *The Preservation of Species; Toward Unity among Environmentalists; Ethics on the Ark; Wolves and Human Communities;* and *Why Preserve Natural Variety?* He has recently published, with Cambridge University Press, *Searching for Sustainability: Interdisciplinary Essays in the Philosophy of Conservation Biology*.

Patricia A. Stokowski is an associate professor in the School of Natural Resources, University of Vermont. Her primary research interests include analysis of the social and cultural aspects of recreation and tourism development in rural and resource-dependent communities. She is the author of *Riches and Regrets: Betting on Gambling in Two Colorado Mountain Towns* and *Leisure in Society: A Network Structural Perspective*.

Bob Pepperman Taylor is professor of political science and director of the John Dewey Honors Program at the University of Vermont. He is the author of *Our Limits Transgressed: Environmental Political Thought in America* and *America's Bachelor Uncle: Henry Thoreau and the American Polity*. Most recently, he has edited, with Ben A. Minteer, *Democracy and the Claims of Nature: Critical Perspectives for a New Century*.

Paul B. Thompson is W. K. Kellogg Chair of Agriculture, Food and Community Ethics at Michigan State University. He has written extensively on the philosophical rationale for conservation ethics within agricultural production systems and has served on National Research Council committees reviewing the environmental effects of genetic engineering. His book *The Spirit of the Soil: Agriculture and Environmental Ethics* is widely regarded as a seminal work on ethics and agriculture.

Stephen C. Trombulak is Albert D. Mead Professor of Biology and Environmental Studies at Middlebury College in Vermont. He is a conservation biologist specializing in terrestrial vertebrates, forest ecosystems, and the design of ecological reserve systems. Most recently, he has edited *So Great a Vision: The Conservation Writings of George Perkins Marsh.*

Luis A. Vivanco is assistant professor of anthropology and director of the Latin American Studies Program at the University of Vermont. His research focuses on the culture and politics of environmental social movements and ecotourism in Costa Rica and southern Mexico. He is co-editor of *Talking about People: Readings in Contemporary Cultural Anthropology.*

INDEX

Ache people, 302
Adams, Thomas, 101
Adaptive management: environmental ethics and, 12, 201–4; Leopold and, 132; reconstructed conservation and, 311, 341–42; in regional planning, 107, 363n40; sustainable use and, 233, 234
Addams, Jane, 143
The African Conservation Centre, 309
Agenda 21, 60
Agrarian vision, 25, 77–92, 341, 342, 344
Agribusiness, 87, 260
Agricultural subsidy programs, 306
Agro-biodiversity, 304–5
Albuquerque Chamber of Commerce, 119–21
Alcibiades, 79
Aldo Leopold National Wildlife Refuge, 132, 368n49
Alienated work, 24–26
Allen, David Grayson, 23
Alternative modernity, 61, 73
Alverson, William S., 269
American Game Conference, 122
American Revolution, 119–20
Andrews, Richard, 23
Animal rights and liberation, 195
Anthropocentrism: in balance-of-nature paradigm, 252, 254, 257; ecological economics and, 232, 236; environmental ethics and, 191–96; Pinchot's views on, 188; sociological surveys of, 207, 215, 217, 221
Appalachian mountain people, 24, 25, 339
Appalachian Trail, 37, 100
Arctic National Wildlife Refuge, 269, 279
Argumedo, Alejandro, 304
Aristotle, 79–80, 126, 192
Arlington County Democratic Committee, 314
Assessment modeling, 203–4
Association of Environmental and Resource Economists, 227
Attitudes survey, 212–14, 217, tables 13.3-13.4
"Axe-in-Hand" (Leopold), 131

Back-casting, 203–4
Backyard wild places, 37, 40
Balance-of-nature paradigm, 239, 249–52, 254, 256
Balds, 28, 354n25

Balogh, Brian, 247
Baron, Hal, 23–24, 25, 353n12
Bass, Rick, 314
Beauty, Health, and Permanence (Hays), 28
Beaver survey, 218–20, table 13.4, fig. 13.2
Beeman, Randal, 176
Bender, Thomas, 282
Bengston, David N., 12, 13, 14, 15, 207, 209, 336, 341, 342, 343, 347
Bentham, Jeremy, 88, 90
Berger, Peter, 284
Berry, Wendell: agrarian vision of, 83–84, 85; Progressive movement and, 167; on reconstructed conservation, 326; rhetorical strengths of, 161; social community and, 145–46, 151–53, 154, 162–63, 293, 374n27
Big tent concept, 315, 346
Billington, Ray Allen, 19
Bill of Rights, 120
bin Laden, Osama, 80, 359n3
Biocentrism, 195, 221, 232
Biodiversity preservation, 258–61
Biological integrity, 266–67, 272–73
Biotic communities, 250, 253–54, 258
"Biotic View of Land, A" (Leopold), 128
Black Hawk (Colo.), 286–89
Black Triangle, 305–6
Blake, Casey, 362n32
Boost, philosophy of, 121, 366n18
Botkin, Daniel, 30
Boulding, Kenneth, 235
Bowden, Martyn J., 23
Bowling Along (Putnam), 317
Bradford, William, 241
Breen, Timothy H., 23
Brick, Philip, 290
Bridger, Jeffrey C., 283, 293
Bridges, metal truss, 40, 42
Brower, David, 248
Brower, Kenneth, 183
Brown, Jessica, 13, 14, 15, 335–36, 340, 344, 345, 346, 347
Brown, Margaret, 24, 25
Brulle, Robert J., 279
Bryant, William Cullen, 38
Buffalo Commons, 45–46, 48, 50–54, 355–56n11
Buffon, Georges Louis Leclerc, 80
Bunch, Lou, 288

Burch, William R., Jr., 280
Bureaucratic slippage, 289, 394n31
Bureau of Indian Affairs, 175
Burke, Edmund, 88, 359–60n14
Burroughs, John, 47
Bush, George W., 181, 330

Callicott, J. Baird, 13, 15, 78, 193–96, 335, 337, 341, 342, 343
Calvinism, 81–82, 241–42, 244
Cambodian immigrants, 307
Campesinos, 65–67, 70–71
CAMPFIRE, 306
Cane River Creole National Historical Park, 316
Capitalism: democracy and, 120; environmental history and, 22–23, 352n9; MacKaye's views on, 38; Nearing's views on, 139–42, 371n34; urban growth and, 99; Weber's views on, 81–82
Carribean: community-based conservation in, 307; participatory planning in, 303, 395n11
Carson, Rachel, 4, 169, 170, 174, 199
Carson National Forest (N.M.), 117
Catastrophic thresholds, 232, 384n23
Central City (Colo.), 286–89
Central High School National Historic Site (Little Rock, Ark.), 316
Centralized authority, 172–79
Changes in the Land (Cronon), 20
Chaos, ecology of, 255–56
Character traits, 83–85
Chase, Stuart, 99
Chatino people, 70–71
Chernela, Janet, 304
Chernobyl nuclear disaster, 330
Chicago Wilderness Habitat Project, 46, 48–50, 53, 54–56, 348, 355–56n11, 368n48
Chin, Jack, 320
Christianity, 190–91, 247–48
Ciriacy-Wantrup, Siegfried V., 227
Citizen involvement, 345
Citizens' Deer Committee, 129–30
Citizenship, 116, 118–23, 126–32, 364–65n3, 367n36, 368nn47–48
Civic dialogue, 315–16
"Civil Disobedience" (Thoreau), 173
Civil society, 68, 305–6, 322–23, 340–41, 345
Clarke-McNary Act (1924), 175
Classical economics, 224, 228, 231, 235, 385n36
Classic conservation tradition. *See* Conservation tradition

Clements, Frederic E., 45, 249–52, 253
Climax communities, 251–52, 257
Clinton, Bill, 181
Cloud forests, 66
Coalitions of diverse interests, 314
Coast Ranges (Ore.), 274
Coggins, George Cameron, 291
Cohen, Anthony P., 282
Cohen, Michael, 33, 35, 36
Cole, Thomas, 38
Collaboration: in community-based conservation, 281, 283, 284, 290–91; in ecosystem management, 234; leadership in, 324–25, 347
Colonial Americans, 22–23
"Coming into the Watershed" (Snyder), 294
Commission for Natural Resources (Zanzibar, Tanzania), 303–4, 396n16
Common ground, 335–49
Communal land use: in Appalachia, 23, 25–26; in colonial America, 23; in Oaxaca, 68–71
Communism, 135, 371n31
Communitarian regional planning movement, 94, 95–104, 361n5
Communities, 13–14, 282, 393n7; Berry's views on, 145, 151–54, 163, 375n36; fighting for, 154–56, 163, 375n36; historic preservation and, 34–35; Leopold's views on, 123–25, 128
Community-based conservation: as contemporary trend, 132, 298, 314–22, 368nn47–48; diversity in, 307–8; global protected areas management and, 302–6; reconstructed conservation and, 343–44, 349; stewardship and, 301; values in, 279–95
Community Conservation Coalition for the Sauk Prairie, 132
Community-conserved areas, 299, 304
Community self-determination, 304–5
Community-supported agriculture (CSA), 92, 342
Community values, 279–95
Complexity theory, 385n36
Confucius, 119
Conscious of a Radical, The (Nearing), 137
Consejo, Juan José, 69–70
Consequentialists, 90
Conservation beef, 319
Conservation biology, 263–76, 316
Conservation easements, 302, 395n11
Conservation economics, 149–51, 319–20, 374n19
"Conservation Economics" (Leopold), 124

Conservation goals, 263–76
Conservation methods and models: conservation philosophy and, 239–61; ecological economics and, 223–38; environmental ethics and, 187–204; landscape-scale conservation and, 263–76; sociology and, 207–21
Conservation philosophy, 239–61
Conservation Study Institute (NPS), 6
Conservation success, measurement of, 317–18
Conservation tradition, 4–11; agrarian vision and, 77–92; contextual reading of, 339–40; ecological economics and, 237–38; four faces of resistance to, 145–64; Leopold and, 4, 10, 115–32, 365n7; Nearing and, 133–44; Progressive movement and, 165–84; regional planning and, 93–113; reintegration of, 182–84; rhetorical deficiencies of, 159–64, 375n43
Consumer economy, 121–22, 128–29, 310
Consumption terms, environment in, 82, 89–91
Contextualism, 208, 215, 218–20, fig. 13.2, table 13.4, 339–40
Contract with America, 181
Control ecosystems, 248–49
Convergence on policy, 215, 217, 220, 382n18
Cooke, Bill, 291
Cooley, Charles Horton, 104
Coon Valley Erosion Project (Wis.), 124–25, 132
Cooperatives, farmer-sportsman, 125
Cooperative Wildlife Research Unit system (1935), 175–76
Corn blight, 86–87, 359n12
Cowan, Stuart, 314
Creativity, 325
Cripple Creek (Colo.), 287
Crocker, David A., 82
Cronon, William, 3–5, 20; capitalist assumptions of, 23, 352n9; wilderness critique of, 33–41, 48, 61, 103, 271, 337
Cultural diversity, 57–73, 308–9
Cultural geography, 23–24, 316, 353n12
Cultural landscapes, 316–17, 338–39, 342
Cultural resources, 33–42
Culture. See Nature and culture
Culture of Cities, The (Mumford), 105, 106
"Cultures, Genuine and Spurious" (Sapir), 60
Culture wars, 159–64, 181
Cumbler, John, 27
Custodianship, 306
Customary laws, 303–4

Daly, Herman, 225, 235
Dann, Kevin, 30
Darling, Jay ("Ding"), 124
Darwin, Charles, 80, 86, 97, 248
Davis, Donald, 24, 25, 339
Debs, Eugene, 136
Deconstructivist critique, 3–4
Deer management, 115, 129–31, 246, 368n43
Delaware Nature Education Society, 314
Democracy: agrarian vision and, 85; citizenship and, 120, 123, 128, 131, 132, 368n47; civic dialogue and, 315–16; community-based conservation and, 283, 285–86, 290; as face of resistance, 157; local interests and, 314–15; Nearing's views on, 142–43; reconstructed conservation and, 347–48; in regional planning, 94–95, 98, 107–10, 363nn43-44, 364n53
Democratic Party, 166–67, 181, 188
Demographic changes, 228–29, 239–40, 267–68
De Voto, Bernard, 178
Dewey, John: pragmatism and, 94–95, 104–10, 113, 196, 359–60n14, 362nn31-32, 363nn43-44, 364n53; on reconstruction, 15
Diamant, Rolf, 13, 14, 15, 335–36, 338, 342, 343, 345, 346, 347
Diderot, Denis, 88
"Dilemmas in a General Theory of Planning" (Rittel and Webber), 198
Dillman, Don A., 208
Dinosaur National Monument, 178–79
Directionality, 190
Discipline, 138, 371n29
Discursive models, 283, 285–86, 291, 293, 294
Disturbance regimes, 259, 261
Disturbances, 46, 252, 253, 254
Diversity in nature, 86–88
Dizard, Jan E., 11, 13, 14, 15, 336, 338, 340, 341, 348
Dominant product sustainability, 232
Dominant-use designations, 269–76, 342
Donahue, Brian, 23
Donahue, Debra, 29
Dracut Land Trust, 307
Dualism, 242, 244, 247
Ducks Unlimited, 55
Dunlap, Rily, 213
Dunlap, Thomas, 33, 35, 37
Durand, Asher B., 38
Dust bowl (1930s), 25, 124, 175
Dwight, Timothy, 24–25
Dynamism, 267

Earth Day, 116, 169, 179, 181
Earth monuments, 28, 29
Earth Summit, 232
Eastern Wilderness Areas Act (1974), 28
East (U.S.) vs. West (U.S.), 12, 19–31, 78
Echo Park dam controversy, 179
Ecocentrism, 195, 207
Ecological Design, 314
Ecological economics, 223–38, 260, 343,
    385n36
Ecological Economics, 235
Ecological lands, 270–74. *See also* Wilderness
    preservation
Ecological Revolutions (Merchant), 20
Ecological services, 259–60, 261, 343
Ecological Society of America, 247
Economic development projects, 286–90
Economics. *See* Conservation economics;
    Ecological economics; Environmental
    economics
"Economy of nature," 250
Ecopolitics, 63–64
Ecosystem concept, 250–53, 258, 266–67
Ecosystem goods, 259, 261
Ecosystem health, 257–58, 260, 261
Ecosystem management, 213, 217, 224, 233–34
Ecosystem services, 259–60, 261, 343
Ecotrust, 319
Education: experiential, 109; place-based, 320
Edwards, Jonathan, 240–41
Elder, John, 315
Ellen, Roy, 62, 72
Elton, Charles, 250
Embodiment, 91, 360n16
Emerson, Ralph Waldo, 85, 91, 240–43
Endangered Species Act (1973), 196, 237, 268,
    275
Endangered Species Coalition, 197
Energy theories of value, 236, 386n40
Engaged citizenry, 345
Enlightenment, 80
Enron, 183
Entrepreneurial models, 319–20
Environmental economics: analyses of, 161,
    163–64; Berry's views on, 153; community
    health and, 154–56, 375n36; environmental
    ethics vs., 82, 89–90, 188, 189–90, 193,
    309; Freeman's views on, 200; history of,
    226–28; Leopold's views on, 82, 149–50,
    374n19; monetary values and, 207
Environmental ethics, 12, 187–204; of
    agrarianism, 78, 83; of community, 146;
    environmental economics vs., 82, 89–90,

188, 189–90, 193, 309; intellectual history
    of, 103, 112–13; of land use, 24–26; of
    preservation, 36, 39; sociology of, 209–12,
    table 13.2, figs. 13.1-2. See also Land ethic
    philosophy
Environmental Ethics, 195
Environmental history, 19–31, 170, 316
Environmental History, 19, 33
Environmentalism, 44–45, 169–70, 175, 176,
    178–82, 279–80
Environmental justice movement, 309
Environmental values: environmental
    economics and, 187–204, 236–38, 379n25;
    global protected areas management and,
    305; sociological surveys of, 209–21, *table
    13.1*
Epistemology of environmental values, 189,
    194–95
Equality as face of resistance, 158–59
Equity, 309
Erie Canal, 254
Erikson, Kai, 330
Espionage Act, 136
Esteva, Gustavo, 69
Ethics, environmental. *See* Environmental
    ethics
Ethnic minorities, 57–73
Eugster, J. Glenn, 13, 14, 15, 335–36, 338, 342,
    343, 345, 346, 347
Europe: civil society in, 305–6; cultural
    landscapes in, 316
Evangelical Environment Network, 181
Experiential education, 109
Extensionism, age of, 189–97
"Externalities," 155

FACT (Farming and Conservation Together),
    132, 368n49
Fall, Albert, 366n18
Farm Bill (1990), 276
Farmer's markets, 92, 342
Farvar, Taghi, 308
Federal Aid in Wildlife Restoration Act (1937),
    176
Federal authority, 171–78, 188
Federal Water Pollution Control Act
    Amendments (1972), 266
Feminist thought, 360n16
Fight for Conservation, The (Pinchot), 171
Fish commissions, 26
Fishery management, 259, 303–4
Fishman, Robert, 97

Flader, Susan, 10, 11, 12, 14, 15, 336, 344, 345, 347

Flexibility, 311

Flood Control Act (1928), 175

Flora, Cornelia Butler, 282, 284

Flora, Jan L., 284

Flux-of-nature paradigm, 239, 252–61

Folkways, 22–24, 25, 339

Food products, 319–20

Forbes, Peter, 317

Forcing the Spring (Gottlieb), 133

Forest banks, 319

Forest exploitation, 166, 172–73, 243, 376n3

Forest Farm, 133, 134–35, 138–40

Forest management, 209–21, *tables 13.1-3*

Forest Products Laboratory (Madison, Wis.), 121

Forestry: environmental ethics and, 198; forest banks and, 319; Leopold's views on, 115, 117–18, 122, 132, 245–46, 368n48

Forest Stewardship Council, 129

Foster, David, 22

Fowler, Verna, 24

Fox, Stephen, 93

Freeman, A. Myrick, III, 200

Free trade, 153, 154–56

"Fresh from Young's Bay" label, 319

Freudenburg, William R., 394n31

Freyfogle, Eric T., 10, 11, 14, 15, 335–36, 338, 341, 344

Friedmann, John, 364n53

Frontier, 21, 23–24, 25, 240

Funders' Forum on Environment and Education, 320

Game management, 44, 118–20, 122–23, 124, 127, 245–47

Game Management (Leopold), 128

Game theory, 385n36

Gaming tourism development, 286–90

Garden cities, 96–97, 99, 100

Garden Cities of Tomorrow (Howard), 96–97

Garfield, James, 173

Garibaldi, Giuseppe, 332

Garkovich, Lori, 282, 285

Gates, Paul W., 19

Gatewood, Steve, 53

Geddes, Patrick, 95–101, 103, 104, 109, 113, 361n5

Genuine-spurious cultures paradigm, 57–73

Geoghegan, Tighe, 307

Georgescu-Roegen, Nicholas, 235

German National Socialism, 80, 123–24, 128, 359n3

Gila National Forest, 246

Gingrich, Newt, 181

Gleason, Henry, 252–53, 256, 258, 261

Glen Canyon Dam, 259

Global economy, 68, 145–46, 153, 154, 307–8, 373n2

Global environmental degradation, 223–24, 228–32, 297–98, 308, 384n19

Global species-extinction crisis, 258

Global trends in protected areas management, 298–301

Goodman, Daniel, 253

Gore, Al, 181

"Gospel of efficiency," 223

Gottlieb, Robert, 133

Government authority, 171–78

Gramling, Robert, 394n31

Gray, L. C., 226

Great Depression, 175

"Great Madness, The" (Nearing), 136

Great Plains Restoration Council (GPRC), 48, 55

Great Smoky Mountains National Park, 28

Greek city-states, 79–80, 85, 120

Green and Permanent Land, A (Beeman and Pritchard), 176

Green Mountain National Forest (GMNF), 208–15, *tables 13.1 and 13.3*, 217, 218, 320

Green primitives, 62–64, 72

Green production, 129, 132

Green revolution technologies, 68, 71

Greider, Thomas, 282, 285

Haberman, Jürgen, 286

Habitat preservation, 258–59, 310

Haeckel, Ernst, 243

Hahn, Steven, 23

Hall, David B., 23

Hanson, Victor Davis, 79–80, 85

Harmonization, 245–49, 257–58, 260–61

Hayden, Dolores, 315

Hays, Samuel, 28, 33, 35, 93

Held values, 209

Hess, Karl, Jr., 280, 294

Hester, Randolph T., Jr., 292–93

Hetch Hetchy Valley, 172, 187

Highest use, 246, 259

Hill, Octavia, 38

Historical reconstructions, 27–29, 31

"Historical Roots of Our Ecologic Crisis, The" (White), 190

Historic preservation, 33–42, 286–89, 316
Holism, 195–96
"Homebuilder Conserves, The" (Leopold), 121
"Home Gardens and Citizenship" (Leopold), 119
Home rule, 321–22
Hoover Dam, 175
Howard, Albert, Sir, 152
Howard, Ebenezer, 95–100, 104, 113, 361n5
Huckleberries (Thoreau), 241
Hudson Guild Farm (Netcong, N.J.), 37
Humanism, 37–38, 111
Human potency, 329–32
Hume, David, 80, 88
Husbandry, 124–25, 127, 131
Hutchinson, G. E., 251
Huxley, Thomas, 97

Iconic cultural landscapes, 28–29
Indigenous peoples, 57–73, 304
Indigenous People's Biodiversity Network, 304
Individualism: in environmental ethics, 195–96; Leopold's views on, 123–25, 128, 162; as resistance to conservation, 146–47; Roosevelt's views on, 167
Industrial ecology, 112
Industrialism, 26–27, 139–40, 371n34
Institutional reforms, 88–91
Institutions and Governance Program (World Resources Institute), 325
Instituto de la Naturaleza y la Sociedad de Oaxaca (INSO), 70–71
Instrumentalism, 105–6, 110, 236, 362n32
Integrative model for conservation, 268–76
Intensive-use lands, 271–75
Interdependency, 255, 284
Intergenerational allocation of resources, 226, 309
International development schemes, 57–73, 344
International Society for Ecological Economics (ISEE), 235
Intrinsic value, 193–97, 199–200, 209, 215, 217, 236–37
Inventories, 291–92
Iowa conservation plan, 122–23
Irland, Lloyd, 28
Islam, 64, 80, 303–4
Iverson, David C., 12, 13, 14, 15, 207, 336, 341, 342, 343, 347
Izaak Walton League of America, 122

Jackson, Wes, 260–61
Janzen, Daniel, 65
Jayber Crow (Berry), 153
Jefferson, Thomas, 83, 84–85, 173, 178
Jizera Mountains, 305–6
John Dewey Lounge, 5, 5–6, 41
Johnstone, Barbara, 285
Journal of Environmental Economics and Management, 227
Journal of Forestry, 37
Journal of the American Institute of Architects, 37
Judd, Richard W., 11, 12, 15, 78, 335–36, 337, 338–39, 339
Judeo-Christian worldview, 190–91, 247–48

Kaibab Plateau, 246
Kant, Immanuel, 80
Katahdin wilderness, 30
Kayapó Indians, 64
Kearney, Michael, 62, 64
Kellner, Hansfried, 284
Kemmis, Daniel, 173, 283
Kenya Wildlife Service, 309
Kindred Spirits (Durand), 38
Klamath Mountains, 274
Klyza, Christopher, 28, 30
Kothari, Uma, 291
Kowanyama (Australia), 304
Kraft, Michael E., 280, 294
Kuhlmann, Walter, 269

Lacy, David, 320
La Follette, Belle Case, 167–68
La Follette, Robert M. ("Fighting Bob"), 165, 167
Land community, 124, 132, 147–48, 373n7
"Land Ethic, The" (Leopold), 127, 132, 177–78
Land ethic philosophy: animal liberation compared to, 195; in conservation tradition, 93, 95, 111–12; as Leopold's legacy, 147, 265; neoclassical economics and, 235; personal responsibility in, 124, 128–29, 132, 162; Progressive movement and, 177–78, 179
Land health: conservation tradition and, 183; harmonization and, 257–58; Leopold's views on, 148–49, 152, 161–62, 248, 260, 373n14; reconstructed conservation and, 341
Landowner responsibility. *See* Private land use
"Land Pathology" (Leopold), 124, 367n29
Land purchases, 66–67
Landscape myths, 84, 359n9

Landscape-scale conservation, 263–76

Land trusts, 132, 302, 307, 317, 344, 345

"Land-Use and Democracy" (Leopold), 122, 128

Larkin, Joyce, 129–30

Lassen National Forest (Calif.), 132

Latin America: genuine-spurious cultures paradigm and, 57–73; private reserves in, 302, 395n11; reconstructed conservation and, 346

Latrines, 71

Leadership, 324–25, 347

Leopold, Aldo: agrarian vision and, 82, 83, 92; Berry compared to, 151–53; citizenship and, 116, 118–23, 126–32, 345; conservation tradition and, 4, 10, 115–32, 154, 365n7, 366nn18-19; harmonization and, 245–49, 260; land ethic of (*see* Land ethic philosophy); land health and (*see* Land health); legacy of, 147–51, 169, 265; private land use and (*see* Private land use); Progressive movement and, 11, 115–32, 170, 174, 177, 179, 377n29; reconstructed conservation and, 340, 344, 347; restoration ecology and, 48, 116, 125; rhetorical strengths of, 160–61, 199; scale and, 30

Le Play, Pierre Guillaume Frédéric, 98

Lewontin, Richard, 46

Ley de Usos y Costumbres (1998), 69

Liberalism, 162–63, 363n44, 375n46

Liberalism and Social Action (Dewey), 108, 363n43

Libertarians, 163–64, 375n49

Liberty as face of resistance, 157

Life-support values, 236–37, 238

Limits, age of, 223–38

Lindeman, Raymond, 250–51

Linnaeus, 251

List, Peter, 213

Living the Good Life (Nearing and Nearing), 134–36, 139

Local interests, 57–73, 171–74, 176, 308, 314–15

Long-settled lands, 21–24, 338, 339

Lorena stoves, 71

Lotka-Volterra logistic equation, 255

Lowenthal, David, 10, 12, 14, 39, 41, 43, 297, 311, 335, 340

Luloff, A. E., 283

Lumber industry, 166, 172, 376n3

Lynch, Kevin, 38–39, 42

Lyon, Larry, 282

MacKaye, Benton: backyard wild places and, 40; reconstructed conservation and, 339; regional planning and, 94, 99–102, 111–12, 113, 361n5, 361–62n19; Stein and, 10, 37–38

Maines, David R., 293

Maine Woods, The (Thoreau), 30

Makah Indians, 63

Malin, James C., 19

Malthus, Thomas, 225

Man and Nature (Marsh), 6, 43–44, 266, 327–28, 332

Man and the Biosphere Program (UNESCO), 273

Manialtepec Initiative, 70–71

Manning, Robert E., 12, 14, 15, 336, 342, 348

Manzanar National Historic Site, 316

Marsh, George Perkins: conservation tradition and, 4, 6, 10, 311; global protected areas management and, 297–98, 300; on mobility, 22; resourcism and, 243–44, 246; restoration ecology and, 43–45, 47; on stewardship, 14, 266, 327–32, 340, 398n8

Marshall, Alfred, 225

Marshall, Robert, 246

Marsh-Billings-Rockefeller National Historical Park, 6

Marx, Karl, 142

MARXAN, 272

Mather, Cotton, 241

Mazmanian, Daniel A., 280, 294

McCullough, Robert, 10, 11, 12, 15, 335–36, 337, 346, 347

McDade, Joseph, 318

McEvoy, Arthur, 26

McIntosh, Robert, 256

McKinley, William, 165–66, 244

McWilliams, Wilson Carey, 142

Meadow management, 305

Measurement: of conservation success, 317–18; of environmental values, 189

Meine, Curt, 10, 12, 14, 15, 340, 341, 345, 346, 361n5

Meller, Helen, 99

Menger, Carl von, 225

Merchant, Carolyn, 20, 295

Migratory Bird Conservation Act (1929), 175

Mill, John Stuart, 90, 225, 235, 245, 363n44

Miller, Char, 171, 174

Miller, Perry, 78, 241

Minteer, Ben A., 10, 11, 12, 14, 15, 335–36, 339, 344, 345, 347

Misali Island Marine Conservation Area
    (Zanzibar, Tanzania), 304
Mitchell, Brent, 13, 14, 15, 335–36, 340, 344,
    345, 346, 347, 395n13
Mitchell, John Hanson, 30, 47–48
Mitchell, Nora J., 13, 14, 15, 335–36, 338, 342,
    343, 345, 346, 347
Moe, Richard, 34–35
Monism, 199–200, 204
Montesquieu, 80, 88
Monte Verde (Costa Rica), 61, 66–67
Monumental natural features, 28, 29
More, Thomas, 233
Muir, Daniel, 242
Muir, Diana, 27, 30
Muir, John: environmental ethics and, 187–88,
    189, 192, 197–98, 199; on indigenous
    peoples, 62; Pinchot and, 93–94, 172, 174,
    187–88, 189, 198, 360n4; reconstructed
    conservation and, 340; wilderness
    preservation and, 3, 47, 241–43
Multi-objective planning and decision making,
    318–19, 342–43
Mumford, Lewis: on Marsh, 6; pragmatic
    conservationism of, 10, 95–113, 362n32,
    364n53; reconstructed conservation and,
    339, 340, 344, 345, 347; regional planning
    and, 12, 94, 95–113, 361n5
Murie, Olaus, 170
Myers, Norman, 64–65

Nader, Ralph, 181
Nash, Roderick, 93
National Environmental Policy Act (1969), 179,
    237, 315
National Forest Management Act (1976), 237
National Forest System, 175
National Historic Preservation Act (1966), 315
National Park Service: Conservation Study
    Institute, 6; fiscal history of, 54; historic
    preservation and, 289; Leopold and, 118;
    preservationism and, 245; Progressive
    movement and, 175; river conservation and,
    318–19, 342
National Park System, 6, 268, 269, 316
National Press Club, 34
National Reclamation Act (1902), 179
National Trust for Historic Preservation, 34, 38
National Trust for Places of Historic Interest or
    Natural Beauty (Great Britain), 38
Native Americans, 30, 63
Natural Lands Trust (Paraguay), 302
"Natural regulation," 45

Natural resource economics, 226
Natural selection, 251, 253
Nature and culture, 11; environmental history
    and, 19–31; genuine-spurious cultures
    paradigm and, 57–73; global protected areas
    management and, 300; historic preservation
    and, 33–42; reconstructed conservation
    and, 337–38; restoration ecology and,
    43–56
The Nature Conservancy, 55, 310, 319
Nature (Emerson), 240
Nazism, 80, 123–24, 128, 359n3
Nearing, Helen, 134–36, 138, 369nn8-10,
    370n14
Nearing, Scott, 10, 12, 133–44, 347–48,
    369nn8-9, 370n14, 370nn19-20, 371n31,
    371n34, 371n39, 371n41, 371–72n43,
    372n47, 372n49, 372–73n51
Neighborhoods. See Communities
Nelson, Robert, 179
Neoclassical economics, 224–28, 234–37, 238,
    385n36, 386n46
Neo-Kantian ethics, 90, 91
Neoliberalism, 68
New Deal, 124, 175, 177
New England paradigms, 19, 23, 25, 26–27,
    351n1
"New England Recreation Plan, A" (MacKaye),
    37
New Entry Sustainable Farming Project, 307
New Face on the Countryside (Silver), 20
Newfont, Kathryn, 25–26
Newman, Paul, 371–72n43
New Republic, 362n32
Newton, Isaac, 247, 251
New urbanism, 112
New World conquest, 239–40
New Yorker magazine, 101
New York Society for Ethical Culture, 38
Noble savages, 62–64
Nonanthropocentrism: biological integrity and,
    266; ecological economics and, 236;
    environmental ethics and, 93, 95, 111, 113,
    191–96, 360n1; sociological surveys of, 217
Norbeck-Anderson Act (1929), 175
Northern Forest Center (NFC), 318
Northern Forest Wealth Index, 318
Norton, Bryan, 12, 14, 15, 111, 217, 336, 342,
    343, 348, 363n40, 382n18
Nuclear waste, 279

Oaxaca (Mexico), 61, 68–71
Odum, Eugene, 45, 251

"Of the Stationary State" (Mill), 225
Ogonowski, John, 307
Old Mill building (University of Vermont), 5, 41
Old World culture, 23
Ontology of environmental values, 189–95, 200
Opie, John, 25
Organic farming, 133, 134, 139–40
Orion magazine, 169
Ostfeld, R. S., 254, 256
Ownership, images of, 150–51. See also Private land use

Palynology, 253
Paper parks, 299, 344
Paradigm shifts: in dominant-use designations, 269; in philosophy of conservation, 239–61, 342; in protected areas management, 299–301, table 18.1; reconstructed conservation and, 346
Parque de la Papa (Pisac Valley), 304
Participatory planning, 303
Partnerships: public-private, 346–47; watershed, 125, 132, 290
Passmore, John, 191
Past Is a Foreign Country, The (Lowenthal), 39
Peasantry, 62, 64, 65–66, 87, 359n12
Peirce, Charles S., 196
Peluso, Nancy L., 292
Peñas Blancas watershed, 66
Perennial polycultures, 261
Personality and landscape, 83–85
Phillips, Adrian, 316
Phillips, John, 250
Philosophy of conservation, 239–61
Physiocrats, 224, 228
Piasecki, Bruce, 20
Pickett, S. T. A., 254, 256
Pinchot, Gifford: on communal land use, 24; conservation tradition and, 10, 168; Muir and, 93–94, 172, 174, 187–88, 189, 198, 360n4; Progressive movement and, 171, 173, 178; reconstructed conservation and, 340; resourcism and, 244–45, 247; USDA Forest Service and, 116, 117, 244; utilitarianism of, 102, 138, 188, 245, 371n25; Yale Forest School and, 245
Pioneering experience, 23, 25, 47
"Pioneers and Gullies" (Leopold), 121
Pisac valley (Peruvian Andes), 304
Pitcaithley, Dwight T., 316
Pittman-Robertson Act (1937), 176
Place-based education, 320

Place knowledge, 324
Plant associations, 249–50, 252
Plato, 79, 251
Plumas National Forest (Calif.), 132
Plumwood, Val, 242
Pluralism, 13–14; environmental ethics and, 199, 202–3; reconstructed conservation and, 343, 349; sociological surveys of, 207–8, 215–16, 220–21; value, 57, 236, 237, 238, 385n31
Political inclusivity, 346–47
Popper, Deborah, 51–52, 54–55
Popper, Frank, 51–52, 54–55
Port Honduras Marine Reserve (Belize), 303
Portney, Paul, 228
Positivism, 223
Potatoes, 304
Powell, John Wesley, 10, 52, 112
Power, Thomas Michael, 82
Power of Place: Urban Landscapes as Public History, The (Hayden), 315
Power relations, 291
Pragmatic conservationism, 94–95, 104–13, 340, 349, 361n5, 363n40, 364n53
Pragmatism, environmental, 196, 220–21, 379n17
Prairie potholes, 55
Prairie restoration, 46, 48–54, 355–56n11
Precapitalist mentalité, 23, 352–53n9
Predator-prey relationships, 246, 248, 253, 255
Preference-based held values, 209, 236–37
Preservationism, 27–29, 240–48, 257, 258, 261, 279. See also Wilderness preservation
President's Council on Sustainable Development, 232
Pritchard, James, 176
Private land use: communities and, 124–25, 154–55; conservation economics and, 149–51, 374n19; custodianship and, 306; dominant-use designations and, 274; as responsibility of citizens, 121, 124, 177, 366n19, 367n29, 377n29; silence on, 161, 164, 375n49; Soil Conservation Service and, 176
Private property: in colonial America, 23; as face of resistance, 157, 375n39, 375n41
Private reserves, 302–3
Process of policy formation, 189, 311
Productive work, 81–83, 84, 91
Professionalism, 116, 117–18, 122–23, 127–32, 368n48
Progressive Era, 165–67, 173, 184, 375n1; Leopold and, 117, 365n7; Marsh and, 44;

Nearing and, 133, 136–39, 142–44, 370nn19-21, 371n24; reconstructed conservation and, 340; USDA Forest Service and, 171

Progressive movement, 11–12, 165–84, 237; Leopold and, 11, 115–32, 170; Nearing and, 134–41; reconstructed conservation and, 346

Protected areas planning and management, 297–311, *table 18.1*, 344. *See also* Wilderness preservation

Protestant Ethic and the Spirit of Capitalism, The (Weber), 81

Public and Its Problems, The (Dewey), 109, 363n43

Public environmentalism, 280. *See also* Community-based conservation

Public land management, 207–21, *tables 13.1-3*

Public-private partnerships, 346–47

Purchase, Eric, 21

Puritanism, 241–42

Putnam, Robert D., 283, 317

QLF/Atlantic Center for the Environment, 395n9

Qualify of life, 314–15

Quincy Library Group, 131, 368n47

Radburn (N.J.), 100

Radical center, 165–84, 340, 346

Raine, Peter, 72

Reclus, Jean Jacques Élisée, 98

Reconceptualizing the Peasantry (Kearney), 62

Reconstructing conservation practice, 162–64; community conservation movements and, 279–95; contemporary trends and, 313–22; global protected areas management and, 297–306; moving forward to, 348–49; principles for, 307–11, 322–25, 335–49

Reconstruction in Philosophy (Dewey), 6, 15

Reflections on the Revolution in France (Burke), 88

Reflex arc, 359–60n14

"Reform environmentalism," 279

Regan, Tom, 193, 195

Regionalism, 20–21, 352n5

Regional planning, 12, 93–113, 339, 344, 345

Regional Planning Association of America. *See* RPAA

Regional Plan of New York and Its Environs, 101

Rehabilitation, 41–42

Relationships to land, 307, 321

Relics and Ruins school, 320

Relph, E. C., 284, 338

Renard, Yves, 307

Republican Party, 166–67, 188

Resource exploitation, 171–74

Resource extraction, 273

Resourcism, 243–48, 257, 258–59, 261

Responsibilities, public, 171–74, 183, 279

Restoration ecology, 43–56, 182–83, 340–41, 348

RESTORE: The North Woods, 45

Rhetorical deficiencies, 159–64, 187–88, 197–98, 375n43

Ricardo, David, 225

Riches and Regrets (Stokowski), 288

Rio+10 World Summit on Sustainable Development, 232

Rittel, Horst, 198–99, 201–3

Robertson, F. Dale, 116

Rockefeller, Laurance S., 6

Rockefeller, Mary French, 6

Rolston, Holmes, III, 193–95

Roosevelt, Franklin Delano, 175

Roosevelt, Theodore, 165–68, 172–75, 179, 244

RPAA (Regional Planning Association of America), 95, 99–101, 104, 361n15

The Rural Sociological Society, 282

Ryden, Kent, 22, 285

Sachs, Wolfgang, 60

Sagebrush rebellion, 181

Sagoff, Mark, 237

Salafsky, Nick, 58, 69

Saltmarsh, John, 135, 140, 143, 370n18

"Sampler of Courses and Programs in Environmental History" (Piasecki), 20

Samuels, Gayle Brandow, 30

Sand County Almanac, A (Leopold): agrarian vision and, 83, 92; conservation tradition and, 115–16; legacy of, 147; new edition of, 183; Progressive movement and, 168, 169, 174; restoration ecology and, 125–27

Sapir, Edward, 60

Sauer, Peter, 169

Sauk County (Wis.), 167–68

Sauk Prairie, 132

Save Wisconsin's Deer, 130

Scale, problems of, 29–31, 153, 273–74

Schama, Simon, 282

Science magazine, 190

Sea Shepherd Conservation Society, 63

Self-determination, community, 304–5

Sense of place, 24, 25, 207, 283, 284–85, 324, 338
Sewall, Hannah Robie, 224
Seymour, Frances J., 325
Shady Ladies of the Motherlode, 288
Shannon, Fred A., 19
Shindler, Bruce, 213
ShoreBank Pacific, 319
Sierra Club, 243, 276
Sierra Madre Occidental, 246, 249
Silent Spring (Carson), 4, 174, 179
Silver, Timothy, 20
Silves (Brazil), 304
Simberloff, Daniel, 251
Simpson, John Warfield, 22, 29
Siskiyou Mountains, 274
Sites, 272
Sky Islands, 274
Slow food movement, 319–20
Smith, Adam, 80
Smuts, Jan, 250
Snow, Donald, 284
Snyder, Gary, 294
Social capital, 283–84, 290, 293, 317–18, 319, 345
Social climate change, 207–21
Social Darwinism, 80
Social engineering, 58, 61
Socialism, 124, 136–38, 371n24
Social justice, 170–71, 346, 376–77n15
Society of American Foresters, 247
Sociology of environmental philosophy, 207–21
Socrates, 79, 119
Soil Conservation Districts, 129
Soil Conservation Service (SCS), 176
Soufriere Marine Management Area (St. Lucia), 303
South Pacific Biodiversity Conservation Programme, 304, 396n18
Spann, Edward K., 101
"Special creation," 46
Speth, Gus, 317
Spurious cultures. See Genuine-spurious cultures paradigm
Steel, Brent, 213
Stegner, Wallace, 19, 285
Stein, Clarence, 10–11, 37–38, 99
Steinberg, Theodore, 27
Stereotypes of indigenous peoples, 60, 61, 62, 72
Stewardship, 14; agrarian vision and, 83; community-based conservation and, 283, 293; conservation economics and, 319–20;

conservation tradition and, 181; cultural diversity and, 308; dominant-use designations and, 270, 272–75; Elder's views on, 315; environmental ethics and, 209, 215; global protected areas management and, 297–311; Marsh's views on, 327–32, 398n8; reconstructed conservation and, 340–41, 345; resourcism and, 247
St. Lucia (Carribean island), 303
Stokowski, Patricia A., 12, 14, 15, 335, 338, 340, 344, 348
Subsistence homesteading, 133, 134–41, 369nn8-10, 370n14, 371n29
Succession, 251–52, 257, 259
Sunnyside Gardens (Queens), 100
Superorganisms, 249–51
Surveys: regional, 98–99, 103, 104, 105, 109–10; sociological, 208–14, tables 13.1-3, 218
Sustainable architecture, 112
Sustainable use: agrarian vision of, 82–83; discourse on, 64–65; dominant-use designations and, 273–74; ecological economics and, 224, 232–37, 238; in forest management, 213; global protected areas management and, 304; history of, 43–45; in Oaxaca, 70; resourcism and, 247

Tahoe National Forest (Calif.), 132
Tansley, Arthur, 250–51, 253
Taylor, Bob Pepperman, 10, 12, 15, 336, 347–48
Taylor, Paul, 193, 195
Taylor Grazing Act (1934), 175, 178
Technological optimism, 190–91
Thinking Like a Mountain (Flader), 115
Thompson, Paul B., 11, 14, 15, 335–36, 338–39, 340, 342, 344
Thoreau, Henry David: agrarian vision and, 91; on government, 173; on nature and culture, 29, 337; Nearing compared to, 135–37, 369n7, 370nn11-12; reconstructed conservation and, 340; scale and, 30; transcendentalism of, 3, 240–43; wilderness preservation and, 241–42, 246
Threatened species, 125, 248, 258–59, 268
Thrupp, Lori Ann, 65
Time, conceptions of, 190
Tocqueville, Alexis de, 120
Toledo, Victor, 69
Tomorrow: A Peaceful Path to Real Reform (Howard), 96

Tourism development, 281, 286–90
Tradition, 22–24. *See also* Conservation
　tradition
Transcendentalism, 84–85, 104, 137, 240–43,
　244, 246
Trombulak, Stephen C., 13, 14, 15, 335–36,
　342, 343, 347
Tropical forests, 63, 64–65
Trout Unlimited, 55
Trustees of Public Reservations (Mass.), 38
Turner, Frederick Jackson, 3, 19, 23, 51,
　377n20
Turner, John Pickett, 104
Turner, Ted, 52–54, 56
Tyranny of small solutions, 321

Udall, Morris, 318
Uncommon Ground (Cronon), 3, 5, 33
UN Conference on Environment and
　Development (UNCED), 232
UNESCO, 273
Unified National Program for Floodplain
　Management, 318
Union of Concerned Scientists, 231
United Auto Workers, 314
UN Population Division, 229
Urban growth boundaries, 96
U.S. Bureau of Land Management, 245
U.S. Bureau of Reclamation, 178–79
U.S. Congress, 172, 275
USDA Forest Service: Leopold and, 117–18,
　121, 131, 245–46; Pinchot and, 171, 244,
　245; Robertson and, 116; western
　resentment toward, 173; wise use movement
　and, 279
U.S. Department of the Interior, 41
U.S. Environmental Protection Agency, 288
U.S. Fish and Wildlife Service, 55, 197, 245
Utilitarianism: agrarian vision vs., 82, 88, 91;
　conservation tradition and, 174, 175, 223;
　regional planning vs., 93–95, 102, 111;
　wilderness preservation vs., 187

Valley section model, 97–99
Value pluralism, 57, 236, 237, 238, 385n31
Van der Ryn, Sim, 314
Van de Wetering, Sarah, 290
Van Hise, Charles, 168
Veblen, Thorstein, 104
Vilas County News Review, 129
Vivanco, Luis A., 11, 15, 335–36, 337, 341,
　344, 346

Walden Pond, 91, 135–36
Walden (Thoreau), 135–36, 138, 241
"Walking" (Thoreau), 241
Waller, Donald M., 269
Walras, Léon, 225
Watershed partnerships, 125, 132, 290
Watt, James, 181
Webb, Walter Prescott, 19
Webber, Melvin, 198–99, 201–3
Weber, Max, 81–82
Weeks Law (1911), 175
Welland Canal, 254
Westbrook, Robert, 362n32
Western, David, 309
West (U.S.) vs. East (U.S.), 12, 19–31, 78
Whaling, 63
What Time Is This Place? (Lynch), 38
Wheeler-Howard Act (1934), 175
Whitaker, Charles, 99
White, Lynn, Jr., 190–93
White Carpathian Mountains, 305
White Clay Creek watershed, 314
White Mountain National Forest (WMNF), 208,
　213, 215, 218
White Sands National Monument, 366n18
Whitfield, Stephen, 136, 369n8, 370n18,
　371n24, 371n31
Wicked problems, 198–99, 201
Wigglesworth, Michael, 241
Wilderness: concept of, 3–4; as metaphor,
　51–52, 55
Wilderness Act (1964), 28, 237, 268
Wilderness critique, 33–41, 47–48, 61, 103,
　169, 271
Wilderness preservation, 33–42; conservation
　tradition and, 174; in Costa Rica, 66; flux-of-
　nature paradigm and, 258; Leopold's views
　on, 245, 248; reconstructed conservation
　and, 338–39; Thoreau's views on, 241–42;
　utilitarianism vs., 172, 187, 377n20
Wilderness recreation, 246, 248
The Wilderness Society, 37, 243, 245–46
Wildlands Project, 53, 273
Willingness to accept (WTA), 235, 236
Willingness to pay (WTP), 235, 236, 237
Winthrop, John, 241
Wise use movement, 93, 168–69, 181, 279
Wood, Gordon, 120
Woodstock, Vt., 6
Work, primacy of, 81–83, 91
Working landscapes, 338–39
World Bank, 64

World Commission on Protected Areas (IUCN), 316
World Conservation Union (IUCN), 316
World Resources Institute, 325
World Scientists' Warning to Humanity, 231
World Trade Center terrorist attack, 307
World Wide Web, 319
World Wildlife Fund, 66
Worster, Donald, 25, 112, 146, 183, 242, 255
Wright, Henry, 99

Yaak Valley Forest Council, 314
Yellowstone National Park, 45, 46
Yosemite National Park, 172
Youth movement, 134, 141, 371nn39-41
Yucca Mountain (Nev.), 330

Zanzibar (Tanzania), 303–4
Zapatista rebellion, 69